Communication and Misinformation

AF214083

Communication and Misinformation

Crisis Events in the Age of Social Media

Edited by

Kevin B. Wright

WILEY Blackwell

Copyright © 2025 by John Wiley & Sons, Inc. All rights reserved, including rights for text and data mining and training of artificial intelligence technologies or similar technologies.

Published by John Wiley & Sons, Inc., Hoboken, New Jersey.
Published simultaneously in Canada.

No part of this publication may be reproduced, stored in a retrieval system, or transmitted in any form or by any means, electronic, mechanical, photocopying, recording, scanning, or otherwise, except as permitted under Section 107 or 108 of the 1976 United States Copyright Act, without either the prior written permission of the Publisher, or authorization through payment of the appropriate per-copy fee to the Copyright Clearance Center, Inc., 222 Rosewood Drive, Danvers, MA 01923, (978) 750-8400, fax (978) 750-4470, or on the web at www.copyright.com. Requests to the Publisher for permission should be addressed to the Permissions Department, John Wiley & Sons, Inc., 111 River Street, Hoboken, NJ 07030, (201) 748-6011, fax (201) 748-6008, or online at http://www.wiley.com/go/permission.

Trademarks: Wiley and the Wiley logo are trademarks or registered trademarks of John Wiley & Sons, Inc. and/or its affiliates in the United States and other countries and may not be used without written permission. All other trademarks are the property of their respective owners. John Wiley & Sons, Inc. is not associated with any product or vendor mentioned in this book.

Limit of Liability/Disclaimer of Warranty
While the publisher and author have used their best efforts in preparing this book, they make no representations or warranties with respect to the accuracy or completeness of the contents of this book and specifically disclaim any implied warranties of merchantability or fitness for a particular purpose. No warranty may be created or extended by sales representatives or written sales materials. The advice and strategies contained herein may not be suitable for your situation. You should consult with a professional where appropriate. Further, readers should be aware that websites listed in this work may have changed or disappeared between when this work was written and when it is read. Neither the publisher nor authors shall be liable for any loss of profit or any other commercial damages, including but not limited to special, incidental, consequential, or other damages.

For general information on our other products and services or for technical support, please contact our Customer Care Department within the United States at (800) 762-2974, outside the United States at (317) 572-3993 or fax (317) 572-4002.

Wiley also publishes its books in a variety of electronic formats. Some content that appears in print may not be available in electronic formats. For more information about Wiley products, visit our web site at www.wiley.com.

Library of Congress Cataloging-in-Publication Data
Names: Wright, Kevin B., editor.
Title: Communication and misinformation : crisis events in the age of social media / edited by Prof. Dr. Kevin B. Wright, George Mason University.
Description: Hoboken : Wiley, 2024. | Series: Communicating science in times of crisis | Includes index.
Identifiers: LCCN 2024031447 (print) | LCCN 2024031448 (ebook) | ISBN 9781394184941 (paperback) | ISBN 9781394184958 (adobe pdf) | ISBN 9781394184965 (epub)
Subjects: LCSH: Communication in crisis management. | Misinformation. | Social media.
Classification: LCC HD49.3 .C655 2024 (print) | LCC HD49.3 (ebook) | DDC 658.45–dc23/eng/20240729
LC record available at https://lccn.loc.gov/2024031447
LC ebook record available at https://lccn.loc.gov/2024031448

Cover Design: Wiley
Cover Image: © AerialPerspective Works/Getty Images

Set in 9.5/12.5pt STIXTwoText by Straive, Pondicherry, India

In Memory of H. Dan O'Hair
friend, mentor, and crisis communication pioneer

Contents

About the Editor

Kevin B. Wright (PhD, University of Oklahoma, 1999) is a professor in the Department of Communication at George Mason University where he teaches classes on health communication, crisis communication, and social media. He has over 20 years of experience as a communication scholar and is the author of eight books (including *Health Communication in the 21st Century*, published by Wiley Blackwell), 115 scholarly journal articles and book chapters, and over 120 papers presented at national and international communication and public health conferences. Much of his research has focused on online social support and health outcomes, online health information and misinformation, risk and crisis communication, and online social networks and health. In addition, he has served as a journal editor for the *Journal of Computer-Mediated Communication*, published by the International Communication Association, and is a frequent reviewer for numerous journals, including *Health Communication*, *Journal of Health Communication*, and *Journal of Medical Internet Research* (*JMIR*).

List of Contributors

Juliana L. Barbati
Department of Communication
University of Arizona

Porismita Borah
Edward R. Murrow College of Communication
Washington State University

Sydney Carver
Department of Communication
George Mason University

Josh Compton
Department of Speech Communication
Dartmouth College

John Cook
Melbourne Centre for Behaviour Change
University of Melbourne

Christopher M. Dobmeier
School of Communication
Northwestern University

Kaylin L. Duncan
Department of Communication Studies
University of Alabama

Sarah A. Geegan
Department of Communication
University of Kentucky

Yan Huang
Jack J. Valenti School of Communication
University of Houston

Bobi Ivanov
Department of Communication
University of Kentucky

Sojung Claire Kim
Department of Communication
George Mason University

Eunsung Lee
Department of Media and Communication
Sungkyunkwan University

Jiyoung Lee
Department of Media and Communication
Sungkyunkwan University

Tong Lin
Department of Communication
University of Maryland

Sai Datta Mikkilineni
College of Communication & Information Sciences
The University of Alabama

Xiaoli Nan
Department of Communication
University of Maryland

Caitlin B. Neal
Hubbard School of Journalism and Mass Communication
University of Minnesota Twin Cities

Kimberly A. Parker
Department of Communication
University of Kentucky

Stephen A. Rains
Department of Communication
University of Arizona

Sergei A. Samoilenko
Department of Communication
George Mason University

Cuihua (Cindy) Shen
Department of Communication
University of California, Davis

Rongwei Tang
Hubbard School of Journalism and Mass Communication
University of Minnesota Twin Cities

Kathryn Thier
Department of Communication
University of Maryland

Ida Tovar
School of Medicine
University of Utah

Cindy Turner
School of Medicine
University of Utah

Emily K. Vraga
Hubbard School of Journalism and Mass Communication
University of Minnesota Twin Cities

Nathan Walter
School of Communication
Northwestern University

Yuan Wang
Department of Communication
University of Maryland

Weirui Wang
Department of Communication
Florida International University

Echo L. Warner
College of Nursing
University of Utah

Kevin B. Wright
Department of Communication
George Mason University

Haoning Xue
Department of Communication
University of Utah

Kun Yan
Department of Communication
University of Arizona

Jessica A. Zier
School of Communication
Northwestern University

Preface

The study of human communication has changed considerably since the turn of the century, with the advent of the Internet, the proliferation of social media platforms, and the many changes in human interaction and information exchange they led to. At the same time, we have witnessed a number of significant crises globally, including climate change, the COVID-19 pandemic, natural disasters, terrorism, and political unrest. During times of crisis, people often turn to social media for information and social support, as both content producers and consumers. The lack of traditional gatekeepers on many social media platforms and Web 2.0 technology has allowed misinformation to spread quickly and widely during times of crisis. Such events and changes in social media have offered a variety of opportunities for scholars to study the development, spread, and impact of online misinformation during crisis events. For example, as we witnessed with COVID-19, views of vaccinations and other preventive measures on social media were often influenced by the spread of misinformation according to differing political viewpoints and agendas, foreign adversary interference, and many other factors that contributed to the sea of misinformation across social media. Social media have become increasingly important sources for information in terms of health and crisis communication, and social media platforms often function as a convenient source of information during crisis situations. Such platforms, including Facebook, X (formerly Twitter), Instagram, and YouTube have accelerated information transmission in crisis contexts across social, cultural, and geographical boundaries. Real-time (mis)information exchange occurs rapidly online via a variety of social media platforms, which makes it challenging for government officials, researchers, public health experts, and other federal, state, and local government entities to identify and potentially correct misinformation about risk and crisis situations.

Communication plays an increasingly critical role in crisis events, particularly in identifying and analyzing the dissemination and impact of misinformation on various segments of the population and in correcting misinformation and/or replacing it with scientific, evidence-based explanations of causes as well as solutions to reduce harm. Social media's ability to tailor information in very specific ways may lead audiences to be exposed to relatively limited or politically biased information about the causes of crisis events or the best policies or course of action to mitigate risk to individuals. During times of crisis, the public may increase their reliance on social media to obtain information from these platforms and from social network members they trust. (Mis)information) is rapidly shared, reshared, and commented on by others online as it is frequently disseminated across multiple social media platforms (e.g., Facebook, X (Twitter), TikTok). Individuals and their social media network members vary in their education level and scientific literacy, and this affects their interpretations of scientific information reported by government officials or the media and their perceptions of the risk and severity of crisis events as well as their behaviors. While social media serve many useful functions by providing multiple sources of good information to the public during a crisis event, there is substantial evidence that misinformation about crisis events has spread rapidly on social media, including information about climate change, vaccinations, and COVID-19. A growing number of researchers have demonstrated, however, that it is possible to preemptively warn social media users about the spread of misinformation during crisis events and also to correct misinformation.

This book addresses these issues and many others in the study of online misinformation during crisis events. The contributors to this volume have extensive research experience of communication of misinformation on social media during times of crisis. They focus on a variety of important questions and issues related to social media misinformation during times of crisis. For example, to what extent can social media play a role in reducing risks to the public during times of crisis? What theoretical frameworks are useful in understanding the spread of misinformation and correcting misinformation on social media during crisis events? What research tools and approaches (e.g., information correction, big data analysis) can researchers use to identify and track misinformation about crisis events on social media? What approaches are most useful for reaching segments of the population who have extreme political views or who may be resistant to changing their perceptions of crisis events?

Kevin B. Wright

1

Characteristics of Crisis Misinformation Messages on Social Media

Christopher M. Dobmeier, Jessica A. Zier, and Nathan Walter

School of Communication, Northwestern University

Crisis and misinformation go hand in hand with what some may call a marriage made in hell. To be sure, during times of crisis, risk and uncertainty are elevated, while the quality and veracity of information tends to drop, contributing to an atmosphere ripe for rumors, misinformation, and outright deceptions. Adding to this mix are a plethora of social media platforms that tend to favor sensational and emotion-laden content; this is another way to say that this is a major problem.

In discussing crisis misinformation and social media, it is important to put some hard truths on the table. First, *misinformation* is as old as its more responsible sibling, *information*, so it is important to firmly foreground any discussion on misinformation in a historical context. Second, because the label of "misinformation" is used to cover a wide array of content, from minor inaccuracies and harmless hoaxes to vicious propaganda and conspiracy theories, the need to define and distinguish different types of misinformation is a challenge in and of itself. Third, that for millennia individuals, groups, and entire societies have fallen victim to misinformation strongly suggests that humans may have a collective blind spot when it comes to accepting untruths. Fourth, whether one supports that technology fundamentally changes humans or it simply allows humans to change, misinformation has an undeniable strong reaction in conjunction with information technology, most recently social media.

Broadly speaking, the structure of this chapter corresponds with these four hard truths. We begin with a brief historical review showing how our understanding of misinformation both is affected by and transcends social and technological evolutions. This review is followed by an attempt to define misinformation, which examines both its general features and its common taxonomies. The bulk of the chapter, however, outlines some of the psychological, sociological, and technological factors that perpetuate humans' susceptibility to misinformation. Then we focus on a series of very different case studies to illustrate how and why misinformation spreads on social media. The chapter concludes with a deceptively optimistic prognosis for social recovery.

Communication and Misinformation: Crisis Events in the Age of Social Media, First Edition.
Edited by Kevin B. Wright.
© 2025 John Wiley & Sons, Inc. Published 2025 by John Wiley & Sons, Inc.

A (Very) Brief History of Misinformation: From Hunter-Gatherers to Russian Bots

> Human beings are the animal that cannot become anything without pretending to be it first.
>
> —*W. H. Auden (1907–1973)*

While a comprehensive review of the history of misinformation or every lie ever told is beyond the scope of this chapter, it is difficult to grasp the role played by misinformation in times of crisis without some historical context. Consider the astonishing fact that humans have spent nearly 99% of their history as hunter-gatherers, living in small groups and dividing their time between fighting and fleeing from predators or other competing groups. This lifestyle highlighted two very important but often scarce resources—food and shelter. Indeed, there are good reasons to suspect that much of human communication in ancestral times revolved around securing these resources. When food and shelter are the two main concerns an individual must grapple with, knowingly or unknowingly misinforming their group is likely to lead to severe consequences. For instance, if they were to tell their tribe that a poisonous berry was edible, that sabretooth cats are docile, or that there was an elephant near the lake but omit to add that hyenas as big as bears also gather there, the result was likely to be swift and bloody. This may explain why estimated murder rates within hunter-gatherer societies were often over 10% (Rosling, Rosling, & Rosling, 2018). Simply put, misinformation had no place during these times.

Over the 10 millennia from the end of hunter-gatherer society to the Greek empire's rise, misinformation evolved considerably. As information gained functions well beyond mere survival, misinformation also served more purposes. One such purpose was found in the ancient Greeks' art of storytelling, and there was no better storyteller than Herodotus (484–425 BCE), who was known as "the father of history." Despite this, depicting Herodotus as a historian is both wrong and a paradox: the label is a misnomer because Herodotus' accounts included more fiction than fact, and a paradox because the English word "history" owes its origin to Herodotus' travelogues, called *Histories*, which are an entertaining cocktail of exaggerated encounters and fanciful tales, garnished with a tiny drizzle of facts. From camel-eating ants in Persia to a 300-foot-thick wall in Babylon, Herodotus had a penchant for not spoiling a good story with facts. Although this part-historian part-fantasist was criticized by his contemporaries for telling lies (Baragwanath & de Bakker, 2012), he was also celebrated as a brilliant storyteller who had an immense influence on generations of orators, particularly those embracing the gray area between embellished truth and deception.

Although early misinformation was characterized by playful and even comical humbuggery, it eventually took a dark turn in the twentieth century, ushering in a new era of far more serious and consequential deceit. As global tensions grew in the lead-up to World War I, misinformation took on a new meaning as European countries began devoting considerable resources to voluntary military recruitment. The result of these efforts was the first large-scale and modern attempt at propaganda (from the Latin *propagare*, to disseminate), which demonized enemies and justified the government's cause. The scale and magnitude of the propaganda machine during World War I ensured that falsehoods about the enemy traveled far and wide, and with great consequences.

Over the next two decades, the traditional propaganda tools of World War I, such as newspapers, leaflets, and full-color posters, were supplanted by more sophisticated media technologies, including radio and film. Although propaganda had become virtually unavoidable during World War I, its influence and impact somehow intensified during the ensuing decades. After Adolf Hitler took over the reins of the national government in 1932, for instance, one of his first political moves was to establish the Ministry of Propaganda and Public Enlightenment, which he placed in the hands of Joseph Goebbels. This meant that for the first time in history a country at peace would have a propaganda ministry, or a lie factory, to glorify its ideology and dehumanize its enemies. Meanwhile, in the West the propaganda machine was picking up steam as well, with award-winning directors such as Frank Capra and John Huston being recruited to create "orientation" (a fancy word for propaganda) films for the US Department of War. One such orientation film series, *Why We Fight*, had been viewed by at least 54 million Americans by the end of the war (Rollins, 1996). While empirical evidence on its impact in swaying public opinion was inconclusive, its cultural significance in offering a coherent and memorable rationale for a total war is undeniable.

Since the emergence of social media, the misinformation playbook has only become more complex. While social media platforms have been associated with the democratization of information and mass communication, they have also opened a Pandora's box of potential threats to democracy. These matters came to the fore when Russia was found meddling in the 2016 US presidential election by employing *bots*—spam accounts that post autonomously using preprogrammed scripts—to spread misinformation and even hijack civic conversations across social media, sowing distrust in electoral procedures and polarizing constituents (Howard, 2018). In an instant, this so-called computational propaganda became an international hazard, as countries near and far grappled with the new cyberreality (Woolley & Howard, 2018). As 2016 drew to a close, Oxford Languages offered the perfect epitaph by declaring its 2016 Word of the Year to be "post-truth": "relating to or denoting circumstances in which objective facts are less influential in shaping public opinion than appeals to emotion and personal belief" (Oxford Languages, 2016).

These new agents of misinformation, social media bots, are just the tip of the iceberg. Artificial intelligence (AI) and machine learning, for example, underlie new misinformation technologies such as the often playful but sometimes nefarious *deepfakes*, programs designed to manipulate pictures, videos, and audio to pass as authentic primary sources of information. As these technologies become more advanced, the misinformation they spread may become more convincing and harder to detect and to deter.

The picture that emerges from this brief overview illustrates that misinformation has been one of the true constants throughout human history from hunter-gatherers to bots and AI. Although cultural, social, and technological environments change, the hold that misinformation has on humans has remained. So, rather than searching for a magical algorithm or a technological fix that would rid the world of misinformation, it is time to look in the mirror and understand what makes humans so vulnerable. To begin, it is necessary to know what exactly misinformation is.

What Is, What Is Not, and What May Be Defined as Misinformation

> You're saying it's a falsehood and ... Sean Spicer, our press secretary, gave alternative facts to that.
>
> —*Kellyanne Conway*

When Kellyanne Conway, counselor to President Trump, used the phrase "alternative facts" to defend the White House press secretary Sean Spicer's false statements about the attendance numbers for Donald Trump's inauguration, she was probably not aware that she was contributing yet another term to the already overcrowded concept of misinformation. Indeed, the exponential growth in misinformation has arguably been outpaced only by ill-fated attempts to define it, as was painfully illustrated in a recent systematic review that yielded more than 30 distinct definitions of this very popular concept (Wang, Their, & Nan, 2022). A closer look at how the literature on misinformation has tackled the challenge of defining its subject of research reveals two distinct approaches: structural definition and taxonomy.

The structural approach attempts to define misinformation by highlighting the essential elements that make up the concept. Consider the following definition of misinformation: "Cases in which people's beliefs about factual matters are not supported by clear evidence and expert opinion" (Nyhan & Reifler, 2010, p. 305). Although similar definitions are commonly used in research and practice, it does not take too long to identify a number of loose ends. To start, the benchmarks for "clear evidence and expert opinion" are fuzzy: how clear should the evidence be, and who has the monopoly on expertise? For instance, next time a dentist who recommends flossing can rightfully be accused of spreading misinformation since the health benefits of routine flossing are not supported by scientific evidence, according to a meta-analysis published by the Cochrane Library, a reputable hub for health information (Berchier et al., 2008). Similarly, one may sneer at an individual who refuses to wear a surgical mask while coughing on a crowded train, but the Surgeon General, Jerome Adams, tweeted "Stop buying masks!" not too long ago. As these examples show, not only do experts sometimes disagree, but the scientific basis for evidence is rarely clear.

Recent attempts have been made to improve existing definitions by emphasizing the dynamic nature of expertise and evidence. One promising attempt comes from Vraga and Bode (2020), who distinguish between different levels of expert consensus from controversial (e.g., astronauts are essential to the future of space programs) to settled (e.g., human activity contributes to climate change), as well as different levels of amount and quality of evidence from controversial (e.g., it is safe to eat foods grown using pesticides) to settled (e.g., there is no evidence that vaccines cause autism). Although this approach retains greater nuance than binary definitions, it has limitations, notably the rarity of near-universal agreement and strong evidence during crises.

Moreover, the distinction definitions make between factual and nonfactual matters is key. On the face of it, the focus on fact-based statements, which can be proved or disproved by objective evidence, makes total sense. On a second glance, however, this distinction raises several concerns. If only fact-based or checkable claims can be labeled as misinformation, the vast majority of public discourse, including opinions, rumors, predictions, and general speculation, is off-limits. This gray area between fact- and opinion-based statements, however, is often what characterizes rumors, innuendo, and pseudoscience. Further, this concern is amplified by people's general tendency to conflate fact and opinion, as revealed by a Pew Research Center (Mitchell et al., 2018) poll showing that only 26% of US adults could accurately and reliably classify them. To this end, if people are unable to distinguish factual from nonfactual matters, the definition is unnecessarily limiting.

Furthermore, this definition of misinformation does not say much about intentionality. Typically, the notion of intentionality helps distinguish misinformation and disinformation, with the latter being defined as false information deliberately created and disseminated with malicious intent (Nan, Thier, & Wang, 2023), whereas the former focuses on instances where there is no clear evidence of intent to mislead or deceive. As with murder cases, where intent is often an essential element in securing a conviction, intent in spreading falsehoods is a major consideration. Antitobacco policymakers and campaigns were successful at dismantling the industry because they were able to show that tobacco companies deliberately deceived the public by minimizing the risk of smoking and by downplaying their responsibility to their customers. Although there is practical value in this distinction, intent is difficult to prove (at least not without litigation), leading some to conclude that "for the purpose of studying misinformation impact, [proving intent] ... is not necessary" (Nan et al., 2023, p. 3).

Structural definitions of misinformation are useful in that they attempt to bound the concept by its underlying components, such as expertise, evidence, checkability, and intent. Still, given the variety of what can be labeled misinformation, perhaps it is an unbounded phenomenon. To address this problem, scholars have offered to pinpoint misinformation not by focusing on its structure but rather by outlining the variety of categories that constitute it. One noteworthy attempt has provided a typology of *fake news* using level of facticity (or the degree to which a message relies on facts) and author's intention to deceive as its delineating factors (Tandoc, Lim, & Ling, 2018). This typology is informative on a number of levels. First, it houses a wide variety of genres—from conventional (e.g., native advertising and fabrication) to unconventional (e.g., parody and news satire) misinformation. Dimensions of facticity and intent further help crystalize similarities and differences between types of fake news. According to this typology, for instance, both fabrication and news parody contain a low degree of facts (low facticity) but whereas the former intends to mislead, news parody (e.g., *The Onion*) forges ludicrous stories to provide a commentary on current affairs. Similarly, while native advertising and news satire tend to share a relatively high degree of factual basis (high facticity), they fulfill drastically different functions: selling products versus using humor and wit to offer constructive social criticism.

All things considered, researchers and practitioners will continue to wrestle with the definitional challenges of misinformation for the foreseeable future, especially as the demand for effective responses to its proliferation grows. Common to all types of misinformation, however, are underlying psychological mechanisms that make individuals vulnerable to their influence.

The Six Degrees of Susceptibility

> When thoughts flow smoothly, people nod along.
>
> —*Schwarz et al. (2016)*

The need for deliberate misinformation control arises from the growing discrepancy between the rapid spread of false information and humans' cognitive capacity to recognize and counteract it. Their brains, with their complex thought, memory, emotional experiences, and information-processing abilities developed over a 200,000-year history, set humans apart from other species. Yet, misinformation has evolved swiftly, taking advantage of individuals' cognitive and emotional vulnerabilities. The six influences that follow exemplify the paradox that the qualities that define humanity also make humans prone to misinformation.

Mental Models

Derived from Craik's (1943) hypothesis that humans hold their own mental maps of the world as they experience it, mental models being internal representations of how the world operates (Johnson-Laird, 2013). More concretely, mental models are intuitive systems that help an individual attend, contextualize, and establish links between prior knowledge and new information, which are used to understand the world before them. Consequently, mental modeling is what coheres all relevant pieces of information, allowing an individual to assess a scenario and ultimately take appropriate action. For example, they may understand the potential consequences of drunk driving through mental modeling (e.g., if they drink alcohol, they will be impaired; and if they drive while impaired, they may cause an accident).

One crucial pitfall of mental modeling is that it is also prone to connecting irrelevant or inaccurate cognitions to form an inaccurate—albeit coherent—inference, paving the perilous path for the flourishing of superstitions and conspiracy theories (Van Prooijen, Douglas, & De Inocencio, 2018). The moon landing conspiracy theory, for example, has survived decades of debunking because it provides people with a relatively simple mental model that easily explains away a lot of questions arising from the moon landing, such as why the iconic moon landing photo shows no stars or why the United States has not conducted another lunar landing since 1972 (for an illustration of the moon landing conspiracy theory mental model, see Figure 1.1). Although these questions often have sound answers, none are as simple and encompassing as the suggestion that the landing was faked by the US government. A well-crafted conspiracy theory like this provides its victims with a coherent story to explain phenomena that are otherwise difficult or tedious to understand, ultimately exploiting the human preference for complete explanations (Korman & Khemlani, 2020). To this end, debunking conspiracy theories is a mammoth task that requires an alternative explanation not for a single piece of misinformation, but for a constellation of misinformation.

Motivated Reasoning

As discussed, the reasoning process of mental modeling can be influenced by external factors such as the quality and completeness of information. Mental modeling may further be biased by one's internal motivations (Kunda, 1990). According to the motivated reasoning approach, individuals are not always motivated to reach the most accurate conclusion and often prefer explanations that align with their preexisting beliefs. Additionally, they tend to accept confirmatory information and to reject disconfirmatory information, which

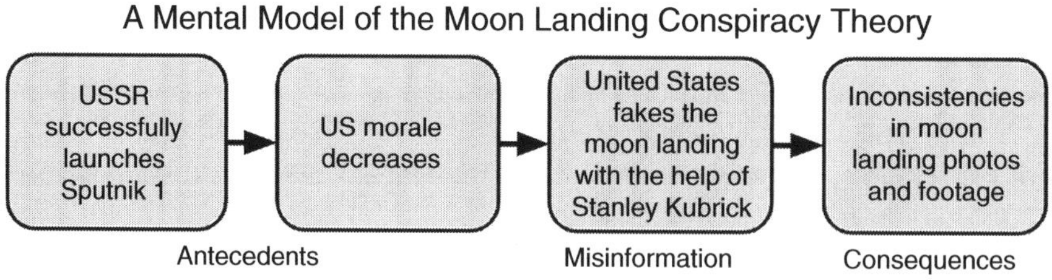

Figure 1.1 A mental model of the moon landing conspiracy theory. Successfully debunking the theory requires the reconciliation not only of its perceived consequences but also of its perceived anteceding motivations—a tall order for standard misinformation corrections.

means that mental models are continually self-reinforcing (Johnson-Laird, 2013; Korman & Khemlani, 2020). Put succinctly, people do not always rationalize in rational ways.

Continuing with the moon landing example, a cynic who naturally distrusts the institutions of government and science is likely more susceptible to the moon landing conspiracy theory than the average person because the conspiracy aligns with their preexisting beliefs (i.e., it fits neatly into their mental model). Further, a cynic may hold implicit or explicit goals to confirm evidence that supports the conspiracy theory and/or to reject or avoid any information intended to debunk the conspiracy theory (e.g., Kahan, 2016; Kim & Cao, 2016). In tandem, these dispositions create the perfect environment for either misinformation or its corrections to thrive—but rarely both.

Memory

Memory is limited, malleable, and prone to error—whether such memories are mundane (e.g., what time one went to the bathroom last night) or significant (e.g., where one was when they received the news of the September 11 attacks). When it comes to communication, not only does one need to remember *what* was said, but maybe also *who* said it and *what the response was* to it, all of which influence the believability of a message. Such details may play a role in distinguishing fact from fiction; for example, if one received a message that President Bush knew about the September 11 attacks before they happened, one might notice that it was from a conspiratorial uncle and promptly ignore it. In this case, the untrustworthiness of the uncle functions as a *discounting cue*, a signal that indicates that the message should be taken with a grain of salt. However, discounting cues are useful only if they are remembered. One may come across misinformation and immediately discount it, but may later remember the misinformation without recalling why it had been discounted or that it was ever discounted. This phenomenon is known as the *sleeper effect*, and it makes people vulnerable to the delayed influence of misinformation (Priester et al., 1999).

Especially in crisis communication, conveying false or incomplete memory can not only lead to suboptimal public action or inaction but also fuel related conspiracy theories that undermine the public's trust in government. Bush's benign lapse in memory recall of the September 11 events heightened public speculation and conspiracy theories that the government had known about the attack before it happened (Greenberg, 2004). And, if one forgot that the person propounding such a theory was one's tin-foil-hat uncle (i.e., the discounting cue), one was just a bit more prone to believe it.

Source Credibility

Echoing the assumptions of the sleeper effect, believability of misinformation falls not only on the message itself but also on the relationship between the messenger and recipient. Swindles, shams, hoaxes, and other fraudulent spectacles have been known throughout history, but their success is often not a testament to the stupidity of the individuals who fall for them but rather to the persuasiveness of the individuals who pedal them. Each fraudster—from the eponymous Charles Ponzi to InfoWars host Alex Jones—played a crucial role for their target audience: a credible source.

More particularly, these sources are seen as competent and trustworthy (O'Keefe, 2018). The InfoWars audience, for example, perceived Alex Jones to be knowledgeable, intelligent, and qualified to speak on the topics at hand and his reporting to be honest, unselfish, and fair. In other words, the audience expected Jones to provide them with accurate information and to have their best interests at heart. Of course, these source perceptions are all subjective: one person's pariah is another's prophet. Faulty information may be readily accepted by an audience that relies on the perceived expertise and trustworthiness of the communicator rather than deliberating on the argument (O'Keefe, 2018). Plainly, misinformation does not have to be compelling to be accepted so long as the person sharing it is compelling.

Negativity Bias

What comes to mind when you think of misinformation? Maybe you think of baseless claims about vaccines causing autism, of climate change as a ploy to push a progressive political agenda, or of the 2020 US presidential election having been stolen. It is no coincidence if all that comes to mind evokes strong negative emotions. Such affect accelerates and broadens the diffusion of misinformation across social media (Vosoughi, Roy, & Aral, 2018) and is therefore a key player in the prominence and longevity of misinformation. The main reason for this is the negativity bias: the human propensity to attend to, learn from, and use negative information rather than positive or emotionally neutral information (Soroka, Fournier, and Nir, 2019).

What makes the negativity bias so dangerous is that it influences the communication process on many levels. First, messages that appeal to negative emotions are more strongly attended to than those with appeals to positive or neutral emotions (Soroka et al., 2019). Second, messages that are not negatively valenced are more likely to turn negative when communicated from one person to another (Bebbington et al., 2017). And third, over time negative emotional experiences can potentially strengthen an individual's ability to recall misinformation (Lee et al., 2023). Taken altogether, messages with misinformation that evoke fear, disgust, or anger do not only linger in one's mind but beg to be communicated to others.

Fluency

Susceptibility to misinformation is also influenced by the metacognitive cue of fluency, which relates to how easily we process information. Judgments and decisions often rely on metacognitive cues, such as the ease or difficulty of recalling information and generating supporting arguments. For example, if a friend asks one to tell them what one loves most about one's job and one struggles to produce any good examples, the metacognitive experience of difficulty is an indication that one may want to start looking for another job.

The ease with which misinformation is processed can contribute to its spread. Take, for instance, "the Big Lie," the false narrative that the 2020 US presidential election had been stolen from Donald Trump and that the Republicans who certified President Biden's victory were complicit. While some estimates suggest that over one-third of the US public continue to believe in widespread election fraud favoring the Democrats, it was a small clique of *big liars* that peddled these falsehoods in the media. Through repetition, the lie became more familiar and easier to process, and this eventually led people to support it. Put differently, people assume that a familiar opinion is a prevalent opinion; and a repetitive voice can sometimes sound like a chorus (Weaver et al., 2007), even if it is spreading dangerous lies. Overall, in combating falsehoods, not only their veracity should be considered but also the relative ease with which they are processed.

Collectively, these six influence mechanisms are products of human evolutionary history, which are deeply ingrained within one's cognitive architecture to assist in the interpretation of and interaction with the information in one's surroundings. The age of social media has unwittingly provided fertile ground for the exploitation of these innate tendencies. To gauge the full extent of the impact of these influences requires an examination of the compounding influence of social media, where the exploitation of human vulnerabilities not only exists but thrives because of its keystone function in the social media business model.

The Compounding Effect of Social Media

The heartbeat of any social media platform is the engagement of its user base. User engagement not only helps these platforms gain sociopolitical capital but is also necessary to sustain their business. Social media platforms rely heavily on advertising revenue; for instance, 97% of Facebook's 2022 global revenue came from advertising (Dixon, 2023). However, this attention and engagement-centered business model works only if social media companies can demonstrate that their platforms attract enough eyeballs to justify advertising campaigns. In other words, user engagement—such as liking, commenting on, sharing, or otherwise interacting with posts—has become meticulously and granularly cataloged (Zuboff, 2019). The amassed data does not just feed in to advertisers' business but also to the creation of individualized cybernetic identities from users' online behaviors (Bollmer, 2018), by which platforms can generate an irresistible content feed for individual users to keep them on the platform for as long as possible.

These precise, user-driven recommendations become a deeper issue when social media platforms act in their own interest at the expense of their customers. If one were to take a minute to scroll through the feed of one's favorite social media platform, paying close attention to the posts. Did we lose you? Oh, good, you're back! Which posts stood out the most? The odds are that one paid less attention to an acquaintance's baby shower updates and more to a conspiratorial uncle's expletive-filled allegation that the government is spying on them through the neighborhood squirrels because it plays into the negativity bias. Social media companies are not oblivious to human tendencies or to the fact that they can be exploited. For example, Facebook whistleblower Frances Haugen revealed evidence that the company not only was aware of the impacts of polarizing and hateful content on its platform but that it deliberately chose not to mitigate the risks because ridding such negative content would negatively impact ad revenue (Zubrow, 2021). Given that archetypal misinformation is also negative and polarizing (albeit captivating), the inaction of Facebook in this case bodes well for its diffusion. Additionally, platforms such as X (formerly Twitter) have cut their information integrity teams, citing ad revenue drops as the reason for layoffs. Operations to mitigate misinformation are simply unprofitable.

The pitfalls of algorithmically curated social media are amplified in times of crisis, during which there is pressing demand from the public for real-time information as events unfold. In one such crisis on November 24, 2017, people were suddenly evacuated from London's Oxford Circus during a Black Friday shopping event and told to take shelter in nearby shops. This led to chaos in the streets. Some people called the police, claiming to have heard gunshots, but the incident was a false alarm. Yet, on social media, content algorithms systematically amplified ambiguous, incorrect, and even propagandistic information, leading to explosive response (Eriksson Krutrök & Lindgren, 2022). According to the principle of fluency, the repetition of misinformation made such claims more certain. In highly uncertain crises, it is understandable how baseless claims gain traction.

The mental susceptibility of humans to misinformation and its exploitation by social media platforms have together created the perfect condition for the dissemination of misleading or downright deceptive messages. The following are some real-world cases that have resulted from this thriving misinformation ecosystem, beginning with a conspiracy of epic proportions.

Case Study 1: As #Plandemic Goes Viral

The early days of the COVID-19 pandemic have provided a steady stream of jaw-dropping moments, from the president of the United States musing about the possibility of injecting disinfectant as a deterrent to the virus to a star-studded Instagram video of two dozen celebrities leading a singalong of John Lennon's "Imagine," with the opening line "Imagine there's no heaven," as the mortality rate soared and hospitals were overwhelmed with COVID-19 patients. These moments pale in comparison to the slickly produced 26-minute video called *Plandemic*, which claimed that "a shadowy cabal of elites was using the virus and a potential vaccine to profit and gain power" (Frenkel, Decker, & Alba, 2020). The video went online on May 4, 2020, and quickly gained steam across the media landscape from legacy outlets, Facebook, YouTube, and Vimeo to networks of shady websites. Just two weeks after it was digitally unleashed, *Plandemic* was estimated to have garnered more than a million interactions, with #Plandemic taking over Twitter and other social media platforms (Kearney, Chiang, & Massey, 2020).

While the video's production quality was not quite that of a Hollywood blockbuster, it told a gripping story. A discredited scientist, Judy Mikovits, cast as the protagonist, accuses the scientific community and pharmaceutical industry of burying her research showing the harms from vaccines and of deliberately trying to infect and then reinfect (with the help of surgical masks, of course) innocent people with COVID-19, which, by the way, was not a novel virus but rather a direct outcome of a flu vaccine gone awry. Dr. Anthony Fauci, the nation's top expert on infectious disease during the early pandemic, was cast as the archnemesis who had been responsible for creating the pandemic. The video was thoroughly fact-checked, always with the same conclusion, that the staggering claims in *Plandemic* were baseless, misleading, and false (Gorski, 2020). However, no amount of fact-checking, rebuttals, and even censorship was able to stop this nonsensical, long-winded, and poorly produced video from circulating. To experts in crisis communication, the popularity and virality of this video is anything but surprising. The 26-minute nightmarish babble had been tailored to exploit some of the vulnerabilities that make misinformation so difficult to fend off.

To begin with, the video was designed to evoke strong negative emotions, which are known to generate engagement (Lee et al., 2023). In crisis communication, negative emotions such as anger, fear, and disgust are abundant and this was certainly true of the COVID-19 pandemic. High public uncertainty and people anxiously sifting through contradictory information from media, public officials, and other experts were the perfect recipe for negative emotions. Humans are drawn to negative information (i.e., the negativity bias), and it is easy to understand why so many people were attentive to this alarmist and sensational content.

While the negativity bias may explain the attention given to the video, it does not fully account for why people accepted its false claims. To better understand this, another concept from the six degrees of influence is necessary. From the mental model perspective, although *Plandemic* made numerous outrageous claims, it imparted no information that conspiracy theory supporters did not already know. Consider the conspiracy theory claiming that pharmaceutical companies leverage political and cultural levers of power and corruption to increase profits while unsuspecting citizens suffer from expensive, ineffective, and outright dangerous treatments. As with most resilient conspiracy theories, the big pharma conspiracy contains a kernel of truth. Corporations, especially large ones, often act in immoral ways to maximize their profits, and health-care disparities are well documented in many countries. But there is quite a distance between this sad reality and the idea of a cabal of evil elites and greedy doctors colluding to infect the public with disease only to sell expensive and dangerous treatments. Notwithstanding the inaccuracy of the claims, this conspiracy theory provides a highly coherent mental model. So, if one already believes that self-interested corporations pay off politicians and doctors to take advantage of defenseless citizens while laughing all the way to the bank, it might not take much more to believe the accusations leveled in *Plandemic*.

The identity of *Plandemic*'s lead character is also likely to have been influential. Although the film reviews Judy Mikovits's troubled career and downfall, she is not painted as the disgraced doctor whose scientific work was found to have involved lab contamination and was later retracted from leading academic journals, and who was discredited by her colleagues and the academic community. Rather, the film portrays Mikovits as a highly credible source and as a martyr who left her lab out of principle.

Case Study 2: Goncharov, Prigozhin, and President Mozzarella Walk into a Bar

Goncharov, arguably the greatest mafia film ever made, is enjoying a resurgence in popularity on social media. In the film the Russian president, Vladimir Putin, offers his condolences to the widow of an opposition leader before a mysterious plane crash kills her husband, and Donald Trump introduces the Italian president, Sergio Mattarella, as President Mozzarella. What do these episodes have in common? They represent completely false events that can be easily discredited without very thorough fact-checking. Unlike the *Plandemic* case study, however, these meme-like examples are by and large innocuous and even somewhat amusing.

Many of the same reasons that humans are susceptible to serious harmful misinformation can also explain how individuals fall victim to seemingly benign hoaxes and rumors. This can even happen to self-proclaimed experts in misinformation, including Nathan Walter, the third author of this chapter, who one day encountered a poster of a 1973 Martin Scorsese film titled *Goncharov*, dubbed "The greatest mafia movie ever made." The initial suspicion ("How is it that I have never hear about this great Scorsese film?") quickly dissipated when other users on social media discussed the film at length, arguing about its plot, soundtrack, and symbolism, and even referencing specific scenes ("Oh, that incredible flashback scene or how would the movie end if Katya had a gun in the hotel room?"). Hollywood mainstays such as Lynda Carter and Henry Winkler claimed that they attended the premiere together and tweeted a photo to prove it. Even Martin Scorsese, the renowned director of this must-watch gangster movie, himself confirmed that he had made the film years ago. The only problem, of course, was that the movie was completely fake.

It is easy to see, from the principles discussed earlier, how one could fall for the well-crafted Goncharov hoax. There was not much evidence to substantiate the existence of the film, and an evaluation of the meme—searching through the International Movie Database, scouting for corroborating evidence, and carefully evaluating the story's sources—would have revealed that it did not exist. But truth evaluations often do not rely on analytical thinking but rather on metacognitive cues such as "When it is easy, it seems familiar, and familiar feels true." Hence, while there was no corroborating evidence for the existence of the film outside of social media, the poster of the film was reminiscent of those of other mafia films from the 1970s. The film's fictional cast—from Robert De Niro in the role of the Goncharov, a hitman with a heart of gold, to his love interest, played by Cybill Shepherd, and the antagonist, played by Harvey Keitel—all made sense as they were actors who would have been working with Scorsese during that period. Every piece of the story was accompanied by an intuitive believability and, hence, it was easy to accept it at face value without analyzing its different components too closely. If there had been anything about the story that felt wrong or at the very least highly surprising, it may have ended up being scrutinized more carefully. At first glance, however, every piece of the Goncharov hoax felt right and so I, Nathan Walter, along with millions of other film buffs, was fooled.

Turning away from fictional Russian mobsters, we now discuss the very real president of Russia. Engulfed in an unpopular and morally difficult to justify war with Ukraine, Russia has experienced an uptick in criticism of its president, Vladimir Putin. On June 23, 2023, longtime Putin associate Yevgeny Prigozhin launched an armed mutiny against the Russian government, seizing control over strategic positions in Russia. Prigozhin quickly turned from a friend to a foe, becoming a serious threat to Putin's grip on power. A few months after the rebellion, Prigozhin and nine other rebels were killed in a plane crash north of Moscow.

To those who follow Russian politics, this outcome was not very surprising. In response, satirists drew attention to the extensive list of Putin's enemies who have died prematurely and under mysterious circumstances, claiming that Putin called Prigozhin's widow to express his condolences *before* the plane actually crashed. These stories were widely circulated on social media, often passing for serious news. This highlights two potential concerns. First, the blurring of the lines between misinformation and satire is not uncommon, and thus helpful definitions of misinformation should be able to distinguish between satire and other forms of entertainment. Second, even though those who read the story may have understood its satirical intent, they may remember the story itself longer than they remember that it is clearly fictional. Given enough time, a sleeper effect may emerge whereby people remember the message (i.e., Putin called Prigozhin's wife about the plane crash before it took place) but forget its source (i.e., satirical news). If the sleeper effect takes hold (Priester et al., 1999), it is no wonder that untrustworthy or even explicitly satirical sources can become hubs for misinformation.

Lastly, while scrolling through social media, one may encounter a post claiming that President Donald Trump referred to the Italian president Sergio Mattarella as President Mozzarella. If one does not have the time or the curiosity to check the transcripts and videos, would one believe it? According to the motivated reasoning approach, the answer is "it depends." A Trump supporter would probably discount this as liberal slander, but a Trump opponent would be more likely to believe that the incident did happen. The viral post about Trump's Oval Office gaffe turned out to be completely false, but this does not guarantee that it will be accepted as such by those who do not share his political ideology.

Conclusion

The interplay between misinformation and age-old human instincts is a remarkable and unpredictable aspect of the evolving information landscape. The early hunter-gatherers who protected their communities from fierce predators could hardly have foreseen into today's anonymous computer geeks spreading misinformation to disrupt society. Challenging misinformation demands a comprehensive approach encompassing policy, technology, and education. While there is much to be done on the policy and technology front, arguably the greatest challenge is arguably education, as humans must somehow learn to stop giving in to their most natural instincts. Although the bell of misinformation cannot be unrung, the persistence of human instincts should inspire praxis rather than paralysis in the ongoing battle against this millennia-old enemy.

References

Baragwanath, E., & de Bakker, M. (2012). *Myth, truth, and narrative in Herodotus*. Oxford University Press.

Bebbington, K., MacLeod, C., Ellison, T. M., & Fay, N. (2017). The sky is falling: Evidence of a negativity bias in the social transmission of information. *Evolution and Human Behavior, 38*(1), 92–101. http://dx.doi.org/10.1016/j.evolhumbehav.2016.07.004

Berchier, C. E., Slot, D. E., Haps, S., & Van der Weijden, G. A. (2008). The efficacy of dental floss in addition to a toothbrush on plaque and parameters of gingival inflammation: A systematic review. *International Journal of Dental Hygiene, 6*(4), 265–279. http://dx.doi.org/10.1111/j.1601-5037.2008.00336.x

Bollmer, G. D. (2018). *Theorizing digital cultures*. SAGE.

Craik, K. (1943). *The nature of explanation*. Cambridge University Press.

Dixon, S. J. (2023, August 29). *Annual revenue generated by Meta Platforms from 2009 to 2022, by segment* [infographic]. Statista. https://www.statista.com/statistics/267031/facebooks-annual-revenue-by-segment

Eriksson Krutrök, M., & Lindgren, S. (2022). Social media amplification loops and false alarms: Towards a sociotechnical understanding of misinformation during emergencies. *The Communication Review, 25*(2), 81–95. http://dx.doi.org/10.1080/10714421.2022.2035165

Frenkel, S., Decker, B., & Alba, D. (2020). How the "Plandemic" movie and its falsehoods spread widely online. *The New York Times*. https://www.nytimes.com/2020/05/20/technology/plandemic-movie-youtube-facebook-coronavirus.html

Gorski, D. (2020, May 6). *Judy Mikovits in Plandemic: An antivax conspiracy theorist becomes a COVID-19 grifter*. Respectful Insolence. https://www.respectfulinsolence.com/2020/05/06/judy-mikovits-pandemic

Greenberg, D. L. (2004). President Bush's false [flashbulb] memory of 9/11/01. *Applied Cognitive Psychology: The Official Journal of the Society for Applied Research in Memory and Cognition, 18*(3), 363–370. http://dx.doi.org/10.1080/10714421.2022.2035165

Howard, P. (2018). How political campaigns weaponize social media bots. *IEEE Spectrum, 55*(11). https://spectrum.ieee.org/how-political-campaigns-weaponize-social-media-bots

Johnson-Laird, P. N. (2013). The mental models perspective. In D. Reisberg (Ed.), *The Oxford handbook of cognitive psychology* (pp. 650–667). Oxford University Press. http://dx.doi.org/10.1093/oxfordhb/9780195376746.013.0041

Kahan, D. M. (2016). The politically motivated reasoning paradigm, part 1: What politically motivated reasoning is and how to measure it. In R. A. Scott, S. M. Kosslyn, & M. Buchmann (Eds.), *Emerging trends in social & behavioral sciences* (pp. 1–16). John Wiley & Sons. http://dx.doi.org/10.1002/9781118900772.etrds0417

Kearney, M. D., Chiang, S. C., & Massey, P. M. (2020). The Twitter origins and evolution of the COVID-19 "Plandemic" conspiracy theory. *Harvard Kennedy School Misinformation Review*, *1*(3). http://dx.doi.org/10.37016/mr-2020-42

Kim, M., & Cao, X. (2016). The impact of exposure to media messages promoting government conspiracy theories on distrust in the government: Evidence from a two-stage randomized experiment. *International Journal of Communication*, *10*, 20. https://ijoc.org/index.php/ijoc/article/view/5127/1740

Korman, J., & Khemlani, S. (2020). Explanatory completeness. *Acta Psychologica*, *209*, 103139. http://dx.doi.org/10.1016/j.actpsy.2020.103139

Kunda, Z. (1990). The case for motivated reasoning. *Psychological Bulletin*, *108*(3), 480–498. http://dx.doi.org/10.1037/0033-2909.108.3.480

Lee, J., Kalny, C., Demetriades, S., & Walter, N. (2023). Angry content for angry people: How anger appeals facilitate health misinformation recall on social media. *Media Psychology*, 1–27. http://dx.doi.org/10.1080/15213269.2023.2269084

Mitchell, A., Gottfried, J., Barthel, M., & Sumida, N. (2018). *Distinguishing between factual and opinion statements in the news*. Pew Research Center. http://www.journalism.org/2018/06/18/distinguishing-between-factual-and-opinion-statements-in-the-news

Nan, X., Thier, K., & Wang, Y. (2023). Health misinformation: What it is, why people believe it, how to counter it. *Annals of the International Communication Association*, *47*(4), 381–410. http://dx.doi.org/10.1080/23808985.2023.2225489

Nyhan, B., & Reifler, J. (2010). When corrections fail: The persistence of political misperceptions. *Political Behavior*, *32*, 303–330. https://doi.org/10.1007/s11109-010-9112-2

O'Keefe, D. J. (2018). Persuasion. In O. Hargie (Ed.), *The handbook of communication skills* (pp. 319–335). Routledge.

Oxford Languages. (2016). *Word of the year 2016*. Oxford University Press. https://languages.oup.com/word-of-the-year/2016

Priester, J., Wegener, D., Petty, R., & Fabrigar, L. (1999). Examining the psychological process underlying the sleeper effect: The elaboration likelihood model explanation. *Media Psychology*, *1*(1), 27–48. http://dx.doi.org/10.1207/s1532785xmep0101_3

Rollins, P. C. (1996). Frank Capra's why we fight film series and our American dream. *The Journal of American Culture*, *19*(4), 81–86. http://dx.doi.org/10.1111/j.1542-734X.1996.1904_81.x

Rosling, H., Rosling, O., & Rosling Rönnlund, A. (2018). *Factfulness: Ten reasons we're wrong about the world—And why things are better than you think*. Flatiron Books.

Schwarz, N., Newman, E., & Leach, W. (2016). Making the truth stick & the myths fade: Lessons from cognitive psychology. *Behavioral Science & Policy*, *2*(1), 85–95. https://doi.org/10.1177/237946151600200110

Soroka, S., Fournier, P., & Nir, L. (2019). Cross-national evidence of a negativity bias in psychophysiological reactions to news. *PNAS*, *116*(38), 18888–18892. http://dx.doi.org/10.1073/pnas.1908369116

Tandoc, E. C., Jr., Lim, Z. W., & Ling, R. (2018). Defining "fake news": A typology of scholarly definitions. *Digital Journalism*, *6*(2), 137–153. http://dx.doi.org/10.1080/21670811.2017.1360143

Van Prooijen, J. W., Douglas, K. M., & De Inocencio, C. (2018). Connecting the dots: Illusory pattern perception predicts belief in conspiracies and the supernatural. *European Journal of Social Psychology*, *48*(3), 320–335. https://doi.org/10.1002%2Fejsp.2331

Vosoughi, S., Roy, D., & Aral, S. (2018). The spread of true and false news online. *Science*, *359*(6380), 1146–1151. http://dx.doi.org/10.1126/science.aap9559

Vraga, E. K., & Bode, L. (2020). Defining misinformation and understanding its bounded nature: Using expertise and evidence for describing misinformation. *Political Communication*, *37*(1), 136–144. http://dx.doi.org/10.1080/10584609.2020.1716500

Wang, Y., Thier, K., & Nan, X. (2022). Defining health misinformation. In A. Keselman, C. A. Smith, & A. Wilson (Eds.), *Combating Online Health Misinformation: A professional's guide to helping the public* (pp. 3–16). Rowman & Littlefield.

Weaver, K., Garcia, S. M., Schwarz, N., & Miller, D. T. (2007). Inferring the popularity of an opinion from its familiarity: A repetitive voice can sound like a chorus. *Journal of Personality and Social Psychology*, *92*(5), 821–833. http://dx.doi.org/10.1037/0022-3514.92.5.821

Woolley, S. C., & Howard, P. N. (2018). *Computational propaganda: Political parties, politicians, and political manipulation on social media*. Oxford University Press.

Zuboff, S. (2019). *The age of surveillance capitalism: The fight for a human future at the new frontier of power*. Profile Books.

Zubrow, K. (2021, October 4). *Facebook whistleblower says company incentivizes "angry, polarizing, divisive content."* CBS News. https://www.cbsnews.com/news/facebook-whistleblower-frances-haugen-60-minutes-polarizing-divisive-content

2

Social Media Networks, Social Support, and Misinformation During Crisis Situations

Kevin B. Wright

Department of Communication, George Mason University

The rapid growth of social media platforms since the turn of the century has influenced people's exposure to misinformation on a variety of issues, including during crisis events such as the COVID-19 pandemic or with ongoing threats to the environment such as climate change (Jin & Austin, 2017). Social media play an important role in both the amplification and attenuation of crises. There has been a growing body of crisis communication research that treats social media as a critical variable or context (Jin & Austin, 2017; Suarez-Lledo & Alvarez-Galvez, 2021; Vosoughi et al., 2018), for example, how organizations use social media during a crisis. Social media can be used in many positive ways to benefit people who have been negatively affected by the crisis. For example, social media platforms such as Facebook, X/Twitter, Reddit, and Weibo have become major venues for people to seek and exchange information as well as offer social support, especially during public crises (Nabity-Grover et al., 2020; Suarez-Lledo & Alvarez-Galvez, 2021; Vosoughi et al., 2018). During crises, audiences increase their social media use and in some situations perceive social media to be more credible than traditional mass media (Procopio & Procopio, 2007). Crisis-related news and information can be conveniently (re)distributed though social media networks, which can reach millions of individuals rapidly without the intervention of gatekeepers such as journalists and editors. There is evidence that some social media platforms are well suited to disseminating crisis information across often overlapping online social networks, and this may stimulate readiness, knowledge, and participation in crisis situations (Nabity-Grover et al., 2020; Saroj & Pal, 2020).

Compared to other types of media, social media provide individuals with the ability to easily produce and distribute content. Social networking technologies can also assist in rapid information exchange between first responders, emergency supervisors, and users (Shen et al., 2021). These characteristics of social media networks can aid in the crowdsourcing of information and data regarding a crisis event while it is underway. Mobile technologies are a key component of social media in crisis management contexts. For example, emergency responders can track data from GPS and other mobile phone data shared on social media to obtain important information about the location of groups within a community that may be more negatively affected by a crisis (Saroj & Pal, 2020). Big data analysis may aid in understanding patterns of behavior among individuals who access crisis information from social media platforms via mobile technology (see Chapter 13). Mobile phones also provide

Communication and Misinformation: Crisis Events in the Age of Social Media, First Edition.
Edited by Kevin B. Wright.
© 2025 John Wiley & Sons, Inc. Published 2025 by John Wiley & Sons, Inc.

emergency managers with a quicker means of distributing information about risks and resources during a crisis than traditional media.

As we witnessed during the COVID-19 shutdowns around the world, social media can be an important channel for people to easily create and maintain relationships with multiple others during times of crisis (Wright et al., 2021). Online communities often overlap with physical communities, raising awareness and providing information about areas where supplies (or other types of tangible support) may be needed following a crisis event. Information support in such cases can generate tangible support (e.g., donations, volunteers, support for victims, and first responders). Government agencies (e.g., National Institutes of Health) and nonprofit organizations also use social media (e.g., Twitter/X) to disseminate important public health information during pandemics and emergencies (Saroj & Pal, 2020). Targeted social media campaigns have also become commonplace among public health organizations such as the Centers for Disease Control and Prevention (CDC) and the World Health Organization (WHO) (Saroj & Pal, 2020). Similarly, local health departments and hospitals have also begun providing up-to-date information via social media during crisis events such as surges in COVID-19 infection. Once considered a novel form of personal networking, social media applications have become an established means of communication in daily life, including during times of crisis. Many government and nonprofit organizations are now using social media to distribute critical preparedness, mitigation, response, and recovery information to citizens across a wide spectrum of emergency scenarios, including public health scares, natural disasters, and even terrorist attacks (Simon et al., 2014).

However, a substantial amount of scholarship has focused on the negative side of social media during crises, particularly the spread of misinformation about issues such as climate change and extreme weather events, COVID-19, vaccines, and many other topics where evidence-based information and misinformation often clash in the social media world. Popular social media platforms (e.g., Twitter/X, Facebook) often lack information gatekeepers, and this leads to the rapid spread of misinformation that can easily contaminate the larger online information ecosystem (Oh et al., 2013). As I shall show in this chapter, the spread of misinformation on social media is often influenced by a variety of factors, from individual perception to the structural characteristics of online social networks. In the United States, people are just as likely to turn to social media as their primary source of crisis-related information as to rely on television and other news media (Su et al., 2015). Individuals seek out social media during crises because they provide both an unfiltered, up-to-date line of communication (Procopio & Procopio, 2007) and unique crisis information that audiences cannot get elsewhere. Audiences also use social media for emotional support and recovery from crises (Choi & Lin, 2009; Stephens & Malone, 2009). Sites such as Flickr and YouTube have been used to collect crisis images and information about larger groups of individuals (Palen, 2008).

Social media have disrupted the traditional hierarchies of communication, including the influence of traditional media gatekeepers such as journalists and news media editors, political parties, and members of the scientific community. While they have allowed average citizens to play a much greater role in shaping public debate about crisis-related issues (Berglez & Al-Saqaf, 2021; Reuter et al., 2020), they have also provided people with a means to post messages based on conspiracy theories, disinformation campaigns from adversaries, and various forms of misinformation during a crisis. Social media platforms have altered the ways in which individuals access news and follow debates on controversial topics related to crises, including online discussions about COVID-19 vaccination (Jin & Austin, 2017;

Suarez-Lledo & Alvarez-Galvez, 2021; Vosoughi et al., 2018). Social media comments by users can influence post-crisis organizational reputations. Negative comments can boost reputational harm while positive comments can assist in moderating the reputational harm for the entity in crisis (Coombs & Holladay, 2014). Social media messages produced by crisis publics can serve or damage the entity in crisis because of their ability to influence assessments of organizational reputations (Coombs & Holladay, 2014).

Finally, there is considerable evidence that social media platforms such as Facebook and X/Twitter, influence how the public receives, consumes, and distributes information about crisis events, particularly during crises such as the COVID-19 pandemic (Ross & Rivers, 2019; Suarez-Lledo & Alvarez-Galvez, 2021; Vraga et al., 2019). Much of this literature has focused on factors that increase the spread of misinformation on social media, the negative effects of misinformation during crises on cognitions, behaviors, and how misinformation can be verified and corrected on social media.

This chapter focuses on research findings related to social media and social networks during times of crisis, specifically how social media platforms can be used to effectively provide important information and support during times of crisis as well as the negative ways in which they can influence people's attitudes, beliefs, and behaviors (with a focus on misinformation). Toward that end, it explores research on both the positive and the negative aspects of social media networks during crisis events. Additionally, the chapter explores characteristics of online social networks on social media platforms that may influence both positive (e.g., social support) and negative (e.g., misinformation) forms of communication.

Positive Aspects of Social Media Networks During Crisis Events

Governments and communities both large and small need to respond to crisis situations with sufficient preparation, and effective crisis communication is one major aspect of this (Jin & Austin, 2017; Sadri et al., 2017). This includes systematic planning and the collection, organization, and circulation of relevant awareness information to the target audience to reach out to every individual in a community (Jin & Austin, 2017). During a crisis, people may obtain critical information from traditional media such as radio or television and from various social media platforms. Social media platforms are different from traditional media in that they can help disseminate targeted information during a crisis as well as facilitate many types of social support (e.g., aid, money, emotional support, information about shelters or government resources). For example, during Hurricane Sandy in the United States, social media also played an important role in crisis communication. New York and New Jersey residents used smartphones to access social media when they lost power and could not use television (Sadri et al., 2017).

During a crisis, people usually suffer from anxiety, uncertainty, and concern about their safety, health, and well-being. Studies have found that people often turn to social media for information during crises in an effort to manage uncertainty or relieve anxiety (McMullan et al., 2019; Pesälä et al., 2017). There are a variety of factors that may influence individuals' beliefs when they seek information during health emergencies (e.g., anxiety about their health) or engage in controlling and preventing potential risks (Pesälä et al., 2017). In other words, people use social media for a variety of reasons during a crisis. They may try to communicate with their family members and friends in the disaster area or inquire about their safety. They may seek or share information about food, shelter, transportation, medical, and other needs. They may wish to gain social support such as information, encouragement, or tangible help to cope with the crisis (Chen et al., 2018).

In addition, unlike many traditional media options, social media can handle a high volume of user activity. Social media is also more interactive than traditional media such as radio and television, and allows users to overcome the barrier of one-way communication. When electricity is cut off or disconnected during a natural disaster, for example, traditional channels of communication (e.g., television) can be disrupted. In such cases, people often reach out on social media for real-time information exchange (Saroj & Pal, 2020) and share their well-being and location with friends and family. In an emergency where there is a high degree of uncertainty, anyone who collects and distributes content on social media is a potential source of information. The increased use of smartphones has been recognized as an important means of access to social media. For example, X/Twitter has been widely used to spread information during crises (such as the number of casualties and the damage, calls for donation, and alerts) and multimedia information such as videos and photos (Saroj & Pal, 2020). Social media platforms can be particularly useful for information dissemination during crises, as evidenced in many empirical studies, because they offer ease and speed of resharing (e.g., retweeting), which leads to greater situational awareness among community members affected by the crisis, better communication with emergency responders, and better disaster relief efforts (Hughes & Tapia, 2015). Further studies examining how practitioners and organizations (rather than individuals) use social media to communicate with and about other organizations during crises (Jin & Austin, 2017) have opened up some interesting new directions for future research.

The collaborative nature of social media facilitates a multidirectional flow of information, allowing citizens to become engaged in the emergency response process by redistributing information, posting incident updates, making requests for information or assistance, and creating news content (Hughes & Tapia, 2015; Yoo et al., 2016). For example, during Hurricane Sandy, private citizens used social media extensively to redistribute emergency updates, connect with loved ones, and provide eyewitness accounts through microblogs and videos, many of which were subsequently used by traditional media outlets reporting on the storm (Stewart & Wilson, 2016).

Previous studies provide empirical evidence that our online social networks influence our behaviors, particularly when we receive encouragement from people with whom we interact in an attempt to alter our behavior, including within social media contexts (Wright & Miller, 2010; Wright et al., 2021). For example, messages within online communities on social media platforms such as Facebook can influence network members to change behaviors (Latkin & Knowlton, 2015; Reuter et al., 2020). Moreover, stronger social network ties such as friends and family can facilitate physical, emotional, and/or financial support during a crisis event (Hurlbert et al., 2000; Nabity-Grover et al., 2020; Suarez-Lledo & Alvarez-Galvez, 2021;Wright et al., 2021). Communities and individuals with stronger social ties tend to be more resilient and to bounce back more quickly during times of crisis than communities and individuals who have fewer strong ties (Metaxa-Kakavouli et al., 2018).

One factor appears to be the different affordances that people obtain from ties of varying strength within online social media networks. For example, a number of researchers have examined the affordances of online weak-tie networks on social media and how these networks can influence health outcomes for individuals seeking certain types of social support (Rains, 2018; Wright & Miller, 2010), These affordances include the ability to vent about problems with little risk and to obtain more heterogeneous information from a diverse pool of community members than is often available in a face-to-face social network, and fewer role obligations in online weak-tie supportive interactions (e.g., the balance between receiving and providing support) compared to seeking social support from stronger social network ties, particularly in the face-to-face world (Wright & Miller, 2010; Wright et al., 2021). These online weak-tie affordances extend into social media use during times of crisis (Jin & Austin, 2017; Wright et al., 2021).

For example, Lu et al. (2022) found that people were more likely to share COVID-19 information within their strong-tie networks than weak-tie networks. COVID-19 information acquisition from strong-tie networks was predictive only of information sharing within strong-tie networks, whereas information acquisition from weak-tie networks was associated with sharing within both strong-tie and weak-tie networks. The findings from this study suggest that individuals tend to share information from casual contacts and strangers with their family members and close friends but not vice versa. However, this study did measure whether respondents' COVID-19 information came from online weak ties or from face-to-face weak ties. Additionally, Lu et al. (2022) found that negative emotions appeared to be the primary psychological predictor of sharing COVID-19 information within weak-tie networks. This finding is consistent with previous research on weak-tie networks that has found that people often like to vent negative emotions and cognitions within weak-tie networks (Wright & Miller, 2010). Weaker ties are often perceived as being safer in terms of allowing people to communicate openly about negative topics compared to stronger ties, who may judge a person more for expressing negative views (see Wright & Miller, 2010).

Wright et al. (2021) explored work–life imbalance and weak-tie social support during the COVID-19 shelter-in-place restrictions of spring 2020 in the United States, and their impact on perceived stress and depression. The findings indicated that, when overall social support was controlled for, work–life imbalance was a significant predictor of both perceived stress and depression during the shelter-in-place restrictions. However, a higher work–life imbalance was a significant predictor of higher weak-tie support preference and interaction or support seeking from weak ties (particularly weak ties on social media), while lower perceived social support from close ties (e.g., friends and family members) predicted higher weak-tie support network preference. In this particular case, people's desire for more heterogeneous information or points of view from online social media weak ties may have motivated them to communicate with other people outside of their immediate face-to-face social network. The pandemic forced many people to limit their interaction to family members or other close-knit ties due to the shutdown and social distancing restrictions. Weak ties provided individuals with access to a social network of diverse information and other types of support at a time when traditional closer-tie support was limited in an effort not to spread the virus.

Negative Aspects of Social Media During Crisis Events

Misinformation Spread on Social Media

A number of scholars have suggested that false or misleading health- and crisis-related information may spread more easily than scientific knowledge through social media (Apuke &

Omar, 2020; Vosoughi et al., 2018). Content on social media platforms such as X/Twitter are mainly user generated and typically lack effective fact-checking mechanisms, which may make them more susceptible to spreading misinformation during crisis events. Studies have shown that, across a variety of recent crisis events, the number of people who use social media to seek information such as health advice or information about resources is high and continues to grow (Apuke & Omar, 2020; Jin & Austin, 2017). Social media have become more influential in recent years in affecting people's health behaviors in crises, including the online controversies at the height of the COVID-19 pandemic over the efficacy of vaccines, social distancing, and the wearing of face masks (Liu et al., 2020). In some cases, sham cures for COVID-19 were promoted via social media as well as a wide array of misinformation about the SARS-CoV-2 virus and infection prevention. The large number of social media platforms and the convenience of their use often help people to find information (both good and bad) more easily and efficiently than traditional media (Liu et al., 2020), particularly in times of crisis.

Researchers have found that the emergence of social media has spread misinformation more quickly and easily among people (Apuke & Omar, 2020; Vosoughi et al., 2018; Vraga et al., 2019) during times of crisis, including health emergencies such as the COVID-19 pandemic. People's lack of professional medical knowledge make it difficult for many to separate misinformation from evidence-based information or advice. As a result, they are more likely to share misinformation without considering whether it is true. While previous studies have indicated vaccine-related misinformation in health emergencies such as those involving the Ebola and Zika viruses (Wang et al., 2019; Waszak et al., 2018), other types of health-related misinformation, including incorrect health advice and fake articles on health help seeking may also be disseminated on social media.

During times of crisis, misinformation on social media can confuse the public and lead to political inaction and stalled support for or rejection of mitigation policies (Brulle, 2018; Cook et al., 2018; Ding et al., 2011; van der Linden et al., 2017). Researchers have found that as many as 20 percent of social media users in the United States have changed their views on a political or social issue as a result of something they saw on social media (Greenwood et al., 2016; Reuter et al., 2020). Crisis situations tend to increase and amplify the number of social media messages that are spread across various platforms. While social media can certainly be used for good during crises, such as a platform that facilitates social support for people in need or works as a public forum to encourage legislators to enact new policies (Reuter et al., 2020), other research underscores the potential harm that can stem from social media during times of crisis (e.g., Brulle, 2018; Pennycook et al., 2018; Reuter et al., 2020). This includes the threat of widespread misinformation on social media during crises that can influence attitudes, beliefs, and behaviors about the crisis or how it can be mitigated.

Some of the vulnerabilities to being influenced by misinformation on social media occur at the psychological level, and these may heighten a person's susceptibility to misinformation during a crisis. People tend to be motivated to protect their beliefs from evidence to the contrary and to subscribe to information that confirms what they already believe to be true or right (Nir, 2011), leading to confirmation bias. For example, previous research findings suggest that, when people are the recipients of fake news that is in line with their preexisting beliefs or values about climate change and/or the causes of extreme weather events, they are less motivated to engage in critical reflection about its accuracy (Drummond et al., 2020; Pennycook et al., 2018).

Social Media Network Influences on Misinformation during Crises

On social media, an individuals' exposure to social media content is largely influenced by the recommendations of their friends or people they follow or whose channels they subscribe to. The ways in which online crisis-related misinformation is communicated via social networks is influenced by the structure and characteristics of these networks, which help facilitate the diffusion of misinformation. Misinformation circulates very easily in online environments (Kouzy et al., 2020), including during times of crisis on social media platforms such as Facebook, YouTube, and Twitter (Carrasco-Polaino et al., 2021; Tang et al., 2021). In some cases, social media platforms such as X/Twitter have been weaponized to promote antivaccine messages through the use of online bots and trolls. Social network factors such as one's social media friends and associates' tendency to share similar interests and opinions, and one's reliance on the recommendations of one's contacts, are likely to create echo chambers where one is repeatedly exposed to conforming opinions (Flaxman et al., 2016; Vraga et al., 2019). In addition, social media content has become more individualized and is determined by the machine learning-based recommendation algorithms of each platform. For example, YouTube will present recommended videos based on a user's prior viewing behaviors. Such personalization of content creates filter bubbles in which algorithms recommend information that users have previously been exposed to and with which they agree (Flaxman et al., 2016; Santos et al., 2021).

Other social characteristics of social media platforms, such as the ability to create content, can influence the ways in which people share information about issues such as vaccines or COVID-19 prevention with members of their online social networks. The lack of effective fact-checking mechanisms makes social media susceptible to the spread of misinformation. Such content can be introduced into a social media network either by mistake or with malicious intention, including the desire to influence public opinion about a politicized issue such as vaccines or COVID-19 prevention behaviors (Flaxman et al., 2016; Vraga et al., 2019). Spreading health-related misinformation or disinformation on social media during health emergencies or other crises can worsen this situation as uncertainty about a crisis may drive people online to seek information from their social network members or weaker ties within online communities that are providing (accurate or not) explanations for certain events or behaviors. Quantitative metrics are used by social media platforms to measure the impact of a message based on the number of replies, retweets, likes, mentions, impressions, and so on a particular social media post has gained (Santos et al., 2021). These measures of user engagement are used in social media platform user recommendation algorithms, which ultimately influence message reach and influence across online social networks.

People often have a strong desire to share their firsthand experiences of a health issue such as vaccines or COVID-19 prevention behaviors (which may or may not be evidence based) on social media communities to help their friends or make a social contribution (Nabity-Grover et al., 2020). Web 2.0 and the rise of easy-to-use social media platforms have made it easier for people to create and share their experiences of health or other crises. Moreover, people are more likely to rely on health information shared by their friends to make decisions than information from online search engines (Zhao & Zhang, 2017). Furthermore, social media connects like-minded people in a closed network where they share similar content, and this amplifies the risks that misinformation causes (Chou et al., 2018). Therefore, unlike health misinformation on websites, which affects individual health, misinformation on social media may lead to community-level problems (Li et al., 2022; Pal et al., 2019).

Misinformation on social media networks on the spread and prevention of COVID-19 are one of the clearest recent examples of how health misinformation can lead to tangible public health problems. For example, researchers have studied topics such as online social network denialist discourses and COVID-19 prevention behaviors (Morel, 2021), doubts about vaccines (Nowak et al., 2020; Subbaraman, 2021; Thelwall et al., 2021), and the popularity of vaccines and their level of controversy on Twitter (Carrasco-Polaino et al., 2021). However, similar types of issues have been seen in other contexts such as the Ebola outbreak in 2014, and in social media discourse on the causes of climate change and extreme weather events (Luckerson, 2014; Vijaykumar et al., 2018).

Moreover, scholars have found that several interconnected characteristics of social networks are frequent factors in how misinformation diffuses. For example, one characteristic that appears to influence the spread of misinformation in online social networks is the perception of homophily or similarity with other participants in the social media platform (Himelboim et al., 2013). Homophily is a ubiquitous tendency for humans to connect with others who share their traits, which can be observed in almost all (offline and online) social networks (Himelboim et al., 2013; McPherson et al., 2001). Perceived homophily is facilitated by many social media platforms that promote connections with individuals who may share similar demographics, backgrounds, and cognitions by suggesting new connections based on matching user profiles or mutual connections, for instance, Facebook "friends" and X/Twitter "followers" (Rains & Wright, 2015).

Homophily can lead to homogeneous clusters of like-minded users, also known as "echo chambers," where information (and misinformation) echoes around the group (Shin et al., 2017; Vicario et al., 2016). Social media platforms, which permit users a high level of selectivity in the discussions in which they can participate (e.g., Reddit "subreddits"), also encourage like-minded groups to form, as it is easy for users to leave groups where their views are not shared. Echo chambers can exacerbate opinion polarization, especially within polarized communities formed around particular issues or types of content. Content is promoted for being engaging rather than for trustworthiness, and this has been found to increase polarization (Sirbu et al., 2019). Other factors leading to the spread of misinformation online include belief systems and confirmation bias whereby users prefer to consume information that is consistent with their belief systems; and social norms, with people tending to trust information received from people within their social network (Vicario et al., 2016).

Previous research using social network analysis of highly active social media users discussing climate change found strong perceptions of homophily between polarized "activist" and "skeptic" groups and evidence of echo chambers (Williams et al., 2015), which suggests that the climate change debate on social media may be susceptible to the diffusion of misinformation. Researchers have found that ideology, values, and social norms play an important role in people's attitudes to climate change (Bhagwat et al., 2016; Corner et al., 2014), indicating that social media users with particular ideologies, belief systems, and perceptions of social norms about controversial issues may be more susceptible to spreading, consuming, and accepting misinformation. In the current social media environment, individuals may selectively expose themselves to news and information that confirms existing biases. This can lead to online silos (or echo chambers) where social media users filter out news and discussions that conflict with the dominant beliefs of the online community (Bakshy et al., 2015; Cinelli et al., 2020; Wang & Qian, 2021).

For example, some studies that used social network analysis have uncovered compelling evidence that climate change discussions on social media platforms tend to exhibit echo chamber-like interactions (Tyagi et al., 2020; Williams et al., 2015). These studies found that more negative framing of climate change issues often prevailed, featuring dismissal of climate change as a hoax, identity-based derailment of conversations, and overall higher levels of incivility (Anderson & Huntington, 2017). Social media platforms extend to include other domains such as discussion sites (e.g., Reddit), video upload sites (e.g., YouTube), and Internet memes (Ross & Rivers, 2019). Discussions about controversial issues such as vaccines, wearing masks to prevent COVID-19 transmission, and climate change are often communicated in the form of multimodal user-generated content, where political commentary, satire, and debates over notions of legitimacy of issues such as climate change research findings can be enacted (Ross & Rivers, 2019). Sharman (2014) used social network analysis to examine blogs skeptical of climate change and found that the central blogs in the network were key in delegitimizing and contesting expert knowledge and reinterpreting existing climate science knowledge claims.

The link between social network member characteristics and polarization within online communities has long been a subject of interest among social media misinformation scholars (Anderson et al., 2014; Bessi et al., 2016; Reuter et al., 2020). For example, Williams et al. (2015) used network analysis to investigate segregation and interaction between communities of X/Twitter users, categorizing users as activist, skeptic, neutral, unknown, ambiguous, or unclassified according to tweet content. They found high levels of polarization and a tendency for active users (either skeptic or activist) to have strong attitudes, which led them to conclude that X/Twitter climate change discussions are characterized by strong attitude-based homophily and widespread segregation of users into like-minded communities. For example, the partisan divide regarding climate change is amplified by factors such as education, scientific literacy, and numeracy (Hamilton et al., 2015; Drummond & Fischhoff, 2017).

Although there is a tendency for echo chambers to form on social media platforms as a result of factors such as homophily, encounters with strangers and weaker ties within social media platform communities can expose users to other individuals who are more heterogeneous in terms of having different life experiences and perspectives. Exposure to more heterogeneous users on social media may be helpful in providing more diverse information or introducing one to individuals who may be willing to challenge misinformation (Kim & Chen, 2016; Vraga & Bode, 2018; Wright & Miller, 2010). As a result, people are likely to come across those who disagree with their views, and this creates opportunities for climate change and extreme misinformation correction to occur. These corrections can be effective, reducing misperceptions in individuals sharing misinformation (Margolin et al., 2018) and for the community witnessing the interaction (Bode & Vraga, 2015; Vraga & Bode, 2018).

Summary

Many types of crises place strains on information networks, and effective crisis communications are essential to successful emergency management (Steelman et al., 2014). Crisis communication situations are typically defined by high levels of ambiguity, fluid conditions, and a diversity of informational needs (Steelman et al., 2014). The study of social media networks during times of crisis is an area of research that draws together a diverse pool of researchers who focus on different types of crises such as public health issues, climate change, or organizational/reputational crises.

There are many gaps in our understanding of social media networks during crisis situations. Social media evolve so fast that scientific gaps frequently appear (Utz et al., 2013). Additionally, Coombs (2008) concluded that the practice of crisis communication in the social media era is ahead of scholarship. Despite its importance, the impact of different social media types on the effects of crisis response strategies remains an understudied area of research (Snoeijers et al., 2014). While some prominent theories such as situational crisis communication theory (Coombs & Holladay, 2002) have been applied to the study of social media networks during crisis situations, much more theoretical development is needed to find frameworks that account for the diverse positive and negative influences of online social networks during crisis situations. Previous research has relied heavily on survey and content analysis research, and there is a particular shortage of studies using experimental designs that are important for examining causal relationships between variables.

However, there are many commonalities and overlaps between these types of crises that can shed light on best practices to manage online misinformation across multiple contexts. Crisis situations evolve quickly, and misinformation spreads widely and rapidly via social media. We need new research methods to better capture the complex and dynamic nature of online misinformation spread by social media in ways that help to mitigate its spread in the midst of a crisis but also to prepare for other potential crises in the future.

References

Anderson, A. A., Brossard, D., Scheufele, D. A., Xenos, M. A., & Ladwig, P. (2014). The "nasty effect": Online incivility and risk perceptions of emerging technologies. *Journal of Computer-Mediated Communication*, *19*(3), 373–387. http://dx.doi.org/10.1111/jcc4.12009

Anderson, A. A., & Huntington, H. E. (2017). Social media, science, and attack discourse: How Twitter discussions of climate change use sarcasm and incivility. *Science Communication*, *39*(5), 598–620. http://dx.doi.org/10.1177/1075547017735113

Apuke, O. D., & Omar, B. (2020). Modelling the antecedent factors that affect online fake news sharing on COVID-19: The moderating role of fake news knowledge. *Health Education Research*, *35*(5), 490–503. http://dx.doi.org/10.1093/her/cyaa030

Bakshy, E., Messing, S., & Adamic, L. A. (2015). Exposure to ideologically diverse news and opinion on Facebook. *Science*, *348*(6239), 1130–1132. http://dx.doi.org/10.1126/science.aaa1160

Berglez, P., & Al-Saqaf, W. (2021). Extreme weather and climate change: Social media results, 2008–2017. *Environmental Hazards*, *20*(4), 382–399. http://dx.doi.org/10.1080/17477891.2020.1829532

Bessi, A., Zollo, F., Del Vicario, M., Puliga, M., Scala, A., Caldarelli, G., Uzzi, B., & Quattrociocchi, W. (2016). Users polarization on Facebook and YouTube. *PLoS ONE*, *11*(8), e0159641. http://dx.doi.org/10.1371/journal.pone.0159641

Bhagwat, S. A., Economou, A., & Thornton, T. F. (2016). The idea of climate change as a belief system: Why climate activism resembles a religious movement. *GAIA: Ecological Perspectives for Science and Society*, *25*(2), 94–98. https://doi.org/%2010.14512/gaia.25.2.8

Bode, L., & Vraga, E. K. (2015). In related news, that was wrong: The correction of misinformation through related stories functionality in social media. *Journal of Communication*, *65*(4), 619–638. http://dx.doi.org/10.1111/jcom.12166

Brulle, R. (2018). *30 years ago global warming became front-page news—And both Republicans and Democrats took it seriously*. The Conversation Media Group. http://theconversation.com/30-years-ago-global-warming-became-frontpage-news-and-both-republicans-and-democrats-took-it-seriously-97658

Carrasco-Polaino, R., Martín-Cárdaba, M. Á., & Villar-Cirujano, E. (2021). Citizen participation in Twitter: Anti-vaccine controversies in times of COVID-19. *Comunicar: Media Education Research Journal*, *29*(69), 21–31. http://eprints.rclis.org/42709

Chen, Y., Moufouma-Okia, W., Masson-Delmotte, V., Zhai, P., & Pirani, A. (2018). Recent progress and emerging topics on weather and climate extremes since the fifth assessment report of the intergovernmental panel on climate change. *Annual Review of Environment and Resources*, *43*, 35–59. http://dx.doi.org/10.1146/annurev-environ-102017-030052

Choi, Y., & Lin, Y. H. (2009). Individual difference in crisis response perception: How do legal experts and lay people perceive apology and compassion responses? *Public Relations Review*, *35*(4), 452–454. http://dx.doi.org/10.1016/j.pubrev.2009.07.002

Chou, W. Y. S., Oh, A., & Klein, W. M. (2018). Addressing health-related misinformation on social media. *JAMA*, *320*(23), 2417–2418. http://dx.doi.org/10.1001/jama.2018.16865

Cinelli, M., Morales, G. D. F., Galeazzi, A., Quattrociocchi, W., & Starnini, M. (2020). *Echo chambers on social media: A comparative analysis*. arXiv. https://arxiv.org/abs/2004.09603

Cook, J., Ellerton, P., & Kinkead, D. (2018). Deconstructing climate misinformation to identify reasoning errors. *Environmental Research Letters*, *2018*, 024018. http://dx.doi.org/10.1088/1748-9326/aaa49f

Coombs, W. T. (2008). Crisis communication. In W. Donsbach (Ed.), *The international encyclopedia of communication*. Wiley. http://dx.doi.org/10.1002/9781405186407.wbiecc156

Coombs, W. T., & Holladay, S. J. (2002). Helping crisis managers protect reputational assets: Initial tests of the situational crisis communication theory. *Management Communication Quarterly*, *16*(2), 165–186. http://dx.doi.org/10.1177/089331802237233

Coombs, W. T., & Holladay, S. J. (2014). Strategic intent and crisis communication: The emergence of a field. In *D. Holtzhausen & A. Zerfass (Eds.), The Routledge handbook of strategic communication* (pp. 497–507). Routledge.

Corner, A., Markowitz, E., & Pidgeon, N. (2014). Public engagement with climate change: The role of human values. *Wiley Interdisciplinary Reviews: Climate Change*, *5*(3), 411–422. http://dx.doi.org/10.1002/wcc.269

Ding, D., Maibach, E. W., Zhao, X., Roser-Renouf, C., & Leiserowitz, A. (2011). Support for climate policy and societal action are linked to perceptions about scientific agreement. *Nature Climate Change*, *1*(9), 462–466. http://dx.doi.org/10.1038/nclimate1295

Drummond, C., & Fischhoff, B. (2017). Individuals with greater science literacy and education have more polarized beliefs on controversial science topics. *PNAS*, *114*(36), 9587–9592. http://dx.doi.org/10.1073/pnas.1704882114

Drummond, C., Siegrist, M., & Árvai, J. (2020). Limited effects of exposure to fake news about climate change. *Environmental Research Communications*, *2*(8), 081003. http://dx.doi.org/10.1088/2515-7620/abae77

Flaxman, S., Goel, S., & Rao, J. M. (2016). Filter bubbles, echo chambers, and online news consumption. *Public Opinion Quarterly*, *80*(S1), 298–320. http://dx.doi.org/10.1093/poq/nfw006

Greenwood, S., Perrin, A., & Duggan, M. (2016, November 11). *Social media update 2016*. Pew Research Center. https://assets.pewresearch.org/wp-content/uploads/sites/14/2016/11/10132827/PI_2016.11.11_Social-Media-Update_FINAL.pdf

Hamilton, L. C., Hartter, J., Lemcke-Stampone, M., Moore, D. W., & Safford, T. G. (2015). Tracking public beliefs about anthropogenic climate change. *PLoS ONE*, *10*(9), e0138208. http://dx.doi.org/10.1371/journal.pone.0138208

Himelboim, I., McCreery, S., & Smith, M. (2013). Birds of a feather tweet together: Integrating network and content analyses to examine cross-ideology exposure on Twitter. *Journal of Computer-Mediated Communication*, *18*, 154–174. http://dx.doi.org/10.1111/jcc4.12001

Hughes, A. L., & Tapia, A. H. (2015). Social media in crisis: When professional responders meet digital volunteers. *Journal of Homeland Security and Emergency Management*, *12*(3), 679–706. http://dx.doi.org/10.1515/jhsem-2014-0080

Hurlbert, J. S., Haines, V. A., & Beggs, J. J. (2000). Core networks and tie activation: What kinds of routine networks allocate resources in nonroutine situations? *American Sociological Review*, *65*(4), 598–618. http://dx.doi.org/10.2307/2657385

Jin, Y., & Austin, L. L. (2017). *Social media and crisis communication*. Taylor & Francis.

Kim, Y., & Chen, H. T. (2016). Social media and online political participation: The mediating role of exposure to cross-cutting and like-minded perspectives. *Telematics and Informatics*, *33*(2), 320–330. http://dx.doi.org/10.1016/j.tele.2015.08.008

Kouzy, R., Abi Jaoude, J., Kraitem, A., El Alam, M. B., Karam, B., Adib, E., Zarka, J., Traboulsi, C., Akl, E. W., & Baddour, K. (2020). Coronavirus goes viral: Quantifying the COVID-19 misinformation epidemic on Twitter. *Cureus*, *12*(3). https://doi.org/10.7759/cureus.7255

Latkin, C. A., & Knowlton, A. R. (2015). Social network assessments and interventions for health behavior change: A critical review. *Behavioral Medicine*, *41*(3), 90–97. http://dx.doi.org/10.1080/08964289.2015.1034645

Li, Y., Kou, G., Li, G., & Peng, Y. (2022). Consensus reaching process in large-scale group decision making based on bounded confidence and social network. *European Journal of Operational Research*, *303*(2), 790–802. http://dx.doi.org/10.1016/j.ejor.2022.03.040

Liu, M., Cheng, S.-Z., Xu, K.-W., Yang, Y., Zhu, Q.-T., Zhang, H., Yang, D.-Y., Cheng, S.-Y., Xiao, H., Wang, J.-W., Yao, H.-R., Cong, Y.-T., Zhou, Y.-Q., Peng, S., Kuang, M., Hou, F.-F., Cheng, K. K., & Xiao, H.-P. (2020). Use of personal protective equipment against coronavirus disease 2019 by healthcare professionals in Wuhan, China: Cross sectional study. *British Medical Journal*, *369*. http://dx.doi.org/10.1136/bmj.m2195

Lu, L., Liu, J., Yuan, Y. C., Lu, E., & Li, D. (2022). Psychological antecedents of COVID-19 information sharing within strong-tie and weak-tie networks. *PEC Innovation*, *1*, 100035. http://dx.doi.org/10.1016/j.pecinn.2022.100035

Luckerson, V. (2014, October 8). Fear, misinformation, and social media complicate Ebola fight. *Time*. https://time.com/3479254/ebola-social-media

Margolin, D. B., Hannak, A., & Weber, I. (2018). Political fact-checking on Twitter: When do corrections have an effect? *Political Communication*, *35*(2), 196–219. http://dx.doi.org/10.1080/10584609.2017.1334018

McMullan, R. D., Berle, D., Arnáez, S., & Starcevic, V. (2019). The relationships between health anxiety, online health information seeking, and cyberchondria: Systematic review and meta-analysis. *Journal of Affective Disorders*, *245*, 270–278. http://dx.doi.org/10.1016/j.jad.2018.11.037

McPherson, M., Smith-Lovin, L., & Cook, J. M. (2001). Birds of a feather: Homophily in social networks. *Annual Review of Sociology*, *27*(1), 415–444. http://dx.doi.org/10.1146/annurev.soc.27.1.415

Metaxa-Kakavouli, D., Maas, P., & Aldrich, D. P. (2018). How social ties influence hurricane evacuation behavior. *Proceedings of the ACM on Human–Computer Interaction*, *2*(CSCW), 1–16. http://dx.doi.org/10.1145/3274391

Morel, A. P. M. (2021). Negationism of the COVID-19 and popular health education: To beyond the necropolitics. *Trabalho, Educação e Saúde, 19*. https://doi.org/10.1590/1981-7746-sol00315

Nabity-Grover, T., Cheung, C. M., & Thatcher, J. B. (2020). Inside out and outside in: How the COVID-19 pandemic affects self-disclosure on social media. *International Journal of Information Management, 55*, 102188. http://dx.doi.org/10.1016/j.ijinfomgt.2020.102188

Nir, L. (2011). Motivated reasoning and public opinion perception. *Public Opinion Quarterly, 75*(3), 504–532. http://dx.doi.org/10.1093/poq/nfq076

Nowak, B., Brzóska, P., Piotrowski, J., Sedikides, C., Żemojtel-Piotrowska, M., & Jonason, P. K. (2020). Adaptive and maladaptive behavior during the COVID-19 pandemic: The roles of dark triad traits, collective narcissism, and health beliefs. *Personality and Individual Differences, 167*, 110232. http://dx.doi.org/10.1016/j.paid.2020.110232

Oh, O., Agrawal, M., & Rao, H. R. (2013). Community intelligence and social media services: A rumor theoretic analysis of tweets during social crises. *MIS Quarterly, 37*(2), 407–426. https://www.jstor.org/stable/43825916

Pal, A., Chua, A. Y., & Goh, D. H. L. (2019). Debunking rumors on social media: The use of denials. *Computers in Human Behavior, 96*, 110–122. http://dx.doi.org/10.1016/j.chb.2019.02.022

Palen, L. (2008). Online social media in crisis events. *Educause Quarterly, 31*(3), 76–78. https://er.educause.edu/articles/2008/8/online-social-media-in-crisis-events

Pennycook, G., Cannon, T. D., & Rand, D. G. (2018). Prior exposure increases perceived accuracy of fake news. *Journal of Experimental Psychology: General, 147*(12), 1865–1880. http://dx.doi.org/10.1037/xge0000465

Pesälä, S., Virtanen, M. J., Sane, J., Mustonen, P., Kaila, M., & Helve, O. (2017). Health information-seeking patterns of the general public and indications for disease surveillance: Register-based study using Lyme disease. *JMIR Public Health and Surveillance, 3*(4), e8306. http://dx.doi.org/10.2196/publichealth.8306

Procopio, C. H., & Procopio, S. T. (2007). Do you know what it means to miss New Orleans? Internet communication, geographic community, and social capital in crisis. *Journal of Applied Communication Research, 35*(1), 67–87. http://dx.doi.org/10.1080/00909880601065722

Rains, S. A. (2018). *Coping with illness digitally*. MIT Press.

Rains, S. A., & Wright, K. B. (2015). Social support and computer-mediated communication: A state-of-the-art review and agenda for future research. *Communication Yearbook, 40*, 175–211. http://dx.doi.org/10.1080/23808985.2015.11735260

Reuter, C., Stieglitz, S., & Imran, M. (2020). Social media in conflicts and crises. *Behaviour & Information Technology, 39*(3), 241–251. http://dx.doi.org/10.1080/0144929X.2019.1629025

Ross, A. S., & Rivers, D. J. (2019). Internet memes, media frames, and the conflicting logics of climate change discourse. *Environmental Communication, 13*(7), 975–994. http://dx.doi.org/10.1080/17524032.2018.1560347

Sadri, A. M., Ukkusuri, S. V., & Gladwin, H. (2017). The role of social networks and information sources on hurricane evacuation decision making. *Natural Hazards Review, 18*(3), 04017005. http://dx.doi.org/10.1061/(ASCE)NH.1527-6996.0000244

Santos, F. P., Lelkes, Y., & Levin, S. A. (2021). Link recommendation algorithms and dynamics of polarization in online social networks. *Proceedings of the National Academy of Sciences, 118*(50), e2102141118. http://dx.doi.org/10.1073/pnas.2102141118

Saroj, A., & Pal, S. (2020). Use of social media in crisis management: A survey. *International Journal of Disaster Risk Reduction, 48*, 101584. http://dx.doi.org/10.1016/j.ijdrr.2020.101584

Sharman, A. (2014). Mapping the climate skeptical blogosphere. *Global Environmental Change, 26*, 159–170. http://dx.doi.org/10.1016/j.gloenvcha.2014.03.003

Shen, H., Shi, J., & Zhang, Y. (2021). CrowdEIM: Crowdsourcing emergency information management tasks to mobile social media users. *International Journal of Disaster Risk Reduction, 54*, 102024. http://dx.doi.org/10.1016/j.ijdrr.2020.102024

Shin, J., Jian, L., Driscoll, K., & Bar, F. (2017). Political rumoring on Twitter during the 2012 US presidential election: Rumor diffusion and correction. *New Media & Society, 19*(8), 1214–1235. http://dx.doi.org/10.1177/1461444816634054

Simon, T., Goldberg, A., Aharonson-Daniel, L., Leykin, D., & Adini, B. (2014). Twitter in the cross fire—The use of social media in the Westgate Mall terror attack in Kenya. *PLoS ONE, 9*(8), e104136. http://dx.doi.org/10.1371/journal.pone.0104136

Sirbu, A., Pedreschi, D., Giannotti, F., & Kertész, J. (2019). Algorithmic bias amplifies opinion fragmentation and polarization: A bounded confidence model. *PLoS ONE, 14*(3), e0213246. http://dx.doi.org/10.1371/journal.pone.0213246

Snoeijers, E. M., Poels, K., & Nicolay, C. (2014). #universitycrisis: The impact of social media type, source, and information on student responses toward a university crisis. *Social Science Computer Review, 32*(5), 647–661. http://dx.doi.org/10.1177/0894439314525025

Steelman, T. A., Nowell, B., Bayoumi, D., & McCaffrey, S. (2014). Understanding information exchange during disaster response: Methodological insights from infocentric analysis. *Administration & Society, 46*(6), 707–743. http://dx.doi.org/10.1177/0095399712469198

Stephens, K. K., & Malone, P. C. (2009). If the organizations won't give us information . . .: The use of multiple new media for crisis technical translation and dialogue. *Journal of Public Relations Research, 21*(2), 229–239. http://dx.doi.org/10.1080/10627260802557605

Stewart, M. C., & Wilson, B. G. (2016). The dynamic role of social media during Hurricane #Sandy: An introduction of the STREMII model to weather the storm of the crisis lifecycle. *Computers in Human Behavior, 54*, 639–646. http://dx.doi.org/10.1016/j.chb.2015.07.009

Su, L. Y. F., Akin, H., Brossard, D., Scheufele, D. A., & Xenos, M. A. (2015). Science news consumption patterns and their implications for public understanding of science. *Journalism & Mass Communication Quarterly, 92*, 597–616. http://dx.doi.org/10.1177/1077699015586415

Suarez-Lledo, V., & Alvarez-Galvez, J. (2021). Prevalence of health misinformation on social media: Systematic review. *Journal of Medical Internet Research, 23*(1), e17187. http://dx.doi.org/10.2196/17187

Subbaraman, N. (2021). How do vaccinated people spread Delta? What the science says. *Nature, 596*(7872), 327–328. https://www.nature.com/articles/d41586-021-02187-1

Tang, Z., Miller, A. S., Zhou, Z., & Warkentin, M. (2021). Does government social media promote users' information security behavior towards COVID-19 scams? Cultivation effects and protective motivations. *Government Information Quarterly, 38*(2), 101572. https://doi.org/10.1016/j.giq.2021.101572

Thelwall, M., Kousha, K., & Thelwall, S. (2021). Covid-19 vaccine hesitancy on English-language Twitter. *Profesional de la Información, 30*(2), e300212. http://dx.doi.org/10.3145/epi.2021.mar.12

Tyagi, A., Babcock, M., Carley, K. M., & Sicker, D. C. (2020). Polarizing tweets on climate change. In *R. Thomson, H. Bisgin, C. Dancy, A. Hyder, & M. Hussain (Eds.), International conference on social computing, behavioral-cultural modeling and prediction and behavior representation in modeling and simulation* (pp. 107–117). Springer.

Utz, S., Schultz, F., & Glocka, S. (2013). Crisis communication online: How medium, crisis type and emotions affected public reactions in the Fukushima Daiichi nuclear disaster. *Public Relations Review, 39*(1), 40–46. http://dx.doi.org/10.1016/j.pubrev.2012.09.010

van der Linden, S., Leiserowitz, A., Rosenthal, S., & Maibach, E. (2017). Inoculating the public against misinformation about climate change. *Global Challenges*, *1*, 1600008. http://dx.doi.org/10.1002/gch2.201600008

Vicario, M. D., Bessi, A., Zollo, F., Petroni, F., Scala, A., Caldarelli, G., Stanley, H. E., & Quattrociocch, W. (2016). The spreading of misinformation online. *PNAS*, *113*(3), 554–559. http://dx.doi.org/10.1073/pnas.1517441113

Vijaykumar, S., Nowak, G., Himelboim, I., & Jin, Y. (2018). Managing social media rumors and misinformation during outbreaks. *American Journal of Infection Control*, *46*(7), 846–850. http://dx.doi.org/10.1016/j.ajic.2018.03.014

Vosoughi, S., Roy, D., & Aral, S. (2018). The spread of true and false news online. *Science*, *359*(6380), 1146–1151. http://dx.doi.org/10.1126/science.aap9559

Vraga, E. K., & Bode, L. (2018). I do not believe you: How providing a source corrects health misperceptions across social media platforms. *Information, Communication & Society*, *21*(10), 1337–1353. http://dx.doi.org/10.1080/1369118X.2017.1313883

Vraga, E. K., Kim, S. C., & Cook, J. (2019). Testing logic-based and humor-based corrections for science, health, and political misinformation on social media. *Journal of Broadcasting & Electronic Media*, *63*(3), 393–414. http://dx.doi.org/10.1080/08838151.2019.1653102

Wang, D., & Qian, Y. (2021). Echo chamber effect in rumor rebuttal discussions about COVID-19 in China: Social media content and network analysis study. *Journal of Medical Internet Research*, *23*(3), e27009. https://doi.org/10.2196/27009

Wang, Y., McKee, M., Torbica, A., & Stuckler, D. (2019). Systematic literature review on the spread of health-related misinformation on social media. *Social Science & Medicine*, *240*, 112552. http://dx.doi.org/10.1016/j.socscimed.2019.112552

Waszak, P. M., Kasprzycka-Waszak, W., & Kubanek, A. (2018). The spread of medical fake news in social media—The pilot quantitative study. *Health Policy and Technology*, *7*(2), 115–118. http://dx.doi.org/10.1016/j.hlpt.2018.03.002

Williams, H. T., McMurray, J. R., Kurz, T., & Lambert, F. H. (2015). Network analysis reveals open forums and echo chambers in social media discussions of climate change. *Global Environmental Change*, *32*, 126–138. http://dx.doi.org/10.1016/j.gloenvcha.2015.03.006

Wright, K. B., & Miller, C. H. (2010). A measure of weak-tie/strong-tie support network preference. *Communication Monographs*, *77*(4), 500–517. http://dx.doi.org/10.1080/03637751.2010.502538

Wright, K. B., Riemann, W., & Fisher, C. L. (2021). Work–life imbalance during the COVID-19 pandemic: Exploring social support behavior and health outcomes. *Journal of Applied Communication Research*, *50*, 54–69. http://dx.doi.org/10.1080/00909882.2021.1965186

Yoo, E., Rand, W., Eftekhar, M., & Rabinovich, E. (2016). Evaluating information diffusion speed and its determinants in social media networks during humanitarian crises. *Journal of Operations Management*, *45*, 123–133. http://dx.doi.org/10.1016/j.jom.2016.05.007

Zhao, Y., & Zhang, J. (2017). Consumer health information seeking in social media: A literature review. *Health Information & Libraries Journal*, *34*(4), 268–283. http://dx.doi.org/10.1111/hir.12192

3

Emerging Media, Emotions, and Misperceptions in Health Crisis

Jiyoung Lee[1], *Sai Datta Mikkilineni*[2], *and Eunsung Lee*[1]

[1] *Department of Media and Communication, Sungkyunkwan University*
[2] *College of Communication & Information Sciences, The University of Alabama*

In times of public crises, the prevalence of uncertainty leads to the rapid proliferation of misinformation on online media platforms. From public health crises such as the COVID-19 pandemic to natural disasters and political unrest, fear-mongering misinformation fuels the accelerated spread of misinformation through diverse online media channels. Although misinformation has been a longstanding issue predating the rise of online media, the advent of media technology has had a profound impact on its production and circulation, presenting both advantageous and potentially harmful outcomes.

The central tenets of misinformation—information identified as false—have not changed drastically throughout history. However, the specifics of misinformation have become unparalleled and unprecedented, and the speed at which it is spread and the magnitude of its influence put it in a different category from its history. Among the factors that influenced the difference that distinguished current misinformation from its older version is the technological advancements in media. Digital media have fulfilled an important role by fostering interactivity and, more recently, with the advancement of artificial intelligence (AI) and immersive media, facilitating the application of multimodal information and computer-generated messages to amplify the influence of misinformation. These technological advancements play a pivotal role in the proliferation of misinformation, further complicating the endeavor to discern truth from falsehood in our digital society.

In this chapter we present a comprehensive examination of the psychological impact that advancements in media technology have had on the dissemination and potency of misinformation, especially in times of crisis. First, drawing from theoretical underpinnings, we delve into the interactive and immersive capabilities of media technology that amplify the influence of misinformation, specifically, the affordances of media technology within the realm of social media, AI, and immersive media. Second, we provide directions for future research and discuss potential solutions to counter misinformation in crises. As misinformation is strategically designed to influence audiences' emotional states, the chapter addresses the emotional ramifications of misinformation across a variety of communication technologies.

Communication and Misinformation: Crisis Events in the Age of Social Media, First Edition.
Edited by Kevin B. Wright.
© 2025 John Wiley & Sons, Inc. Published 2025 by John Wiley & Sons, Inc.

The Interactive Affordances of Social Media and Misinformation

Social Media as a Two-Way Communication Channel for the Amplification of Misinformation

One of the distinctive characteristics of social media is its capacity to facilitate user interaction and engagement. Social media engagement encompasses "all forms of interaction in an online environment, ranging from simple one-click interactions (e.g., like-clicking, leaving reactive emojis) to in-depth communication about controversial issues" (Lee et al., 2023b, p. 1232). Indeed, the concept of interactivity has been often discussed from a multifaceted perspective in traditional communication scholarship (Kiousis, 2002; McMillan & Hwang, 2002). By enabling users to actively engage and collaborate with each other, social media has been a place for two-way communication that co-creates information. During crises, such two-way communication can help navigate uncertainty. Organizations and individuals can quickly gather and share crucial information through open channels of communication, leading to better-informed decisions.

However, not all two-way communication lead to positive outcomes to manage uncertainty during crises. Based on a public relations perspective, two-way communication can be differentiated into asymmetric (i.e., conveying persuasive messages with the intention of influencing audiences) and symmetric communication (i.e., emphasizing mutual respect while being open to changes of organizational operations to align with public perspectives; Dozier et al., 1995; Grunig & Grunig, 2008). Asymmetric, in contrast to symmetric, two-way communication has been found to be less effective for establishing trust between an organization and the public.

Considering the drawback of asymmetric communication, authoritative organizations such as the Centers for Disease Control and Prevention have endeavored to participate in symmetric two-way communication by actively prompting feedback from their audience via X/Twitter chats. Despite these efforts, the participatory space of social media has often remained a place for asymmetric two-way communication in which experts unilaterally delivered advice and answered questions from the public (Dalrymple et al., 2016). This top-down communicative practice may inadvertently result in situations where audiences may need to seek additional information from questionable and unverified sources. Jang and Baek (2019), for instance, explored how the public adapted their health-information-seeking behaviors during the 2015 Middle East Respiratory Syndrome (MERS) outbreak in South Korea when asymmetric two-way communication from public health officials failed to deliver satisfactory information. Their research revealed that individuals turned to alternative communication platforms, including online news and social media, to seek more comprehensive and trustworthy information than that provided by public health authorities. However, relying on these alternative sources led unexpectedly to individuals being influenced by misinformation.

Taken together, these results suggest that the use of asymmetric two-way communication by authoritative sources during a crisis, rather than alleviating anxiety during crises, can have unintended consequences (See Table 3.1). It may exacerbate the chaos and ultimately drive the public to seek out alternative information—often unverified or false information provided by nonauthoritative sources. Is adopting two-way symmetric interaction on social media a foolproof solution to protect the public from succumbing to misinformation?

Table 3.1 Defining Misinformation Across Emerging Media and Relevant Variables that Influence Users' Susceptibility to Misinformation.

Medium		**How is misinformation manifested?**	**Examples of affordances that lead to misinformation susceptibility**	**Psychological drivers behind misinformation susceptibility**
Social media		The dissemination of false or misleading information through online platforms, fueled by emotional reactions and amplified by users, contributing to false beliefs and perceptions.	• Two-way communication (symmetric or asymmetric)	• Interactivity • Source credibility
AI	Misinformation generator	The generation of false or misleading information, including text-based misinformation from large language models (e.g., ChatGPT), and the creation of fabricated content through AI-generated images and deepfakes. This misleading content can appear highly convincing, leading to misperceptions, eroded trust, and increased susceptibility to false information.	• Generative language model • AI-generated multimodality • Virtual human	• (Multimodal AI) hallucination
	Misinformation facilitator	The strategic dissemination of platform or user-generated content through algorithms specifically designed to create filter bubbles and echo chambers, which reinforce misinformation during crises. These algorithms exploit emotional responses, amplifying the impact of emotionally charged but misleading information.	• Recommendation engines • Biased algorithms	• Homophily heuristic
Immersive media		The deliberate or unintentional dissemination of false or misleading information within immersive virtual environments, where the heightened sense of presence and embodiment can lead users to misexperience fabricated narratives as factual and emotionally compelling, thus distorting their perceptions of reality.	• 3D formats • Virtual reality • Virtual avatar	• Spatial presence • Social presence • Embodiment

Notwithstanding that active interaction based on mutual respect between two entities on social media has the potential to encourage audiences to engage more deeply with the shared information (Dozier et al., 1995; Grunig & Grunig, 2008), this very aspect of symmetric two-way communication can also give rise to the spread of misinformation during public crises. The openness of information exchange, whereby information flows freely without any restrictions, can provide a place for unauthorized individuals to engage in low-quality discussions and share misinformation either intentionally or unintentionally. In contrast to the asymmetrical and top-down approach used by authoritative sources such as fact-checking organizations or government agencies to correct misinformation, social media users can engage in symmetrical communication by sharing misinformation with good intentions such as to inform other users about uncertain situations. Thus the lack of gatekeeping by authoritative sources in two-way symmetric communication can easily make users more susceptible to misinformation that can spread widely without the facts being checked. A recent study categorizing the types of social media users who gain influence in misinformation-related discussions during crises lends support to the notion that peer-to-peer communication on social media can trigger cycles of misinformation (Lee et al., 2023a).

Emotions and Misinformation on Social Media

In the context of misinformation-related discussions, it has become evident that social media platforms function as amplification hubs for misinformation because users are frequently exposed to and actively propagate misinformation on these platforms (Lee et al., 2023b; Zhang & Cozma, 2022). The role of social media in disseminating misinformation during crises is explained through the theoretical lens of the social amplification of risk framework (SARF), which posits that "risk events interact with psychological, social, and cultural processes in ways that can heighten or attenuate public perceptions of risk and related risk behavior" (Kasperson et al., 1988, pp. 178–179). That said, while transmitting risk-related information, stations for social amplification either enhance or reduce particular elements of the information, thereby influencing the public's comprehension of the associated hazard in various ways. In the case of mask wearing during the COVID-19 pandemic, Twitter emerged as a platform that highlighted contrasting opinions regarding the CDC guidelines, eroding credibility and trust in government agencies and attenuating the public's perception of the risks posed by COVID-19 (Hopfer et al., 2021). Similarly, Strekalova and Krieger (2017) examined audience engagement of the National Cancer Institute (NCI) Facebook posts concerning cancer risks and found that social media platforms served to amplify cancer-related risks. More specifically related to misinformation during health crises, previous research uncovered the widespread circulation of conspiracy theories concerning the causes and risks associated with the Zika virus on social media (Wirz et al., 2018). A crucial point in relation to SARF is that social media plays a role in spreading misinformation by evoking negative emotions. This perspective is in line with the theory of social sharing of emotion (Rimé, 2009), which posits that individuals experiencing intense emotions are inclined to share (mis)information with others.

The alarming concern here is that emotional states can prompt the sharing of the information, regardless of its accuracy (Song et al., 2023). The influence of negative emotions on amplifying the susceptibility to misinformation can be further elucidated through the lens of affective heuristics (Finucane et al., 2000; Slovic et al., 2007). According to this perspective, emotional arousal serves as a cognitive shortcut that prompts individuals to make rapid decisions rather than engaging in deliberate and thoughtful reasoning. Recent cases related to COVID-19 vaccine hesitancy are typical examples of how extreme anxiety regarding vaccine side effects immediately led to a strong aversion to get vaccinated (Chou & Budenz, 2020). Especially during public health crises involving novel infections, scientific uncertainty hinders authorities from providing definitive knowledge (Sommariva et al., 2018). Although users at times create and spread misinformation without realizing its falsehood, malicious actors on social media also intentionally manipulate and exploit uncertainty by deliberately disseminating false information. The challenge lies in correcting misinformation that has been intentionally designed to provoke uncertainty. Lee's (2022b) research, for example, demonstrates that misinformation on social media that stirs up fear in the context of public health crises is notably resistant to correction, which increases users' vulnerability to misinformation.

Apart from the deliberate intentions of malicious actors on social media to exploit fear and induce inaccurate judgments, users tend to alleviate anxiety through interactions with other users on social media at times of public crises. Particularly salient is the possibility that such social media interaction often undermines the severity of public health crises, leading to the formation of misperceptions. For instance, a recent panel study revealed that merely engaging in interactions on social media platforms (i.e., sharing emotions, discussing contentious topics related to the virus, and responding to others' posts) was associated with a decreased perception of the risk of COVID-19. This diminished risk perception consequently contributed to an increase in misperceptions regarding the virus (Lee et al., 2023b). Similarly, another panel study discovered that individuals who relied heavily on social media as their primary source of news were more prone to believe and subsequently share COVID-19 misinformation (Ahmed & Rasul, 2022).

In both cases where social media serves as a channel to attenuate or to amplify negative emotions, it becomes a potent misinformation station that can disseminate false or misleading information to a wide range of users. Of even greater concern is the phenomenon whereby AI-driven algorithms exacerbate people's vulnerability to misinformation by actively amplifying and disseminating content that reinforces their preconceived beliefs or triggers emotional responses. In the following section, we delve deeper into the role of AI in misinformation and discuss its multifaceted role.

AI-driven Misinformation

Recent innovations in communication technologies have revolutionized the ways in which information is created, curated, and transmitted, consequently shaping users' attitudes toward misinformation. With the rise and ubiquity in modern communication technologies, AI is at the forefront of such discussions. While most of the scholarship has focused on identifying different approaches in leveraging AI for satisfying communication goals, misinformation scholars have raised alarming concerns for its ability to generate or aid the spread of malicious content (Bontridder & Poullet, 2021; Vizoso et al., 2021; Zhou et al., 2023). Indeed, the potential of AI to effortlessly fabricate and convincingly communicate with millions of users is far beyond our ability to understand. Drawing upon Bontridder and Poullet's (2021) conceptualization, we argue that AI can manifest in two ways, facilitating both the creation (i.e., misinformation generator) and dissemination of misinformation (i.e., misinformation facilitator).

AI as a Misinformation Generator: Multimodality and Emotion

Despite AI being viewed as the remedy for the misinformation crisis (Ozbay & Alatas, 2019; Shu et al., 2017), the current focus has shifted to exploring how AI can autonomously generate misinformation, utilizing both text-only or multimodal approaches (i.e., text-plus-synthetic image or deepfakes). The evolution of generative AI allows for the creation of misleading messages that are far from the truth but appear highly plausible, thereby impeding the effective handling of uncertain crisis scenarios. As an example, ChatGPT often offers responses with unwarranted confidence, providing information that is disconnected from reality, a phenomenon commonly referred to as hallucination (Alkaissi & McFarlane, 2023). Hallucination in large language models (LLMs) can occur when the model generates information that seems plausible on the surface but is entirely fabricated or lacks factual basis to support the claims. A matter of concern is that people tend to rely on generative AI in the fields of medicine and law to reach conclusions. Not only does hallucination in AI language models pose immediate risks that make people susceptible to misinformation, but also has the capacity to erode trust in information systems as a whole, prevailing fear and uncertainty.

Aside from text-based AI such as ChatGPT, it is important to note the emergence of AI-edited images or deepfakes that AI generates from scratch, which fall into the category of what we call *multimodal AI hallucinations* in this chapter. Specifically, we define multimodal AI hallucinations as a phenomenon in which AI systems produce or modify the content across multiple modes (i.e., text, images, and audio), ultimately leading to the creation of fabricated messages that appear convincingly realistic. Deepfakes are synthetic audio-visual materials that are developed using a deep learning technique called generative adversarial networks (GANs) (Rana & Sung, 2020; Whyte, 2020). Using GANs, one can seamlessly swap visual elements in a picture or a video and insert features that were not originally part of the content. For instance, deepfakes are routinely used to swap the faces of celebrities for a variety of material ranging from parody to purposeful deception. In fact, many manual input-reliant procedures have been automated, and once closely protected software is now open-source, enabling individuals with little-to-no experience to generate deepfakes through simple clicks (Hancock & Bailenson, 2021; Vizoso et al., 2021). Consequently, a report from 2019 identified close to 15,000 deepfakes on the internet (Castro, 2019) and the number spiked almost certainly to over 1 million at the time of the writing (Byman et al., 2023).

To delve deeper into the multifaceted nature of AI-induced misinformation, it is essential to tap into the role of virtual humans (in other words, AI-generated entities) as they can exert substantial influence in individuals' responses to misinformation. These virtual humans, serving as embodied agents, are endowed with the capacity to engage with users in a manner akin to real-world interactions. That said, their human-like appearance and interaction abilities render the spread of misinformation more impactful. In the field of medicine, for example, virtual humans have the capability to replicate the appearance of health-care professionals and leverage their authoritative personas, fostering a perception of credibility. Consequently, individuals may place trust in and adhere to the guidance offered by these virtual entities, presuming them to be trustworthy sources. These misperceptions concerning health can result in individuals making ill-informed decisions about their health behaviors.

The potential influences of multimodal disinformation can be explained by the heuristic-systematic model (HSM; Eagly & Chaiken, 1993). For example, a study by Lee and Shin (2022) found that deepfakes were perceived as more credible when compared to text-only and text-photo disinformation, especially among those who relied on *vividness heuristics* of the face-swapped person in the deepfake content (Lee & Shin, 2022). Although Hameleers et al. (2022) found contradicting evidence on political deepfakes, which demonstrated that deepfakes were not perceived to be significantly more credible than textual disinformation, the nonsignificant effects regarding deepfakes could be partially attributed to the implausibility of the extremist political claims associated with the less extreme political figure. Although deepfakes in some cases can be perceived to be less credible than the authentic content (Shin & Lee, 2022), these results do not negate the potential risks associated with AI-generated deepfakes. Indeed, the impact of multimodal deepfakes is connected to the heuristic processing of fabricated content, leading to misperceptions.

The fundamental process at play herein is that visuals provide a more direct index of reality and are capable of triggering emotional responses through an automatic process (Powell et al., 2015). This argument underscores the power of multimodal information on our misperceptions, often overriding conscious thought when assessing the accuracy of information. In support of this perspective, recent research in the context of health disinformation about the flu vaccine has revealed that multimodal disinformation, manipulated as videos featuring interviews with health experts and individuals claiming to have experienced negative effects from the vaccine, induced the feelings of anxiety, leading to a greater acceptance of the misinformation presented (Lee et al., 2023c).

However, it should be acknowledged that even AI agents with singular modality (e.g., text-only) are influential in spreading disinformation by making people feel anxious about uncertain situations. AI chatbots such as ChatGPT that are developed on the principles of LLMs manifest as another AI-enabled apparatus that generate disinformation (Hsu & Thompson, 2023), particularly posing a threat to public health (De Angelis et al., 2023). Given that users believe that machines are objective and free of ideological biases based on the machine heuristics (Sundar, 2008), the content generated by ChatGPT would be deemed credible by users, irrespective of its truthfulness. Importantly, since generative AI like ChatGPT takes away users' agency (Sundar & Liao, 2023), the approach by which users typically assess the accuracy of information through active interaction with the content would become infeasible in AI-dominated systems, potentially leading to a heightened susceptibility to misinformation.

Given these discussions, the rise of LLMs and other generative AI that creates multimodal content (e.g., Midjourney) emphasizes the need to revisit and retest our prior assumptions of how users psychologically respond to AI-produced misinformation with different modalities. This entails examining users' emotional responses, particularly when they encounter (multimodal) disinformation created by AI that challenges their agency to validate the authenticity of the message. In all, the intricate relationship between multimodalities and emotions in the context of misinformation underscores the need to consider the psychological dynamics at play when assessing the impact of AI-generated misinformation.

AI as a Misinformation Facilitator: Algorithm and Emotion

Beyond AI's role as a producer of misinformation, where AI serves as a *source* of false information, we are now addressing concerns related to how AI plays a role as a *disseminator* of preexisting fabricated content. One of the representative examples is algorithmic personalization which was at the core of discussion over several years. AI-driven recommendation engines are known to contribute to the formation of filter bubbles or echo chambers on social media by exposing users predominantly to content that aligns with their existing attitudes. For instance, a user who fell for vaccine-related misinformation is more likely to be recommended such misinformation from other like-minded individuals. This leads to a homogeneous social media ecosystem, making it more challenging to combat misinformation especially during times of crisis when unverified information tends to proliferate.

An overview of previous research shows how misinformation can be spread through AI-driven algorithms. Although some empirical findings indicate that social media platforms facilitate users in acquiring diverse perspectives through unintentional exposure (Beam et al., 2020), there are concerns that algorithms utilize users' individual-level characteristics and tailor content by learning from other like-minded users (Bi et al., 2019; Huang et al., 2007). This personalization creates filter bubbles, where the content that aligns with one's own interests and other like-minded individuals garners extensive engagement. This algorithmically curated homogenous digital space has the potential to trigger *homophily heuristic*, a mental shortcut that leads users to believe that "if others similar to me like something, I should like it too" (Liao, 2023, p. 8). Such heuristic encourages users to place trust in and be susceptible to misinformation as it leads users to accept the widely shared information among like-minded users to be aligned with their own beliefs or characteristics, regardless of its accuracy or reliability.

Filter bubbles become significantly more pronounced in situations where health crises are intertwined with politics, leading individuals to blindly trust information coming from their own in-group. Instances of this nature have been observed amid the COVID-19 pandemic, where right-leaning communities have exhibited a strong affinity for antivaccine narratives (Sharma et al., 2022). Likewise, as users started engaging with health-related misinformation, they were directed toward antivaccine videos (Tang et al., 2021). Their misperceptions were further fueled by the algorithms that prevent any accurate information from reaching them. Research has also noted that users who consume ideologically extreme-right content on YouTube are more likely to be further recommended the similar videos (O'Callaghan et al., 2014).

Importantly, AI-driven algorithms that contribute to the spread of misinformation can not only fabricate content based on users' existing attitudes but also exploit their emotional states during the persuasion process by presenting emotionally provocative but misleading content. Given that misinformation tends to evoke stronger negative emotions compared to fact-based information (Paschen, 2020), users may find themselves exposed more frequently to emotionally charged misleading content. Furthermore, users are often inclined to engage with and share content that elicits strong emotional responses, such as anger, even if it contains misleading claims (Lee et al., 2023d). This suggests that when users are predominantly exposed to emotionally charged misinformation that resonates with their emotional states or alleviates their anxiety during health crises, the influence of misinformation on shaping users' misconceptions can become even more pronounced. Hence, the repetitive presentation of emotionally charged misleading content, curated by algorithms, can lead users to become more engaged with such emotionally provocative messages, thereby impeding their ability to accurately discern the content.

Immersive Media and Emotions and Misexperience

Immersive media technologies such as mixed reality (MR) have been developed to enhance the level of immersion, interactivity, and vividness in mediated experiences. This can be accomplished, for instance, by representing information in 3D formats or leveraging spatial audio that mimics sound waves in the real world. A recent systematic review has indicated that immersive media forms lead to stronger persuasive effects primarily through various psychological mechanisms, with a sense of presence playing a key role (see Breves, 2023 for a review).

Unexpectedly, the immersive capabilities of these technologies, which can be harnessed to promote health behaviors, can also be exploited for antisocial purposes, such as disseminating disinformation and inciting discord—a classic double-edged-sword dilemma. The influential potential of immersive media have led scholars recently to begin examining how they can be used as a weapon for disinformation (Brown et al., 2023). There has been a lack of empirical scholarship on this matter, with the exception of Verhulst et al.'s (2020) pilot study, which tested the relative influence of fake news on virtual reality (VR) versus 2D. The study had six participants, half of whom were assigned to the VR condition and the other half to the 2D condition. Results showed that participants in the VR condition rated the disinformation as more credible and fairer than participants in the 2D condition.

While the study is in its early stages, these findings are unsurprising when we consider the theoretical mechanisms that have been identified as amplifying the impact of immersive media on users' perceptions, that is, presence and embodiment. In line with Brown et al.'s (2023, p. 4) research, we argue that immersive media give rise to what they term *misexperiences*, wherein users engage experientially with misinformation within immersive environments that nurture distorted beliefs about reality. For example, when individuals are completely immersed in a virtual environment, to the extent that they are disconnected from the real world, they may encounter challenges in verifying the accuracy of information. To delve deeper into this phenomenon, we concentrate on two fundamental mechanisms during the experience of immersive media, namely *presence* and *embodiment*, and their associations with emotional arousal, as they can play a pivotal role in shaping misexperiences.

Presence, as an illusion of nonmediation, entails the sensation of being within a mediated environment (Lombard & Ditton, 1997). That is, when utilizing an immersive media device such as a VR head-mounted display (HMD), users momentarily perceive that they are positioned inside a mediated environment and are also able to interact with virtual objects in the scene. The psychological experience of being deeply immersed in media content plays a pivotal role in shaping misexperiences, as users perceive it to be reality even when they are engaging with a fabricated narrative.

In particular, spatial presence triggers what is known as the "being there" heuristic (Sundar, 2008). This means that, when individuals know they are within a mediated environment, it heightens their perception of the material's authenticity. In this context, users may come to believe that the information is unadulterated and is a direct reflection of a real-life experience (Kim & Biocca, 1997). As a result, the sense of presence can lead users to misconstrue an event, increasing their vulnerability to misinformation and distorting their perceptions of reality. This heightened feeling of spatial presence is often accompanied by intensified emotions (Riva et al., 2007; Wirth et al., 2012). When users find themselves situated within mediated environments, their emotional responses can become heightened, making the content in the mediated environment feel even more genuine and compelling.

Embodiment is another key theoretical construct that can shape users' misexperiences in immersive media. Embodiment is defined as a psychological state of involvement with a virtual character, where the user believes they are located inside the virtual being and has agency and ownership over its actions (Kilteni et al., 2012). Making a first-person perspective of the virtual character readily available to the user enhances the sense of body ownership (Kilteni et al., 2012). This perspective taking has been found to shape attitudes and behaviors toward a variety of issues as users feel they are personally experiencing the actions and/or the consequences in the virtual simulation (for a review, see Niedenthal et al., 2005).

Relatedly, it is understood that the emotions, experiences, and thoughts that are held by the virtual character (or an avatar) may be transferred to the audience (Slater et al., 2010). This concept is referred to as *emotion contagion* in virtual environments; when users become deeply immersed and embodied in virtual characters, they may not only adopt the character's perspective but also experience similar emotions that the avatar experiences. As a result, conspiracy theorists could exploit such embodied experiences and immerse users in virtual characters that are engaged in a fabricated narrative, thereby intensifying their misperceptions. For instance, one of the popular misinformation claims during the pandemic was that COVID-19 vaccines were used to implant citizens with trackable microchips. Theoretically, to promote these conspiracy theories, all the vaccine hoaxers need to do is generate a misexperience of a virtual character developing complications after vaccination and expressing anxiety toward the vaccine. When users are embodied in this character, they may perceive the negative effects as real and accurate, and thus their perceptions are biased against vaccination.

Call to Actions for Human–Computer Interaction, Emotion, and Misinformation Scholars

As the preceding sections have demonstrated, it is evident that the disinformation crisis is immense across a variety of interactive media and is highly likely to grow as more and more individuals use social and emerging media for their informational and entertainment needs. In this context, it is important to recognize that emotions play a significant role in the spread and impact of misinformation. As the costs of social and immersive media (e.g., head-mounted devices) come down, access and vulnerability to misinformation through psychological mechanisms rooted in emotional responses increase. Conflicts will increasingly be manifested as information wars that aim to sway public opinion, often by exploiting emotional triggers. In the face of this adversity, the onus is on all stakeholders to safely navigate the disinformation era.

At the individual level, it is necessary for users to maintain a state of vigilance while engaging with any form of online content. For instance, Appel and Prietzel (2022) found that users who engaged in analytical thinking were more likely to deduce that the deepfake they had watched was indeed fake, which highlights the importance of cognitive processes in managing emotional responses to deceptive content. As such, users must embrace critical thinking and be skeptical of the content they encounter online, even when it elicits strong a emotional reaction.

Relatedly, users must also expose themselves to a diversity of information for cross-checking whenever they encounter suspicious content. This not only helps in fact checking but also serves as an emotional buffer against the persuasive power of emotionally manipulative misinformation. For instance, as mentioned, algorithms play a central role in recommending content. However, the effortful actions of the users themselves play a major part in how these algorithms function (Shin et al., 2022). In addition, individuals must actively embrace certain behaviors, such as following counterattitudinal sources (e.g., a liberal user following Fox News on X/Twitter), referring to multiple sources, and frequently scanning independent fact-checking websites. Finally, users must also take responsibility for their part in debunking disinformation and making other users aware of unverified, suspicious content. For people to be resilient to misinformation, it is crucial to take such actions, given that people tend to respond to corrective information when it is sent to them by familiar groups or networks (Tandoc et al., 2023). Independent users may therefore be more likely to influence their ingroup networks and to nudge them toward corrective information.

From a broader, macrolevel perspective, governments, technology companies, and educational institutions are equally responsible for mitigating this crisis. For governments, this responsibility involves enacting and enforcing regulations that promote transparency and accountability in online content and platforms. It also requires them to allocate resources to public education campaigns on media literacy and critical thinking to empower citizens to navigate the digital landscape more effectively, which includes recognizing and managing the emotional impact of misleading content. The crucial consideration here is to expand existing media literacy interventions in a more nuanced way to encompass the diverse features of computational media, including AI and other immersive technologies. For technology companies, the responsibility lies in designing and implementing algorithms and platform features that prioritize the dissemination of accurate information over misleading content in real time. This can be achieved, for instance, by using AI-based fake news detection tools (Lee, 2022a; Ozbay & Alatas, 2019), which can not only identify false information but also help to reduce the emotional impact of misinformation. Furthermore, such automated tools can be used to flag questionable content and nudge users regarding its veracity.

Alternatively, rather than relying solely on follow-up measures, media companies should inoculate users by exposing them to a variety of disinformation techniques while informing them about strategies to detect and counteract them across different interactive and immersive media platforms. As future generations rely more on digital platforms for various tasks, it becomes increasingly vital for educational institutions to integrate media literacy interventions that address disinformation features within diverse immersive platforms. This includes instructing students in critical information evaluation, the identification of disinformation tactics, and the use of effective verification strategies, all within the context of evolving digital media environments where both media content and message sources can be manipulated or faked. More active discussions on this crisis are necessary and the interventions for mitigation must be continually revisited, with a focus on emotional resilience in the face of misinformation.

References

Ahmed, S., & Rasul, M. E. (2022). Social media news use and COVID-19 misinformation engagement: Survey study. *Journal of Medical Internet Research*, *24*(9), e38944. http://dx.doi.org/10.2196/38944

Alkaissi, H., & McFarlane, S. I. (2023). Artificial hallucinations in ChatGPT: Implications in scientific writing. *Cureus*, *15*(2), e35179. http://dx.doi.org/10.7759/cureus.35179

Appel, M., & Prietzel, F. (2022). The detection of political deepfakes. *Journal of Computer-Mediated Communication*, *27*(4), zmacc008. http://dx.doi.org/10.1093/jcmc/zmac008

Beam, M. A., Hutchens, M. J., & Hmielowski, J. D. (2020). Facebook news and (de)polarization: Reinforcing spirals in the 2016 US election. In M. Beaufort (Ed.), *Digital media, political polarization and challenges to democracy* (pp. 26–44). Routledge. http://dx.doi.org/10.4324/9780429243912

Bi, J.-W., Liu, Y., & Fan, Z.-P. (2019). A deep neural networks based recommendation algorithm using user and item basic data. *International Journal of Machine Learning and Cybernetics, 11*, 763–777. http://dx.doi.org/10.1007/s13042-019-00981-y

Bontridder, N., & Poullet, Y. (2021). The role of artificial intelligence in disinformation. *Data & Policy, 3*, e32. http://dx.doi.org/10.1017/dap.2021.20

Breves, P. (2023). Persuasive communication and spatial presence: A systematic literature review and conceptual model. *Annals of the International Communication Association, 47*(2), 222–241. http://dx.doi.org/10.1080/23808985.2023.2169952

Brown, J. G., Bailenson, J. N., & Hancock, J. (2023). Misinformation in virtual reality. *Journal of Online Trust and Safety, 1*(5). http://dx.doi.org/10.54501/jots.v1i5.120

Byman, D., Meserole, C., & Subrahmanian, V. S. (2023, February 23). The deepfake dangers ahead. *The Wall Street Journal*. https://www.wsj.com/articles/the-deepfake-dangers-ahead-b08e4ecf

Castro, D. (2019). *Deepfakes are on the rise—How should government respond?* GovTech. https://www.govtech.com/policy/deepfakes-are-on-the-rise-how-should-government-respond.html#

Chou, W. Y. S., & Budenz, A. (2020). Considering emotion in COVID-19 vaccine communication: Addressing vaccine hesitancy and fostering vaccine confidence. *Health Communication, 35*(14), 1718–1722. http://dx.doi.org/10.1080/10410236.2020.1838096

Dalrymple, K. E., Young, R., & Tully, M. (2016). "Facts, not fear": Negotiating uncertainty on social media during the 2014 Ebola crisis. *Science Communication, 38*(4), 442–467. https://doi.org10.1177/1075547016655546

De Angelis, L., Baglivo, F., Arzilli, G., Privitera, G. P., Ferragina, P., Tozzi, A. E., & Rizzo, C. (2023). ChatGPT and the gerise of large language models: The new AI-driven infodemic threat in public health. *Frontiers in Public Health, 11*, 1166120. https://doi.org/10.3389/fpubh.2023.1166120

Dozier, D. M., Grunig, L. A., & Grunig, J. E. (1995). *Manager's guide to excellence in public relations and communication management*. Routledge.

Eagly, A. H., & Chaiken, S. (1993). *The psychology of attitudes*. Harcourt Brace Jovanovich.

Finucane, M. L., Alhakami, A., Slovic, P., & Johnson, S. M. (2000). The affect heuristic in judgments of risks and benefits. *Journal of Behavioral Decision Making, 13*(1), 1–17. http://dx.doi.org/10.1002/(SICI)1099-0771(200001/03)13:1%3c1::AID-BDM333%3e3.0.CO;2-S

Grunig, J. E., & Grunig, L. A. (2008). Excellence theory in public relations: Past, present, and future. In A. Zerfass, B. van Ruler, & K. Sriramesh (Eds.), *Public relations research*. VS Verlag für Sozialwissenschaften. http://dx.doi.org/10.1007/978-3-531-90918-9_22

Hameleers, M., van der Meer, T. G. L. A., & Dobber, T. (2022). You won't believe what they just said! The effects of political deepfakes embedded as vox populi on social media. *Social Media + Society, 8*(3). http://dx.doi.org/10.1177/205630512211163

Hancock, J. T., & Bailenson, J. N. (2021). The social impact of deepfakes. *Cyberpsychology, Behavior, and Social Networking, 24*(3), 149–152. http://dx.doi.org/10.1089/cyber.2021.29208.jth

Hopfer, S., Fields, E. J., Lu, Y., Ramakrishnan, G., Grover, T., Bai, Q., Huang, Y., Li, C., & Mark, G. (2021). The social amplification and attenuation of COVID-19 risk perception shaping mask wearing behavior: A longitudinal twitter analysis. *PLoS One*, *16*(9), e0257428. http://dx.doi.org/10.1371/journal.pone.0257428

Hsu, T., & Thompson, S. A. (2023, February 8). Disinformation researchers raise alarms about A.I. chatbots. *The New York Times*. https://www.nytimes.com/2023/02/08/technology/ai-chatbots-disinformation.html

Huang, Z., Zeng, D., & Chen, H. (2007). A comparison of collaborative-filtering recommendation algorithms for e-commerce. *IEEE Intelligent Systems*, *22*(5), 68–78. http://dx.doi.org/10.1109/mis.2007.4338497

Jang, K., & Baek, Y. M. (2019). When information from public health officials is untrustworthy: The use of online news, interpersonal networks, and social media during the MERS outbreak in South Korea. *Health Communication*, *34*(9), 991–998. http://dx.doi.org/10.1080/10410236.2018.1449552

Kasperson, R. E., Renn, O., Slovic, P., Brown, H. S., Emel, J., Goble, R., Kasperson, J. X., & Ratick, S. (1988). The social amplification of risk: A conceptual framework. *Risk Analysis*, *8*(2), 177–187. http://dx.doi.org/10.1111/j.1539-6924.1988.tb01168.x

Kilteni, K., Groten, R., & Slater, M. (2012). The sense of embodiment in virtual reality. *Presence: Teleoperators & Virtual Environments*, *21*(4), 373–387. http://dx.doi.org/10.1162/pres_a_00124

Kim, T., & Biocca, F. (1997). Telepresence via television: Two dimensions of telepresence may have different connections to memory and persuasion. *Journal of Computer-Mediated Communication*, *3*(2). http://dx.doi.org/10.1111/j.1083-6101.1997.tb00073.x

Kiousis, S. (2002). Interactivity: A concept explication. *New Media & Society*, *4*(3), 355–383. http://dx.doi.org/10.1177/146144480200400303

Lee, J. (2022a). The effect of web add-on correction and narrative correction on belief in misinformation depending on motivations for using social media. *Behaviour & Information Technology*, *41*(3), 629–643. http://dx.doi.org/10.1080/0144929X.2020.1829708

Lee, J. (2022b). When web add-on correction comes with fear-arousing misinformation in public health crisis: Focusing on the role of risk perception in belief in misinformation. *Journal of Applied Communication Research*, *50*(1), 70–90. http://dx.doi.org/10.1080/00909882.2021.1964574

Lee, J., Britt, B. C., & Kanthawala, S. (2023a). Taking the lead in misinformation-related conversations in social media networks during a mass shooting crisis. *Internet Research*, *33*(2), 638–663. http://dx.doi.org/10.1108/INTR-02-2021-0120

Lee, J., Choi, J., & Britt, R. K. (2023b). Social media as risk-attenuation and misinformation-amplification station: How social media interaction affects misperceptions about COVID-19. *Health Communication*, *38*(6), 1232–1242.

Lee, J., Hameleers, M., & Shin, S. Y. (2023c). The emotional effects of multimodal disinformation: How multimodality, issue relevance, and anxiety affect misperceptions about the flu vaccine. *New Media & Society*. http://dx.doi.org/10.1177/14614448231153959

Lee, J., Kim, Y., & Zhu, X. (2023d). Liked and shared tweets during the pandemic: The relationship between intrinsic message features and (mis) information engagement. *Behaviour & Information Technology*, *43*(8), 1596–1613. http://dx.doi.org/10.1080/0144929X.2023.2222192

Lee, J., & Shin, S. Y. (2022). Something that they never said: Multimodal disinformation and source vividness in understanding the power of AI-enabled deepfake news. *Media Psychology*, *25*(4), 531–546. http://dx.doi.org/10.1080/15213269.2021.2007489

Liao, M. (2023). Understanding the effects of personalized recommender systems on political news perceptions: A comparison of content-based, collaborative, and editorial choice-based news recommender system. *Journal of Broadcasting & Electronic Media*, *67*(3), 1–29. http://dx.doi.org/10.1080/08838151.2023.2206662

Lombard, M., & Ditton, T. (1997). At the heart of it all: The concept of presence. *Journal of Computer-Mediated Communication*, *3*(2). http://dx.doi.org/10.1111/j.1083-6101.1997.tb00072.x

McMillan, S. J., & Hwang, J. S. (2002). Measures of perceived interactivity: An exploration of the role of direction of communication, user control, and time in shaping perceptions of interactivity. *Journal of Advertising*, *31*(3), 29–42.

Niedenthal, P. M., Barsalou, L. W., Winkielman, P., Krauth-Gruber, S., & Ric, F. (2005). Embodiment in attitudes, social perception, and emotion. *Personality and Social Psychology Review*, *9*(3), 184–211. http://dx.doi.org/10.1207/s15327957pspr0903_1

O'Callaghan, D., Greene, D., Conway, M., Carthy, J., & Cunningham, P. (2014). Down the (white) rabbit hole: The extreme right and online recommender systems. *Social Science Computer Review*, *33*(4), 459–478. http://dx.doi.org/10.1177/0894439314555329

Ozbay, F. A., & Alatas, B. (2019). Fake news detection within online social media using supervised artificial intelligence algorithms. *Physica A: Statistical Mechanics and Its Applications*, *540*, 123174. http://dx.doi.org/10.1016/j.physa.2019.123174

Paschen, J. (2020). Investigating the emotional appeal of fake news using artificial intelligence and human contributions. *Journal of Product & Brand Management*, *29*(2), 223–233. http://dx.doi.org/10.1108/JPBM-12-2018-2179

Powell, T. E., Boomgaarden, H. G., De Swert, K., & de Vreese, C. H. (2015). A clearer picture: The contribution of visuals and text to framing effects. *Journal of Communication*, *65*(6), 997–1017. http://dx.doi.org/10.1111/jcom.12184

Rana, Md. S., & Sung, A. H. (2020). DeepfakeStack: A deep ensemble-based learning technique for deepfake detection. In 2020 7th IEEE international conference on cyber security and cloud computing (CSCloud)/2020 6th IEEE international conference on edge computing and scalable cloud (EdgeCom) (pp. 70–75). http://dx.doi.org/10.1109/cscloud-edgecom49738.2020.00021

Rimé, B. (2009). Emotion elicits the social sharing of emotion: Theory and empirical review. *Emotion Review*, *1*(1), 60–85. https://doi.org/10.1177/1754073908097189

Riva, G., Mantovani, F., Capideville, C. S., Preziosa, A., Morganti, F., Villani, D., Gaggioli, A., Botella, C., & Alcañiz, M. (2007). Affective interactions using virtual reality: The link between presence and emotions. *Cyberpsychology & Behavior*, *10*(1), 45–56. http://dx.doi.org/10.1089/cpb.2006.9993

Sharma, K., Zhang, Y., & Liu, Y. (2022). COVID-19 vaccine misinformation campaigns and social media narratives. *Proceedings of the International AAAI Conference on Web and Social Media*, *16*, 920–931. http://dx.doi.org/10.1609/icwsm.v16i1.19346

Shin, D., Hameleers, M., Park, Y. J., Kim, J. N., Trielli, D., Diakopoulos, N., Helberger, N., Lewis, S. C., Westlund, O., & Baumann, S. (2022). Countering algorithmic bias and disinformation and effectively harnessing the power of AI in media. *Journalism & Mass Communication Quarterly*, *99*(4), 887–907. http://dx.doi.org/10.1177/10776990221129245

Shin, S. Y., & Lee, J. (2022). The effect of deepfake video on news credibility and corrective influence of cost-based knowledge about deepfakes. *Digital Journalism*, *10*(3), 412–432. http://dx.doi.org/10.1080/21670811.2022.2026797

Shu, K., Sliva, A., Wang, S., Tang, J., & Liu, H. (2017). Fake news detection on social media: A data mining perspective. *ACM SIGKDD Explorations Newsletter*, *19*(1), 22–36. http://dx.doi.org/10.1145/3137597.3137600

Slater, M., Spanlang, B., Sanchez-Vives, M. V., & Blanke, O. (2010). First person experience of body transfer in virtual reality. *PLoS One*, *5*(5), e10564. http://dx.doi.org/10.1371/journal.pone.0010564

Slovic, P., Finucane, M. L., Peters, E., & MacGregor, D. G. (2007). The affect heuristic. *European Journal of Operational Research*, *177*(3), 1333–1352. http://dx.doi.org/10.1016/j.ejor.2005.04.006

Sommariva, S., Vamos, C., Mantzarlis, A., Đào, L. U. L., & Martinez Tyson, D. (2018). Spreading the (fake) news: Exploring health messages on social media and the implications for health professionals using a case study. *American Journal of Health Education*, *49*(4), 246–255. http://dx.doi.org/10.1080/19325037.2018.1473178

Song, H., So, J., Shim, M., Kim, J., Kim, E., & Lee, K. (2023). What message features influence the intention to share misinformation about COVID-19 on social media? The role of efficacy and novelty. *Computers in Human Behavior*, *138*, 107439. http://dx.doi.org/10.1016/j.chb.2022.107439

Strekalova, Y. A., & Krieger, J. L. (2017). Beyond words: Amplification of cancer risk communication on social media. *Journal of Health Communication*, *22*(10), 849–857. http://dx.doi.org/10.1080/10810730.2017.1367336

Sundar, S. S. (2008). The MAIN model: A heuristic approach to understanding technology effects on credibility. In M. J. Metzger & J. Flanagin (Eds.), *Digital media, youth, and credibility* (pp. 73–100). MIT Press. http://dx.doi.org/10.1162/dmal.9780262562324.073

Sundar, S. S., & Liao, M. (2023). Calling BS on ChatGPT: Reflections on AI as a communication source. *Journalism & Communication Monographs*, *25*(2), 165–180. http://dx.doi.org/10.1177/15226379231167135

Tandoc, E. C., Jr., Lee, J. C. B., Lee, C. S., Sin, J. S. C., & Seet, S. K. (2023). No “me” in misinformation: The role of social groups in the spread of, and fight against, fake news. In C. Soon (Ed.), *Mobile communication and online falsehoods in Asia. Mobile communication in Asia: Local insights, global implications* (pp. 131–148). Springer.

Tang, L., Fujimoto, K., Amith, M., Cunningham, R., Costantini, R. A., York, F., Xiong, G., Boom, J. A., & Tao, C. (2021). “Down the rabbit hole” of vaccine misinformation on YouTube: Network exposure study. *Journal of Medical Internet Research*, *23*(1), e23262. http://dx.doi.org/10.2196/23262

Verhulst, A., Zhao, W., Nakamura, F., Fukuoka, M., Sugimoto, M., & Inami, M. (2020). Impact of fake news in VR compared to fake news on social media, a pilot study. In *Proceedings of 2020 IEEE Conference on Virtual Reality and 3D User Interfaces Abstracts and Workshops (VRW)* (pp. 576–577). IEEE. https://doi.org/10.1109/VRW50115.2020.00139.

Vizoso, Á., Vaz-Álvarez, M., & López-García, X. (2021). Fighting deepfakes: Media and internet giants’ converging and diverging strategies against hi-tech misinformation. *Media and Communication*, *9*(1), 291–300. http://dx.doi.org/10.17645/mac.v9i1.3494

Whyte, C. (2020). Deepfake news: AI-enabled disinformation as a multi-level public policy challenge. *Journal of Cyber Policy*, *5*(2), 1–19. http://dx.doi.org/10.1080/23738871.2020.1797135

Wirth, W., Hofer, M., & Schramm, H. (2012). The role of emotional involvement and trait absorption in the formation of spatial presence. *Media Psychology*, *15*(1), 19–43. http://dx.doi.org/10.1080/15213269.2011.648536

Wirz, C. D., Xenos, M. A., Brossard, D., Scheufele, D., Chung, J. H., & Massarani, L. (2018). Rethinking social amplification of risk: Social media and Zika in three languages. *Risk Analysis*, *38*(12), 2599–2624. http://dx.doi.org/10.1111/risa.13228

Zhang, X. A., & Cozma, R. (2022). Risk sharing on Twitter: Social amplification and attenuation of risk in the early stages of the COVID-19 pandemic. *Computers in Human Behavior*, *126*, 106983. http://dx.doi.org/10.1016/j.chb.2021.106983

Zhou, J., Zhang, Y., Luo, Q., Parker, A. G., & De Choudhury, M. (2023, April). Synthetic lies: Understanding AI-generated misinformation and evaluating algorithmic and human solutions. In *Proceedings of the 2023 CHI Conference on Human Factors in Computing Systems* (pp. 1–20). Association for Computing Machinery. http://dx.doi.org/10.1145/3544548.3581318

4

Persuasion, Resistance, and Online Misinformation During Crisis

Sarah A. Geegan, Bobi Ivanov, and Kimberly A. Parker

Department of Communication, University of Kentucky

A precise definition of *crisis*, and consequently its management, are debated in the scientific community as a result of differing worldviews and cross-disciplinary approaches to studying this concept (Jaques, 2009). Less debated is how crisis is understood on an individual level as

> a state of feeling; an internal experience of confusion and anxiety to the degree that formerly successful coping mechanisms fail us and ineffective decisions and behaviors take their place. As a result, the person in crisis may feel confused, vulnerable, anxious, afraid, angry, guilty, hopeless, and helpless. (National Interagency Fire Center [NIFC], n.d.)

While this state depicts a time of danger, it simultaneously signals a time of opportunity for individuals to reach beyond their current coping skills, which have proven ineffective in dealing with the crisis. Through the acquisition of proper information and constructive skills, a crisis may present an opportunity for individuals to increase their autonomy and competence in dealing with the crisis event (NIFC, n.d.). The most appropriate resource to provide accurate information and help build these skills, according to Ivanov and colleagues, is scientific-based evidence, which should function as the "decision-informing source for determining when drinking water is safe after a storm, deciding where to shelter during a tornado, and weighing the risks of a new vaccine" (Ivanov, Dillingham, Hester, & Parker, 2022, p. 49). A question of significant import, however, is how to deliver this pertinent scientific evidence in times of crisis.

Depending on the accuracy and intent to harm (or deceive), false information can be further organized into three broader categories (Mayorga et al., 2020; Wardle & Derakhshan, 2017): *misinformation*—false information shared without the intent to harm; *disinformation*—false information shared with the intent to harm; or *malinformation*—accurate information manipulated and presented out of context with the intent to harm. This chapter will focus on strategies to address all of these forms of inaccurate information collectively and on the use of social media to deliver and share accurate science-based information before and during crises. As such, the term "misinformation," in the context of this chapter, is used as an umbrella term for all three forms of false information.

Communication and Misinformation: Crisis Events in the Age of Social Media, First Edition.
Edited by Kevin B. Wright.
© 2025 John Wiley & Sons, Inc. Published 2025 by John Wiley & Sons, Inc.

As such, this chapter will first examine the role that social media occupy with different audiences and their information-seeking behaviors. It will then discuss different psychological motivations that drive individuals' crisis-related information pursuit. The chapter will also propose motivation-specific strategic approaches to encourage the pursuit and sharing of accurate science-based crisis information. The conclusion of the chapter will feature a discussion of the future directions and some practical considerations.

The Role of Social Media in Crises

How to deliver pertinent scientific evidence to the public in times of crisis may depend on the type of crisis and audience composition (Liu et al., 2015; Park & Avery, 2018). Park and Avery's (2018) research led the authors to conclude that, during crises that present immediate danger (e.g., natural disasters, acts of violence or terrorism, transportation crises), people seek trusted and verified sources to ease their immediate concerns, thus turning to traditional sources such as television and radio. For other crisis types, such as public health and political crises, however, people are more likely to turn to social media where they can seek multiple voices and a variety of expert opinions, as, unlike the first set of crises, public health and political crises may be more subjective and less straightforward, and thus necessitate a deeper dive into supplementary information and evidence (Park & Avery, 2018). In addition to the type of crisis at hand, Liu et al. (2015) argued that traditional and social media have different effects on different audiences regarding the motivation to follow instructions and recommended behaviors during crises. For example, although younger audiences seem to favor social media to traditional media sources during times of crisis (Kapp, 2013; Park & Avery, 2018), older audiences indicate a preference for traditional media (Park & Avery, 2018). Thus, both traditional and social media play a prominent role in delivering important scientific information to the public during crises. Additionally, when the emergency does not threaten immediate danger (e.g., political and public health crises), social media becomes the preferred information-seeking platform for the general audience, not just youth (Park & Avery, 2018).

Traditional media generally take on the responsibility of performing critical science reviews and authenticating the information shared with the public to ensure that the best scientifically based evidence is communicated to their audiences (Rehman, 2013). Social media, however, provides a direct link for private individuals to spread unauthenticated and frequently false information (Khanday et al., 2020). As such, scientific evidence and messages disseminated by crisis managers via social media platforms must compete for public attention in an informational space that affords an equal voice to unverified crisis communication messages. To best understand how to successfully attract the public's attention on social media when communicating crisis information and to ensure that accurate science-based information is given attentional preference, Ståhl & Van Prooijen (2018) suggest that we should understand the *motivation* that drives social media information-seeking behavior. Thus, the next question of significant consequence for crisis managers is what motivates individuals to pursue crisis information disseminated via social media. Stated differently, in their pursuit for pertinent information about a given crisis, are individuals motivated to seek the most accurate information (accuracy-seeking individuals) or the information most consistent with their current beliefs (confirmation-seeking individuals)?

The next section of the chapter will explore the motivations driving the pursuit of crisis information disseminated via social media platforms. It will also offer recommended corresponding strategies designed to increase the search for, and assimilation of, verified science-based crisis information. It will provide an overview of each approach, followed by a discussion of how the approach may be used before a crisis even begins (precrisis strategies) and/or during a crisis (peri-crisis strategies).

Audience Motivations

The information-attainment routes mentioned (accuracy seeking and confirmation seeking) are grounded in the social-psychological notion of motivated reasoning. Under this framework, the process by which an individual acquires and contemplates information is inextricably tied to their goals (James & Van Ryzin, 2017; Kruglanski, 1980; Kunda, 1990). Accordingly, an individual's motivations are theorized as oriented around either (1) reaching a valid, accurate conclusion based on consideration of accurate facts or (2) reaching a conclusion that confirms or preserves existing attitudes, identities, or behaviors (Kunda, 1990). Scholars refer to these information-processing goals as accuracy and directional goals, respectively (James & Van Ryzin, 2017).

Particularly during a crisis, strategies aiming to increase consumption of—and trust in—science-based information distributed through social media should reflect an understanding of these two information-processing routes. Strategic communication and persuasion efforts can be conceptualized in terms of two separate target audiences with specific needs, perspectives, and motives: individuals with accuracy goals and individuals with directional goals.

Accuracy Goals

Strategic communication targeting the former group may take a variety of forms, all of which should capitalize on the audience's existing motivation to acquire valid information. This audience wants to avoid being misled by inaccurate information. Thus, three strategies outlined by O'Keefe (2016) may prove fruitful in reducing this susceptibility: skills building, warning, and inoculation. These may be disseminated at different times, including during precrisis and peri-crisis periods.

Promoting Training and Skills Building

Discerning the difference between accurate and inaccurate information online is a difficult task that requires a skill set. Indeed, research demonstrates that individuals with lower levels of general analytical ability are less successful at distinguishing between true and false information (Ståhl & Van Prooijen, 2018) and more likely to believe information contradicted by scientific evidence (Swami et al., 2014). Thus, scholars have called for efforts to enhance general analytical skills among the public (Lewandowsky et al., 2017; Mayorga et al., 2020) and for efforts directly focused on misinformation (Lewandowsky et al., 2017; Mayorga et al., 2020).

Research demonstrates the effectiveness of skills building; as an example, an initiative named "Satyameve Jayate" orchestrated in Kerala, India, effectively enhanced information literacy among school children (Christopher, 2018). Additionally, instruction focused on undergraduates has also enhanced individuals' abilities to reject unreliable information

(Walton & Hepworth, 2011). Taken together, these findings underscore the value of training resources and the importance of providing such instruction in teaching environments. As such, it may be prudent for educators to embed these topics into curricula.

Of course, practitioners aiming to strengthen the public's information literacy lack the advantage of a captive audience inside a classroom. Rather, they face a more difficult task: persuading individuals to build literacy in their own time. As such, the accuracy-seeking audience represents the segment most likely to engage. Interventions supporting skills-building ideally would be deployed before a crisis occurs, allowing individuals to respond to emergencies having already established online literacy. However, crises don't provide ideal circumstances.

Precrisis. Scholars have recommended broad public information campaigns that incorporate a variety of content, such as digestible material or quick tips, to enhance online literacy and reliance on science-based evidence (Komendantova et al., 2021). For example, National Public Radio (NPR) utilized this approach when it produced a story titled "Fake news: How to spot misinformation" (Parks & Douglis, 2019). Additionally, organizations may consider promoting literacy-boosting games, which have shown effectiveness in building relevant skills (Angell & Tewell, 2014). Importantly, practitioners should note that these strategies are likely only to generate interest among accuracy-seeking individuals.

Organizations with sufficient resources may consider developing such material internally. At the same time, content is available from several nonprofit organizations (NPOs) focused on issues of online literacy. For example, the News Literacy Project, a nonpartisan education NPO, offers a suite of educational tools as part of its movement to advance information literacy throughout the United States (News Literacy Project, 2023), and Microsoft recently partnered with the Trust Project, creating a list of indicators for determining an online source's credibility (Klepper, 2023). These are just two examples of many. Organizations responsible for protecting public safety and/or communicating evidence-based information may consider either partnering with an NPOs or directing individuals to relevant content. Additionally, practitioners should consider infusing this content into their routine communications and positioning the opportunities toward the accuracy-seeking audience who are more likely to make use of them.

Peri-crisis. Although skills building should ideally occur before a crisis strikes, it may nevertheless be prudent to encourage literacy development during a crisis. Particularly when targeting accuracy-motivated audiences, crisis communicators may position skills building as vital to safely navigating an ongoing crisis. The Centers for Disease Control and Prevention employed this strategy throughout the COVID-19 pandemic, posting crisis-related information on the CDC website alongside links to literacy-boosting content such as "Finding credible vaccine information" (CDC, 2021). In this example, the title of the content appeals directly to an accuracy-seeking audience—the individuals most likely to consume skills-building resources, in alignment with their goals.

Strengthening Accuracy Motivation with Forewarning

In tandem with strategies that enhance *skills* in detection of inaccurate content, a second approach, forewarning, would strengthen individuals' *motivation* to reject false information. In the persuasion literature, forewarning is conceptualized as content that "alerts message recipients to the vulnerability of their current attitude or behavior" (Ivanov, 2017, p. 25). The emphasis on the *current* attitude or behavior is significant for the accuracy-seeking audience, as they already espouse the "desired" inclination; they want to discern accurate from inaccurate material. As such, strategists may find value in strengthening this existing drive.

Communication research demonstrates that forewarning of impending persuasion increases an individual's desire to defend their attitude (Compton & Ivanov, 2012). In other words, when they are told that their current attitudes are vulnerable, they respond by building up a desire to minimize that vulnerability. Research into forewarning in the online information context is limited, but extant evidence has revealed some promise.

For instance, Ecker et al. (2010) exposed participants to content that cautioned, "sometimes reported 'facts' are not double-checked before they are released" and found that forewarnings diminished reliance on misinformation (p. 1089). Even with small effect sizes, these results are encouraging, particularly when we consider that participants represented a general audience, likely composed of individuals at both ends of the motivated reasoning spectrum.

Because accuracy-seeking individuals are already motivated to detect and reject inaccurate information, a forewarning strategy may involve messages suggesting that individuals are more susceptible to being fooled than they realize—that they may be passively accepting information that undermines their goals to form accurate conclusions. Theoretically, the consequential increase in motivation should result in a boosted desire for online vigilance. As described by Petty and Cacioppo (1977), "a person forewarned is forearmed!" (p. 654).

At the same time, it is important to consider the degree to which individuals are forearmed. Among individuals with high levels of online literacy or analytical skills, enhanced motivation should result in expanded use of those skills. For individuals with less developed cognitive resources, enhanced vigilance may serve as the best available line of defense in combating misinformation. In both cases, enhanced motivation should yield a positive effect; however, the comparison highlights how forewarning is best employed in a precrisis rather than a peri-crisis scenario.

Precrisis. As previously discussed, less-skilled individuals are more susceptible to false information (Ståhl & Van Prooijen, 2018). Thus, in a precrisis context, forewarning offers an avenue to persuade individuals toward proactive skills building. Organizations entrusted to protect the public should consider infusing forewarning into their routine communication efforts, with messaging potentially mirroring Ecker et al.'s (2010) language—cautioning that online information generally may not be fact-checked. Importantly, messages should also emphasize the audience's vulnerability to being fooled by fake news. As an example, messages might state, "You might be misled by online information that is not fact-checked. Learn how to spot misinformation here." Importantly, these messages should also point to training resources (such as those mentioned in the previous section) by which people can build their online literacy.

Peri-crisis. Forewarning strategies may also prove useful in a peri-crisis context, where messages can be used to warn users about misinformation related to a specific emergency. In parallel with the precrisis forewarning, strategies should be used to enhance individuals' motivation (Ivanov et al., 2017), not as mechanisms to develop skills. Thus, ideally, messages should be presented alongside skills-building content.

For example, the social network formerly known as Twitter made use of a forewarning strategy against misinformation during the 2020 presidential elections in the United States. The platform posted at the top of users' feeds, "you might encounter unconfirmed claims that voting by mail leads to election fraud ahead of the 2020 US elections" (Ingram, 2020). Importantly, the message also included a link to literacy resources specific to the elections. However, even if individuals did not engage, the forewarning likely propelled them to consume all election-related content with bolstered scrutiny.

Protecting Accuracy Motivation with Inoculation Theory

The first approach focuses on skill development and the second on motivation; an additional approach would combine both to shore up individuals' motivation to seek accurate information *and* provide content, within the message itself, that enhances their ability to reject false information. Such interventions would be grounded in inoculation theory (McGuire, 1964; see Chapter 12 of this book).

Rooted in a biological metaphor, inoculation theory is a theory of resistance by which messages targeting individuals' attitudes are thought to simulate the process of medical immunization in the body (Ivanov, 2017). To that end, inoculation messages begin with a forewarning and subsequently present weakened arguments that contradict an existing desired attitude; messages then systematically refute those weakened points with strong counterarguments, mimicking immune responses to vaccines containing weakened virus strains (Compton, 2013). As such, inoculation messages are thought to encourage individuals to defend their attitudes *and* to provide relevant content and guided practice in refuting an opposing argument (Ivanov, 2017). Meta-analytic findings have demonstrated the efficacy of the approach across a variety of contexts (Banas & Rains, 2010).

The context of inaccurate online information itself consists of multiple domains in which scholars have evaluated the efficacy of inoculation strategies. They have effectively inoculated individuals against deception efforts by groups withholding their true identities (Boman & Schneider, 2021; Pfau et al., 2007) and in the context of political misinformation from global adversaries (Zerback & Töpfl, 2022). Two studies (Cook et al., 2017; van der Linden et al., 2017) found inoculation effective in protecting individuals against climate change misinformation. Finally, Roozenbeek and van der Linden (2019) developed a game that inoculated individuals against online misinformation.

In line with the biological metaphor, the strategy is designed for individuals already espousing the desired goals (accuracy seeking). Given the proliferation of online information, the process of detecting fake news may seem daunting; this would explain Pew Research Center's findings indicating that nearly half (48 percent) of American adults in 2021 supported government action restricting online false information, up from 39 percent in 2018 (Mitchell & Walker, 2021). Against this backdrop, inoculation offers guidance for content in both precrisis environments, when messaging should be broad, and peri-crisis environments, when messaging should be specific.

Precrisis. Given these Pew Research Center findings, precrisis inoculation strategies present an opportunity to combat messaging that may undermine people's confidence in their ability—or erode their inclination—to seek accuracy. Organizations charged with protecting the public should incorporate inoculation strategies into their routine communication to combat the influence of misinformation.

For instance, precrisis messages could include advice such as:

> You will probably hear that striving to tell the difference between accurate information and misinformation is a waste of time, or that it's hard to recognize official sources. But these ideas are false. Reading accurate information helps you make

informed decisions for the safety of your loved ones. You can learn how to spot the difference between accurate and inaccurate information by following official government accounts, available on the organizations' websites.

This message, following the format of forewarning ("You will probably hear ..."), weakened counterargument ("it's hard to recognize official sources"), and refutations ("following official government accounts"), should protect accuracy-seeking individuals' from misinformation as they pursue factual information in advance of a crisis.

Peri-crisis. Inoculation theory also has value as a peri-crisis strategy for individuals who prize accuracy by orienting messages toward specific circumstances. As an example, inoculation messages utilized by van der Linden et al. (2017) targeted misinformation relating to climate change. The messages began with a forewarning, alerting individuals that "some politically motivated groups use misleading tactics to try to convince the public that there is a lot of disagreement [about climate change] among scientists" (p. 3). The messages then offered a series of refutations to the weakened false idea that scientists disagree on the topic; those refutations outlined research demonstrating nearly unanimous consensus among climate scientists that climate change is caused by human activity (van der Linden et al., 2017). Messages relating to any given crisis could follow this format to generate resistance to influences that may weaken the audience's attitude toward vigilance.

Directional Goals

This chapter now turns to individuals with directional goals. This audience operates with confirmation bias, a psychological phenomenon referring to "the seeking or interpreting of evidence in ways that are partial to existing beliefs, expectations, or a hypothesis in hand" (Nickerson, 1998, p. 1089). Both pieces of the reasoning process mentioned in this definition are relevant: directionally motivated individuals have been shown to search for evidence that supports their existing beliefs (Epley & Gilovich, 2016) and to evaluate information in ways that are consistent with their existing beliefs (Babcock & Loewenstein, 1997).

Importantly, biased information gathering and interpretation in a directionally motivated audience should not be viewed as exclusively conscious or active. Rather, these individuals "are still responsive to reality and don't simply believe whatever they want to believe" (Epley & Gilovich, 2016). Instead, they seek sources and subsets of the germane information that reflect their bias (Kunda, 1990). In other words, they often believe that they *are* seeking valid information. As such, simplistic appeals to striving for accuracy will not resonate with this audience. Instead, messages must create trigger motivations related to other values or ideas.

Combating False Information with Cognitive Dissonance Theory

One approach may involve messages leveraging cognitive dissonance theory (Festinger, 1954). The theory, which is based on the importance of cognitive consistency and cohesion, holds that individuals become uncomfortable when they have to hold two divergent ideas simultaneously; this psychological discomfort catalyzes their desire to resolve the tension (Dickerson et al., 1992). Accordingly, crisis communicators may find value in crafting precrisis and peri-crisis messages to elicit cognitive dissonance. Messages should then position behavioral changes in online information consumption as a way to defuse the tension.

Precrisis. Practitioners designing precrisis messages may consider inducing hypocrisy among directionally motivated individuals. Because these audience members believe that they regularly seek information without bias, messages should highlight the common pitfalls of confirmation bias in online behaviors, encouraging individuals to recognize their own behavior in the portrayal. Perceiving the discrepancy between one's beliefs and one's past behavior should generate cognitive dissonance.

A classic advertising example that leveraged hypocrisy illustrates how to operationalize this strategy. During the 2004 US presidential election, George Bush's campaign used footage of the candidate John Kerry, referring to the war in Afghanistan and Iraq, in which he stated "I actually did vote for the $87 billion before I voted against it" (Roberts, 2004). Messages targeting patterns of information consumption should aim to induce a similar, but self-reflective, feeling of hypocrisy. Such efforts may find value in following the format utilized by Aronson et al. (1991) who presented messages to college students reminding them of instances where they had failed to use condoms. Their induced hypocrisy led to heightened intention for future condom use, compared to peers who had not been triggered to feel hypocritical.

Following this format, message strategies may utilize a variety of advertising appeals such as dramatization, in which fictional characters dramatize instances highlighting the common pitfalls of biased processing. Testimonials from individuals previously fooled by inaccurate information may also prove effective (Belch & Belch, 2020). In other words, depictions that allow individuals to see themselves in a portrayal of hypocritical behavior may incite them to self-reflect. These approaches may be employed outside the context of a specific crisis.

Peri-crisis. For peri-crisis messaging, appeals to other values may induce cognitive dissonance. For example, research demonstrates that general information-sharing behaviors during a disaster are often motivated by the intrinsic satisfaction associated with helping others (Constant et al., 1994). Altruism has been shown to significantly impact people's intention to share online crisis information (Zhang et al., 2017). Thus, crisis-specific messages leveraging cognitive dissonance may illuminate the disconnect between individuals' desire to help others and the potential damage that may result from inadvertently sharing false information. The resultant dissonance may cause individuals to reconsider their online behavior. Moreover, research demonstrates that, when people become aware that their prior behaviors are incongruent with basic morality, they undergo ethical dissonance and alter their behaviors (Gamma et al., 2020).

Kim and Ryoo (2022) effectively induced hypocrisy related to COVID-19 safety. Their design involved a series of questions proposed by a chatbot that prompted individuals to reflect on their risky behavior, illuminating the discrepancy between their actions and their desire to promote safety. Following this format, a message targeting information consumption could resources mentioned earlier to develop a question series such as:

> Misinformation about H1N1 is harming people in our community. Ask yourself: Have you shared information without checking that it comes from a verified source? Did you check for a byline? Did you check for grammar or punctuation errors? Have you checked to ensure the media outlet is independent? We know you want to protect our community. Make sure you aren't fooled by content that fails those tests. Follow @cdcgov for accurate information. Let's keep everyone safe!

These questions were adapted from resources published by the News Literacy Project (2023).

As these examples demonstrate, practitioners can leverage different values or ideals that induce cognitive dissonance, positioning increased online vigilance as a mechanism for resolving tension. The important point when designing strategies for this audience is to identify an appropriate value outside of simple accuracy seeking to overcome barriers associated with confirmation bias.

Combating False Information with Narrative Theory

An additional approach for directionally motivated individuals lies in narrative theory or the use of storytelling to influence how individuals scrutinize online information. Bilandzic and Busselle (2013) defined a narrative as a "symbolic representation of events" (p. 201). According to the transportation imagery model, narratives exert persuasive influence via two mechanisms: transportation and identification (Green & Brock, 2000). Transportation is conceptualized as the combination of imagery, attention, and emotion devoted to the story's events (Mazocco et al., 2010). Identification refers to individuals' feelings that they, or someone they know, are similar to a character (Slater & Rouner, 2002). Both mechanisms cause individuals to lower their attitudinal defenses, rendering them more likely to accept positions depicted in the story.

A wide swath of research has demonstrated the persuasive power of narratives across contexts, including advertising (e.g., Chang, 2019; Escalas, 2004), but also outside the marketing realm, such as communication about social issues (e.g., Slater et al., 2006) and messaging about risky health behaviors (e.g., Geegan et al., 2023). Further, meta-analytic results have illustrated that individuals who view narratives have reported attitudinal change in alignment with the narrative (Braddock & Dillard, 2016). In other words, compelling stories have been shown to serve as effective persuasive tools. Narratives represent a particularly appropriate strategy for the directionally motivated audience, as increased levels of identification and transportation may trigger them to consider information they would have otherwise disregarded as a function of their motivated reasoning.

A limited amount of research has focused on narrative persuasion in the context of misinformation amid a crisis, but the results are promising. Sangalang et al. (2019) specifically focused on the use of narratives as correctives—or information that provides an alternative (accurate) account of, or corrects, the misinformation. Evidence illustrated that such narratives designed to correct false online information were effective in curtailing misinformed attitudes and intentions (Sangalang et al., 2019). More specifically, this investigation revealed that narratives with emotional endings were more effective in altering beliefs.

The primary difference between precrisis and peri-crisis narratives lies in whether or not a story portrays an immediate ongoing crisis. In both cases, the strategies are appropriate for directionally motivated audiences, who are more likely to be swayed when experiencing identification and transportation.

Precrisis. Precrisis strategies should take into account communities' (particularly marginalized communities') potential mistrust of media outlets that would issue disaster warnings. As just one example, data from New Orleans residents revealed that more than half of participants stated that they did not trust the media to deliver accurate information relating to Hurricane Katrina (Voorhees et al., 2007) In the absence of a crisis, practitioners may also consider referencing past crises that individuals would recognize and, through the framework of storytelling, portray how false online information generated negative impacts. For example, a video utilizing this strategy, posted on social media, may depict two characters with whom the audience can easily identify discussing the impact of misinformation during the H1N1 outbreak. Their conversation could include key details about the impact of misleading or inaccurate information and the importance of seeking evidence-based information. This format may reveal tips useful in debunking inaccurate rumors, misunderstandings, or other forms of misinformation.

Peri-crisis. The narrative approach lends itself even more to peri-crisis strategies because information specific to an ongoing crisis is likely more eye-catching. A message utilizing this strategy may follow the same format as the one mentioned earlier, with the details of the immediate crisis replaced with more specific information.

Combating False Information with Social Judgment Theory

As suggested, directionally motivated information seekers and sharers genuinely believe that they are pursuing accurate information (Epley & Gilovich, 2016) but may disagree on which sources produce such information and what may be accurate. Stated differently, they seek information that confirms their current beliefs (Kunda, 1990). In such circumstances, any discrepant information may be disregarded and any sources disseminating such information ignored and/or discredited.

A possible approach to this audience may be offered by social judgment theory (SJT). SJT conceptualizes individuals' current attitudes or positions as anchors. When people encounter information or message-advocated positions characterized as significantly discrepant from their anchors, they may overestimate the degree of difference between the two positions, a phenomenon known as contrast (Griffin, 2011; Sherif et al., 1965). In such a case, they will reject the information or message-advocated position. Thus, presenting this audience via social media with evidence-based crisis information that significantly deviates from their anchor positions may backfire (Griffin, 2011; Sherif et al., 1965). However, SJT also suggests that, when individuals encounter information or a message-advocated position characterized as *closer* to their anchor position, they consider it to be closer than it really is, a phenomenon known as assimilation (Griffin, 2011; Sherif et al., 1965). Thus, a third approach to reach this audience would involve initially delivering only pieces of science-based information that are closer to the positions already held by these individuals. This approach, according to SJT, may lead to the assimilation of the new information into the audience member's current position and result in a movement toward the position advocated by the crisis manager. While this approach does not produce the assimilation of the entire content the crisis manager hopes to share, it does elicit movement toward that goal. This process can then be repeated, gradually moving the message recipient's position toward the assimilation of the comprehensive science-based crisis information. This approach can be effectively implemented both before and during crises.

Precrisis. A recent CDC survey of coastal residents indicated that the main reason people avoid using shelters during hurricane evacuations is their lack of faith in the information provided by the media (58 percent; CDC, 2021). Simply disseminating evidence showing past media accuracy during hurricane evacuations may effectively persuade accuracy-seeking individuals. However, the approach may backfire with directionally motivated individuals, who may consider the evidence to be significantly discrepant from their current beliefs and, as such, dismiss it (a contrast effect). Instead, a better approach may be to advocate a position that is closer to, but more positive than, the audience's current position on the issue.

For example, by emphasizing that there are at least a few news media outlets that may deliver accurate evacuation information, the crisis manager delivers pertinent information that may be easier for directionally motivated individuals to assimilate (e.g., Greitemeyer, 2023). These individuals may still maintain their general belief that news media evacuation information is unreliable but also allow for the possibility that at least a few media news sources provide accurate information. The result is a positional movement in the desired direction. Using this gradual approach, crisis managers can attempt to move people's positions in the desired direction methodically. Thus, an SJT-based approach may be a valuable tool to use in crisis preparation.

Peri-crisis. An SJT-based approach may also prove useful in the context of an immediate crisis. Consider the example of nuclear waste disposal and the threat of contamination, which represent a global crisis as waste volume continues to rise (Roche et al., 2018). All countries reviewed in a report recently commissioned by Greenpeace lacked a sustainable safe solution to this problem (Roche et al., 2018). However, a possible breakthrough solution recently emerged from Finland that involves building underground bunkers to contain nuclear waste for at least 100,000 years (Igini, 2022). The challenge, however, lies in the diverging opinions about the solution's efficacy due to the novelty of the idea and the risk of contamination (Igini, 2022). This crisis offers a backdrop for designing crisis messaging, through the SJT framework, building support for, and assimilation of, this scientifically supported solution.

Accordingly, a gradual approach may provide promise. In 2004 Finland used a similar, but much smaller-scale approach to its nuclear waste problem by entombing 2,300 tons of high-level waste in an underground rock mine, that to date has proven successful. Building support for the larger project (i.e., assimilating the scientific information that supports the soundness of this big idea) may be more successful by starting on a smaller scale. Messages could first present the idea that this approach has already shown past success, albeit at a much smaller level and evidenced over a relatively shorter time. It is hoped that this SJT-based approach will create a gradual movement toward acceptance of the science-based solution.

Some evidence already suggests such a possibility. In an agent-based social simulation, using survey data from more than 1,300 Swiss citizens, Stefanelli and Siedl (2014) explored the efficacy of SJT. Their findings showed evidence of both assimilation and contrast effects regarding the citizens' attitudes toward building a deep underground repository for nuclear waste. These results show promise for the application of an SJT-based approach during crises.

Practical Considerations

As detailed, crisis managers should consider a variety of message strategies based on the key differences in audience members' motivations and information-seeking tendencies. Of course, organizations charged with protecting public safety are responsible for protecting all citizens in their jurisdictions, not only individuals who fall into particular information-processing categories. This underscores the need for comprehensive crisis communication planning and the use of the various approaches discussed throughout this chapter, which are designed for various audience members, in message strategies for disaster planning, response, and recovery.

Importantly, all the approaches described in this chapter reflect the importance of social listening, or the process of monitoring, analyzing, and responding to information being shared about a crisis on social media (Young et al., 2019). All strategic communication rooted in these approaches should be driven by a thorough understanding of the misinformation being shared on social media with respect to a given issue and how science-based evidence is being misconstrued, refuted, misrepresented, or disregarded by social media users.

Particularly as many of the strategies described involve directly alluding to rumors or misconceptions posted on digital platforms, a robust social listening operation will enhance the effectiveness of crisis messaging.

Additionally, these strategies should be used in tandem with mechanical solutions, as proposed by Mayorga et al. (2020), such as investments in new software development and the employment of new systems and algorithms capable of detecting, flagging, tagging, and/or removing false information from social media platforms such as Google, YouTube, and Facebook (Mayorga et al., 2020). This chapter has focused on psychological solutions that can be deployed by individual organizations, but the importance of technological mechanisms for combating misinformation cannot be overstated.

The importance of case studies, best practices, and collaboration also cannot be overstated. As scholars and practitioners continue to grapple with this issue, there is great opportunity to learn from each other regarding which strategies have proven most effective, for which types of crisis, and among which types of audiences. This chapter has provided a foundation of strategies rooted in persuasion. Future research should continue to explore the nuances of these solutions.

References

Angell, K., & Tewell, E. (2014). Far from a trivial pursuit: Assessing the effectiveness of games in information literacy instruction. *Evidence Based Library and Information Practice*, *10*(1), 20–33. http://dx.doi.org/10.18438/B8B60X

Aronson, E., Fried, C., & Stone, J. (1991). Overcoming denial and increasing the intention to use condoms through the induction of hypocrisy. *American Journal of Public Health*, *81*(12), 1636–1638. http://dx.doi.org/10.2105/ajph.81.12.1636

Babcock, L., & Loewenstein, G. (1997). Explaining bargaining impasse: The role of self-serving biases. *Journal of Economic Perspectives*, *11*(1), 109–126. http://dx.doi.org/10.1257/jep.11.1.109

Banas, J. A., & Rains, S. A. (2010). A meta-analysis of research on inoculation theory. *Communication Monographs*, *77*, 281–311. https://doi.org/10.1080/03637751003758193

Belch, G., & Belch, M. (2020). *Advertising and promotion*. In *An integrated marketing communications perspective*. McGraw-Hill.

Bilandzic, H., & Busselle, R. (2013). Narrative persuasion. In J. P. Dillard & L. Shen (Eds.), *The SAGE handbook of persuasion: Developments in theory and practic* (pp. 200–219). SAGE.

Boman, C. D., & Schneider, E. J. (2021). Finding an antidote: Testing the use of proactive crisis strategies to protect organizations from astroturf attacks. *Public Relations Review*, *47*(1), 102004. https://doi.org/10.1016/j.pubrev.2020.102004

Braddock, K., & Dillard, J. P. (2016). Meta-analytic evidence for the persuasive effect of narratives on beliefs, attitudes, intentions, and behaviors. *Communication monographs*, *83*(4), 446–467. https://doi.org/10.1080/03637751.2015.1128555

Centers for Disease Control and Prevention. (2021). *Finding credible vaccine information*. https://www.cdc.gov/vaccines/vac-gen/evalwebs.htm

Chang, C. (2019). Narrative advertisements and narrative processing. In *Advertising theory* (pp. 275–292). Routledge.

Christopher, A. J. (2018, August 27). Kerala: Kannur district teaches school kids to spot fake news. *The Week*. https://www.theweek.in/news/india/2018/08/27/kerala-kannur-teaches-school-kids-spot-fake-news.html

Compton, J. (2013). Inoculation theory. In J. P. Dillard & L. Shen (Eds.), *The SAGE handbook of persuasion: Developments in theory and practice* (2nd ed., pp. 220–236). SAGE. https://doi.org/10.1177/0093650206296083

Compton, J., & Ivanov, B. (2012). Untangling threat during inoculation-conferred resistance to influence. *Communication Reports*, *25*(1), 1–13. http://dx.doi.org/10.1080/08934215.2012.661018

Constant, D., Kiesler, S., & Sproull, L. (1994). What's mine is ours, or is it? A study of attitudes about information sharing. *Information Systems Research*, *5*(4), 400–421. https://doi.org/10.1287/isre.5.4.400

Cook, J., Lewandowsky, S., & Ecker Ullrich, K. H. (2017). Neutralizing misinformation through inoculation: Exposing misleading argumentation techniques reduces their influence. *PLoS ONE*, *12*(5), e0175799. https://doi.org/10.1371/journal.pone.0175799

Dickerson, C. A., Thibodeau, R., Aronson, E., & Miller, D. (1992). Using cognitive dissonance to encourage water conservation 1. *Journal of Applied Social Psychology*, *22*(11), 841–854. http://dx.doi.org/10.1111/j.1559-1816.1992.tb00928.x

Ecker, U. K. H., Lewandowsky, S., & Tang, D. T. W. (2010). Explicit warnings reduce but do not eliminate the continued influence of misinformation. *Memory and Cognition*, *38*, 1087–1100. http://dx.doi.org/10.3758/MC.38.8.1087

Epley, N., & Gilovich, T. (2016). The mechanics of motivated reasoning. *Journal of Economic Perspectives*, *30*(3), 133–140. http://dx.doi.org/10.1257/jep.30.3.133

Escalas, J. E. (2004). Narrative processing: Building consumer connections to brands. *Journal of Consumer Psychology*, *14*(1–2), 168–180. https://doi.org/10.1207/s15327663jcp1401&2_19

Festinger, L. (1954). A theory of social comparison processes. *Human Relations*, *7*(2), 117–140. https://doi.org/%2010.1177/001872675400700202

Gamma, K., Mai, R., & Loock, M. (2020). The double-edged sword of ethical nudges: Does inducing hypocrisy help or hinder the adoption of pro-environmental behaviors? *Journal of Business Ethics*, *161*, 351–373.

Geegan, S. A., Ivanov, B., & Parker, K. A. (2023). Inoculation within character limits: Terse messages to promote Gen Z mental health. *Journal of Communication and Media Studies*, *8*(2), 65–86. https://doi.org/10.18848/2470-9247/CGP/v08i02/65-86

Green, M. C., & Brock, T. C. (2000). The role of transportation in the persuasiveness of public narratives. *Journal of Personality and Social Psychology*, *79*(5), 701–721. http://dx.doi.org/10.1037/0022-3514.79.5.701

Greitemeyer, T. (2023). Counter explanation and consider the opposite: Do corrective strategies reduce biased assimilation and attitude polarization in the context of the COVID-19 pandemic? *Journal of Applied Social Psychology*, *53*, 785–795. http://dx.doi.org/10.1111/jasp.12968

Griffin, E. (2011). *A first look at communication theory*. McGraw-Hill.

Igini, M. (2022, September 12). *The nuclear waste disposal dilemma*. Earth.org. https://earth.org/nuclear-waste-disposal/

Ingram, D. (2020). *Twitter launches "pre-bunks" to get ahead of voting misinformation*. National Broadcasting Company. https://www.nbcnews.com/tech/tech-news/twitter-launches-pre-bunks-get-ahead-voting-misinformation-n1244777

Ivanov, B. (2017). Inoculation theory applied in health and risk messaging. In M. Powers (Ed.), *Oxford Research Encyclopedia of Communication*. Oxford University Press. http://dx.doi.org/10.1093/acrefore/9780190228613.013.254

Ivanov, B., Dillingham, L. L., Hester, E. B., & Parker, K. A. (2022). Enhancing catastrophic event preparedness and response: The inoculation approach. In H. D. O'Hair & M. J. O'Hair (Eds.),

Communication and Catastrophic Events: Strategic Risk and Crisis Management (pp. 49–64). Wiley Blackwell.

Ivanov, B., Rains, S. A., Geegan, S. A., Vos, S. C., Haarstad, N. D., & Parker, K. A. (2017). Beyond simple inoculation: Examining the persuasive value of inoculation for audiences with initially neutral or opposing attitudes. *Western Journal of Communication*, *81*(1), 105–126. http://dx.doi.org/10.1080/10570314.2016.1224917

James, O., & Van Ryzin, G. G. (2017). Motivated reasoning about public performance: An experimental study of how citizens judge the affordable care act. *Journal of Public Administration Research and Theory*, *27*(1), 197–209. http://dx.doi.org/10.1093/jopart/muw049

Jaques, T. (2009). Issues and crisis management: Quicksand in the definitional landscape. *Public Relations Review*, *35*(3), 280–286. http://dx.doi.org/10.1016/j.pubrev.2009.03.003

Kapp, L. (2013). *Recruiting and retention: An overview of FY2011 and FY2012 results for active and reserve component enlisted personnel.* CRS Report for Congress. http://www.fas.org/sgp/crs/natsec/RL32965.pdf

Khanday, A., Khan, Q. R., & Rabani, S. T. (2020). Identifying propaganda from online social networks during COVID-19 using machine learning techniques. *International Journal of Information Technology*, *13*, 115–122. http://dx.doi.org/10.1007/s41870-020-00550-5

Kim, W., & Ryoo, Y. (2022). Hypocrisy induction: Using chatbots to promote COVID-19 social distancing. *Cyberpsychology, Behavior, and Social Networking*, *25*(1), 27–36.

Klepper, D. (2023). *Microsoft's media literacy program aims to empower Internet users and combat online misinformation.* Associated Press. https://apnews.com/article/microsoft-misinformation-twitter-facebook-youtube-media-literacy-1e086a5f9fc258ddb7391557b9f73401

Komendantova, N., Ekenberg, L., Svahn, M., Larsson, A., Shah, S. I. H., Glinos, M., Koulolias, V., & Danielson, M. (2021). A value-driven approach to addressing misinformation in social media. *Humanities and Social Sciences Communications*, *8*, 33. http://dx.doi.org/10.1057/s41599-020-00702-9

Kruglanski, A. W. (1980). Lay epistemology process and contents. *Psychological Review*, *87*, 70–87. http://dx.doi.org/10.1037/0033-295X.87.1.70

Kunda, Z. (1990). The case for motivated reasoning. *Psychological Bulletin*, *108*(3), 480–498. http://dx.doi.org/10.1037/0033-2909.108.3.480

Lewandowsky, S., Ecker, U. K., & Cook, J. (2017). Beyond misinformation: Understanding and coping with the "post-truth" era. *Journal of Applied Research in Memory and Cognition*, *6*(4), 353–369. http://dx.doi.org/10.1016/j.jarmac.2017.07.008

Liu, B. F., Fraustino, J. D., & Jin, Y. (2015). Social media use during disasters: How information form and source influence intended behavioral responses. *Communication Research*, *43*(5), 626–646. http://dx.doi.org/10.1177/0093650214565917

Mayorga, M. W., Hester, E. B., Helsel, E., Ivanov, B., Sellnow, T. L., Slovic, P., Burns, W. J., & Frakes, D. (2020). Enhancing public resistance to deliberate fake news: A review of the problem and strategic solutions. In H. D. O'Hair & M. J. O'Hair (Eds.), *Handbook of applied communication research* (Vol. 1, pp. 197–212). Wiley Blackwell. http://dx.doi.org/10.1002/9781119399926.ch12

Mazocco, P. J., Green, M. C., Sasota, J. A., & Jones, N. W. (2010). This story is not for everyone: Transportability and narrative persuasion. *Social Psychological and Personality Science*, *1*(4), 361–368. http://dx.doi.org/10.1177/1948550610376600

McGuire, W. J. (1964). Inducing resistance to persuasion: Some contemporary approaches. In L. Berkowitz (Ed.), *Advances in experimental social psychology* (Vol. 1, pp. 191–229). Academic Press.

Mitchell, A., & Walker, M., (2021). *More Americans now say government should take steps to restrict false information online than in*. Pew Research Center. https://www.pewresearch.org/short-reads/2021/08/18/more-americans-now-say-government-should-take-steps-to-restrict-false-information-online-than-in-2018

National Interagency Fire Center. (n.d.). *What is crisis?* https://www.nifc.gov/sites/default/files/document-media/CrisisIntervention.pdf

News Literacy Project. (2023). *Our mission*. https://newslit.org/about/mission/#nlp-mission

Nickerson, R. S. (1998). Confirmation bias: A ubiquitous phenomenon in many guises. *Review of General Psychology*, *2*(2), 175–220.

O'Keefe, D. (2016). *Persuasion: Theory and research* (3rd ed.). SAGE.

Park, S., & Avery, E. J. (2018). Effects of media channel, crisis type and demographics on audience intent to follow instructing information during crisis. *Journal of Contingencies and Crisis Management*, *26*(1), 69–78. http://dx.doi.org/10.1111/1468-5973.12137

Parks, M., & Douglis, S. (2019, October 31). *Fake news: How to spot misinformation*. National Public Radio. https://www.npr.org/2019/10/29/774541010/fake-news-is-scary-heres-how-to-spot-misinformation

Petty, R. E., & Cacioppo, J. T. (1977). Forewarning, cognitive responding, and resistance to persuasion. *Journal of Personality and Social Psychology*, *35*(9), 645–655. http://dx.doi.org/10.1037/0022-3514.35.9.645

Pfau, M., Haigh, M. M., Sims, J., & Wigley, S. (2007). The influence of corporate front group stealth campaigns. *Communication Research*, *34*, 73–99. https://doi.org/10.1177/0093650206296083

Rehman, J. (2013, May 16). The need for critical science journalism: Too much contemporary science writing falls under the category of "infotainment". *The Guardian*. https://www.theguardian.com/science/blog/2013/may/16/need-for-critical-science-journalism

Roberts, J. (2004, September 29). *Kerry's Top Ten Flip-Flops*. CBS News. https://www.cbsnews.com/news/kerrys-top-ten-flip-flops

Roche, P., Thuiller, B., Laponche, B., Goldstick, M., Swahn, J., Ban, H., & Alvarez, R. (2018). *The global crisis of nuclear waste: A report commissioned by GP France*. Greenpeace. https://www.greenpeace.org/static/planet4-belgium-stateless/2019/03/f7da075b-18.11.gp-report-global-crisis of nuclear waste.pdf

Roozenbeek, J., & van der Linden, S. (2019). Fake news game confers psychological resistance against online misinformation. *Palgrave Communications*, *5*(1), 1–10. https://doi.org/10.1207/s15327663jcp1401&2_19

Sangalang, A., Ophir, Y., & Cappella, J. N. (2019). The potential for narrative correctives to combat misinformation. *Journal of Communication*, *69*(3), 298–319. http://dx.doi.org/10.1093/joc/jqz014

Sherif, C. W., Sherif, M., & Nebergall, R. E. (1965). *Attitude and attitude change: The social-involvement approach*. Saunders.

Slater, M. D., & Rouner, D. (2002). Entertainment—Education and elaboration likelihood: Understanding the processing of narrative persuasion. *Communication Theory*, *12*(2), 173–191. http://dx.doi.org/10.1111/j.1468-2885.2002.tb00265.x

Slater, M. D., Rouner, D., & Long, M. (2006). Television dramas and support for controversial public policies: Effects and mechanisms. *Journal of Communication*, *56*(2), 235–252. https://doi.org/10.1111/j.1460-2466.2006.00017.x

Ståhl, T., & Van Prooijen, J. W. (2018). Epistemic rationality: Skepticism toward unfounded beliefs requires sufficient cognitive ability and motivation to be rational. *Personality and Individual Differences*, *122*, 155–163. http://dx.doi.org/10.1111/j.1468-2885.2002.tb00265.x

Stefanelli, A., & Siedl, R. (2014). Moderate and polarized opinions. Using empirical data for an agent-based simulation. Paper presented at the Social Simulation Conference. Bellaterra, Cerdanyola del Vallès.

Swami, V., Voracek, M., Stieger, S., Tran, U. S., & Furnham, A. (2014). Analytic thinking reduces belief in conspiracy theories. *Cognition*, *133*(3), 572–585. http://dx.doi.org/10.1016/j.cognition.2014.08.006

van der Linden, S., Leiserowitz, A., Rosenthal, S., & Maibach, E. (2017). Inoculating the public against misinformation about climate change. *Global Challenges*, *1*(2), 1600008. https://doi.org/10.1002/gch2.201600008

Voorhees, C. C., Vick, J., & Perkins, D. D. (2007). "Came hell and high water": The intersection of Hurricane Katrina, the news media, race and poverty. *Journal of Community & Applied Social Psychology*, *17*(6), 415–429. https://doi.org/10.1002/casp.945

Walton, G., & Hepworth, M. (2011). A longitudinal study of changes in learners' cognitive states during and following an information literacy teaching intervention. *Journal of Documentation*, *67*(3), 449–479. http://dx.doi.org/10.1108/00220411111124541

Wardle, C., & Derakhshan, H. (2017). *Information disorder: Toward an interdisciplinary framework for research and policymaking*. Council of Europe. http://tverezo.info/wp-content/uploads/2017/11/PREMS-162317-GBR-2018-Report-desinformation-A4-BAT.pdf

Young, C., Simmons, H., & Stewart, M. (2019). Social listening during crises: A practitioner guide for crisis communication on social media. http://dx.doi.org/10.30658/icrcc.2019.11

Zerback, T., & Töpfl, F. (2022). Forged examples as disinformation: The biasing effects of political astroturfing comments on public opinion perceptions and how to prevent them. *Political Psychology*, *43*(3), 399–418. https://doi.org/10.1111/pops.12767

Zhang, X., Liu, S., Deng, Z., & Cheng, X. (2017). Knowledge sharing motivations in online health communities: A comparative study of health professionals and normal users. *Computers in Human Behavior*, *75*, 797–810. https://doi.org/10.1016/j.chb.2017.06.028

5

Emergent Conceptual Frameworks of Disruption, Character Assassination, and Visual Disinformation in Crisis Communication Research

Sergei A. Samoilenko

Department of Communication, George Mason University

Introduction

To maintain relevancy, communication theory must shift its focus to examining the effects of subversive practices on institutional trust and public reputation in the context of collapsing economic optimism, mounting public disapproval of governments, and low trust in traditional and social media (Edelman, 2023). This is especially apposite for communication scholars who advise practices on adequate crisis response strategies. Recent technological developments have created new possibilities for subversive actors to manipulate and undermine organizational safety and national security worldwide (Pashentsev, 2023). This chapter discusses three innovative concepts—disruption, visual disinformation, and character assassination—in the context of crisis communication theory.

The evolution of digital communications has created new forms of visibility and provided the conditions for permanent scandal (Haller & Michael, 2023). Today, the pervasiveness of subversive communication has been associated with many factors, including the effects of mediatization on society, political polarization, and declining confidence in traditional institutions, among others (Samoilenko, 2020). Subversion here refers to the process through which the values and principles of a system are contradicted or reversed in an attempt to sabotage the operations of political and social institutions and undermine the established social order (Blackstock, 1964). The concept of subversion is convoluted and defies simple explanations because of the variety of forms and contexts in which it takes place. For example, in cultural and social movement studies, "subversion of purpose, principle, or design" (Leach & Wilson, 2014, p. 237) entails acts of nonconformity to established rules that are shared by many grassroots and activist campaigns (Hollander & Einwohner, 2004; Williams, 2011). Cause-driven campaigns and social movements have traditionally used subversive communications in protests and boycotts to advocate for justice in the form of public apologies, legal proceedings, or revised policies (Jasper & King, 2020).

In this chapter, I discuss primarily subversive campaigns that entail practices of disruption, character assassination, and visual disinformation. Subversive campaigns using AI technologies enable the mass creation of fake visual content that could potentially contribute to the public's distrust in visual information and create new reputational risks for political

Communication and Misinformation: Crisis Events in the Age of Social Media, First Edition.
Edited by Kevin B. Wright.
© 2025 John Wiley & Sons, Inc. Published 2025 by John Wiley & Sons, Inc.

and public institutions (Samoilenko & Suvorova, 2023). These campaigns have the capacity to discredit individuals and organizations by lowering their credibility to a degree that is unacceptable to a specific populace. Ultimately, their intention is to trigger a reputational crisis or highly mediated event (e.g., scandal) that can be linked to character-based issues or highly contested social conflicts.

This chapter discusses the relevancy of emergent research on subversive communication in the context of crisis communication and reputation management. This chapter also provides suggestions for countering the effects of subversive communication and offers insights that could potentially direct future academic investigations.

Disruption

Sometimes, using social media and crowdsourcing for public relations can backfire, especially when a social media conversation can be disrupted and hijacked by angry followers. For example, in April 2014 the New York City Police Department (NYPD) invited people to tweet pictures highlighting the best of police officers' work with the hashtag #myNYPD. This seemingly innocuous tweet, however, ignited a Twitter storm when users flooded the hashtag with images of brutal arrests and shooting victims, sparking widespread national coverage (Tran, 2014).

Pranks can also be powerful. Donald Trump learned this the hard way after a viral TikTok video encouraged people to rack up fake ticket reservations to his June campaign rally in Tulsa in an attempt to keep seats empty. Ultimately, fewer than 6,200 people attended—less than one-third of the arena's 19,000 capacity (Upton-Clark, 2020).

As alluded to in these examples, in this chapter I define *disruption* as the use of strategic communication campaigns by one party for the purpose of interrupting the narrative of another party, reframing its messaging, subverting the original agenda, and ultimately gaining control or influence over the audience. In recent literature, many disruptive "game-breaking" online behaviors, such as trolling or conspiracy fictioning, have been referred to as *dark play* (Linderoth & Mortensen, 2015; also see de Zeeuw & Gekker, 2023). Within this practice, strategic actors can hijack an opponent's media event in a way that creatively reframes the issue while leveraging media presence to draw attention to their side of the story (Boyd, 2012). Trolling, pranking, and brandjacking are some of the most notorious disruptive practices widely used online today.

Online *trolling* involves the posting of provocative content, including deliberately misleading and pointless comments, with the intention of provoking and mocking other users to drag them into an empty argument or quarrel (Klyueva, 2013). Trolling is often described as being playful, ironic, and transgressive and may be associated with identity play and collective storytelling (Phillips, 2015; Phillips & Milner, 2017). Online echo chambers can make political discourse dysfunctional and foster polarization in open societies (Kratzke, 2023). Today, it is possible to repeat and reproduce a multitude of subversive messages automatically through the use of bots and algorithms for better organic placement in newsfeeds. Howard and Kollanyi (2016) analyzed the role of bots in the run-up to the UK's vote to exit the EU and found that they were deployed in an effort "to attack opponents, choke off hashtags, and promote political platforms for amplifying messages" (p. 5). Political parties or military and business enterprises may hire trolls to spread disinformation and manipulate online opinions (Fichman & Akter, 2023; Marcondes et al., 2024).

A related disruptive technique is *pranking*, which constitutes a powerful tool of subversive humor. Pranks are practical jokes played on an individual to ridicule them and cause them embarrassment and discomfort. As Upton-Clark (2020) notes, "Pranks can be a powerful means of disrupting the spectacle of hegemony, giving a voice to the voiceless and opening up new forms of ideological interaction." Pranks can be used to set the media agenda, influence the public perception of events, and highlight certain issues as key topics of public debate (Harold, 2004; McLeod, 2014). However, political pranksters can often play the role of state proxies by pranking public figures who hold dissenting views or oppose their governments (Wootson, 2017). State-affiliated pranksters look for opportunities to reinforce the strategic narratives of their governments by discrediting targeted policymakers. For example, Russian pranksters Vovan and Lexus have a history of fooling Western politicians and high-ranking figures (Cooper, 2023). The strategic use of hoaxes and ridicule produces a compare-and-contrast effect, making foreign political actors appear dumb and incompetent compared to national state actors and diplomats, who are conversely given an impression of being more serious and legitimate to domestic audiences (Sukhodolov et al., 2018).

Media-jacking is another disruptive tactic that seeks to assume control of an organization's media event, refocus an audience's attention, and highlight a different side of a given story (Boyd, 2012). In some cases, the original messaging is challenged and reframed by counternarratives, as was the case when Greenpeace campaigners used a YouTube video that parodied Nestlé's KitKat "Take a Break" advertising campaign to draw attention to the conglomerate's use of palm oil from unsustainable operations in Indonesia. Protesters outside Nestlé's UK head office carried signs with the words "Give me a break" printed in the distinctive red and white Gill Sans font (Dunlevy, 2010).

In corporate communication, a similar term, *brandjacking*, is used to describe cases when a brand's narrative is disrupted and its corporate identity appropriated by third parties (Langley, 2014). In corporate contests, brandjacking can complement obstructive marketing, which seeks to reduce the operational capacity of competitors through activities designed to prevent the distribution of a product by making it seem less valuable or damaging it in some way (Hyslop, 2014). Brandjacking is also associated with the unauthorized use of a brand by impersonators and fraudsters who take over campaigns and hashtags by pretending to be brand marketers (Siano et al., 2021). Brandjacks promoting fake corporate statements are especially harmful, as they can affect brand trust if they are perceived as credible (Chan-Olmsted & Qin, 2021). Some brandjacks utilize smear efforts to provoke social media outrage against politicians and corporate CEOs.

Crisis communicators must understand that disruptive techniques are strategic in nature because they are derived from the opinions and attitudes of members representing various communities on a range of different social issues and hold the capacity for inciting moral outrage (Samoilenko, 2021). They also appeal to invested stakeholders (e.g., journalists, activist groups, and competitors) who profit from the tarnishing of reputations. In the following section, I shall discuss the deliberate destruction of reputation through character attacks.

Character Assassination

In March 2020 *The Washington Post* obtained internal emails indicating that Facebook's parent company, Meta, had been paying one of the world's most prominent consulting agencies, Targeted Victory, to orchestrate a nationwide campaign to turn the public against

TikTok (Lorenz & Harwell, 2022). News of Facebook's decision to hire the firm came only a few weeks after the company declared that it was losing users for the first time in its 18-year history. The campaign included placing op-eds and letters to the editor in major regional news outlets promoting dubious stories about alleged TikTok trends that originated on Facebook and pushing political reporters and local politicians into helping take down its biggest competitor. The idea was to portray the rapidly growing app, owned by the Beijing-based company ByteDance, as a danger to American children and society.

This vignette exemplifies the concept of character assassination, which refers to the strategic effort to discredit an individual or group through character attacks (Shiraev et al., 2022). Character attacks can take various forms, ranging from an offensive caricature in a newspaper to a virulent conspiracy theory trending online. Character assassination is both a process of communication (e.g., a smear campaign) and the outcome of this process (e.g., a damaged reputation). The purpose of these negative campaigns using subversive messaging is to undermine a target's reputation and credibility, weaken their social support, and force them to waste their time, energy, and resources.

Character assassination has been conceptually linked to a number of other concepts and theories, including systems theory (Samoilenko, 2020), stigma communication (Smith & Eberly, 2021), public shaming (Stephenson, 2021), and Burke's approach to framing (Schumacher-Rutherford & Muddiman, 2021). Scholars have argued that public attacks on one's character are intended to instigate a public event that yields a negative opinion about the intended target. The audience-centric nature of character assassination campaigns is discussed by Simons (2020). This view is supported by Klicperová-Baker (2020), who writes about show trials or propagandistic spectacles that are widely publicized and highly promoted by their producers. Show trials involve smearing the character of an innocent victim who is accused, publicly shamed, and then forced to confess.

A recurring theme in research on the topic is state-run character assassination campaigns attacking and denigrating opposition parties through techniques such as labeling, othering, and creating an enemy image (Saleh, 2020). Another trend is discussed by Laruelle (2020), who notes a recent escalation in the use of *Reductio ad Hitlerum* (i.e., comparing one's opponent to Hitler) in the public sphere as a tool for framing political and geopolitical legitimacy by exercising control over the labeling of opponents.

Although character assassination has been studied by researchers across multiple disciplines and contexts, there are two predominant theoretical frameworks that have produced substantial scholarship on the topic. The first is the theory of persuasive attack (Benoit, 2020). According to Benoit (2024), persuasive attack messages can address two basic topics: actions (behavior) and character (personality). This theory posits that each of these elements includes a variety of strategies for enhancing an attack that corresponds to beliefs (blame) and values (offensiveness). At its core, a character attack is a persuasive attack targeting public opinion. A persuasive attack on someone's character asserts that they possesses a certain trait that is inherently offensive. For instance, an accusation questioning the moral standing of a politician or a corporate CEO is likely to trigger the social evaluation and judgment of their reputation. When someone's reputation comes under attack, audiences may change their opinion about them regardless of whether the allegations are true or false.

The second theoretical framework is the character assassination typology conceptualized by scholars at the CARP Lab at George Mason University (Icks et al., 2020). This typology features five pillars of character assassination, including the attacker, the target, the medium, the audience, and the context. These pillars are usually discussed together when assessing the probability of a reputational crisis and public outrage following a character attack. Shiraev et al. (2022) highlight three cardinal media strategies in a character assassination attack: provocation, contamination, and obliteration. *Provocation* strategies aim to intercept the media agenda and create highly mediated scandals, often amplifying a hot-button issue to further exacerbate the public's scorn for the target (Samoilenko, 2020). *Contamination* strategies involve spreading falsehoods, rumors, and conspiracy theories. The idea here is to insert a small dose of disinformation about the target into public discourse and gradually poison the well, so to speak, in an effort to sway public opinion against the target (Marwick & Lewis, 2017). Finally, *obliteration* strategies attempt to purge the public's memory of a target's positive achievements and accomplishments (Waymer & Heath, 2019).

Though the term *character assassination* was initially used only in cases involving individuals (Icks & Shiraev, 2014), later contributions have also applied it to cases involving collectives, such as corporations (Coombs & Holladay, 2020) and nations (Aspriadis et al., 2020). In their analysis of corporate character assassination, Coombs and Holladay (2020) discuss how some angry stakeholders will resort to adopting such strategies when they are seeking revenge or even complete reputational or physical termination. Media outlets often amplify challenge crises by focusing on conflict, negativity, and the victimization aspect of news stories as a way of increasing online traffic and revenues. Laufer et al. (2023) found that reporting irrelevant information on a victim's negative character traits impacts their reputation and the potential empathy they may receive during a crisis. However, this can also potentially backfire and negatively affect the reputation of the news organization. Crisis communicators should study character assassination in the social context of their organizations and communities, which will help to explain the history of relationships between attackers, targets, and their multiple audiences.

Visual Disinformation

The use of compromising videos to destroy reputations has a long history (Shiraev et al., 2022). Lately, reputational attacks have proliferated with the development of automated systems circulating misinformation and synthetic media technologies used for smear campaigns. Visual disinformation can add a powerful spin to a message, especially when it comes to persuading audiences about complex social and political issues (Powell et al., 2015). AI-generated disinformation has become notorious for its manipulation of human psychographic profiles, which allows AI systems to tailor disruptive, persuasive, and intimidating messaging in a more targeted manner. Of particular concern is how deepfakes—synthesized media manipulated by AI—will be weaponized in politics. The following discussion elaborates on a few examples of how deepfakes have been deployed in recent US politics, particularly within the context of the 2024 presidential election (see Farid, 2024) when a political action committee (PAC) supporting Ron DeSantis created an ad criticizing former President Donald Trump and his attack on Iowa Governor Kim Reynolds. The video features Trump's voice disparaging Reynolds, and the text appears to be based on a post by Trump on Truth Social (Isenstadt, 2023).

A video of the Florida governor Ron DeSantis announcing his withdrawal from the 2024 presidential race circulated on social media. "BREAKING NEWS: Governor Ron DeSantis drops out of the 2024 Republican presidential primary," proclaimed a September 1, 2023, post on X (formerly Twitter) that showed a two-minute video in which DeSantis sits at a desk and appears to announce that he is terminating his campaign. The clip shows DeSantis saying:

> I've realized that I need to drop out of this race immediately. I was told I could be president by some very powerful people, and I took some very bad advice ... I never should have challenged President Trump, the greatest president of my lifetime ... It's time to right this ship and help President Trump get reelected to make America great again. (Suciu, 2023)

These examples show that deepfake technology has become a popular campaign tool used to land a political attack or spread false information. Visual disinformation has mushroomed with new technologies facilitating strategic deception in online spaces. Typically, strategic deception refers to the application of deceptive stratagems by pragmatic actors intending to create a believable communication performance within a particular media system (Chiluwa & Samoilenko, 2019). Like traditional compromising videos, deepfakes tend to exploit more taboo topics like sex (especially cheating on one's spouse or partner), drug use, inappropriate behavior, and age-related incompetency (Diakopoulos & Johnson, 2021; Samoilenko & Suvorova, 2023).

A popular way of using deepfake technology is in character assassination through ridicule. A recorded speech originally given by Vice President Kamala Harris at Howard University on April 25, 2023, was digitally altered to replace the original voice track with a seemingly inebriated and rambling voice saying, "Today is today, and yesterday was today yesterday, tomorrow will be today tomorrow, so live today so the future today will be as the past today as it is tomorrow." As Professor Hany Farid (2024) from UC Berkeley stated, it is not entirely clear whether the video is a lip-sync deepfake or just a classic audio/video dubbing. The proliferation of technologies such as deepfakes are effectively shaping political landscapes in nefarious ways. Scholars need to make more concerted efforts to grapple with the effects of these emerging phenomena.

Emergent Conceptual Frameworks for Reputation Management and Crisis Communication

In an era of extreme political polarization and heightened scrutiny, governments and corporations "constantly are in crisis management mode" (Waymer & Hill, 2023). As Benoit (in press) notes, persuasive attacks and defenses in both society and politics are frequent occurrences because human behavior often provokes criticism. Contemporary subversive communication campaigns are produced by strategic actors across multiple online communities and digital platforms involving multiple contributors, including popular media personalities, bloggers, YouTube influencers, and other active opinion leaders with digital power and the capability of amplifying the effects of subversive messaging. Scholars and organizations must be cognizant of emergent theories in the areas of crisis communication and reputation management to foresee, minimize, or counter subversive efforts that threaten personal or organizational survival.

Paracrisis and Issues Management

The most efficient strategy for individuals to protect their reputation is to ensure that they do not get compromised in the first place. That is why preparedness and prevention measures are crucial. Such measures seek to identify issues, reduce risks, and prepare response strategies against reputational crises.

According to Coombs and Halladay (2020), one of the strongest links between subversive communication (e.g., character assassination) and crisis communication is the "challenge crisis," or situations where stakeholders claim that an organization is acting in an irresponsible or immoral manner (Lerbinger, 1997). These crises begin as "paracrises," situations where a crisis risk must be managed in public before it escalates into a full reputational crisis (Chen & Holladay, 2023). A paracrisis warrants attention because it threatens an organization's reputation and its related assets. For instance, an accusation of corruption or abuse of human rights against a corporate CEO may be considered a paracrisis (Seifert-Brockmann et al., 2018).

Recent scholarship on *scansis* situations is of particular interest here (Coombs & Tachkova, 2019). A scansis occurs when a crisis situation also becomes a scandal involving perceptions of a moral violation. A crisis transmogrifies into a scansis when media coverage raises awareness of a situation in such a way that incites moral outrage. It is the moral outrage associated with a scansis that makes it particularly enduring (Coombs & Tachkova, in press).

The recent scholarship on paracrisis and scansis has profound implications for developing new approaches to *issues management*. Issues management, according to Coombs (2019), "means taking steps to prevent a problem from maturing into a crisis" (p. 11). Issues management is critical because it involves proactive attempts to identify and resolve high-priority issues that present imminent challenges to organizations. Because issues change their characteristics and develop according to a life cycle, a matter that was not an issue for the public at one point in time may become a problem for the same public at another point (Botan, 2018). Issues management involves scanning the environment, identifying potential problems, and trying to address these problems before they become full-blown crises. It also attempts to monitor the development of new social trends and prognosticate reputational threats by following emergent discourses around issues, events, and conversations concerning gender, race, identity, and other relevant social topics.

One way for crisis management to foresee subversive efforts is to become synergetic with the communities of interest. Since connected citizens and communities have the power to criticize and challenge official narratives and promote their own agendas, it is crucial for crisis practitioners and scholars to actively participate in the lives of online communities and work toward understanding their cultures, social norms, and needs. Additionally, they should learn to identify the signals of discontent or resentment toward formal narratives and systemic practices and become voluntary agents of change by suggesting new ideas for positive development to their stakeholders. Recent research on issues management has suggested that social media storms may influence the broader discourse about an organization when this discourse converges and reaches a tipping point. Hence, it is paramount to study the tipping point after which issues become impactful and explore new ways to analyze the influence of actors within certain discourses (Illia et al., 2023).

The rise of paracrises has prompted the use of social media and AI in processing risk information for pre-crisis management and communication. Social media, in particular, provides opportunities for crisis managers to gain insights into online conversations, identify potential warning signs, and prognosticate the likelihood and impact of crises (Guthrie & Rich, 2022; Senarath et al., 2021). As various aspects of crisis communication become digitalized, research should focus on how to integrate digital channels into crisis communication. For example, Coombs & Holladay (2023) illustrate the digitalization of crisis communication using the case of VW's advertisements in 2020 while launching its 2021 Golf; the advertisements attracted widespread condemnation across social and traditional media platforms for being racist, thereby tarnishing VW's reputation. Focusing on the #DeleteUber boycott, Illia and Colleoni (2023) illustrated how organizations use digital technology to strategically monitor, analyze, and respond to emerging sociopolitical issues that may be important to stakeholders.

Preemptive Inoculation and Image Prepare

The pre-crisis stage is also where crisis managers identify potential vulnerabilities by examining which crises are likely to occur and to have the most impact once they do. As part of this process, crisis managers may design pre-crisis *inoculation* messaging for stakeholders based on the most likely and impactful potential crises (Compton et al., 2021). The basic idea of inoculation theory is "that a position (an attitude, a belief, etc.) can be made resistant to future persuasive attacks in much the same way a body can be made resistant to future viral attacks: through preexposure to weakened forms of the impending challenge" (Compton & Braddock, in press). When an organization is open about its possible shortcomings and criticisms, inoculation strategies can build trust and credibility with stakeholders. Compton (2020) argues that inoculation-informed campaigns offer a preemptive, protective reputational management strategy. Crisis managers can identify threats and then try to inoculate their key audiences against such threats, such as online astroturfing (coordinated attacks from paid pollsters, trolls, or social bots; Boman & Schneider, 2021) and attacks on source credibility (Pfau & Burgoon, 1988). By identifying common strategies used to make character attacks, inoculation messages can help spot fallacies and respond with logic (Cook et al., 2017). In paracrisis situations, inoculation approaches could be combined with other preventive strategies, such as *stealing thunder* or releasing information about a potential crisis before it becomes widely circulated (Compton et al., 2021).

Another relevant framework here is *image prepare*, a conceptual model elaborated by Compton (2020). The idea of image prepare is to make preemptive use of the image repair typology (see Benoit, 2014) that is typically employed to study reactive strategies or attempts at image repair after an attack. Persuasive defense can address elements of an attack (or of suspicion), blame (denial, evading responsibility), or offensiveness (Benoit, 2024). For example, as suggested by Compton (2016), an organization could point toward previous or current handlings of challenges to establish precedence and anticipate future responses. Similarly, Wan and Pfau (2004) highlighted how positive evidence, such as the positive image of a corporation in the past, can bolster respondents' perceptions of and attitudes toward the company.

Another study used Benoit's typology (2014) to show how vice-presidential nominee Kamala Harris crafted a rhetorical persona defined by a socially acceptable construction of Black identity that corroborated her legitimacy and warded off scathing character attacks (Waymer & Hill, 2023). At the same time, Harris was able to maintain the Biden–Harris ticket's appeal to the Black community. The rhetorical strategies used by Harris (e.g., bolstering, denial, and attacking the accuser) can also be used proactively for inoculation messaging and reputation management.

One suggestion is to use provocation as a preemptive strategy. In image repair theory, this tactic falls under the broader strategy of evading responsibility, as when someone seeks to explain unflattering behavior by asserting that the act was provoked by another party. In inoculation messaging, a politician using provocation will tell their constituency that their political opponents are most likely running negative ads to smear their character. Hence, attacking an accuser as part of one's defense strategy against character assassination may be seen as legitimate and efficient.

Additionally, image prepare seems especially promising when used to preempt the effects of visual disinformation such as deepfake technology. Although deepfake detection has improved significantly, there are still a number of problems with current detection algorithms (Naitali et al., 2023). Used for image repair, the presence of deepfake technology gives public figures a viable excuse for denying and evading responsibility in the aftermath of unfortunate events. As previous research has shown, excuses citing causes that are unintentional, uncontrollable, and external are more effective in achieving forgiveness than excuses that cite causes that are intentional, controllable, and internal (Weiner et al., 1987).

A case in point is when European parliamentarians participated in video calls in April 2021 with a hoaxer pretending to be a Russian opposition politician and claimed to have fallen victim to a sophisticated deepfake. Yet, as the notorious Russian pranksters Vovan and Lexus, who staged the video interviews, told *The Verge*, their doppelgänger was using simple makeup and an obscure camera angle (Vincent, 2021). As this example illustrates, a simple reference to deepfake gives individuals the possibility of denying real scenarios by claiming a lack of knowledge or self-efficacy to deal with this type of disinformation or casting doubt on the veracity of video materials and makes it possible to reject any criticism or allegations. With image prepare, politicians and their campaign managers have a promising conceptual framework in place for developing a pre-crisis strategy that allows them to forewarn their key constituents about the damaging effects of deepfakes.

Conclusions and Future Research

This chapter has discussed new trends in subversive communication, including disruption, character assassination, and visual disinformation. These practices have become pervasive in recent years, exerting a tremendous impact on society. In the context of digital activism, cancel culture, and manipulated media, these practices are functional tools in the hands of subversive actors who seek to achieve goals ranging from settling personal scores to changing societal power dynamics. It is imperative that crisis communication scholars revisit established theories and models and embrace emergent concepts to stay in tune with changing sociopolitical realities, generational shifts, and technological advancements. Understanding contemporary trends in subversive communication is especially relevant for reputational pre-crisis scenarios, offering multiple directions for further research.

This chapter calls for greater interdisciplinary synergy between scholars to further study the negative impacts of these subversive campaigns. The emerging concepts of paracrisis, scansis, and image prepare allow for a closer examination of cases dealing with moral outrage and suggest ways of countering their effects. Though image prepare, in particular, requires further empirical testing and validation, this conceptual framework provides an effective antidote to disruptive, invective, and deceptive strategies and can help the public develop critical skills to properly assess the content of news media and popular culture. Future scholarship will further increase our knowledge of subversive communication by testing, refining, and elaborating existing theories.

References

Aspriadis, N., Takas, E., & Samaras, A. N. (2020). Country reputation assassination during the Greek memorandum re-negotiations. In S. A. Samoilenko, M. Icks, J. Keohane, & E. Shiraev (Eds.), *Routledge handbook of character assassination and reputation management* (pp. 236–250). Routledge.

Benoit, W. L. (2014). *Accounts, excuses, apologies: A theory of image restoration strategies* (2nd ed.). State University of New York Press.

Benoit, W. L. (2020). Character assassination and persuasive attack on CBS's face the nation. In S. A. Samoilenko, M. Icks, J. Keohane, & E. Shiraev (Eds.), *Routledge handbook of character assassination*. (pp. 295–307). Routledge.

Benoit, W. L. (in press). Persuasive attack and defense in social and political conflict. In S. A. Samoilenko & S. Simmons (Eds.), *The Wiley handbook of political and social conflict*. Wiley.

Blackstock, P. W. (1964). *The strategy of subversion: Manipulating the politics of other nations*. Quadrangle Books.

Boman, C. D., & Schneider, E. J. (2021). Finding an antidote: Testing the use of proactive crisis strategies to protect organizations from astroturf attacks. *Public Relations Review, 47*(1), 102004. http://dx.doi.org/10.1016/j.pubrev.2020.102004

Botan, C. H. (2018). *Strategic communication: Theory and practice*. Wiley Blackwell.

Boyd, A. (2012). *Beautiful trouble: A toolbox for revolution*. OR Books.

Chan-Olmsted, S. M., & Qin, Y. S. (2021). The impact of fake news on its sponsor's brand trust. *Journal of Brand Strategy, 9*(4), 446–465.

Chen, F., & Holladay, S. J. (2023). Identifying and responding to social media risks: Towards an organizational paracrisis communication framework. *Corporate Communications, 28*(1), 103–117.

Chiluwa, I. E., & Samoilenko, S. A. (2019). *Handbook of research on deception, fake new and misinformation online*. IGI Global.

Compton, J. (2016). Image prepare: Image repair, inoculation theory, and anticipated attacks on credibility. *International Journal of the Image, 8*(1), 1–9.

Compton, J. (2020). Inoculation against/as character assassination. In S. A. Samoilenko, M. Icks, J. Keohane, & E. Shiraev (Eds.), *The Routledge handbook of character assassination* (pp. 25–35). Routledge.

Compton, J., & Braddock, K. (in press). Inoculation theory and conspiracy, radicalization, and violent extremism. In S. A. Samoilenko & S. Simmons (Eds.), *The Wiley handbook of political and social conflict*. Wiley.

Compton, J., Wigley, S., & Samoilenko, S. A. (2021). Inoculation theory and public relations. *Public Relations Review, 47*(5), 102116. http://dx.doi.org/10.1016/j.pubrev.2021.102116

Cook, J., Lewandowsky, S., & Ecker, U. K. H. (2017). Neutralizing misinformation through inoculation: Exposing misleading argumentation techniques reduces their influence. *PLoS One, 12*(5). http://dx.doi.org/10.1371/journal.pone.0175799

Coombs, T., & Holladay, S. (2023). Digital corporate communication and paracrises and AI. In V. Luoma-aho & M. Badham (Eds.), *Handbook on digital corporate communication.* (pp. 165–178). Edward Elgar.

Coombs, T. W. (2019). *Ongoing crisis communication: Planning, managing, and responding* (5th ed.). SAGE.

Coombs, W. T., & Holladay, S. (2020). Corporate character assassination and crisis communication. In S. A. Samoilenko, M. Icks, J. Keohane, & E. Shiraev (Eds.), *Routledge handbook of character assassination* (pp. 225–235). Routledge.

Coombs, W. T., & Tachkova, E. R. (2019). Scansis as a unique crisis type: Theoretical and practical implications. *Journal of Communication Management*, *23*(1), 72–88.

Coombs, W. T., & Tachkova, E. R. (in press). How political and social conflict enter into the corporate realm: Scansis as an exemplar of moral outrage inducing crises. In S. A. Samoilenko & S. Simmons (Eds.), *The Wiley handbook of political and social conflict.* Wiley.

Cooper, A. (2023, May 27). *How Russian pranksters are tricking influential foreign leaders.* CNN. https://edition.cnn.com/videos/world/2023/05/27/russian-prank-callers-chance-dnt-ac360-vpx.cnn

de Zeeuw, D., & Gekker, A. (2023). A god-tier LARP? QAnon as conspiracy fictioning. *Social Media + Society*, *9*(1). http://dx.doi.org/10.1177/20563051231157300

Diakopoulos, N., & Johnson, D. (2021). Anticipating and addressing the ethical implications of deepfakes in the context of elections. *New Media & Society*, *23*(7), 2072–2098.

Dunlevy, G. (2010, March 18). Gory Greenpeace KitKat video goes viral. *The Daily Telegraph* (Sydney). https://www.dailytelegraph.com.au/gory-greenpeace-kitkat-video-goes-viral/news-story/

Edelman. (2023). *2023 Edelman trust barometer: Navigating a polarized world.* https://www.edelman.com/trust/2023/trust-barometer

Farid, H. (2024). *Deepfakes in the 2024 US Presidential Election.* Berkeley University. https://farid.berkeley.edu/deepfakes2024election

Fichman, P., & Akter, S. (2023). Trolling asymmetry toward republicans and democrats and the shift from foreign to domestic trolling. *Telematics and Informatics*, *82*, 101998. http://dx.doi.org/10.1016/j.tele.2023.101998

Guthrie, W. S., & Rich, J. (2022). New technology, big data, and artificial intelligence. In Y. Jin & L. L. Austin (Eds.), *Social media and crisis communication.* (pp. 180–192). Routledge.

Haller, A., & Michael, H. (2023). *Scandalogy 4: Political scandals in the age of populism, partisanship, and polarization.* Springer.

Heath, R. L., Liao, S., & Douglas, W. (1995). Effects of perceived economic harms and benefits on issue involvement, use of information sources, and actions: A study in risk communication. *Journal of Public Relations Research*, *7*, 89–109.

Hollander, J. A., & Einwohner, R. L. (2004). Conceptualizing resistance. *Sociological Forum*, *19*(4), 533–554.

Howard, P. N., & Kollanyi, B. (2016). *Bots, #Strongerin, and #Brexit: Computational propaganda during the UK-EU referendum.* Comprop Research Note 2016. 1. http://dx.doi.org/10.2139/ssrn.2798311

Hyslop, M. (2014). *Obstructive marketing: Restricting distribution of products and services in the age of asymmetric warfare.* Ashgate.

Icks, M., & Shiraev, E. (2014). *Character assassination throughout the ages.* Palgrave Macmillan.

Icks, M., Shiraev, E., Keohane, J., & Samoilenko, S. A. (2020). Character assassination: Theoretical framework. In S. A. Samoilenko, M. Icks, J. Keohane, & E. Shiraev (Eds.),

Routledge handbook of character assassination and reputation management (pp. 11–24). Routledge.

Illia, L., & Colleoni, E. (2023). Digital corporate communication and issues management. In V. Luoma-aho & M. Badham (Eds.), *Handbook on digital corporate communication* (pp. 135–151). Edward Elgar.

Illia, L., Colleoni, E., Etter, M., & Meggiorin, K. (2023). Finding the tipping point: When heterogeneous evaluations in social media converge and influence organizational legitimacy. *Business & Society, 62*(1), 117–150.

Isenstadt, A. (2023, July 17). *DeSantis PAC uses AI-generated Trump voice in ad attacking ex-president.* Politico. https://www.politico.com/news/2023/07/17/desantis-pac-ai-generated-trump-in-ad-00106695

Jasper, J. M., & King, B. (2020). *Protestors and their targets.* Temple University Press.

Klicperová-Baker, M. (2020). Show trials in communist countries: Psychology of the ultimate cases of character assassination. In S. A. Samoilenko, M. Icks, J. Keohane, & E. Shiraev (Eds.), *The Routledge handbook of character assassination* (pp. 320–334). Routledge.

Klyueva, A. (2013). Trolling. In R. Heath (Ed.), *Encyclopedia of public relations* (pp. 933–934). SAGE.

Kratzke, N. (2023). How to find orchestrated trolls? A case study on identifying polarized Twitter Echo Chambers. *Computers, 12*(3), 57. http://dx.doi.org/10.3390/computers12030057

Langley, Q. (2014). *Brandjack: How your reputation is at risk from brand pirates and what to do about it.* Palgrave Macmillan.

Laruelle, M. (2020). Reductio ad Hitlerum as a new frame for political and geopolitical conflicts. In S. A. Samoilenko, M. Icks, J. Keohane, & E. Shiraev (Eds.), *The Routledge handbook of character assassination* (pp. 307–319). Routledge.

Laufer, D., Einwiller, S., & Neureiter, A. (2023). All the news that is fit to print? Reporting on a victim's character during a crisis. *Journal of Contingencies and Crisis Management, 31*, 592–598. http://dx.doi.org/10.1111/1468-5973.1246

Leach, J., & Wilson, L. (2014). Subversion, conversion, development: Imaginaries, knowledge forms, and the uses of ICTs. In J. Leach & L. Wilson (Eds.), *Subversion, conversion, development. Cross-cultural knowledge exchange and the politics of design* (pp. 231–244). MIT Press.

Lerbinger, O. (1997). *The crisis manager: Facing risk and responsibility.* Lawrence Erlbaum.

Linderoth, J., & Mortensen, T. E. (2015). Dark play: The aesthetics of controversial playfulness. In J. Linderoth, T. E. Mortensen, & A. M. L. Brown (Eds.), *The dark side of game play* (pp. 3–12). Routledge.

Lorenz, T., & Harwell, D. (2022, March 30). Facebook paid GOP firm to malign TikTok. *The Washington Post.* https://www.washingtonpost.com/technology/2022/03/30/facebook-tiktok-targeted-victory

Marcondes, F. S., Almeida, J. J., & Novais, P. J. (2024). An exploratory design science research on troll factories. *Integrated Computer-Aided Engineering, 31*(1), 95–115.

Marwick, A., & Lewis, R. (2017). *Media manipulation and disinformation online.* Data and Society Research Institute. https://datasociety.net/wp-content/uploads/2017/05/DataAndSociety_MediaManipulationAndDisinformationOnline-1.pdf

McLeod, K. (2014). *Pranksters: Making mischief in the modern world.* New York University Press.

Naitali, A., Ridouani, M., Salahdine, F., & Kaabouch, N. (2023). Deepfake attacks: Generation, detection, datasets, challenges, and research directions. *Computers, 12*(10). http://dx.doi.org/10.3390/computers12100216

Pashentsev, E. (2023). *The Palgrave handbook of malicious use of AI and psychological security.* Palgrave Macmillan.

Pfau, M., & Burgoon, M. (1988). Inoculation in political campaign communication. *Human Communication Research, 15*, 91–111.

Phillips, W. (2015). *This is why we can't have nice things: Mapping the relationship between online trolling and mainstream culture.* MIT Press.

Phillips, W., & Milner, R. M. (2017). *The ambivalent Internet.* Polity Press.

Powell, T. E., Boomgaarden, H. G., De Swert, K., & de Vreese, C. H. (2015). A clearer picture: The contribution of visuals and text to framing effects. *Journal of Communication, 65*(6), 997–1017.

Saleh, A. S. (2020). Character assassination of activists in Egypt: ElBaradei as a target. In S. A. Samoilenko, M. Icks, J. Keohane, & E. Shiraev (Eds.), *The Routledge handbook of character assassination* (pp. 105–116). Routledge.

Samoilenko, S. A. (2020). Character assassination in the context of mediated complexity. In K. Sriramesh & D. Verčič (Eds.), *The global public relations handbook: Theory, research, and practice* (pp. 268–282). Routledge.

Samoilenko, S. A. (2021). The cocreational view of character assassination. In C. H. Botan (Ed.), *The handbook of strategic communication* (pp. 76–90). Wiley.

Samoilenko, S. A., & Suvorova, I. (2023). Deepfakes in strategic deception campaigns. In E. Pashentsev (Ed.), *The Palgrave handbook of malicious use of AI and psychological security.* Palgrave Macmillan.

Schumacher-Rutherford, A., & Muddiman, A. (2021). The bullying pulpit: The audience effects of a partisan character-attacking speaker. *Journal of Applied Social Theory, 1*(3), 31–61.

Seifert-Brockmann, J., Einwiller, S., & Stranzl, J. (2018). Character assassination of CEOs in crises—Questioning CEOs' character and values in corporate crises. *European Journal of Communication, 33*(4), 413–429. http://dx.doi.org/10.1177/0267323118763860

Senarath, Y., Peterson, S., Purohit, H., Hughes, A. L., & Stephens, K. K. (2021). Mining risk behaviors from social media for pandemic crisis preparedness and response. In *Proceedings of the 2021 international conference on social computing, behavioral-cultural modeling & prediction and behavior representation in modeling and simulation.* https://sbp-brims.org/2021/papers/working-papers/2021_SBP-BRiMS_FinalPDF_55.pdf

Shiraev, E., Keohane, J., Icks, M., & Samoilenko, S. A. (2022). *Character assassination and reputation management: Theory and applications.* Routledge.

Siano, A., Confetto, M. G., Vollero, A., & Covucci, C. (2021). Redefining brand hijacking from a non-collaborative brand co-creation perspective. *Journal of Product & Brand Management, 31*(1), 110–126.

Simons, G. (2020). The role of propaganda in the character assassination of world leaders in international affairs. In S. A. Samoilenko, M. Icks, J. Keohane, & E. Shiraev (Eds.), *Routledge handbook of character assassination and reputation management* (pp. 163–180). Routledge.

Smith, R., & Eberly, R. A. (2021). Advancing research on character assassination and stigma communication: A dynamics of character. *Journal of Applied Social Theory, 1*(3), 134–157.

Stephenson, S. (2021). A ritual civil execution: Public shaming meetings in the post-Stalin Soviet Union. *Journal of Applied Social Theory, 1*(3), 112–133.

Suciu, P. (2023, September 2). There is now a deep fake video of Ron DeSantis dropping out of the 2024 race. *Forbes.* https://bit.ly/3ujRyDR

Sukhodolov, A. P., Kudlik, E. S., & Antonova, A. B. (2018). Prank journalism as a new genre in Russian media landscape. *Theoretical and Practical Issues of Journalism*, *7*(3), 361–370.

Tran, M. (2014, April 23). #myNYPD Twitter callout backfires for New York police department. The Guardian. https://bit.ly/3UkgdTx

Upton-Clark, E. (2020, July 29). Pranks as political activism: From the yippies to TikTok. *TeenVogue*. https://www.teenvogue.com/story/pranks-political-activism-history

Vincent, J. (2021, April 30). "Deepfake" that supposedly fooled European politicians was just a look-alike, say pranksters. *The Verge*. https://bit.ly/34XC0Zp

Wan, H.-H., & Pfau, M. (2004). The relative effectiveness of inoculation, bolstering, and combined approaches in crisis communication. *Journal of Public Relations Research*, *16*(3), 301–328.

Waymer, D., & Heath, R. L. (2019). The public relations paradox of erasure: Damnatio memoriae as public relations strategy and tactic. *Public Relations Review*, *45*(3), 1–11. http://dx.doi.org/10.1016/j.pubrev.2019.04.011

Waymer, D., & Hill, T. E. (2023). A conceptual update to image restoration theory (IRT) via an analysis of the vice-presidential campaign of Kamala Harris. *Public Relations Review*, *49*(2), 102306. http://dx.doi.org/10.1016/j.pubrev.2023.102306

Weiner, B., Amirkhan, J., Folkes, V. S., & Verette, J. A. (1987). An attributional analysis of excuse giving: Studies of a naive theory of emotion. *Journal of Personality and Social Psychology*, *52*(2), 316–324. http://dx.doi.org/10.1037/0022-3514.52.2.316

Williams, J. P. (2011). *Subcultural theory: Traditions and concepts*. Polity Press.

Wootson, C. R., Jr. (2017, July 26). It was a prank call. Listen to Russian pranksters trick Rick Perry into a conversation about pig manure. *The Washington Post*. https://wapo.st/3go6l5Y

6

Politicization of Health Issues: Misinformation and Social Media

Porismita Borah

Edward R. Murrow College of Communication, Washington State University

Past research has examined the causes, mechanisms, and consequences of the politicization of health issues. It is an area of research that continues to grow as "health issues are increasingly becoming politicized" (Fowler & Gollust, 2015, p. 155). Previous studies have identified three dimensions of the politicization of health issues: the dispute about science and health topics in the public sphere; the exaggeration and exploitation of the inherent uncertainty of science to evoke doubt; and the inclusion of political conflict and partisan disagreement in the discussions related to health and science (Fowler et al., 2022). Several studies have examined topics such as the human papillomavirus (HPV; Fowler & Gollust, 2015); mammography (Fowler & Gollust, 2015); and COVID-19 (Borah et al., 2023, 2024; Motta et al., 2020; Stroebe et al., 2015; Van Scoy et al., 2021). The findings show that the entangling of politics with health and science has serious repercussions on health attitudes and behavior. The politicization of a number of health issues, such as controversies over the efficacy and risks of vaccinations or other prevention measures, has become more prominent in recent years and is often amplified by the media during times of crisis. For example, partisan media use was associated with a lower likelihood of social distancing behavior during the COVID-19 pandemic (Borah et al., 2024). Partisan media play important functions in the process of shaping the public's health attitudes and behaviors, particularly during times of health crises. Much past research demonstrated the conservative media's negative effects on public health (e.g., decreasing users' health behaviors). For instance, Motta and Stecula (2023) found that Fox News's COVID-19 vaccine-related coverage was significantly more negative than other media. Their research also found that self-reported Fox News exposure is associated with increased vaccine refusal.

The politicization of health and science can lead to individuals processing information through a political lens. Political ideology can impact information-processing (Chan & Palmeira, 2021; Jost et al., 2003), which may be associated with misperceptions. Nan et al. (2022) conducted a systematic review to explore who is susceptible to health misinformation. They found that political ideology is associated with health misperceptions and that conservatives held higher misperceptions. Nan and colleagues used "identity-motivated

Communication and Misinformation: Crisis Events in the Age of Social Media, First Edition.
Edited by Kevin B. Wright.
© 2025 John Wiley & Sons, Inc. Published 2025 by John Wiley & Sons, Inc.

thinking" to shed light on the psychological mechanisms of this process. A variety of empirical studies also supported the close association between conservative identification and misinformation beliefs (e.g., Agley & Xiao, 2021; Marwick & Lewis, 2017). Such motivated reasoning can be problematic for various health outcomes but particularly so in the presence of misinformation and disinformation, such as during the COVID-19 pandemic.

Over the years, health information seeking has evolved with emerging technologies such as mobile phones and social media. Very often, individuals seek health information from social media (Himelboim et al., 2020). Social media platforms make it easy for people to receive health information as well as share their opinions (Hong et al., 2021). This is a double-edged sword such as has never before in health communication. A plethora of health information is easily available but, at the same time, these platforms can be full of unconfirmed information often containing false details. Add predispositions and politically motivated information-processing to the mix, and we face a critical information crisis such as the COVID-19 pandemic. The situation during the pandemic became so critical that the World Health Organization declared it an "infodemic." In this chapter, I review the literature related to the politicization of health and misinformation and end with potential directions for future research.

Politicization of Health Issues and Its Consequences

The politicization of health issues is an umbrella term encompassing a variety of research topics. Many studies examine, on the one hand, how health issues are framed from a political perspective and, on the other, the consequences of politicizing health issues.

Framing of Health Issues

A variety of studies examined how the COVID-19 pandemic was framed by the media and by different political stakeholders. Most of these studies conducted content analysis of one or several media outlets. Hubner (2021) used a combination of manual and computational coding methods and found that political response was one of the major frames for *The New York Times*' and *The Washington Post*'s COVID-19 reports. Using both quantitative and qualitative methods we (Borah et al., 2024) found differences between right-leaning and left-leaning media outlets. We studied 15 different media organizations, which included a total of 17,322 articles from left-leaning and 21,820 articles from right-leaning media outlets. Our findings showed that the right-leaning media downplayed the virus, while the left leaning media focused on the risks associated with the virus. Our findings also showed that the left-leaning media portrayed the COVID-19 crisis as "out of control" but the right-leaning media often depicted the virus as "under control" (Borah et al., 2024, p. 6).

Consequences of the Politicization of Health Issues

Past research has demonstrated the severe consequences of the politicization of health, especially during crises. For example, in the case of the COVID-19 pandemic, Stroebe et al. (2015) examined survey data from the United States and found that political ideology predicted people's risk perceptions and health protective behaviors. Taking a qualitative approach,

Van Scoy et al. (2021) analyzed participants' responses to open-ended questions. They found that people were concerned about the politicization of the pandemic. Participants also shared their concerns about media bias and disinformation from the government. They were aware of the politicization of the pandemic and were anxious about the distrust around information about the public health crisis. Trust in intuitional information and science is critical for health communication. However, distrust in science is at an all-time low.

Even before the pandemic, research has paid attention to the politicization of health issues. For example, Fowler and Gollust (2015) studied the politicization of mammogram screening. They used both content analysis and survey data to examine how fast an issue such as mammogram screening can become politicized. The authors also studied the public's reaction to the politicization of mammogram screening. They were able to understand the changes in public opinion related to mammogram screening and HPV vaccines just as the issue became increasingly politicized. Fowler and Gollust's (2015) research added a dynamic dimension by examining the mammogram screening rapidly became politicized. Their findings showed how trust in medical institutions decreased as a result of the issue becoming which in turn could impact attitudes and behaviors around the issue.

In recent years, the COVID-19 pandemic has been a stark example of the politicization of health issues. People's reactions to the pandemic were often contingent on their political orientation. Gollwitzer et al. (2020) found that partisanship was closely associated with physical distancing. Specifically, US counties that voted for Donald Trump over Hillary Clinton in the 2016 presidential election exhibited 14 percent less physical distancing. Moreover, they also found that county-level consumption of conservative media (Fox News) was related to reduced physical distancing (Gollwitzer et al., 2020). These findings show that partisan factors played important roles in influencing the public's health beliefs and behaviors. The problems of misinformation are amplified when individuals seek out congruent information or stay within circles with similar worldviews. Han and Lee (2023) found that risk perceptions of the pandemic were particularly different for individuals who selectively consumed like-minded news outlets. Using a three-wave longitudinal survey Romer and Jamieson (2021) demonstrated the negative effects of conservative media use. Specifically, their research results showed that, though some users of conservative media supported vaccination and trusted the Centers for Disease Control at the outset of their study, continued exposure to conservative media reduced support for both.

One of the health issues that is often politicized and that has significant consequences is vaccines. In general, vaccine attitudes and behavior are divided along partisan lines. For example, Jiang et al. (2022) found that conservatives were less likely to get vaccinated against COVID-19. Moreover, Ji (2021) found that, though exposure to proximal others' vaccination posts on social media was positively associated with readers' vaccination intention through positive affective responses, this relationship was moderated by partisan media use. Specifically, conservative media use enhanced readers' negative affective response to vaccination posts while liberal media use was associated with positive affective response. Kareklas et al. (2023) considered the politicization of COVID-19 within the context of the US presidential election. The authors found that Trump voters reported a lower likelihood than Biden voters to be vaccinated in the future and expressly indicated a lower desire to receive the COVID-19 vaccine. Mistrust toward vaccines caused by politicization of the issue by government figures serves as a major vaccine acceptance barrier (Fowler et al., 2022; Galbraith-Gyan et al., 2019; Saulsberry et al., 2019).

Misinformation and the Politicization of Health Issues

Scholars have differentiated misinformation and disinformation such that disinformation is "designed, presented and promoted to intentionally cause public harm or for profit" and misinformation is shared without the "disseminators' knowledge" (Freelon & Wells, 2020, p. 1).

Past studies have posited that conservatives share misinformation more often than liberals (e.g., Marwick & Lewis, 2017). Vosoughi et al. (2018) claimed that, in general, conservatives follow and trust news outlets that include false information in their content. Research also confirmed that information from in-group members and sources are often considered accurate (Ardèvol-Abreu et al., 2017; Garrett et al., 2019). Indeed, political orientation may play a role in various media effects, which means that individual attitudes and behaviors can be impacted by preexisting ideology (e.g., Reedy et al., 2014). Reedy et al. (2014) showed that individuals' political ideology was often associated with false beliefs. In this sense, individuals are more susceptible to misinformation and disinformation that are congruent with their predispositions and political orientation.

Political ideology plays a critical role in individuals' information-processing (Chan & Palmeira, 2021; Jost et al., 2003). Ideology can often serve as "epistemic motivation" (Federico et al., 2012, p. 381), which can enable people to situate themselves on the ideological spectrum. As such, people may construct a reality that is congruent with their placement on the spectrum. Thus political ideology impacts information-processing and leads to reality construction and perceptions that may be biased (Federico et al., 2012). Liberals and conservatives use different approaches to processing information (Amodio et al., 2007). For example, Amodio et al. (2007) found that conservatives were often persistent in their attitudes, while liberals were more tolerant and open to new experiences and heterogeneous news sources.

A variety of research from multiple fields have shown that people process information that may benefit them and perceive this information through the lens of their preexisting ideologies (e.g., Balcetis & Dunning 2006; Long & Toppino 2004). Individuals want to protect their own preexisting attitudes (Chaiken et al., 1996). This biased information-processing (Lodge & Hamill, 1986) can make individuals highly susceptible to misinformation. "The desire to hold attitudes and beliefs that are congruent with existing self-definitional attitudes and beliefs" (Chaiken et al., 1996, p. 577) may often be true when processing false information. Heuristic processing has been shown to be a significant predictor of misinformation acceptance in past studies. Hwang and Jeong (2023) found that those who used heuristic processing in understanding information about COVID-19 were also more likely to accept COVID-19-related misinformation and, of course, misinformation beliefs meant not following health recommendations. For example, higher misperceptions about COVID-19 were negatively associated with people's vaccination intention (e.g., Husain et al., 2021; Kim et al., 2022).

A related topic that is integral to the politicization of health issues is the discussion about public trust. The public's trust in the government, institutions, political leaders, and scientific experts is crucial to their health attitudes and behavior. Trust in health institutions such as CDC and WHO is related to health attitudes and behavior (Borah et al., 2024; Lewandowsky et al., 2012; Nyhan & Reifler, 2010). Jennings et al. (2021) found that trust in government and health institutions is a positive predictor of an individual's willingness to get the COVID-19 vaccine, a finding that was repeated in countries outside of the United States. In a survey conducted in Austria, Schernhammer et al. (2022) demonstrated that COVID-19 vaccine hesitancy was closely related to public trust in government. Beyond COVID-19, research has the shown the importance of public trust in other health attitudes and behaviors. For instance, Blair et al. (2017) found that people who distrusted the government were less likely to adopt prevention behaviors against the Ebola virus and were less compliant with Ebola control policies. Moreover, Pak et al. (2021) found that higher public trust in government could double the impact of policy restrictions and affect public compliance. Just as political ideology may influence information-processing, these predispositions can impact the public's trust in various organizations. Agley (2020) found that political orientation was associated with people's trust in science and scientists. Thus, when topics of health and science are politicized, people no longer process information as just a matter of health but see it through a political lens, which may impact everything from scientific trust to health behaviors.

Politicization of Health Issues, Misinformation, and Social Media

Social media platforms have brought us immeasurable opportunities to gather information. However, along with facts, misinformation and disinformation can also be easily shared on these platforms (Wang et al., 2019). As a result, the probability of being exposed to misinformation online is higher. When the false information is processed with heuristics and filters such as political orientation, the situation becomes grave. In such a scenario, the consequences of the politicization of health issues become significantly complex. Disinformation campaigns use strategic communication tactics and Peng et al. (2022) conducted a systematic review of the persuasive strategies of online health misinformation. They concluded 12 thematic groups including fabricating narrative with details, citing anecdotes and personal experience as evidence, distrusting government or pharmaceutical companies, politicizing health issues, highlighting uncertainty and risk, using scientific evidence inappropriately, employing rhetorical tricks, and making emotional appeals. In a recent study we examined strategies of sharing conspiracy theories about the pandemic (Himelboim et al., 2023). We found that statements of belief, malicious purposes, conspirators, authentication, and secretive actions were most commonly used to discuss these conspiracy theories. For example, conspirators such as Bill Gates were mostly commonly cited and the content often used authenticating sources such as the CDC to validate the conspiracy theory.

The dissemination of health misinformation and disinformation can be often attributed to political purposes. For instance, Yan et al. (2022) explored how Russian "trolls" were used to post antivaccination information on Twitter during the COVID-19 pandemic. Their results indicated that misinformation was more likely to be perpetuated by partisan trolls. In another related study, Muric et al. (2021) analyzed Twitter posts regarding COVID-19 antivaccine information. They found that the accounts engaged in the antivaccine narratives lean to the right of the political spectrum. Comparing social media platforms such as Twitter with news media outlets, past research has shown that the prevalence of misinformation is higher on social media platforms. For instance, Bridgman et al. (2020) found that misinformation was more prevalent on Twitter compared to news media. Although the political slant of the news media outlets would be an important factor in these evaluations, in general social media platforms were a hotbed for misinformation because of their unverified information. Research has demonstrated that exposure to social media is positively associated with misperceptions (e.g., Zhang et al., 2023). Whether people are exposed to information on social or news media or both, conservatives were consistently found to be more likely to generate and share misinformation (e.g., Marwick & Lewis, 2017) compared to liberals. Social media use was also often found to be associated with holding higher misperceptions. For example, Islam et al. (2020) found that during the COVID-19 pandemic people driven by self-promotion were more likely to share unverified information.

The impact of false information has been extensively studied, and research has shown various negative consequences of exposure to misinformation. Individuals may ignore recommended health behaviors (Tan et al., 2015) because of misperceptions. Misinformation may cause fear, anxiety, anger, and panic (Borah et al., 2022; Luo and Cheng, 2021). Misinformation has effects on people's cognitive and emotional states. Borges do Nascimento's (2022) systematic review of health misinformation found several serious consequences caused by the dissemination of misinformation, including an increase in misleading interpretations of the available evidence, a negative impact on mental health, the misallocation of health resources, and an increase in vaccination hesitancy.

Scholars have also explored the mechanisms of why some people are particularly susceptible to misinformation. Distrust of science and partisan-motivated reasoning serve as two main explanations. Studies found that conservatives generally hold negative views toward science and expertise (e.g., Gauchat, 2012) and that distrust of experts can facilitate partisan polarization concerning the endorsement of antiscience conspiracy theories (e.g., Miller, 2020). Motta's (2021) research also supported the mediating effect of antiexpert attitudes in the relationship between political orientation and misinformation endorsement. Moreover, whether people find a message credible or not depends on their group affiliations (Tanis & Postmes, 2005).

To understand the variety of research on health misinformation and social media, Li et al. (2019) conducted a systematic review of studies regarding health misinformation on social media. They found that the studies include four key topics: characteristics of health misinformation, spread of health misinformation, impact of health misinformation, and coping strategy. In a more recent study Li et al. (2022) conducted another systematic review where they discuss a stage-based framework of health misinformation on social media to synthesize the results of prior studies by dividing the process into originating stage, transmitting stage, and consuming stage. The systematic reviews, as well as the discussion of past research, give us a sense of the problem and of the prevalence of health misinformation on social media. As discussed, the politicization of health issues adds an additional layer of complexity to the situation. One prominent question for researchers and health organizations is whether there are any solutions. What can be done to mitigate some of these consequences?

Potential Solutions and Future Directions

Beyond examining the spread of misinformation and its consequences, much research has examined the ways to mitigate misinformation (Bode & Vraga, 2018; Lewandowsky et al., 2012; Sangalang et al., 2019). Past research has shown that there are ways to fight misinformation with corrective measures (Bode & Vraga, 2018; Borah et al., 2021), inoculation (Bolsen & Druckman, 2015), and media literacy (Craft et al., 2013; Guess et al., 2020). There is an abundance of research on corrective and inoculation messages as strategies for fighting misinformation on social media. Inoculation messages are widely used to conduct preemptive refutation of misinformation. Compton et al. (2016) claimed that inoculation messages were effective in decreasing misperceptions. Roozenbeek et al. (2022) tested five short videos that inoculate people against manipulation techniques commonly used in fake information. They found that these videos improved the recognition of manipulation techniques, boosted confidence in spotting such techniques, increased people's ability to discern trustworthy from untrustworthy content, and improved the quality of their sharing decisions. Similarly, the use of corrective messages has also been shown shown to reduce misperceptions. Vraga et al. (2019) found that both logic-based and humor-based corrections could reduce HPV vaccination-related misperceptions. Other researchers have tested fact-based corrective messages (Lewandowsky et al., 2012), social correction using family and friends (Bode & Vraga, 2018), and loss- and gain-framed messages (Borah et al., 2021).

An extensive list of studies has explored ways to correct misinformation. Some studies have shown that the source of the corrective messages plays a key role. Vraga and Bode (2017a, 2017b) proposed that, to be effective, the corrective message should provide a source and that an expert source is more impactful. Other studies examined the effectiveness of different sources from a social network perspective. Margolin et al. (2018) found that individuals who follow and are followed by the people who correct them are significantly more likely to accept the correction than individuals confronted by strangers.

Fact checking is another way to correct misinformation mentioned in misinformation correction studies. The central form of fact-checking is debunking, which means presenting a warning and corrective information before exposure to the misinformation (Chan et al., 2017). Past studies (e.g., Zhang et al., 2021) have also found that exposure to fact-checking labels on misinformation can generate more positive attitudes toward vaccines compared to misinformation without fact-checking labels. Moreover, if the fact-checking labels are from trusted health institutions, users will have higher perceptions of the expertise and more positive attitudes. Similarly, Moon et al. (2023) explored the effects of the source of fact-checking labels on users' bias in information-processing. The authors found that AI-sourced labels on fact-checking messages significantly reduced partisan-based motivated reasoning in the participants. Moreover, Lee et al. (2022) found that a fact-checking label attached to misinformation significantly reduced MMR (measles, mumps and rubella) vaccine conspiracy beliefs compared to the no fact-checking condition. Past research has also shown that media literacy can also be helpful to mitigate misinformation (Craft et al., 2013; Guess et al., 2020). However, some of the positive impact of media literacy variables may be diminished by factors such as political orientation (Borah, 2022; Borah et al., 2022).

Most of the literature in this area of research discusses the potential of political variables to dismiss the impact of certain strategies to fight misinformation. However, not many studies have empirically tested how (if at all possible) to minimize the influence of political factors such as political orientation and motivated reasoning. This area is wide open to future researchers. There are at least five important areas to explore in future research. The first is to examine the different political variables that may influence the process of health information gathering and health attitudes and behavior. Second, future research should examine the psychological mechanisms involved in the processing of health information and misinformation exclusively among partisans. Third, the different strategies that may be successful in targeting partisans and understanding their health behavior should be studied. For example, Sylvester et al. (2023) explored if co-partisan source cues serve as an effective means to facilitate vaccination in right-leaning individuals. Their results showed that exposing middle-of-the-road partisans to pro-vaccine messages from co-partisan source cues reduced vaccine hesitancy. Fourth, strategies for correcting misinformation that may work across ideological lines should be explored. Finally, future research should study the different media literacy variables and their potential to work across different political orientations.

Although recent years have seen a significant increase in misinformation studies, this research does not always account for the impact of the politicization of health and science. For example, media literacy studies do not always examine if literacy can help individuals across party lines. This is important because recent research has shown that literacy may not be helpful for everyone (Borah et al., 2022). Similarly, in correction studies, it would be important to understand the role of motivated reasoning and information-processing, especially with issues that are politicized. It will be critical for future research to examine these dynamics so that solutions to combat misinformation can be successful. As mentioned earlier, it is not possible to eradicate misinformation and disinformation completely. Our goal should be to minimize their impact, and understanding the complex dynamics of the politicization of health and science is a crucial step forward.

References

Agley, J. (2020). Assessing changes in US public trust in science amid the COVID-19 pandemic. *Public Health*, *183*, 122–125. http://dx.doi.org/10.1016/j.puhe.2020.05.004

Agley, J., & Xiao, Y. (2021). Misinformation about COVID-19: Evidence for differential latent profiles and a strong association with trust in science. *BMC Public Health*, *21*, 1–12. https://doi.org/10.1186/s12889-020-10103-x

Amodio, D. M., Jost, J. T., Master, S. L., & Yee, C. M. (2007). Neurocognitive correlates of liberalism and conservatism. *Nature Neuroscience*, *10*(10), 1246–1247. https://doi.org/10.1038/nn1979

Ardèvol-Abreu, A., Hooker, C. M., & Gil de Zúñiga, H. (2017). Online news creation, trust in the media, and political participation: Direct and moderating effects over time. *Journalism*, *19*(5), 611–631.

Balcetis, E., & Dunning, D. (2006). See what you want to see: Motivational influences on visual perception. *Journal of Personality and Social Psychology*, *91*(4), 612–625. https://psycnet.apa.org/doi/10.1037/0022-3514.91.4.612

Blair, R. A., Morse, B. S., & Tsai, L. L. (2017). Public health and public trust: Survey evidence from the Ebola virus disease epidemic in Liberia. *Social Science & Medicine*, *172*, 89–97. http://dx.doi.org/10.1016/j.socscimed.2016.11.016

Bode, L., & Vraga, E. K. (2018). See something, say something: Correction of global health misinformation on social media. *Health Communication*, *33*(9), 1131–1140. http://dx.doi.org/10.1080/10410236.2017.1331312

Bolsen, T., & Druckman, J. N. (2015). Counteracting the politicization of science. *Journal of Communication*, *65*(5), 745–769. http://dx.doi.org/10.1111/jcom.12171

Borah, P. (2022). The moderating role of political ideology: Need for cognition, media locus of control, misinformation efficacy, and misperceptions about COVID-19. *International Journal of Communication*, *16*, 26.

Borah, P., Austin, E., & Su, Y. (2023). Injecting disinfectants to kill the virus: The role of literacy, information gathering sources, credibility perceptions, and political ideology on misinformation perceptions about COVID-19. *Mass Communication and Society*, *26*(4), 566–592. http://dx.doi.org/10.1080/15205436.2022.2045324

Borah, P., Ghosh, S., Hwang, J., Shah, D. V., & Brauer, M. (2024). Red media vs. blue media: Social distancing and partisan news media use during the COVID-19 pandemic. *Health Communication*, *39*(2), 417–427. http://dx.doi.org/10.1080/10410236.2023.2167584

Borah, P., Kim, S., & Hsu, Y. C. (2022). "Masks do not work": COVID-19 misperceptions and theory-driven corrective strategies on Facebook. *Online Information Review*, *47*(5), 880–905. http://dx.doi.org/10.1108/OIR-11-2021-0600

Borah, P., Kim, S., Xiao, X., & Lee, D. K. L. (2021). Correcting misinformation using theory-driven messages: HPV vaccine misperceptions, information seeking, and the moderating role of reflection. *Atlantic Journal of Communication*, *30*(3), 316–331. http://dx.doi.org/10.1080/15456870.2021.1912046

Borges do Nascimento, I. J. B., Pizarro, A. B., Almeida, J. M., Azzopardi-Muscat, N., Gonçalves, M. A., Björklund, M., & Novillo-Ortiz, D. (2022). Infodemics and health misinformation: A systematic review of reviews. *Bulletin of the World Health Organization*, *100*(9), 544–561. https://doi.org/10.2471%2FBLT.21.287654

Bridgman, A., Merkley, E., Loewen, P. J., Owen, T., Ruths, D., Teichmann, L., & Zhilin, O. (2020). The causes and consequences of COVID-19 misperceptions: Understanding the role of news and social media. *Harvard Kennedy School Misinformation Review*, *1*(3). https://doi.org/10.37016/mr-2020-028

Chaiken, S., Giner-Sorolla, R., & Chen, S. (1996). Beyond accuracy: Defense and impression motives in heuristic and systematic information processing. In P. M. Gollwitzer & J. A. Bargh (Eds.), *The psychology of action: Linking cognition and motivation to behavior* (pp. 553–578). Guilford Press.

Chan, E. Y., & Palmeira, M. (2021). Political ideology moderates consumer response to brand crisis apologies for data breaches. *Computers in Human Behavior*, *121*, 106801. https://doi.org/10.1016/j.chb.2021.106801

Chan, M. P. S., Jones, C. R., Hall Jamieson, K., & Albarracín, D. (2017). Debunking: A meta-analysis of the psychological efficacy of messages countering misinformation. *Psychological Science*, *28*(11), 1531–1546. http://dx.doi.org/10.1177/0956797617714579

Compton, J., Jackson, B., & Dimmock, J. A. (2016). Persuading others to avoid persuasion: Inoculation theory and resistant health attitudes. *Frontiers in Psychology*, *7*, 122. http://dx.doi.org/10.3389/fpsyg.2016.00122

Craft, S., Maksl, A., & Ashley, S. (2013). *Measuring news media literacy*. Robert R. https://core.ac.uk/download/pdf/61726967.pdf

Federico, C. M., Deason, G., & Fisher, E. L. (2012). Ideological asymmetry in the relationship between epistemic motivation and political attitudes. *Journal of Personality and Social Psychology*, *103*(3), 381–398.

Fowler, E. F., & Gollust, S. E. (2015). The content and effect of politicized health controversies. *Annals of the American Academy of Political and Social Science*, *658*(1), 155–171. https://doi.org/10.1177/0002716214555505

Fowler, E. F., Nagler, R. H., Banka, D., & Gollust, S. E. (2022). Effects of politicized media coverage: Experimental evidence from the HPV vaccine and COVID-19. *Progress in Molecular Biology and Translational Science*, *188*(1), 101–134. http://dx.doi.org/10.1016/bs.pmbts.2021.11.008

Freelon, D., & Wells, C. (2020). Disinformation as political communication. *Political Communication*, *37*(2), 145–156. https://doi.org/10.1080/10584609.2020.1723755

Galbraith-Gyan, K. V., Lechuga, J., Jenerette, C. M., Palmer, M. H., Moore, A. D., & Hamilton, J. B. (2019). African-American parents' and daughters' beliefs about HPV infection and the HPV vaccine. *Public Health Nursing*, *36*(2), 134–143. http://dx.doi.org/10.1111/phn.12565

Garrett, R. K., Long, J. A., & Jeong, M. S. (2019). From partisan media to misperception: Affective polarization as mediator. *Journal of Communication*, *69*(5), 490–512.

Gauchat, G. (2012). Politicization of science in the public sphere: A study of public trust in the United States, 1974 to 2010. *American Sociological Review*, *77*(2), 167–187. http://dx.doi.org/10.1177/0003122412438225

Gollwitzer, A., Martel, C., Brady, W. J., Pärnamets, P., Freedman, I. G., Knowles, E. D., & Van Bavel, J. J. (2020). Partisan differences in physical distancing are linked to health outcomes during the COVID-19 pandemic. *Nature Human Behaviour*, *4*(11), 1186–1197. http://dx.doi.org/10.1038/s41562-020-00977-7

Guess, A. M., Lerner, M., Lyons, B., Montgomery, J. M., Nyhan, B., Reifler, J., & Sircar, N. (2020). A digital media literacy intervention increases discernment between mainstream and false news in the United States and India. *PNAS*, *117*(27), 15536–15545.

Han, J., & Lee, E. J. (2023). Polarization or mainstreaming? How COVID-19 news exposure affects perceived seriousness of the pandemic and the susceptibility to COVID-19 misinformation? *Science Communication*, *45*(3). http://dx.doi.org/10.1177/10755470231186396

Himelboim, I., Lee, J. J., Cacciatore, M. A., Kim, S., Krause, D., Miller-Bains, K., Mattson, K., & Reynolds, J. (2023). Vaccine support and hesitancy on Twitter: Opposing views, similar strategies, and the mixed impact of conspiracy theories. In *Vaccine Communication Online: Counteracting Misinformation, Rumors and Lies* (pp. 81–101). Springer. https://doi.org/10.1007/978-3-031-24490-2_5

Himelboim, I., Xiao, X., Lee, D. K. L., Wang, M. Y., & Borah, P. (2020). A social networks approach to understanding vaccine conversations on Twitter: Network clusters, sentiment, and certainty in HPV social networks. *Health Communication*, *35*(5), 607–615. https://doi.org/10.1080/10410236.2019.1573446

Hong, Y., Wan, M., & Li, Z. (2021). Understanding the health information sharing behavior of social media users: an empirical study on WeChat. *Journal of Organizational and End User Computing (JOEUC)*, *33*(5), 180–203. https://doi.org/10.4018/JOEUC.20210901.oa9

Hubner, A. (2021). How did we get here? A framing and source analysis of early COVID-19 media coverage. *Communication Research Reports*, *38*(2), 112–120. http://dx.doi.org/10.1080/08824096.2021.1894112

Husain, F., Shahnawaz, M. G., Khan, N. H., Parveen, H., & Savani, K. (2021). Intention to get COVID-19 vaccines: Exploring the role of attitudes, subjective norms, perceived behavioral control, belief in COVID-19 misinformation, and vaccine confidence in Northern India. *Human Vaccines & Immunotherapeutics*, *17*(11), 3941–3953. http://dx.doi.org/10.1080/21645515.2021.1967039

Hwang, Y., & Jeong, S. H. (2023). Misinformation exposure and acceptance: The role of information seeking and processing. *Health Communication*, *38*(3), 585–593. http://dx.doi.org/10.1080/10410236.2021.1964187

Islam, A. N., Laato, S., Talukder, S., & Sutinen, E. (2020). Misinformation sharing and social media fatigue during COVID-19: An affordance and cognitive load perspective. *Technological Forecasting and Social Change*, *159*, 120201. http://dx.doi.org/10.1016/j.techfore.2020.120201

Jennings, W., Stoker, G., Bunting, H., Valgarðsson, V. O., Gaskell, J., Devine, D., ... Mills, M. C. (2021). Lack of trust, conspiracy beliefs, and social media use predict COVID-19 vaccine hesitancy. *Vaccine*, *9*(6), 593. http://dx.doi.org/10.3390/vaccines9060593

Ji, Y. (2021). Exposure to "vaccination selfies" relate to readers' vaccination intention: The moderating role of partisan media use and the mediating role of affective responses. *Journal of Health Communication*, *26*(12), 867–876. http://dx.doi.org/10.1080/10810730.2021.2025174

Jiang, X., Hwang, J., Su, M. H., Wagner, M. W., & Shah, D. (2022). Ideology and COVID-19 vaccination intention: Perceptual mediators and communication moderators. *Journal of Health Communication*, *27*(6), 416–426. http://dx.doi.org/10.1080/10810730.2022.2117438

Jost, J. T., Glaser, J., Kruglanski, A. W., & Sulloway, F. J. (2003). Exceptions that prove the rule—Using a theory of motivated social cognition to account for ideological incongruities and political anomalies: Reply to Greenberg and Jonas (2003). *Psychological Bulletin*, *129*(3), 383–393. https://psycnet.apa.org/doi/10.1037/0033-2909.129.3.383

Kareklas, I., Bhattacharya, D., Muehling, D. D., & Kisekka, V. (2023). Reexamining health messages in the political age: The politicization of the COVID-19 pandemic and its detrimental effects on vaccine hesitancy. *Journal of Consumer Affairs*, *57*(3), 1120–1150. http://dx.doi.org/10.1111/joca.12553

Kim, K., Lee, C. J., Ihm, J., & Kim, Y. (2022). A comprehensive examination of association between belief in vaccine misinformation and vaccination intention in the COVID-19 context. *Journal of Health Communication*, *27*(7), 495–509. http://dx.doi.org/10.1080/10810730.2022.2130479

Lee, S. J., Lee, C. J., & Hwang, H. (2022). The role of deliberative cognitive styles in preventing belief in politicized COVID-19 misinformation. *Health Communication*, *38*, 13, 2904–2914. http://dx.doi.org/10.1080/10410236.2022.2125119

Lewandowsky, S., Ecker, U. K., Seifert, C. M., Schwarz, N., & Cook, J. (2012). Misinformation and its correction: Continued influence and successful debiasing. *Psychological Science in the Public Interest*, *13*(3), 106–131.

Li, Y. J., Cheung, C. M., Shen, X. L., & Lee, M. K. (2019). Health misinformation on social media: A literature review. *PACIS 2019 Proceedings*, 194. https://aisel.aisnet.org/pacis2019/194

Li, Y. J., Marga, J. J., Cheung, C. M., Shen, X. L., & Lee, M. (2022). Health misinformation on social media: A systematic literature review and future research directions. *AIS Transactions on Human-Computer Interaction*, *14*(2), 116–149. http://dx.doi.org/10.17705/1thci.00164

Lodge, M., & Hamill, R. (1986). A partisan schema for political information processing. *American Political Science Review*, *80*(2), 505–519. https://doi.org/10.2307/1958271

Long, G. M., & Toppino, T. C. (2004). Enduring interest in perceptual ambiguity: Alternating views of reversible figures. *Psychological Bulletin*, *130*(5), 748–768.

Luo, Y., & Cheng, Y. (2021). The presumed influence of COVID-19 misinformation on social media: Survey research from two countries in the global health crisis. *International Journal of Environmental Research and Public Health*, *18*(11), 5505. https://doi.org/10.3390/ijerph18115505

Margolin, D. B., Hannak, A., & Weber, I. (2018). Political fact-checking on Twitter: When do corrections have an effect? *Political Communication*, *35*(2), 196–219. http://dx.doi.org/10.1080/10584609.2017.1334018

Marwick, A., & Lewis, R. (2017). Media manipulation and disinformation online. *Data & Society*. https://datasociety.net/library/media-manipulation-and-disinfo-online/

Miller, J. M. (2020). Psychological, political, and situational factors combine to boost COVID-19 conspiracy theory beliefs. *Canadian Journal of Political Science/Revue Canadienne de Science Politique*, *53*(2), 327–334. http://dx.doi.org/10.1017/S000842392000058X

Moon, W. K., Chung, M., & Jones-Jang, S. M. (2023). How can we fight partisan biases in the COVID-19 pandemic? AI source labels on fact-checking messages reduce motivated reasoning. *Mass Communication and Society*, *26*(4), 646–670. http://dx.doi.org/10.1080/15205436.2022.2097926

Motta, M. (2021). Republicans, not Democrats, are more likely to endorse anti-vaccine misinformation. *American Politics Research*, *49*(5), 428–438. http://dx.doi.org/10.1177/1532673X211022639

Motta, M., & Stecula, D. (2023). The effects of partisan media in the face of global pandemic: How news shaped COVID-19 vaccine hesitancy. *Political Communication*, *40*(5), 505–526. http://dx.doi.org/10.1080/10584609.2023.2187496

Motta, M., Stecula, D., & Farhart, C. (2020). How right-leaning media coverage of COVID-19 facilitated the spread of misinformation in the early stages of the pandemic in the US. *Canadian Journal of Political Science / Revue Canadienne de Science Politique*, *53*(2), 335–342. https://doi.org/10.1017/S0008423920000396

Muric, G., Wu, Y., & Ferrara, E. (2021). COVID-19 vaccine hesitancy on social media: Building a public Twitter data set of antivaccine content, vaccine misinformation, and conspiracies. *JMIR Public Health and Surveillance*, *7*(11), e30642. http://dx.doi.org/10.2196/30642

Nan, X., Wang, Y., & Thier, K. (2022). Why people believe health misinformation and who are at risk? A systematic review of individual differences in susceptibility to health misinformation. *Social Science & Medicine*, *314*, 115398. http://dx.doi.org/10.1016/j.socscimed.2022.115398

Nyhan, B., & Reifler, J. (2010). When corrections fail: The persistence of political misperceptions. *Political Behavior*, *32*(2), 303–330. http://dx.doi.org/10.1007/s11109-010-9112-2

Pak, A., McBryde, E., & Adegboye, O. A. (2021). Does high public trust amplify compliance with stringent COVID-19 government health guidelines? A multi-country analysis using data from 102,627 individuals. *Risk Management and Healthcare Policy*, 293–302. http://dx.doi.org/10.2147/RMHP.S278774

Peng, W., Lim, S., & Meng, J. (2022). Persuasive strategies in online health misinformation: A systematic review. *Information, Communication & Society*, *26*(11), 2131–2148. https://doi.org/10.1080/1369118X.2022.2085615

Reedy, J., Wells, C., & Gastil, J. (2014). How voters become misinformed: An investigation of the emergence and consequences of false factual beliefs. *Social Science Quarterly*, *95*(5), 1399–1418. https://doi.org/10.1111/ssqu.12102

Romer, D., & Jamieson, K. H. (2021). Conspiratorial thinking, selective exposure to conservative media, and response to COVID-19 in the US. *Social Science & Medicine*, *291*, 114480. http://dx.doi.org/10.1016/j.socscimed.2021.114480

Roozenbeek, J., Van Der Linden, S., Goldberg, B., Rathje, S., & Lewandowsky, S. (2022). Psychological inoculation improves resilience against misinformation on social media. *Science Advances*, *8*(34), eabo6254. http://dx.doi.org/10.1126/sciadv.abo6254

Sangalang, A., Ophir, Y., & Cappella, J. N. (2019). The potential for narrative correctives to combat misinformation. *Journal of Communication*, *69*(3), 298–319. https://doi.org/10.1093/joc/jqz014

Saulsberry, L., Fowler, E. F., Nagler, R. H., & Gollust, S. E. (2019). Perceptions of politicization and HPV vaccine policy support. *Vaccine*, *37*(35), 5121–5128. http://dx.doi.org/10.1016/j.vaccine.2019.05.062

Schernhammer, E., Weitzer, J., Laubichler, M. D., Birmann, B. M., Bertau, M., Zenk, L., ... Steiner, G. (2022). Correlates of COVID-19 vaccine hesitancy in Austria: Trust and the government. *Journal of Public Health*, *44*(1), e106–e116. http://dx.doi.org/10.1093/pubmed/fdab122

Stroebe, W., vanDellen, M. R., Abakoumkin, G., Lemay, E. P., Schiavone, W. M., Agostini, M., Tan, A. S., Lee, C. J., & Chae, J. (2015). Exposure to health (mis) information: Lagged effects on young adults' health behaviors and potential pathways. *Journal of Communication*, *65*(4), 674–698. https://doi.org/10.1111/jcom.12163

Sylvester, S., Motta, M., Trujillo, K. L., & Callaghan, T. (2023). Vaccinating across the aisle: Using co-partisan source cues to encourage COVID-19 vaccine uptake in the ideological right. *Journal of Behavioral Medicine*, *46*(1–2), 311–323. http://dx.doi.org/10.1007/s10865-022-00323-4

Tan, A. S., Lee, C. J., & Chae, J. (2015). Exposure to health (mis) information: Lagged effects on young adults' health behaviors and potential pathways. *Journal of Communication*, *65*(4), 674–698. https://doi.org/10.1111/jcom.12163

Tanis, M., & Postmes, T. (2005). A social identity approach to trust: Interpersonal perception, group membership and trusting behaviour. *European Journal of Social Psychology*, *35*(3), 413–424. http://dx.doi.org/10.1002/ejsp.256

Van Scoy, L. J., Snyder, B., Miller, E. L., Toyobo, O., Grewel, A., Ha, G., Gillespie, S., Patel, M., Reilly, J., Zgierska, A. E., & Lennon, R. P. (2021). Public anxiety and distrust due to perceived politicization and media sensationalism during early COVID-19 media messaging. *Journal of Communication in Healthcare*, *14*(3), 193–205.

Vosoughi, S., Roy, D., & Aral, S. (2018). The spread of true and false news online. *Science*, *359*(6380), 1146–1151. https://doi.org/10.1126/science.aap9559

Vraga, E. K., & Bode, L. (2017a). I do not believe you: How providing a source corrects health misperceptions across social media platforms. *Information, Communication & Society*, *21*(10), 1337–1353. http://dx.doi.org/10.1080/1369118X.2017.1313883

Vraga, E. K., & Bode, L. (2017b). Using expert sources to correct health misinformation in social media. *Science Communication*, *39*(5), 621–645.

Vraga, E. K., Kim, S. C., & Cook, J. (2019). Testing logic-based and humor-based corrections for science, health, and political misinformation on social media. *Journal of Broadcasting & Electronic Media*, *63*(3), 393–414. http://dx.doi.org/10.1080/08838151.2019.1653102

Wang, Y., McKee, M., Torbica, A., & Stuckler, D. (2019). Systematic literature review on the spread of health-related misinformation on social media. *Social Science & Medicine*, *240*, 112552. http://dx.doi.org/10.1016/j.socscimed.2019.112552

Yan, K., Barbati, J. L., Duncan, K. L., Warner, E. L., & Rains, S. A. (2022). Russian troll vaccine misinformation dissemination on Twitter: The role of political partisanship. *Health Communication*, *38*(8), 1591–1600. https://doi.org/10.1080/10410236.2021.2021692

Zhang, J., Featherstone, J. D., Calabrese, C., & Wojcieszak, M. (2021). Effects of fact-checking social media vaccine misinformation on attitudes toward vaccines. *Preventive Medicine*, *145*, 106408. http://dx.doi.org/10.1016/j.ypmed.2020.106408

Zhang, Y., Chen, F., & Lukito, J. (2023). Network amplification of politicized information and misinformation about COVID-19 by conservative media and partisan influencers on Twitter. *Political Communication*, *40*(1), 24–47. http://dx.doi.org/10.1080/10584609.2022.2113844

7

Understanding and Mitigating Vaccine Misinformation on Social Media

Tong Lin, Yuan Wang, Kathryn Thier, and Xiaoli Nan

Department of Communication, University of Maryland

Health scholars and practitioners are concerned about the rapid spread of misinformation on health-related topics, including healthy habits and medical information for disease prevention (Nan et al., 2021; Wang et al., 2023). Social media provide an unprecedented opportunity for individuals and organizations to post, share, reshare, and seek information, thereby increasing health literacy and self-efficacy and aiding health decisions, especially during crises marked by information overload and uncertainty (Hong et al., 2021). However, their flexibility and accessibility have also enabled social media platforms to become conduits for the faster spread of misinformation compared to scientific information (Vosoughi et al., 2018). Recent survey results from the Health Information National Trends Survey (HINTS) (2022) show that over 50 percent of participants find it somewhat hard to distinguish true from false health information on social media. Additionally, approximately 33 percent of participants believe that the primary responsibility for reducing false or misleading health information on social media lies with the platforms (e.g., Twitter, or YouTube) themselves (HINTS, 2022).

Considered by the World Health Organization as one of the top 10 threats to global health, vaccine hesitancy is heavily impacted by the misinformation prevalent on social media and other information channels. Misinformation affects scientific knowledge about vaccine safety or effectiveness, vaccine perceptions, vaccine acceptance, and concerns about immunization against future diseases (Garett & Young, 2021). Achieving expected vaccination levels has become challenging because of the well-documented evidence of misinformation spreading widely, particularly through various social media platforms (Muric et al., 2021). While empirical data show that detecting misinformation is not an easy one-step effort, social media companies have taken measures to control the spread of misinformation about vaccines on their platforms (Puri et al., 2020; Skafle et al., 2022). Such efforts are evidenced in numerous studies on vaccines including the vaccines for SARS-CoV-2 (i.e., COVID-19; Muric et al., 2021), human papillomavirus infection (Wang et al., 2023), and influenza (Abrams & Greenhawt, 2020). Despite these efforts, the prevalence of vaccine misinformation on social media platforms has not diminished significantly. Therefore, scholars persist in exploring whether and how misinformation affects individuals' attitudes and behaviors

Communication and Misinformation: Crisis Events in the Age of Social Media, First Edition.
Edited by Kevin B. Wright.
© 2025 John Wiley & Sons, Inc. Published 2025 by John Wiley & Sons, Inc.

toward vaccines and vaccination. The recognition of the challenges involved in countering misinformation and its potential impacts on individuals continues to drive multiple research inquiries:

1) What are the characteristics of vaccine misinformation and what are the popular social media platforms known to disseminate vaccine misinformation?
2) Who is vulnerable to misinformation and how does it impact vaccine perceptions and acceptance?
3) What might be some strategies for countering vaccine misinformation on social media?

Before discussing and attempting to answer these questions, we first need to define what *health misinformation* is and how we—as individuals and as social media users—may detect whether a piece of information is false or misleading. "Health misinformation" is a broad term and includes a wide variety of definitions in the literature. According to a recent study that exclusively analyzed the existing definitions of health misinformation (Wang et al., 2022), health misinformation is "a health-related claim of fact that is currently false due to its contradiction to expert consensus and/or best available evidence at the time, inaccurate due to its use of incomplete evidence, or unsubstantiated due to a lack of evidence" (p. 11). Whether the false information is created with or without the intention of causing harm to individuals, social groups, or institutions is immaterial (Wang et al., 2022). Relying on this definition, we provide an overview of the prevalence of vaccine misinformation across various social media platforms and describe key message and diffusion characteristics. We then discuss factors that have been shown to influence individual susceptibility to vaccine misinformation, focusing on findings from empirical studies. Finally, we look into strategies and approaches for counteracting vaccine misinformation, including research initiatives and practical interventions. We conclude with proposed mitigation strategies for institutions and individuals in mitigating the impact of vaccine misinformation, particularly on social media.

Social Media Platforms and the Dissemination of Vaccine Misinformation

Following scholars who systematically reviewed the spread of health misinformation on social media (Wang et al., 2019; Wardle & Derakhshan, 2017), we identified three major components—sender, message, and receiver—involved in the creation, production, distribution, and reproduction process. In this section, we will examine the role played by each of the components in the spread of vaccine misinformation on a larger scale. This will involve an analysis of the patterns and characteristics of the misinformation circulating on social media.

Prevalence of Vaccine Misinformation on Social Media

The magnitude of health misinformation on social media remains unknown; however, empirical studies have found that vaccines and vaccination dominate the wide range of health topics on social media platforms. Suarez-Lledo and Alvarez-Galvez (2021) reviewed a number of articles focusing on health misinformation in social media and found that 32 percent (22 out of 69) of these were related to vaccines or were opposed to vaccination. These studies revealed that a significant portion of the information on social media was associated with misinformation, accounting for 43 percent of the content. Furthermore, HPV vaccine misinformation was identified as the most prevalent (e.g., Keelan et al., 2010). The large portion of studies about vaccine misinformation revealed not only the prevalence of vaccine misinformation but also the challenges of implementing misinformation prevention measures, especially among vulnerable populations. Although vaccine misinformation can impact many different areas (which we will discuss in the following sections), we can foresee that information plays a role in influencing individuals' decision-making process, specifically in their perceptions of vaccination, which could subsequently influence their behavioral intentions and actual behaviors.

Studies have shown that an extensive range of vaccine-related content is available on social media, particularly on platforms such as Twitter, now X (e.g., Broniatowski et al., 2018; Muric et al., 2021; Radzikowski et al., 2016), Facebook (e.g., Buchanan & Beckett, 2014; Schmidt et al., 2018; Yang et al., 2021), and YouTube (e.g., Basch et al., 2017; Li et al., 2022; Tuells et al., 2015). Basch et al.'s (2017) study found that a significant majority of the videos (65.5 percent of their study sample) advised against the use of vaccines and that the videos had a wide range of views with an average of approximately 62,000 views per video. Their findings highlighted the potential influence of vaccine misinformation on public opinion. The predominance of YouTube videos that discourage vaccination underscores the challenge faced by health professionals in combating vaccine misinformation.

Amid the diverse array of vaccines, HPV and COVID-19 vaccines have garnered the most attention and debate on social media, drawing significant interest from health practitioners and communication scholars alike. Regarding the HPV vaccine, scholars have highlighted the prevalence of negative content in online platforms, the significant impact of social media on public opinion, and the influences of mixed information on individuals' attitudes toward the vaccine, and they emphasize the need to address misinformation about HPV vaccines circulating on social media (e.g., Briones et al., 2012; Dunn et al., 2015; Dunn et al., 2017). In a study examining the nature of pro- and anti-HPV vaccine content on Instagram, Massey et al. (2020) found that nearly half of the HPV vaccine-related posts (44.1 percent) were anti-HPV vaccine. The posts were more likely to come from individuals and often included personal narratives. The mounting vaccine-related infodemic that proliferated during the COVID-19 pandemic has raised concerns about vaccine hesitancy and vaccine uptake (Loomba et al., 2021; Muric et al., 2021). Pierri et al.'s (2023) study revealed a concerning trend in the prevalence of COVID-19 vaccine misinformation on social media throughout 2021. While low-credibility information did not dominate mainstream news in terms of overall presence, the most popular sources of such misinformation had reshared volumes comparable to mainstream outlets and even exceeded those of authoritative health organizations such as the CDC and WHO. An alarming aspect was the identification of a small number of "super-spreaders," approximately 800 verified Twitter accounts, who were disproportionately responsible for the spread of this misinformation. These super-spreaders accounted for about 35 percent of all misinformation shares on an average day, with the top individual alone being responsible for over 13 percent of such retweets.

Characteristics of Vaccine Misinformation on Social Media

While recognizing that vaccine misinformation is prevalent on social media, we should also know about the characteristics of these types of information so that we can spot and respond in the appropriate way (Massey et al., 2020; Wang et al., 2023). We shall focus on two specific trends: descriptive features of the message (i.e., message content) and diffusion characteristics (i.e., durability and distribution of misinformation).

Message Characteristics. Instances of vaccine misinformation can be found circulating across social media platforms; for example, some claim a connection between 5G mobile networks and the virus, a theory without scientific basis (Ahmed et al., 2020), or that six individuals have died as a result of receiving the Pfizer-BioNTech COVID-19 vaccine (Reuters, 2020). In decoding this type of message, we notice two major components of the message content, sentiment and evidence, which have also been emphasized in previous studies detailing the characteristics of health misinformation (Nan et al., 2021). Regarding sentiment, vaccine misinformation tends to be more negative in tone than scientific messages (Xu and Guo, 2018). For instance, an anti-vaccine tweet with a negative tone would be "Another Childhood #Vaccine Link to #Autism: Dr. Andrew Wakefield has proven right again," whereas a pro-vaccine tweet with positive sentiment would state "Gardasil the vaccine that can prevent #cervical cancer in girls won FDA blessing as #vaccine to #prevent #anal #cancer" (Blankenship et al., 2018, p. 3). Negative sentiments arising from vaccine misinformation can provoke a range of emotional reactions such as fear, anger, worry, or empathy, particularly in relation to individuals who might have experienced adverse side effects from vaccination. Featherstone and Zhang's (2020) study highlighted that misinformation spread on social media can influence vaccine beliefs and behaviors, showing that exposure to vaccine misinformation can decrease pro-vaccination attitudes, with this effect mediated by emotions such as anger.

While misinformation tends to shift the focus from scientific facts to emotional arousal, studies have also underscored the common themes on which those messages are based. One theme is related to conspiracy theories or a search for truth regarding vaccinations. In Klimiuk et al.'s (2021) study, this theme was found to be the most dominant comment category of the analyzed Facebook posts. Several unique theories about the purposes of vaccination were prominent, which include "depopulation/genocide claims," "preparation for organ donation and global government control," and "microchips are inserted during COVID-19 vaccination" (Bok et al., 2023; Klimiuk et al., 2021). Other messages also involve comments suggesting that vaccination programs are driven solely by profit. These comments often implicate politicians, pharmaceutical companies, and health-care professionals as beneficiaries of this profiteering. Briones et al.'s (2012) study found that around 8.7 percent of the YouTube videos analyzed referenced a potential conspiracy theory concerning the HPV vaccine, implicating entities such as the government, pharmaceutical companies, or medical professionals. Another theme centers on personal stories or anecdotes (Nan et al., 2021). This type of misinformation is associated with several subcategories. One could be "falsehoods" such as claims of vaccinated people spreading diseases that they have gained immunity to or that any viral vaccine destroys the intestines (Bok et al., 2023; Frenkel et al., 2020). The other categories may include *vaccine effectiveness* and *harmed individuals/negative experiences.* A significant portion of content related to vaccine effectiveness often discusses potential adverse reactions to vaccines and suggests alternative medications. However, these messages typically lack scientific evidence or credible sources. For instance, Bok et al. (2023) cite examples such as claims that "COVID-19 vaccines could damage the spinal cord" or that "vitamins and minerals are as effective as COVID-19 vaccines" (p. 4). Klimiuk et al. (2021) also noted that claims of vaccine ineffectiveness in posts often include references to anti-vaccination "experts" to enhance credibility. Regarding personal harm and negative experiences, narratives frequently focus on children adversely affected by vaccinations. These accounts typically cite conditions such as autism, epilepsy, and convulsions (Gabis et al., 2022; Gawronski et al., 2022) along with perceived behavioral changes such as mental illness and mood variations (Skafle et al., 2022).

Diffusion Characteristics. The dissemination of vaccine misinformation on social media, although difficult to quantify precisely, is discernibly more prevalent compared to other vaccine-related communications (Wang et al., 2023). Research indicates that social media platforms such as Twitter, YouTube, and Facebook are predominant in spreading vaccine misinformation (Basch et al., 2017; Suarez-Lledo and Alvarez-Galvez, 2021). Chin et al. (2020) found that misinformation about HPV vaccines on Twitter spread through various cascades that differed in both time and size, implying a wider and more frequent dissemination compared to factual information. The COVID-19 pandemic underscored this trend, with numerous studies highlighting the rapid viral spread of misleading messages and their consequential impact on vaccination behavior. Notably, Kalichman et al. (2022) analyzed early 2020 Facebook posts, revealing that major anti-vaccine groups disseminated misinformation preceding the US government's Operation Warp Speed, outstripping public health messaging and adversely influencing the vaccine rollout. Furthermore, studies reveal that misinformation on YouTube channels often involves topics such as vaccines causing autism, undisclosed risks, adverse reactions, and the presence of thimerosal or mercury (Basch et al., 2017). Additionally, YouTube videos on the topic are frequently created by consumers, news outlets, and health professionals. Studies also indicated that automated accounts, or bots, and political activists on Twitter, as well as Russian troll accounts, play a role in disseminating anti-vaccine messages, creating an illusion of parity and challenging the consensus on vaccination acceptance (Broniatowski et al., 2018; Wawrzuta et al., 2021; Yousefinaghani et al., 2021).

Taking a further look at the activities initiated on social media platforms, empirical research indicates a higher propensity for misinformation to be interacted with via likes, shares, and comments (Wang et al., 2023; Xu and Guo, 2018). For instance, Daradkeh (2021) conducted a study examining the diffusion characteristics of COVID-19 vaccine misinformation on Twitter and found that the number of retweets was higher for tweets with negative sentiment than those with positive sentiment; tweets with negative sentiment had more likes than those with positive sentiment. Despite the growing interest in examining characteristics of vaccine misinformation and their dissemination, there is a need for more research to understand the factors that influence the spread of misinformation on social media platforms and how these factors affect people's engagement in discussions about the safety and efficacy of vaccines and the actions taken.

Summary

Overall, existing studies indicate a high prevalence of vaccine misinformation on social media, highlighting the potential challenges this poses to public health and underscoring the need for targeted interventions. We observed that misinformation, particularly about HPV and COVID-19 vaccines, tends to be shared more widely than factual information. Prominent platforms for this misinformation include X/Twitter, Facebook, and YouTube, where automated bots, political activists, and even Russian troll accounts play a significant role in dissemination. Our findings emphasize the challenges of countering vaccine misinformation and its potential impact on public perception and vaccine acceptance.

Impacts of Vaccine Misinformation and Susceptibility to Misinformation

Research about the prevalence and characteristics of vaccine misinformation on social media raises questions about the extent of its influence on vaccine perceptions, beliefs, and acceptance, and the factors that make people more susceptible to such misinformation. While public health professionals express growing concern about the potential adverse effects of vaccine misinformation on public acceptance, there remains limited empirical evidence linking exposure to misinformation with decreased vaccine uptake. However, growing evidence suggests that exposure to vaccine misinformation can significantly influence belief in misinformation and conspiracy theories, which in turn impact the decision to vaccinate.

Previous research indicates that exposure to vaccine misinformation or negative portrayals of vaccines can shape trust and belief in vaccines, thereby influencing motivation and the willingness to be vaccinated. Jennings et al. (2021) conducted a survey and focus groups in the UK and found that trust, belief in conspiracy theories, and misinformation disseminated through platforms such as YouTube significantly heighten vaccine hesitancy. Their study underscores the role of unregulated information sources in fostering distrust in vaccines and government health initiatives. Echoing these sentiments, Crouse and Dupuis (2022) found that COVID-19 misinformation encountered on social media could influence individual behaviors and heighten vaccine hesitancy. Additionally, Demuyakor et al. (2021) surveyed university students in Ghana and found that exposure to COVID-19 vaccine misinformation on social media incited fear and mistrust of vaccines. In the context of HPV vaccines, Dunn et al. (2015) found that exposure to negative tweets increased the likelihood of users expressing similar sentiments, demonstrating the sway of social media misinformation in shaping vaccine perceptions.

The impact of vaccine misinformation is more convincingly shown in experimental studies. Carrieri et al. (2019) used a quasi-experimental design to examine the impact of misinformation on immunization rates in Italy following a court ruling linking the measles, mumps, and rubella vaccine to autism. Their results indicated a decrease in child immunization rates across various vaccines as a result of the spread of misinformation. Similarly, Calo et al. (2021) conducted an experiment involving tweets to examine the influence of misinformation on HPV vaccination intentions among US parents, discovering that misinformation-laden tweets drastically reduced vaccination motivation. Loomba et al. (2021) conducted experiments and found that exposure to misinformation about COVID-19 vaccines lowered participants' vaccination intentions both in the United States and the United Kingdom.

Collectively, these studies underscore the profound impact of social media misinformation on public perception and acceptance of vaccines and the need for effective communication strategies to counteract misinformation and foster trust in vaccination campaigns. However, it should be noted that overemphasizing the impact of the anti-vaccination movement may inadvertently amplify the very anti-vaccination messages health professionals seek to mitigate. For example, Edelstein et al. (2020) examined the relationship between anti-vaccine views and the reduction in childhood immunization rates in England. Their results showed inconsistent trends in vaccine coverage, including a notable rise in vaccine confidence during the period examined. Their study suggested that vaccine coverage trends may be influenced by elements beyond anti-vaccination attitudes. Therefore, understanding what drives differences in susceptibility to misinformation is crucial.

So, what factors contribute to the varying impact of health misinformation? Through in-depth systematic reviews, Nan et al. (2022, 2023) suggest that susceptibility to health misinformation is driven by various psychological processes. For instance, individuals equipped with extensive scientific knowledge and with advanced literacy, numeracy, and analytical thinking abilities, coupled with high trust in science, generally exhibit a stronger resistance to health misinformation (Nan et al., 2022, 2023). Conversely, a propensity for conspiracy thinking, religious beliefs, adherence to conservative ideologies, and alignment with conservative political parties correlate with increased susceptibility to such misinformation (Nan et al., 2022, 2023). Demographic characteristics also matter: susceptibility to misinformation diminishes with age and higher educational attainment, while members of racial minority groups appear more vulnerable to its influence (Nan et al., 2022, 2023). Additionally, these studies highlight a behavioral pattern: reliance on information from professional health sources tends to reduce susceptibility to health misinformation, whereas frequent engagement with social media has been found to heighten it (Nan et al., 2022, 2023).

Acknowledging the necessity for further study into how vaccine misinformation on social media impacts public perception, researchers have examined how specific vaccines affect different vulnerable groups. Riad et al. (2021) found that COVID-19 vaccine hesitancy was more common among university students who relied on social media for information, held personal beliefs or misconceptions about immunity, had prior COVID-19 infections, harbored doubts about vaccine safety and efficacy, or were suspicious about the local availability of the vaccines. While the study did not explicitly link misinformation exposure to vaccine hesitancy or uptake, it suggested that vaccine safety concerns were closely tied to misinformation exposure on social media, particularly among university students. Moreover, Loomba et al. (2021) suggested that the impact of exposure to misinformation varied across different sociodemographic groups. For example, in the United States, females were more susceptible to misinformation about COVID-19 vaccines than males where it pertained to their decision to get vaccinated to protect others. In the United Kingdom, individuals identifying as Christians were found to be more vulnerable to COVID-19 vaccine misinformation compared to those of other religious affiliations (Loomba et al., 2021). Furthermore, Ngai et al. (2022) identified that safety concerns were the most prevalent theme negatively impacting social media engagement, such as liking or sharing posts. Their study highlighted concerns about the dissemination of misinformation through posts that imitate the style and language of news or scientific reports, noting that such imitation positively influences user engagement. This underscores the complexity and nuances in the spread and impact of health misinformation.

Summary

Understanding vaccine misinformation on social media is critical because it significantly impacts public perceptions and vaccine acceptance. Empirical studies have demonstrated that misinformation can shape trust and beliefs about vaccines, leading to increased hesitancy, especially when it originates from popular social media platforms such as YouTube and X/Twitter. This hesitancy is further exacerbated by factors such as personal beliefs, reliance on social media for information, and misconceptions about vaccine safety and efficacy. Reviews indicate that individuals with higher scientific literacy and analytical thinking skills are less susceptible to misinformation, while those prone to conspiracy thinking and certain ideological beliefs are more vulnerable. These studies collectively suggest that tackling health misinformation requires a nuanced understanding of the psychological, demographic, and behavioral dimensions that influence individuals' acceptance of such information. More importantly, there is a need for the development of effective communication strategies and public health interventions tailored to address the impacts of vaccine misinformation on vulnerable populations.

Strategies for Counteracting Vaccine Misinformation on Social Media

Despite the limited evidence that vaccine misinformation on social media directly leads to a reduction in vaccination rates, public health researchers and professionals are rightly concerned about the potential of online misinformation to compromise vaccination efforts. Existing studies have emphasized two main approaches in mitigating the spread or impact of health misinformation with varying degrees of success: correcting misinformation through strategic communication interventions (e.g., Walter & Murphy, 2018) and building inoculating resistance against the influence of misinformation (e.g., Iles et al., 2021).

Regarding correction methods, studies have shown mixed findings. Nyhan et al. (2014) conducted a two-wave online survey experiment with a large sample of US parents whose children were aged 17 years or younger. Participants were randomly assigned to one of the four intervention groups, with one being CDC information debunking the MMR–autism link. While the refutation of the MMR–autism link effectively reduced false beliefs about vaccines causing autism, it paradoxically decreased vaccination intent among parents with the least favorable attitudes toward vaccines. The findings suggest that prevailing public health communications about vaccines may not be effective and, in some cases, may worsen misconceptions or reduce vaccination intent. Bautista et al. (2023) examined the impact of six different social correction methods on the willingness of vaccine skeptics to receive the COVID-19 vaccine. The study found that, when vaccine skeptics were exposed to corrections using the priming method by any corrector, their intention to take the COVID-19 vaccine increased but only if they perceived the information to be trustworthy. Additionally, among participants with moderate vaccine skepticism, the study found that exposure to either priming (regardless of corrector) or rebuttal corrections (by either an ordinary person or a medical doctor) positively influenced their intention to receive the vaccine, provided they viewed the corrector as an expert. In another experimental study, Nyhan and Reifler (2015) found that the corrective information from the CDC successfully reduced belief in the myth and concerns about flu vaccine safety. However, it also unintentionally decreased the willingness to be vaccinated among participants who were already highly concerned about vaccine side effects. This reduction in vaccination intent was not seen in those with low concern levels. This finding aligns with previous research on misperceptions about the MMR vaccine, indicating that merely correcting myths about vaccines might not be an effective method to boost immunization rates. This suggests the need for more nuanced approaches in public health communication strategies to address vaccine hesitancy and misconceptions.

Proactive measures such as the development of preinterventions are also found to be effective strategies for enhancing public resilience to vaccine misinformation. Wong (2016) evaluated the effectiveness of two distinct inoculation messages in safeguarding against persuasive claims challenging the efficacy and safety of the HPV vaccine. The findings revealed that general inoculation messages affirming the safety and efficacy of vaccines overall (i.e., promoting the idea that all vaccines are safe and effective) were equally effective in counteracting negative messages specifically about the HPV vaccine as the inoculation messages that were specifically tailored to the HPV vaccine (i.e., asserting that the HPV vaccine is safe and effective). Other scholars have also emphasized the need for proactive efforts in addressing the escalating issue of vaccine misinformation. For instance, van der Linden et al. (2021) stressed the importance of applying inoculation messages that focus on the medical consensus regarding the safety and efficacy of vaccines. Vivion et al.'s (2022) study also concluded that prebunking messages can be an effective public health communication strategy to counteract vaccine misinformation and improve vaccination intentions, particularly among older populations who have a higher susceptibility to disease.

Some research has explored the effects of efforts by social media companies to stem the distribution of vaccine misinformation. For instance, Walter et al. (2021) found that the effectiveness of real-time corrections, community-based fact checking, and algorithmic identification of false claims was notably higher when participants had an existing interest in the health topic, when misinformation originated from news sources (as opposed to peers), and when it was debunked by experts rather than laypersons. Similarly, Whitehead et al. (2023) conducted a systematic review of nine widely used communication interventions aimed at combating vaccine misinformation. Their findings suggest that some strategies, such as communicating with certainty, might have counterproductive effects. Conversely, promising strategies include communicating the weight of evidence, highlighting scientific consensus, employing humor appeals, and providing warnings about encountering misinformation. The results from these reviews not only provide a snapshot of the current research landscape but also offer targeted recommendations for more effectively combating the spread of health misinformation on social media.

Summary

Existing research about strategies to counter vaccine misinformation on social media highlights the complexity and mixed effectiveness of these approaches. Key studies such as Nyhan et al. (2014) and Bautista et al. (2023) show that, while debunking myths can reduce misperceptions, it oftentimes paradoxically lowers vaccination intent. In contrast, inoculation strategies saffirming the general safety and efficacy of vaccines, as examined by Wong (2016) and others, are effective in countering misinformation. However, the success of these strategies often depends on the trustworthiness and perceived expertise of the source. These findings underscore the importance of using credible sources and effective communication strategies in public health messaging, especially in addressing vaccine skepticism on social media platforms.

Directions for Future Research

The emerging body of research on vaccine-related misinformation on social media, especially on platforms such as YouTube, X/Twitter, and Facebook has begun to show the influence such content can have on public opinion. Future studies should look into the dynamics of information discourse, particularly focusing on the predominance of anti-vaccination narratives and their impact on public health. Furthermore, research is needed about how combating online vaccine misinformation fits within a larger accessibility acceptance framework for countering health misinformation more generally (Nan et al., 2023). In terms of accessibility, Nan et al. (2023) suggest decreasing the accessibility of health misinformation and increasing the accessibility of reliable health information. Similarly, they propose an exploration of efforts to decrease susceptibility to health misinformation and increase the acceptability of reliable health information. In these veins, we suggest potential directions for future research.

Decreasing Accessibility of Online Vaccine Misinformation

An important strategy in the quest to mitigate the pervasive spread of vaccine misinformation on social media is to decrease its accessibility. This involves a multifaceted approach that engages both social media platforms and public health authorities. Key approaches include the refinement of algorithms by social media companies to identify and limit the spread of misinformation (de Beer & Matthee, 2020). This requires the development of more sophisticated AI tools that are capable of distinguishing between misinformation and legitimate discourse. Collaboration with health experts would ensure that content moderation policies are grounded in scientific accuracy. Moreover, there is a need for transparent reporting systems for social media users to flag misleading content and for these systems to be bolstered by response teams that can assess and act on these reports. These measures, combined with the promotion of verified information through targeted advertising and suggested content, can potentially reduce the accessibility of vaccine misinformation (Jamison et al., 2020). By reducing the ease of access to misinformation, we can create a digital environment that favors informed decision making and public trust in vaccines.

Increasing Accessibility of Reliable Online Vaccine Information

Collaborative approaches involving health-care institutions, social media companies, and public health organizations are needed to evaluate the effectiveness of strategic interventions aimed at promoting factual, science-based information about vaccines and their safety. Additionally, given the influence of vaccine misinformation on public perception (Leader et al., 2021) and the limited participation of the medical community in vaccine discussions on social media, there is a need for further research on how health-care professionals can more effectively engage in public health education on social media and whether there are barriers to their engagement and strategies to increase their presence and influence in these conversations. Future studies could explore strategies for health-care providers to actively participate in online discourse, perhaps through creating or endorsing informative content that addresses common misconceptions and provides evidence-based information about vaccines.

Decreasing Susceptibility to Online Vaccine Misinformation

Research should continue to dissect the themes and communication strategies of vaccine misinformation, as identified in studies such as Massey et al. (2020) and Ngai et al. (2022). This could involve an analysis of the use of specific hashtags, claims, and narrative styles in spreading misinformation and how these elements resonate with different audience segments. Following Loomba et al.'s (2021) findings on the polarization of vaccine discourse on platforms such as Twitter, future research should investigate the drivers of this polarization. Understanding the role of political and nonmedical influencers in shaping vaccine-related discussions could inform strategies to mitigate their impact. Past reviews (Nan et al., 2022;

Walter et al., 2021; Wang et al., 2023) have indicated that health misinformation research has been predominantly conducted within Western contexts, particularly in the United States. Future research with a more culturally diverse sample is needed to examine whether and how the impact of and susceptibility to vaccine misinformation varies across groups with different cultural backgrounds. Such efforts are crucial for developing culturally sensitive interventions against vaccine misinformation. Investigating the efficacy of various forms of corrective information in altering vaccine hesitancy would be valuable. This includes exploring how different demographics respond to such corrections and identifying the most effective methods for changing misconceptions. While extensive research has been conducted on the impact of misinformation and corrective interventions on public perceptions about vaccines, there is a notable gap in understanding how these perceptions translate into actual behavioral outcomes (Wang et al., 2023; Whitehead et al., 2023). This highlights a critical need for future research not only to assess beliefs and intentions but also to measure the direct impact of misinformation and corrective interventions on real-world vaccine uptake.

Increasing Acceptability of Reliable Vaccine Information Online

While empirical evidence indicates that social media interventions may yield a mix of both positive and negative impacts on vaccine acceptance and uptake, research underscores the importance of refining the approach to social media to effectively improve vaccination rates. Information disseminated through social media requires strict monitoring for accuracy and reliability by competent authorities and health-care professionals. This vigilance paves the way for social media to become a powerful channel for circulating vaccine information and advancing immunization coverage. Future research should focus on developing methods to proficiently surveil media narratives of vaccines and develop strategic interventions to bolster the surveillance and analysis of vaccine acceptance and adherence rates.

Concluding Remarks

Our chapter presents the pervasiveness of vaccine misinformation on social platforms as a significant challenge to public health efforts. The findings from various studies underscore the complexities of public perception shaped by misinformation and the resultant vaccine hesitancy that arises. These studies reveal the intricate web of psychological, demographic, and behavioral factors that influence individuals' reception of misinformation. The mixed outcomes of interventions to combat the issue highlight the need for reliable resources and communication strategies that resonate with the target audience. Enhancing public health education on social media requires a multifaceted approach, leveraging trustworthy information and engaging health-care professionals to mitigate the impact of misinformation and promote vaccine uptake.

References

Abrams, E. M., & Greenhawt, M. (2020). Mitigating misinformation and changing the social narrative. *The Journal of Allergy and Clinical Immunology: In Practice*, *8*(10), 3261–3263. http://dx.doi.org/10.1016/j.jaip.2020.08.001

Ahmed, W., Vidal-Alaball, J., Downing, J., & Seguí, F. L. (2020). COVID-19 and the 5G conspiracy theory: Social network analysis of Twitter data. *Journal of Medical Internet Research*, *22*(5), e19458. http://dx.doi.org/10.2196/19458

Basch, C. H., Zybert, P., Reeves, R., & Basch, C. E. (2017). What do popular YouTube videos say about vaccines? *Child: Care, Health and Development*, *43*(4), 499–503. http://dx.doi.org/10.1111/cch.12442

Bautista, J. R., Zhang, Y., & Gwizdka, J. (2023). Correcting vaccine misinformation on social media: Effect of social correction methods on vaccine skeptics' intention to take COVID-19 vaccine. New Media & Society. http://dx.doi.org/10.1177/14614448231169697

Blankenship, E. B., Goff, M. E., Yin, J., Tse, Z. T. H., Fu, K.-W., Liang, H., Saroha, N., & Fung, I. C.-H. (2018). Sentiment, contents, and retweets: A study of two vaccine-related twitter datasets. *The Permanente Journal*, *22*(3), 17–138. http://dx.doi.org/10.7812/TPP/17-123

Bok, S., Martin, D., Acosta, E., Shum, J., Harvie, J., & Lee, M. (2023). Psychometric development of the COVID-19 vaccine misinformation scale and effects on vaccine hesitancy. *Preventive Medicine Reports*, *31*, 102087. http://dx.doi.org/10.1016/j.pmedr.2023.102087

Briones, R., Nan, X., Madden, K., & Waks, L. (2012). When vaccines go viral: An analysis of HPV vaccine coverage on YouTube. *Health Communication*, *27*(5), 478–485. http://dx.doi.org/10.1080/10410236.2011.610258

Broniatowski, D. A., Jamison, A. M., Qi, S., AlKulaib, L., Chen, T., Benton, A., et al. (2018). Weaponized health communication: Twitter bots and Russian trolls amplify the vaccine debate. *American Journal of Public Health*, *108*(10), 1378–1384. http://dx.doi.org/10.2105/AJPH.2018.304567

Buchanan, R., & Beckett, R. D. (2014). Assessment of vaccination-related information for consumers available on Facebook. *Health Information and Libraries Journal*, *31*(3), 227–234. http://dx.doi.org/10.1111/hir.12080

Calo, W. A., Gilkey, M. B., Shah, P. D., Dyer, A. M., Margolis, M. A., Dailey, S. A., & Brewer, N. T. (2021). Misinformation and other elements in HPV vaccine tweets: An experimental comparison. *Journal of Behavioral Medicine*, *44*, 310–319. http://dx.doi.org/10.1007/s10865-020-00197-0

Carrieri, V., Madio, L., & Principe, F. (2019). Vaccine hesitancy and (fake) news: Quasi-experimental evidence from Italy. *Health Economics*, *28*(11), 1377–1382. http://dx.doi.org/10.1002/hec.3937

Chin, J., Chin, C. L., Panday, S., Ghazanfari, A., Jagadeesan, G., Wang, Z., Ontengco, A., Chang, A., Liu, B., Schwartz, A., & Caskey, R. (2020). Tracking the human papillomavirus vaccine risk misinformation: An explorative study to examine how the misinformation has spread in user-generated content. *Human Factors and Ergonomics Society*, *9*(1), 312–316. http://dx.doi.org/10.1177/2327857920091069

Crouse, L., & Dupuis, M. (2022, September). A dangerous infodemic: An examination of the impact social media misinformation has on covid-19 vaccination status. In *Proceedings of the 23rd Annual Conference on Information Technology Education* (pp. 37–43). Association for Computing Machinery. http://dx.doi.org/10.1145/3537674.3554754

Daradkeh, M. (2021). Analyzing sentiments and diffusion characteristics of COVID-19 vaccine misinformation topics in social media. *International Journal of Business Analytics*, *9*(3), 1–22. http://dx.doi.org/10.4018/ijban.292056

de Beer, D., & Matthee, M. (2020). Approaches to identify fake news: A systematic literature review. *In Integrated Science in Digital Age, 2020*, 13–22). Springer. http://dx.doi.org/10.1007/978-3-030-49264-9_2

Demuyakor, J., Nyatuame, I. N., & Obiri, S. (2021). Unmasking Covid-19 vaccine "infodemic" in the social media. *Online Journal of Communication and Media Technologies, 11*(4), e202119. http://dx.doi.org/10.30935/ojcmt/11200

Dunn, A. G., Leask, J., Zhou, X., Mandl, K. D., & Coiera, E. (2015). Associations between exposure to and expression of negative opinions about human papillomavirus vaccines on social media: An observational study. *Journal of Medical Internet Research, 17*(6), e4343. http://dx.doi.org/10.2196/jmir.4343

Dunn, A. G., Surian, D., Leask, J., Dey, A., Mandl, K. D., & Coiera, E. (2017). Mapping information exposure on social media to explain differences in HPV vaccine coverage in the United States. *Vaccine, 35*(23), 3033–3040. http://dx.doi.org/10.1016/j.vaccine.2017.04.060

Edelstein, M., Müller, M., Ladhani, S., Yarwood, J., Salathé, M., & Ramsay, M. (2020). Keep calm and carry on vaccinating: Is anti-vaccination sentiment contributing to declining vaccine coverage in England? *Vaccine, 38*(33), 5297–5304. http://dx.doi.org/10.1016/j.vaccine.2020.06.020

Featherstone, J. D., & Zhang, J. (2020). Feeling angry: The effects of vaccine misinformation and refutational messages on negative emotions and vaccination attitude. *Journal of Health Communication, 25*(9), 692–702. http://dx.doi.org/10.1080/10810730.2020.1805350

Frenkel, S., Decker, B., & Alba, D. (2020, May 20). How the "Plandemic" movie and its falsehoods spread widely online. The New York Times. https://www.nytimes.com/2020/05/20/technology/plandemic-movie-youtube-facebook-coronavirus.html

Gabis, L. V., Attia, O. L., Goldman, M., Barak, N., Tefera, P., Shefer, S., ... Lerman-Sagie, T. (2022). The myth of vaccination and autism spectrum. *European Journal of Paediatric Neurology, 36*, 151–158. http://dx.doi.org/10.1016/j.ejpn.2021.11.001

Garett, R., & Young, S. D. (2021). Online misinformation and vaccine hesitancy. *Translational Behavioral Medicine, 11*(12), 2194–2199. http://dx.doi.org/10.1093/tbm/ibab075

Gawronski, B., Brannon, S. M., & Ng, N. L. (2022). Debunking misinformation about a causal link between vaccines and autism: Two preregistered tests of dual-process versus single-process predictions (with conflicting results). *Social Cognition, 40*(6), 580–599. http://dx.doi.org/10.1521/soco.2022.40.6.580

Health Information National Trends Survey. (2022). HINTS 6 methodology report. https://hints.cancer.gov/data/methodology-reports.aspx

Hong, Y., Wan, M., & Li, Z. (2021). Understanding the health information sharing behavior of social media users: An empirical study on WeChat. *Journal of Organizational and End User Computing, 33*(5), 180–203. http://dx.doi.org/10.4018/joeuc.20210901.oa9

Iles, I. A., Gillman, A. S., Platter, H. N., Ferrer, R. A., & Klein, W. M. (2021). Investigating the potential of inoculation messages and self-affirmation in reducing the effects of health misinformation. *Science Communication, 43*(6), 768–804.

Jamison, A. M., Broniatowski, D. A., Dredze, M., Wood-Doughty, Z., Khan, D., & Quinn, S. C. (2020). Vaccine-related advertising in the Facebook Ad Archive. *Vaccine, 38*(3), 512–520. http://dx.doi.org/10.1016/j.vaccine.2019.10.066

Jennings, W., Stoker, G., Bunting, H., Valgarðsson, V. O., Gaskell, J., Devine, D., McKay, L., & Mills, M. C. (2021). Lack of trust, conspiracy beliefs, and social media use predict COVID-19 vaccine hesitancy. *Vaccine, 9*(6), 593. https://doi.org/10.3390/vaccines9060593

Kalichman, S. C., Eaton, L. A., Earnshaw, V. A., & Brousseau, N. (2022). Faster than warp speed: Early attention to COVD-19 by anti-vaccine groups on Facebook. *Journal of Public Health, 44*(1), e96–e105. http://dx.doi.org/10.1093/pubmed/fdab093

Keelan, J., Pavri, V., Balakrishnan, R., & Wilson, K. (2010). An analysis of the human papilloma virus vaccine debate on MySpace blogs. *Vaccine*, *28*(6), 1535–1540. http://dx.doi.org/10.1016/j.vaccine.2009.11.060

Klimiuk, K., Czoska, A., Biernacka, K., & Balwicki, Ł. (2021). Vaccine misinformation on social media—Topic-based content and sentiment analysis of Polish vaccine-deniers' comments on Facebook. *Human Vaccines & Immunotherapeutics*, *17*(7), 2026–2035. http://dx.doi.org/10.1080/21645515.2020.1850072

Leader, A. E., Burke-Garcia, A., Massey, P. M., & Roark, J. B. (2021). Understanding the messages and motivation of vaccine hesitant or refusing social media influencers. *Vaccine*, *39*(2), 350–356. http://dx.doi.org/10.1016/j.vaccine.2020.11.058

Li, H. O. Y., Pastukhova, E., Brandts-Longtin, O., Tan, M. G., & Kirchhof, M. G. (2022). YouTube as a source of misinformation on COVID-19 vaccination: A systematic analysis. *BMJ Global Health*, *7*(3), e008334. http://dx.doi.org/10.1136/bmjgh-2021-008334

Loomba, S., de Figueiredo, A., Piatek, S. J., de Graaf, K., & Larson, H. J. (2021). Measuring the impact of COVID-19 vaccine misinformation on vaccination intent in the UK and USA. *Nature Human Behaviour*, *5*(3), 337–348. http://dx.doi.org/10.1038/s41562-021-01056-1

Massey, P. M., Kearney, M. D., Hauer, M. K., Selvan, P., Koku, E., & Leader, A. E. (2020). Dimensions of misinformation about the HPV vaccine on Instagram: Content and network analysis of social media characteristics. *Journal of Medical Internet Research*, *22*(12), e21451. http://dx.doi.org/10.2196/21451

Muric, G., Wu, Y., & Ferrara, E. (2021). COVID-19 vaccine hesitancy on social media: Building a public Twitter data set of antivaccine content, vaccine misinformation, and conspiracies. *JMIR Public Health and Surveillance*, *7*(11), e30642. http://dx.doi.org/10.2196/30642

Nan, X., Thier, K., & Wang, Y. (2023). Health misinformation: What it is, why people believe it, how to counter it. *Annals of the International Communication Association*, *47*(4), 381–410. http://dx.doi.org/10.1080/23808985.2023.2225489

Nan, X., Wang, Y., & Thier, K. (2021). Health misinformation. In T. Thompson & N. Harrington (Eds.), *The Routledge handbook of health communication* (pp. 318–332). Routledge.

Nan, X., Wang, Y., & Thier, K. (2022). Why people believe health misinformation and who are at risk? A systematic review of individual differences in susceptibility to health misinformation. *Social Science & Medicine*, *314*, 115398. http://dx.doi.org/10.1016/j.socscimed.2022.115398

Ngai, C. S. B., Singh, R. G., & Yao, L. (2022). Impact of COVID-19 vaccine misinformation on social media virality: Content analysis of message themes and writing strategies. *Journal of Medical Internet Research*, *24*(7), e37806. http://dx.doi.org/10.2196/37806

Nyhan, B., & Reifler, J. (2015). Does correcting myths about the flu vaccine work? An experimental evaluation of the effects of corrective information. *Vaccine*, *33*(3), 459–464. http://dx.doi.org/10.1016/j.vaccine.2014.11.017

Nyhan, B., Reifler, J., Richey, S., & Freed, G. L. (2014). Effective messages in vaccine promotion: A randomized trial. *Pediatrics*, *133*(4), e835–e842. https://doi.org/10.1542/peds.2013-2365

Pierri, F., DeVerna, M. R., Yang, K. C., Axelrod, D., Bryden, J., & Menczer, F. (2023). One year of COVID-19 vaccine misinformation on Twitter: Longitudinal study. *Journal of Medical Internet Research*, *25*, e42227. http://dx.doi.org/10.2196/42227

Puri, N., Coomes, E. A., Haghbayan, H., & Gunaratne, K. (2020). Social media and vaccine hesitancy: New updates for the era of COVID-19 and globalized infectious diseases. *Human Vaccines & Immunotherapeutic*, *16*(11), 2586–2593. http://dx.doi.org/10.1080/21645515.2020.1780846

Radzikowski, J., Stefanidis, A., Jacobsen, K. H., Croitoru, A., Crooks, A., & Delamater, P. L. (2016). The measles vaccination narrative in Twitter: A quantitative analysis. *JMIR Public Health and Surveillance*, *2*(1), e5059. http://dx.doi.org/10.2196/publichealth.5059

Reuters. (2020, December 16). Fact check: Six people have not died from the Pfizer-BioNTech COVID-19 vaccine. https://www.reuters.com/article/uk-factcheck-trials/fact-check-six-people-have-not-died-from-the-pfizer-biontech-covid-19-vaccine-idUSKBN28Q2X4

Riad, A., Pokorná, A., Antalová, N., Krobot, M., Zviadadze, N., Serdiuk, I., ... Klugar, M. (2021). Prevalence and drivers of COVID-19 vaccine hesitancy among Czech university students: National cross-sectional study. *Vaccine*, *9*(9), 948. http://dx.doi.org/10.3390/vaccines9090948

Schmidt, A. L., Zollo, F., Scala, A., Betsch, C., & Quattrociocchi, W. (2018). Polarization of the vaccination debate on Facebook. *Vaccine*, *36*(25), 3606–3612. http://dx.doi.org/10.1016/j.vaccine.2018.05.040

Skafle, I., Nordahl-Hansen, A., Quintana, D. S., Wynn, R., & Gabarron, E. (2022). Misinformation about COVID-19 vaccines on social media: Rapid review. *Journal of Medical Internet Research*, *24*(8), e37367. http://dx.doi.org/10.2196/37367

Suarez-Lledo, V., & Alvarez-Galvez, J. (2021). Prevalence of health misinformation on social media: Systematic review. *Journal of Medical Internet Research*, *23*(1), e17187. http://dx.doi.org/10.2196/17187

Tuells, J., Martínez-Martínez, P. J., Duro-Torrijos, J. L., Caballero, P., Fraga-Freijeiro, P., & Navarro-López, V. (2015). Characteristics of the videos in Spanish posted on YouTube about human papillomavirus vaccines. *Revista Española de Salud Publica*, *89*(1), 107–115. http://dx.doi.org/10.4321/s1135-57272015000100012

van der Linden, S., Dixon, G., Clarke, C., & Cook, J. (2021). Inoculating against COVID-19 vaccine misinformation. *eClinicalMedicine*, *33*, 100772. http://dx.doi.org/10.1016/j.eclinm.2021.100772

Vivion, M., Anassour Laouan Sidi, E., Betsch, C., Dionne, M., Dubé, E., Driedger, S. M., Gagnon, D., Graham, J., Greyson, D., Hamel, D., Lewandowsky, S., MacDonald, N., Malo, B., Meyer, S. B., Schmid, P., Steenbeek, A., van der Linden, S., Verger, P., Witteman, H. O., et al. (2022). Prebunking messaging to inoculate against COVID-19 vaccine misinformation: An effective strategy for public health. *Journal of Communication in Healthcare*, *15*(3), 232–242. http://dx.doi.org/10.1080/17538068.2022.2044606

Vosoughi, S., Roy, D., & Aral, S. (2018). The spread of true and false news online. *Science*, *359*(6380), 1146–1151. http://dx.doi.org/10.1126/science.aap9559

Walter, N., Brooks, J. J., Saucier, C. J., & Suresh, S. (2021). Evaluating the impact of attempts to correct health misinformation on social media: A meta-analysis. *Health Communication*, *36*(13), 1776–1784. http://dx.doi.org/10.1080/10410236.2020.1794553

Walter, N., & Murphy, S. T. (2018). How to unring the bell: A meta-analytic approach to correction of misinformation. *Communication Monographs*, *85*(3), 423–441. http://dx.doi.org/10.1080/03637751.2018.1467564

Wang, Y., McKee, M., Torbica, A., & Stuckler, D. (2019). Systematic literature review on the spread of health-related misinformation on social media. *Social Science & Medicine*, *240*, 112552. http://dx.doi.org/10.1016/j.socscimed.2019.112552

Wang, Y., Thier, K., & Nan, X. (2022). Defining health misinformation. In A. Keselman, C. A. Smith, & A. J. Wilson (Eds.), *Combating online health misinformation: A professional's guide to helping the public* (pp. 3–16). Rowman & Littlefield. http://dx.doi.org/10.31234/osf.io/jt9f7

Wang, Y., Thier, K., & Nan, X. (2023). HPV vaccine misinformation online: A narrative scoping review. In T. Ginossar, S. F. A. Shah, & D. Weiss (Eds.), *Vaccine communication online: Counteracting misinformation, rumors and lies* (pp. 33–55). Palgrave Macmillan. http://dx.doi.org/10.1007/978-3-031-24490-2_3

Wardle, C., & Derakhshan, H. (2017). Information disorder: Toward an interdisciplinary framework for research and policy making. Council of Europe. https://firstdraftnews.org:443/coe-report

Wawrzuta, D., Jaworski, M., Gotlib, J., & Panczyk, M. (2021). Characteristics of antivaccine messages on social media: Systematic review. *Journal of Medical Internet Research*, *23*(6), e24564. http://dx.doi.org/10.2196/24564

Whitehead, H. S., French, C. E., Caldwell, D. M., Letley, L., & Mounier-Jack, S. (2023). A systematic review of communication interventions for countering vaccine misinformation. *Vaccine*, *41*(5), 1018–1034. http://dx.doi.org/10.1016/j.vaccine.2022.12.059

Wong, N. C. (2016). "Vaccinations are safe and effective": Inoculating positive HPV vaccine attitudes against antivaccination attack messages. *Communication Reports*, *29*(3), 127–138. http://dx.doi.org/10.1080/08934215.2015.1083599

Xu, Z., & Guo, H. (2018). Using text mining to compare online pro-and anti-vaccine headlines: Word usage, sentiments, and online popularity. *Communication Studies*, *69*(1), 103–122. http://dx.doi.org/10.1080/10510974.2017.1414068

Yang, A., Shin, J., Zhou, A., Huang-Isherwood, K. M., Lee, E., Dong, C., Kim, H. M., Zhang, Y., Sun, J., Li, Y., Nan, Y., Zhen, L., & Liu, W. (2021). The battleground of COVID-19 vaccine misinformation on Facebook: Fact checkers vs. misinformation spreaders. *Harvard Kennedy School Misinformation Review*. http://dx.doi.org/10.37016/mr-2020-78

Yousefinaghani, S., Dara, R., Mubareka, S., Papadopoulos, A., & Sharif, S. (2021). An analysis of COVID-19 vaccine sentiments and opinions on Twitter. *International Journal of Infectious Diseases*, *108*, 256–262. http://dx.doi.org/10.1016/j.ijid.2021.05.059

8

The Scope and Effects of Vaccine Misinformation on Social Media

Juliana L. Barbati[1], Kaylin L. Duncan[2], Kun Yan[1], Cindy Turner[3], Ida Tovar[3], Stephen A. Rains[1], and Echo L. Warner[4]

[1] *Department of Communication, University of Arizona*
[2] *Department of Communication Studies, University of Alabama*
[3] *School of Medicine, University of Utah*
[4] *College of Nursing, University of Utah*

Despite the potential of social media for communicating about science and health, misinformation looms as a persistent threat. The networked nature of social media in which people are connected to a large number of friends and acquaintances makes it easy for misinformation to spread. When it does, misinformation makes it difficult for people to know what to believe and encourages a broader culture of mistrust that undermines legitimate efforts to promote public health. Misinformation is also notoriously persistent, continuing to influence people even after they have been supplied with accurate information (Ecker et al., 2022).

Vaccination is one topic where misinformation has been particularly problematic on social media. Vaccination is critical for promoting public health by reducing the likelihood and severity of illness along with the associated burdens on health-care systems. Despite overwhelming scientific agreement about the utility and safety of vaccinations, scholars have regularly reported the presence of vaccine misinformation on social media. The presence of misinformation has also been cited as a key reason for suboptimal vaccination rates (Schmid & Betsch, 2022).

In this chapter, we spotlight the role of social media in the spread of vaccine misinformation. We begin by defining key terms and considering existing theory on this topic. We next review extant research examining vaccine misinformation on social media. We consider the scope and content of vaccine misinformation on social media, its effects, its politicization, beliefs in misinformation, and how it can be combatted. We conclude the chapter with a discussion of the practical implications and possible future directions born from the existing research on this topic. It is our hope that readers will gain a better understanding of the nature and scope of the problem posed by vaccine misinformation on social media and of some of the ways in which it can be mitigated.

Communication and Misinformation: Crisis Events in the Age of Social Media, First Edition.
Edited by Kevin B. Wright.
© 2025 John Wiley & Sons, Inc. Published 2025 by John Wiley & Sons, Inc.

Background and Definitions

The advent of vaccinations marked a change in public health and medicine. When vaccines first became available to the public, they represented a major shift toward preventive medicine. This shift was at the forefront of the growth of public health in the United States and other developed countries. Although the benefits of vaccination have been widely documented, a long history of vaccine hesitancy has perplexed scientists and public health officials alike. Beginning with Andrew Wakefield's rebutted publication falsely claiming a link between autism and the measles, mumps, and rubella vaccine, there has been growing resistance to timely and complete vaccination for children (Flaherty, 2011). This movement has persisted despite scientific evidence to the contrary and, largely as a result of Internet diffusion, has cultivated what we now know as modern vaccine misinformation.

Health misinformation is broadly defined as any health-related claim that is false or misleading based on current scientific consensus (Chou et al., 2020). Some scholars differentiate between misinformation and disinformation, where the former refers to information that is inadvertently false and the latter information that has been knowingly created to cause harm (Wardle & Derakhshan, 2017). In this chapter, we use *misinformation* as an umbrella term to capture all forms of inaccurate health information to avoid assumptions about the creator's intent, which cannot always be ascertained. Similarly, we define *social media* broadly to include different genres of technologies such as video and image-sharing sites (e.g., TikTok and Instagram), microblogs (e.g., X, formerly known as Twitter), social network sites (e.g., Facebook), and related technologies. What unites these technologies under the umbrella of social media is the potential for users to create, view, and share content (Carr & Hayes, 2015). Sharing can occur with a narrow and targeted audience such as friends and family or a broad and undifferentiated audience such as everyone who uses a platform. Social media is particularly relevant to vaccine misinformation because it enables content to spread rapidly with relatively minimal interference from traditional gatekeepers (e.g., news organizations).

The rise of misinformation on social media has become a growing public health concern since the 2010s, as studies have revealed the unique characteristics of this medium. False stories have been shown to spread more quickly than the truth and are more likely to achieve virality on social media platforms (Vosoughi et al., 2018; Wang et al., 2019). Social media misinformation is also challenging to quantify and combat because of the lack of formal regulations and algorithms that can modify individual exposure and decentralize information (Southwell et al., 2019). Two recently published systematic reviews aiming to characterize health misinformation on social media independently concluded that vaccination was the most prevalent topic (Suarez-Lledo & Alvarez-Galvez, 2021; Wang et al., 2019).

In defining key constructs, it is also important to identify the scope conditions for our chapter. While we have made a concerted effort to discuss research specific to vaccine misinformation on social media, we have also drawn from broader bodies of research examining health misinformation and misinformation on social media where appropriate. Our chapter is similarly intended to be representative but not exhaustive. We have endeavored to cover the breadth of scholarship examining vaccine misinformation on social media with the understanding that not all studies could be included in our review. Toward this end, the following section includes theoretical frameworks we deemed relevant to social media and vaccine misinformation research.

Theoretical Perspectives Related to Vaccine Misinformation on Social Media

Given the complex web of issues associated with misinformation on social media, it is perhaps not surprising that there is no single overarching theory to explain this phenomenon. Rather, several frameworks have been advanced by scholars working to explain different dimensions. These works are not specific to vaccine misinformation or even social media but are nonetheless informative. They focus on explaining vaccination behavior, why people believe misinformation, the effects of misinformation exposure, and motivations for engaging in misinformation correction.

Vaccination behavior has been widely understood through the theory of planned behavior. It explains how people's attitudes, subjective norms, and perceived behavioral control influence whether or not they choose to engage in a particular behavior. Attitudes and subjective norms are particularly influenced by online health information and likewise misinformation. Gerend and Shepherd (2012) explored how these concepts influenced human papillomavirus vaccine uptake. They found that intentions, self-efficacy, and subjective norms significantly predicted HPV vaccination. Social media portrays attitudes and social norms about health behaviors from an individual's social network, including peers, family, friends, and colleagues, who may hold more influence over their intention to engage in vaccination than traditional public health messaging.

Researchers have also attempted to understand why people believe misinformation. Although several different individual factors have been studied, scholars have consolidated these influences into cognitive and socioaffective factors (Ecker et al., 2022). Cognitive factors involve the way people think about and perceive the world and include things such as intuitive thinking, cognitive failures, and information-processing biases. Socio-affective factors stem from social context and involve cues associated with the misinformation source and with the emotions and worldview people hold. Notably, these factors are not thought to be different from the mechanisms that give rise to correct or accurate beliefs. A second and related line of inquiry has involved the effects of exposure to misinformation. Scholars have regularly documented what has been deemed the continued influence effect wherein the effects of misinformation can persist despite correction (Ecker et al., 2022). Even after misinformation has been corrected, it can continue to impact some people's beliefs, attitudes, and behavior.

One final dimension of misinformation that has received attention involves the motivation to engage in correction. Scholars have adopted theories from other domains and applied them to predict misinformation correction behavior (e.g., Koo et al., 2021). Sun et al. (2022), for example, drew from theories involving presumed influence and emotion appraisal. They predicted that, when people perceive others to be susceptible to misinformation and expect the influence of misinformation to be severe, they feel anxiety, anger, and anticipated guilt that lead them to engage in misinformation correction. Sun et al.'s study showed that anticipated guilt was the most important factor directly contributing to misinformation correction. People who reported greater potential remorse for not correcting misinformation had greater intentions to engage in this behavior (Koo et al., 2021). With this theoretical background in place, we next consider the state of research examining the effects of vaccine misinformation on social media.

Summarizing Research Examining Vaccine Misinformation on Social Media

Scope and Content of Vaccine Misinformation

Misinformation about vaccines is widely circulated online. For instance, over 88 percent of antivaccine websites were found to contain unreliable sources, false conclusions, or unsupported arguments (Kata, 2010). Half of parents with children under five reported in a UK survey that they were "often or sometimes" exposed to negative information about vaccines on social media (Royal Society of Public Health, 2019). A review of approximately 100 studies examining COVID-19 vaccine misinformation found that misinformation ranged from 0.1 to 41.3 percent across different online platforms (Zhao et al., 2023). Thus, it is perhaps not surprising that misinformation on social media has been named a "global threat" (World Economic Forum, 2023) and that the World Health Organization (2023) has declared an infodemic, that is, widespread misinformation that can negatively impact health and lead to mistrust in authorities.

Researchers have attempted to identify themes in antivaccine messages online (Jamison et al., 2020; Kata, 2010). Although these themes are not specific to misinformation, they are informative in understanding the different ways in which vaccines have been questioned. One common class of antivaccine messages involves safety and personal danger (e.g., exaggerated side effects, questioning vaccine ingredients, highlighting negative outcomes). Another type focuses on raising doubts about vaccine efficacy and advocates alternative medicine. A third category involves conspiracies wherein sinister activities or actors (e.g., pharmacies and the government) operate against public interests. Anti-vaccine messages regarding civil liberties, a common fourth category, position vaccination requirements as infringements of personal liberty. "Educational" anti-vaccination messages depict doctors with inadequate knowledge or who use their expertise to pedal falsehoods. A final type of antivaccine message argues that vaccination violates ethical or moral codes by mistreating animals or using fetal tissues in vaccine development. One study showed that, between 2014 and 2017, conspiracy- and safety-related themes were the most common types of antivaccine information appearing on the microblog Twitter (Jamison et al., 2020).

A growing area in vaccine misinformation research concerns how people discuss vaccines and is explored by examining the psycholinguistic properties (i.e., words that indicate particular emotions or cognitive processes) of relevant online messages using dictionary-based content analysis tools. The language users choose to use online has the potential to reveal much about their inner thoughts, motivations, and emotions (Chung & Pennebaker, 2007; Pennebaker et al., 2003). The features of social media that reflect audience engagement (e.g., likes, retweets, comments) allow further insight into the type of language that resonates with particular audiences (Rains et al., 2023). Scholars have uncovered patterns of language use in both pro- and antivaccine movements, as well as how such language use connects with their respective audiences.

This area of research has examined messages from microblogs such as Twitter (Argyris et al., 2022; Mitra et al., 2016; Rains et al., 2023; Shi et al., 2022) and social network sites such as Facebook (Faasse et al., 2016). Regardless of the platform where vaccine misinformation is encountered, relatively consistent patterns appear in language use. Compared to messages that are either characterized as pro-vaccination or identified as not containing misinformation, antivaccine sources are more likely to appear certain and assured in their language use, which may reflect an effort to present themselves as an authority on their content (Faasse et al., 2016; Mitra et al., 2016; Rains et al., 2023). For example, tweets containing COVID-19 conspiracy theories were less likely to be retweeted if they exhibited tentative language (Rains et al., 2023). Moreover, such sources were also less likely to use words indicating anxiety to signal that they are a reliable source of information (Faasse et al., 2016; Mitra et al., 2016).

In addition, online messages containing misinformation—compared to those without—are more likely to signal negative affective processes in general and anger in particular (Mitra et al., 2016; Rains et al., 2023; Shi et al., 2022). Even though antivaccination messages may be overtly deceptive (Argyris et al., 2022; Faasse et al., 2016), they are more likely to be shared, liked, commented on, and quoted by other users (Argyris et al., 2022; Mitra et al., 2016). Anti-vaccination messages are also more likely to include words indicating ingroup identity, which may point to the antivaccination movement's effort to invoke group solidarity (Mitra et al., 2016). Relatedly, tweets about COVID-19 conspiracy theories that used first-person plural pronouns (e.g., *we*, *us*) were more likely to be retweeted (Rains et al., 2023).

Vaccine Misinformation Effects

Researchers have also begun to examine the effects of vaccine misinformation on social media. Several experimental studies show that exposure to vaccine misinformation reduces people's intention to vaccinate. For instance, after browsing an antivaccine website for 5–10 minutes, participants reported a heightened sense of the risks of vaccination and of the lower risk of skipping vaccination and reduced intention to be vaccinated compared to participants who browsed a control website (Betsch et al., 2010). In a large nationally representative sample from the United States and the United Kingdom, exposure to online COVID-19 vaccine misinformation was found to reduce intentions to receive the vaccination (Loomba et al., 2021). Similarly, Calo et al. (2021) found that US parents exposed to tweets with (compared to without) misinformation reported lower motivation to vaccinate their children. The mechanisms responsible for these effects have received relatively less attention from researchers. Anger, perceived danger of vaccination, perceived powerlessness, disillusionment with government or pharmacies, and distrust in authorities may explain some responses (Featherstone & Zhang, 2020; Jolley & Douglas, 2014).

Although experimental studies have collectively found short-term or acute effects of vaccine misinformation on vaccine hesitancy, nonexperimental work exploring longer-term implications presents a mixed and complicated picture. One study found that greater exposure to tweets about safety issues and conspiracies relating to the HPV vaccine correlated with lower vaccine coverage in the United States (Dunn et al., 2017), whereas another showed no connection between antivaccine messages on Twitter and vaccine coverage in the United Kingdom (Edelstein et al., 2020). A three-wave panel study showed that exposure to COVID-19 vaccine misinformation at the first measurement point did not predict subsequent misperceptions and attitudes toward vaccines (Xu et al., 2022). However, misperceptions (i.e., how accurate people think the misinformation is) were responsible for later unfavorable attitudes toward vaccines. Additional research is critical to understand the long-term effects of vaccine misinformation exposure on social media.

Politicization of Vaccination and Social Identity

In a representative democracy such as the United States and in other countries, accurate information is essential for political decisions, policy, and morale. Inaccurate information can affect the public's judgment about political policies (Hochschild & Einstein, 2015) and figures (Flynn et al., 2017). Opinions and knowledge surrounding vaccination have become highly politicized (Saulsberry et al., 2019) to the point where extreme vaccine hesitancy and attitudes toward vaccines are seemingly related to political party (Howard, 2023). Coincidentally, political party and ideology are large drivers of politicized information spread online, and vaccine misinformation is no different (Li et al., 2023; Yan et al., 2023). The politicization of vaccination has had important implications for both accurate information and misinformation.

Several researchers have reported nuanced connections in the United States between political affiliation and perception of vaccines. For instance, liberals and conservatives endorse pro-vaccination statements more than antivaccination statements, and both groups are also more likely to perceive pro-vaccination statements as facts rather than beliefs (Rabinowitz et al., 2016). However, Democrats are more likely to trust scientific findings on vaccines compared to Republicans (Hamilton, 2015). Conservatism is also associated with decreased accuracy of COVID-19 knowledge and a lower ability to discern between real and fake headlines (Calvillo et al., 2020).

Political leaders can also greatly influence antivaccination sentiment. Approval of former president Donald Trump mediated the association between conservative ideology and perceived vulnerability, such that those who favored Trump perceived a lower vulnerability to the COVID-19 virus (Calvillo et al., 2020). Furthermore, Hornsey et al. (2020) conducted an experiment in which Trump voters were assigned to view either actual tweets endorsing antivaccine sentiments from Donald Trump or tweets about an unrelated topic. Exposure to tweets about antivaccination led to a significant increase in concerns about vaccines compared to the control condition. Trump's antivaccination tweets, however, did not affect non-Trump voters' concerns about vaccination.

Liberals and conservatives alike are susceptible to adopting and endorsing misinformation. Liberals are more likely than conservatives to believe that vaccinations engender autism in children (Wolters & Steel, 2017). Conservatives, however, are more likely than other partisan groups to endorse vaccine conspiracy theories. Jiang et al. (2021) analyzed users' messages posted on Twitter from March to June 2020, finding that both conservatives and liberals' tweets addressed COVID-19 conspiracy theories, conservative tweets emphasized surveillance and mandatory immunizations, and liberal tweets focused on Big Pharma and inequality. Twitter users identifying as conservative also shared more unfavorable attitudes toward the COVID-19 vaccine and expressed greater concerns about the side effects than liberals (Jiang et al., 2021).

One framework that can be used to understand the implications of political ideology for vaccine misinformation on social media is social identity theory (Tajfel & Turner, 1979). This theory explains how people's social group membership influences their attitudes and behavior. In the context of vaccine misinformation, social identity theory can help to explain how political ideology contributes to misinformation diffusion. When people's social identities—for example, their political ideology (Greene, 2004)—are made salient, they work to distinguish their group from other related social groups in a way that reflects on their own group positively. Such affiliations can be observed in messages that correspond to people's in-groups or respective out-groups and, theoretically, occurs as a consequence of the consumption of polarized vaccine information online (Li et al., 2023; Yan et al., 2023). Yan et al. (2023), for example, examined how operatives working for the Russian Internet Research Agency (i.e., trolls) used Twitter to present themselves as either conservative or liberal and tweeted vaccine misinformation. Conservative and liberal trolls were significantly more likely than nonpartisan trolls to share vaccine misinformation. However, this partisan distinction did not lead to greater tweet engagement (i.e., liking, retweeting, quote tweeting, or commenting) among Twitter users. The relationships between social identity and misinformation dissemination warrant further attention from scholars.

Belief in Misinformation

Some groups of people are more susceptible to believing misinformation than others. Understanding which groups are most vulnerable can aid efforts to reduce the harm and spread of misinformation. Inattention and confirmation bias are two factors that contribute to the risk of believing misinformation (van der Linden, 2022). Inattention involves the lack of effort and evaluation necessary to distinguish fact from fiction. Conversely, confirmation bias involves a tendency to seek out and accept ideas that align with one's own stance and to reject ideas that do not support it.

Inattention, confirmation bias, and related problems are fueled by the structure and design of social media platforms. Social media companies often tailor news feeds to consumers' specific interests and tastes to increase engagement. In this way, users are likely to view information that fits their interests but may also be more susceptible to consuming misinformation online. Misinformation generally affects people who passively consume content on social media rather than those who critically appraise it. People do not typically verify sources of information when browsing social media for entertainment purposes (Oh et al., 2013). In contrast, people who possess strong digital literacy skills are generally less inclined to accept health misinformation (Pickles et al., 2021).

Knowledge of a subject can also affect how people process misinformation. For example, people are more likely to accept health misinformation if they lack knowledge on the topic and if they have strong preexisting attitudes on the topic (Scherer et al., 2021). People who overestimate their knowledge on a topic are also more likely than those who do not to perceive fake news as being accurate (Pennycook & Rand, 2020). A systematic review (Nan et al., 2022) revealed that analytic thinking and numeracy skills serve as buffers against misinformation because of their link to reduced susceptibility (Pennycook & Rand, 2019; Roozenbeek et al., 2020). Reliance on scientific and health-care sources is also negatively correlated with susceptibility to health misinformation, whereas increased social media use is linked with greater susceptibility (Nan et al., 2022).

Demographically, older people are more likely to engage with online misinformation than younger people (Grinberg et al., 2019). This age-related discrepancy may stem from lower digital literacy among older adults. However, older adults are generally less inclined than younger adults to believe misinformation concerning health-related content (Nan et al., 2022).

Additionally, susceptibility to online health misinformation is related to lower educational level, decreased health literacy and trust in healthcare, and more favorable attitudes toward alternative medicine. Acceptance of misinformation has also been linked to conservative political orientations (Motta, 2021) and racial minority groups (Nan et al., 2022). Additional research into the characteristics of people who are most susceptible to misinformation is essential to develop strategies and policies to combat its dissemination on social media.

Combating Vaccine Misinformation

Given the significant problems associated with misinformation, scholars have worked to develop approaches to combat it both online and offline. Two general classes of misinformation correction strategies are prebunking and debunking (Ecker et al., 2022). Prebunking is a preemptive strategy to raise awareness of specific instances or the general presence of misinformation before it is encountered. This approach involves forewarning an audience about the possibility that they may encounter misinformation and/or identifying and refuting a specific piece of misinformation before they encounter it in their everyday lives. Prebunking helps people to become resistant to misinformation.

Debunking is a second general correction strategy that involves targeting misinformation that has already been shared (Ecker et al., 2022). Once misinformation is circulated, debunking serves as a post hoc means to help people see why it is inaccurate and to learn the correct information. Debunking often takes the form of fact-based correction through pointing out inaccuracies and providing correct information. Other approaches include challenging the credibility of an information source or addressing logical fallacies that are present in misinformation. One key for debunking is to include an alternate explanation for misinformation that is rooted in factual information (Ecker et al., 2022).

On social media, both prebunking and debunking can come from different sources such as algorithms, organizations, or other users (Ecker et al., 2022). Researchers have shown that debunking approaches can be effective on social media. Across 20 studies, Walter et al. (2021) found that correction attempts were more effective than instances without correction. Misinformation was more difficult to correct when it was delivered by peers rather than by news agencies, and corrections were more effective when they came from experts than from nonexperts. Although relatively less research has been conducted to examine prebunking strategies, there is evidence that they can be effective. One group of scholars created a browser game that improved the ability of users to identify misinformation about COVID-19 and reduced their willingness to share the information (Basol et al., 2021). Despite the value of research showing that prebunking and debunking can be effective strategies for addressing vaccine misinformation, researchers should keep in mind the broader context of social media whereby vaccine misinformation promotes a general distrust in health care, medicine, and pharmaceutical companies.

Practical Implications and Future Directions

Practical Implications

The results of our review suggest three practical implications for addressing vaccine misinformation on social media. One is the need to improve the dialog relating to misinformation identification and correction in discussions among the public on social media.

A major barrier to addressing online misinformation begins at an individual level, where constructive dialogue to address health misinformation on social media platforms has been halted by a polarizing political climate. Interpersonal dialogue about misinformation needs to shift from a simple information exchange to a more nuanced model based on principles of actively open-minded thinking and curiosity. Actively open-minded thinking, or the ability to weigh new evidence against personally held beliefs and the opinions of others, is associated with increased objective reasoning independent of prior belief and is effective in addressing claims that are strongly rooted in ideologies (Stanovich & West, 1997). We propose emphasizing nonjudgmental dialogue to pave the way for more shared ground and better relational connection. Curious question asking invites all people to make connections between their personally held beliefs and their experiences of misinformation (Dyche & Epstein, 2011). Practically speaking, this approach can involve open-ended questions to people sharing misinformation online such as "Why do you trust this source?" or "Why does you feel it is important to share this message?", The goal is to elicit a conversation that involves understanding the other person's perspective and correcting misinformation in a way that does not alienate or fuel societal divides rather than to levy an accusation.

In addition to advocating for conversation about online misinformation on an interpersonal level, a second practical implication involves promoting literacy. We propose macrolevel efforts to inhibit the spread of misinformation on social media. One possibility is to normalize the importance and use of social media and different types of literacy to understand the source, intention, and potential influence of misinformed messages, and the importance of these components (Center for Media Literacy, 2008). With the rise of misinformation and fake news, many nonprofit and academic organizations have sought to educate and spread awareness of media and news literacy (Center for Media Literacy, n.d.; Pennsylvania State University News Literacy Initiative, 2023). Moreover, empirical research supports the efficacy of different forms of literacy (e.g., media, news, digital, and/or information literacy) to combat the influence of online misinformation (Arechar et al., 2023; Pickles et al., 2021; Vraga et al., 2020). Although legislation for literacy educational programming has been passed in multiple states (McNeill, 2023), there is no universal curriculum or enacted policy that dictates the teaching of media and news literacy skills in K–12 schools. We believe that there has never been a better opportunity for legislators to advocate for this type of education through policy, such as with the introduction of the Digital Citizenship and Media Literacy Act (117th Congress, 2021–2022).

A final practical implication involves the role of technology companies. Policies to hold social media platforms more accountable for misinformation posted on their sites can also ameliorate the spread of such messages. Some argue that Section 230, or the "Internet Immunity" clause of the Communications Decency Act (i.e., social media platforms are not liable for content posted on their sites), should be repealed so that the impetus to remove misinformation is shifted to social media companies. However, opponents have raised concerns that social media platforms will simply apply algorithms to automatically remove all content containing keywords that may suggest misinformation. Such processes could silence marginalized voices or inadvertently censor accurate information (McDermott, 2023). Although systematic misinformation bans may not be feasible, there is evidence to suggest that the application of warning labels on misinformation, particularly around vaccines, is an effective way to change attitudes (Zhang et al., 2021). We believe this to be a pragmatic and effective mitigation strategy that social media platforms can and should prioritize.

Future Directions

The results of our review suggest three areas for future research on misinformation on social media. One involves the long-term effects of vaccine misinformation exposure on social media. Research concerning the effects of vaccine misinformation makes use primarily of experiments and captures immediate effects such as an increase in vaccine hesitancy after exposure. However, the consequences of misinformation may persist after correction, given that misinformation and its subsequent correction both exist in memory and have the potential to be reactivated (Ecker et al., 2022). We therefore suggest that the long-term or repeated exposure effects of vaccine misinformation on social media be explored. In addition, exposure to vaccine misinformation may have broader societal implications beyond individual health. For instance, Balcaen et al. (2023) found that the effect of exposure to vaccine misinformation can be extended to the economic sphere; vaccine misinformation decreased perceptions of vaccination effectiveness, which further resulted in a pessimistic view of the economy. Society suffers when fewer individuals are vaccinated and the disease is allowed to spread across communities and nations and worldwide. Future studies should continue to explore these broader implications of vaccine misinformation.

A second general future direction involves adopting more nuanced approaches to identifying the mechanisms associated with the sharing and effects of different types of vaccine misinformation. As various forms of or frames for antivaccine messages (e.g., safety concerns, alternative medicine, conspiracy theories, deprivation of civil rights) circulate on social media, it is essential to scrutinize each type of vaccine misinformation and to unpack the underlying mechanisms. For example, conspiracy theories about vaccination are effective in provoking anger and distrust in authorities among their audiences (Featherstone & Zhang, 2020; Jolley & Douglas, 2014), whereas messages about freedom or civil rights often capitalize on feelings of protection, vulnerability, and sacredness (Hughes et al., 2021). More research is needed to understand the motivation behind the belief and dissemination of each type of misinformation, and why each type of vaccine misinformation goes viral and becomes problematic on social media. Further understanding the impact of viral vaccine misinformation on personal health behaviors may shed light on how to intervene when exposure to online vaccine misinformation on social media results in problematic beliefs.

A final area in which we encourage future research is in combating the spread of online misinformation. We highlight one strategy in particular—inoculation messaging—that has much potential in combating misinformation. Inoculation theory (McGuire, 1964) likens people's attitudes to their immune system. In a similar way to how a person's immunity can be strengthened by vaccination (i.e., being exposed to a dead or weakened form of a virus), people's attitudes toward any particular topic can be strengthened as a result of being exposed to oppositional arguments. According to the original formulation of the theory, inoculation messages must be used preemptively, and much misinformation correction research already utilizes inoculation as a theoretical framework to explain prebunking (Ecker et al., 2022). More recently, inoculation messaging has been used to change negative or neutral attitudes, that is, therapeutic inoculation (Ivanov et al., 2017), and has the potential also to be used as a debunking strategy.

Recent misinformation research has considered the perceived threat of encountering misinformation, the perceived threat of attitudinal change, the counterargument to misinformation, and prior vaccine attitudes (Amazeen et al., 2022; Jiang et al., 2022). We believe that misinformation research can benefit from further considering core constructs (i.e., perceived threat, counterarguing, issue involvement) and different strategies (i.e., logic based versus fact based) that appear in contemporary inoculation research (Banas et al., 2023). For instance, a worthy endeavor would be to establish the differences between logic-based and fact-based inoculation strategies and which of the two is more effective at promoting resistance to vaccine misinformation. It may also be worth further unpacking the implications of motivational threat and how differing levels of this construct impacts vaccine attitudes and the intention to be vaccinated (e.g., Jiang et al., 2022).

Conclusion

If the past is any guide, it seems likely that vaccine misinformation on social media will continue to be a problem for some time. Our review has focused on vaccine misinformation and evaluated existing empirical research: its scope and content, its effects, its politicization, belief in misinformation, and how it can be countered. We have also considered some practical implications and directions for future research. It is our hope that readers better understand the problem posed by vaccine misinformation on social media, feel more empowered to navigate it in their own lives, and start their own constructive conversations about its prevalence and impact on their personal networks.

References

Amazeen, M. A., Krishna, A., & Eschmann, R. (2022). Cutting the bunk: Comparing the solo and aggregate effects of prebunking and debunking Covid-19 vaccine misinformation. *Science Communication*, *44*(4), 387–417. http://dx.doi.org/10.1177/10755470221111558

Arechar, A. A., Allen, J., Berinsky, A. J., Cole, R., Epstein, Z., Garimella, K., Gully, A., Lu, J. G., Ross, R. M., Stagnaro, M. N., Zhang, Y., Pennycook, G., & Rand, D. G. (2023). Understanding and combatting misinformation across 16 countries on six continents. *Nature Human Behavior*, *7*, 1502–1513. http://dx.doi.org/10.1038/s41562-023-01641-6

Argyris, Y. A., Zhang, N., Bashyal, B., & Tan, P. N. (2022). Using deep learning to identify linguistic features that facilitate or inhibit the propogation of anti- and pro-vaccine content on social media. *IEEE International Conference on Digital Health, In 2022*, 107–116. IEEE. http://dx.doi.org/10.1109/ICDH55609.2022.00025

Balcaen, P., Buts, C., Du Bois, C., & Tkacheva, O. (2023). The effect of disinformation about COVID-19 on consumer confidence: Insights from a survey experiment. *Journal of Behavioral and Experimental Economics*, *102*, 101968. http://dx.doi.org/10.1016/j.socec.2022.101968

Banas, J. A., Bessarabova, E., Penkauskas, M. C., & Talbert, N. (2023). Inoculating against anti-vaccination conspiracies. *Health Communication*, *39*(9), 1760–1768. http://dx.doi.org/10.1080/10410236.2023.2235733

Basol, M., Roozenbeek, J., Berriche, M., Uenal, F., McClanahan, W. P., & van der Linden, S. (2021). Towards psychological herd immunity: Cross-cultural evidence for two prebunking interventions against COVID-19 misinformation. *Big Data & Society*, *8*(1). http://dx.doi.org/10.1177/20539517211013868

Betsch, C., Renkewitz, F., Betsch, T., & Ulshöfer, C. (2010). The influence of vaccine-critical websites on perceiving vaccination risks. *Journal of Health Psychology*, *15*(3), 446–455. http://dx.doi.org/10.1177/1359105309353647

Calo, W. A., Gilkey, M. B., Shah, P. D., Dyer, A. M., Margolis, M. A., Dailey, S. A., & Brewer, N. T. (2021). Misinformation and other elements in HPV vaccine tweets: An experimental comparison. *Journal of Behavioral Medicine*, *44*, 310–319. http://dx.doi.org/10.1007/s10865-021-00203-3

Calvillo, D. P., Ross, B. J., Garcia, R. J., Smelter, T. J., & Rutchick, A. M. (2020). Political ideology predicts perceptions of the threat of COVID-19 (and susceptibility to fake news about it). *Social Psychological and Personality Science*, *11*(8), 1119–1128. http://dx.doi.org/10.1177/1948550620940539

Carr, C. T., & Hayes, R. A. (2015). Social media: Defining, developing, and divining. *Atlantic Journal of Communication*, *23*(1), 46–65. http://dx.doi.org/10.1080/15456870.2015.972282

Center for Media Literacy. (2008). *Literacy for the 21st Century: An overview & orientation guide to media literacy education* (2nd ed.). https://www.medialit.org/literacy-21st-century

Center for Media Literacy. (n.d.). *Getting started: Strategies for introducing media literacy in your school or district.* https://www.medialit.org/getting-started-strategies-introducing-media-literacy-your-school-or-district

Chou, W.-Y., Gaysynsky, A., & Cappella, J. N. (2020). Where we go from here: Health misinformation on social media. *American Journal of Public Health*, *110*(S3), S273–S275. http://dx.doi.org/10.2105/AJPH.2020.305905

Chung, C., & Pennebaker, J. (2007). The psychological functions of function words. In K. Fiedler (Ed.), *Social communication* (pp. 343–359). Routledge. http://dx.doi.org/10.4324/9780203837702

Digital Citizenship and Media Literacy Act, S. Bill, 4490 Cong. (2021–2022). https://www.congress.gov/bill/117th-congress/senate-bill/4490/text?r=15&s=1

Dunn, A. G., Surian, D., Leask, J., Dey, A., Mandl, K. D., & Coiera, E. (2017). Mapping information exposure on social media to explain differences in HPV vaccine coverage in the United States. *Vaccine*, *35*(23), 3033–3040. http://dx.doi.org/10.1016/j.vaccine.2017.04.060

Dyche, L., & Epstein, R. M. (2011). Curiosity and medical education. *Medical Education*, *45*(7), 663–668. http://dx.doi.org/10.1111/j.1365-2923.2011.03944.x

Ecker, U. K., Lewandowsky, S., Cook, J., Schmid, P., Fazio, L. K., Brashier, N., Kendeou, P., Vraga, E. K., & Amazeen, M. A. (2022). The psychological drivers of misinformation belief and its resistance to correction. *Nature Reviews Psychology*, *1*(1), 13–29. http://dx.doi.org/10.1038/s44159 021 00006 y

Edelstein, M., Müller, M., Ladhani, S., Yarwood, J., Salathé, M., & Ramsay, M. (2020). Keep calm and carry on vaccinating: Is anti-vaccination sentiment contributing to declining vaccine coverage in England? *Vaccine*, *38*(33), 5297–5304. http://dx.doi.org/10.1016/j.vaccine.2020.05.082

Faasse, K., Chatman, C. J., & Martin, L. R. (2016). A comparison of language use in pro- and anti-vaccination comments in response to a high profile Facebook post. *Vaccine*, *34*(47), 5808–5814. https://doi.org/10.1016/j.vaccine.2016.09.029

Featherstone, J. D., & Zhang, J. (2020). Feeling angry: The effects of vaccine misinformation and refutational messages on negative emotions and vaccination attitude. *Journal of Health Communication*, *25*(9), 692–702. http://dx.doi.org/10.1080/10810730.2020.1838671

Flaherty, D. K. (2011). The vaccine-autism connection: A public health crisis caused by unethical medical practices and fraudulent science. *Annals of Pharmacotherapy*, *45*(10), 1302–1304. http://dx.doi.org/10.1345/aph.1Q318

Flynn, D. J., Nyhan, B., & Reifler, J. (2017). The nature and origins of misperceptions: Understanding false and unsupported beliefs about politics. *Political Psychology*, *38*(1), 127–150. http://dx.doi.org/10.1111/pops.12394

Gerend, M. A., & Shepherd, J. E. (2012). Predicting human papillomavirus vaccine update in young adult women: Comparing the health belief model and theory of planned behavior. *Annals of Behavioral Medicine*, *44*(2), 171–180. http://dx.doi.org/10.1007/s12160-012-9366-5

Greene, S. (2004). Social identity theory and party identification. *Social Science Quarterly*, *85*(1), 136–153. http://dx.doi.org/10.1111/j.0038-4941.2004.08501010.x

Grinberg, N., Joseph, K., Friedland, L., Swire-Thompson, B., & Lazer, D. (2019). Fake news on Twitter during the 2016 U.S. presidential election. *Science*, *363*(6425), 374–378. http://dx.doi.org/10.1126/science.aau2706

Hamilton, L. C. (2015). Conservative and liberal views of science: Does trust depend on topic? The Carsey School of Public Policy. https://scholars.unh.edu/carsey/252

Hochschild, J. L., & Einstein, K. L. (2015). Do facts matter? Information and misinformation in American politics. *Political Science Quarterly*, *130*(4), 585–624. http://dx.doi.org/10.1002/polq.12398

Hornsey, M. J., Finlayson, M., Chatwood, G., & Begeny, C. T. (2020). Donald Trump and vaccination: The effect of political identity, conspiracist ideation and presidential tweets on vaccine hesitancy. *Journal of Experimental Social Psychology*, *88*, 103947. http://dx.doi.org/10.1016/j.jesp.2019.103947

Howard, M. C. (2023). Integrating the person-centered approach with the study of vaccine hesitancy: Applying latent profile analysis to identify vaccine hesitancy subpopulations and assess their relations with correlates and vaccination outcomes. *Vaccine*, *41*, 4823–4835. http://dx.doi.org/10.1016/j.vaccine.2023.06.057

Hughes, B., Miller-Idriss, C., Piltch-Loeb, R., Goldberg, B., White, K., Criezis, M., & Savoia, E. (2021). Development of a codebook of online anti-vaccination rhetoric to manage COVID-19 vaccine misinformation. *International Journal of Environmental Research and Public Health*, *18*(14), 7556. http://dx.doi.org/10.3390/ijerph18147556

Ivanov, B., Rains, S. A., Geegan, S. A., Vos, S. C., Haarstad, N. D., & Parker, K. A. (2017). Beyond simple inoculation: Examining the persuasive value of inoculation for audiences with initially neutral or opposing attitudes. *Western Journal of Communication*, *81*(1), 105–126. http://dx.doi.org/10.1080/10570314.2016.1224917

Jamison, A., Broniatowski, D. A., Smith, M. C., Parikh, K. S., Malik, A., Dredze, M., & Quinn, S. C. (2020). Adapting and extending a typology to identify vaccine misinformation on Twitter. *American Journal of Public Health*, *110*(S3), S331–S339. http://dx.doi.org/10.2105/AJPH.2020.305940

Jiang, L. C., Sun, M., Chu, T. H., & Chia, S. C. (2022). Inoculation works and health advocacy backfires: Building resistance to COVID-19 vaccine misinformation in a low political trust context. *Frontiers in Psychology*, *13*, 1–11. http://dx.doi.org/10.3389/fpsyg.2022.976091

Jiang, X., Su, M. H., Hwang, J., Lian, R., Brauer, M., Kim, S., & Shah, D. (2021). Polarization over vaccination: Ideological differences in Twitter expression about COVID-19 vaccine favorability and specific hesitancy concerns. *Social Media + Society*, *7*(3). https://doi.org/10.1177/20563051211048413

Jolley, D., & Douglas, K. M. (2014). The effects of anti-vaccine conspiracy theories on vaccination intentions. *PLoS ONE*, *9*(2), 1–9. http://dx.doi.org/10.1371/journal.pone.0089177

Kata, A. (2010). A postmodern Pandora's box: Anti-vaccination misinformation on the Internet. *Vaccine*, *28*(7), 1709–1716. http://dx.doi.org/10.1016/j.vaccine.2009.12.022

Koo, A. Z. X., Su, M. H., Lee, S., Ahn, S. Y., & Rojas, H. (2021). What motivates people to correct misinformation? Examining the effects of third-person perceptions and perceived norms.

Journal of Broadcasting & Electronic Media, *65*(1), 111–134. http://dx.doi.org/10.1080/08838151.2021.1903896

Li, Y., Gee, W., Jin, K., & Bond, R. (2023). Examining homophily, language coordination, and analytical thinking in web-based conversations about vaccines on Reddit: Study using deep neural network language models and computer-assisted conversational analyses. *Journal of Medical Internet Research*, *25*, 1–16. https://www.jmir.org/2023/1/e41882

Loomba, S., de Figueiredo, A., Piatek, S. J., de Graaf, K., & Larson, H. J. (2021). Measuring the impact of COVID-19 vaccine misinformation on vaccination intent in the UK and U.S.A. *Nature Human Behaviour*, *5*(3), 337–348. http://dx.doi.org/10.1038/s41562-021-01056-1

McDermott, M. E. (2023). Mitigating misinformation on social media platforms: Treating section 230 of the Communications Decency Act as a quid pro quo benefit note. *Connecticut Law Review*, *558*. https://digitalcommons.lib.uconn.edu/law_review/558/

McGuire, W. J. (1964). Inducing resistance to persuasion: Some contemporary approaches. In L. Berkowitz (Ed.), *Advances in experimental social psychology* (Vol. 1, pp. 191–229). Academic Press.

McNeill, E. (2023, February). *U.S. media literacy policy report 2022: A state-by-state status of media literacy education laws for K–12 schools*. Media Literacy Now. https://medialiteracynow.org/document/u-s-media-literacy-policy-report-2022

Mitra, T., Counts, S., & Pennebaker, J. (2016). Understanding anti-vaccination attitudes in social media. *Proceedings of the International AAAI Conference on Web and Social Media*, *10*(1), 269–278. https://doi.org/10.1609/icwsm.v10i1.14729

Motta, M. (2021). Republicans, not Democrats, are more likely to endorse anti-vaccine misinformation. *American Politics Research*, *49*(5), 428–438. http://dx.doi.org/10.1177/1532673X211022639

Nan, X., Wang, Y., & Thier, K. (2022). Why people believe health misinformation and who are at risk? A systematic review of individual differences in susceptibility to health misinformation. *Social Science & Medicine*, *314*, 115398. http://dx.doi.org/10.1016/j.socscimed.2022.115398

Oh, O., Agrawal, M., & Rao, H. R. (2013). Community intelligence and social media services: A rumor theoretic analysis of tweets during social crises. *MIS Quarterly*, *37*(2), 407–426. http://www.jstor.org/stable/43825916

Pennebaker, J., Mehl, M., & Niederhoffer, K. (2003). Psychological aspects of natural language use: Our words, our selves. *Annual Review of Psychology*, *54*, 547–577. http://dx.doi.org/10.1146/annurev.psych.54.101601.145041

Pennsylvania State University News Literacy Initiative. (2023). *The basics: You have the power to choose your news*. https://newsliteracy.psu.edu/basics

Pennycook, G., & Rand, D. G. (2019). Lazy, not biased: Susceptibility to partisan fake news is better explained by lack of reasoning than by motivated reasoning. *Cognition*, *188*, 39–50. http://dx.doi.org/10.1016/j.cognition.2018.06.011

Pennycook, G., & Rand, D. G. (2020). Who falls for fake news? The roles of bullshit receptivity, overclaiming, familiarity, and analytic thinking. *Journal of Personality*, *88*(2), 185–200. http://dx.doi.org/10.1111/jopy.12476

Pickles, K., Cvejic, E., Nickel, B., Copp, T., Bonner, C., Leask, J., Ayre, J., Batcup, C., Cornell, S., Dakin, T., Dodd, R. H., Isautier, J. M. J., & McCaffery, K. J. (2021). COVID-19 misinformation trends in Australia: Prospective longitudinal national survey. *Journal of Medical Internet Research*, *23*(1), e23805. http://dx.doi.org/10.2196/23805

Rabinowitz, M., Latella, L., Stern, C., & Jost, J. T. (2016). Beliefs about childhood vaccination in the United States: Political ideology, false consensus, and the illusion of uniqueness. *PLoS ONE*, *11*(7), 1–19. http://dx.doi.org/10.1371/journal.pone.0158382

Rains, S. A., Leroy, G., Warner, E. L., & Harber, P. (2023). Psycholinguistic markers of COVID-19 conspiracy tweets and predictors of tweet dissemination. *Health Communication*, *38*(1), 21–30. http://dx.doi.org/10.1080/10410236.2021.1929691

Roozenbeek, J., Schneider, C. R., Dryhurst, S., Kerr, J., Freeman, A. L., Recchia, G., van der Bies, A. M., & van der Linden, S. (2020). Susceptibility to misinformation about COVID-19 around the world. *Royal Society Open Science*, *7*(10), 201199. http://dx.doi.org/10.1098/rsos.201199

Royal Society of Public Health. (2019, January). *Moving the needle: Promoting vaccination uptake across the life course*. www.rsph.org.uk/our-work/policy/vaccinations/moving-the-needle-promoting-vaccination-uptake-across-the-life-course.html

Saulsberry, L., Fowler, E. F., Nagler, R. H., & Gollust, S. E. (2019). Perceptions of politicization and HPV vaccine policy support. *Vaccine*, *37*(35), 5121–5128. http://dx.doi.org/10.1016/j.vaccine.2019.05.062

Scherer, L. D., McPhetres, J., Pennycook, G., Kempe, A., Allen, L. A., Knoepke, C. E., Tate, C. E., & Matlock, D. D. (2021). Who is susceptible to online health misinformation? A test of four psychosocial hypotheses. *Health Psychology*, *40*(4), 274–284. http://dx.doi.org/10.1037/hea0000978

Schmid, P., & Betsch, C. (2022). Benefits and pitfalls of debunking interventions to counter mRNA vaccination misinformation during the COVID-19 pandemic. *Science Communication*, *44*(5), 531–558. http://dx.doi.org/10.1177/10755470221129

Shi, J., Ghasiya, P., & Sasahara, K. (2022). Psycho-linguistic differences among competing vaccination communities on social media. *APSIPA Transactions on Signal and Information Processing*, *11*, 1–21. http://dx.doi.org/10.1561/116.00000056

Southwell, B. G., Niederdeppe, J., Cappella, J. N., Gaysynsky, A., Kelley, D. E., Oh, A., Peterson, E. B., & Chou, W.-Y. S. (2019). Misinformation as a misunderstood challenge to public health. *American Journal of Preventive Medicine*, *57*(2), 282–285. http://dx.doi.org/10.1016/j.amepre.2019.03.009

Stanovich, K. E., & West, R. F. (1997). Reasoning independently of prior belief and individual differences in actively open-minded thinking. *Journal of Educational Psychology*, *89*(2), 342–357. http://dx.doi.org/10.1037/0022-0663.89.2.342

Suarez-Lledo, V., & Alvarez-Galvez, J. (2021). Prevalence of health misinformation on social media: Systematic review. *Journal of Medical Internet Research*, *23*(1), 1–17. http://dx.doi.org/10.2196/17187

Sun, Y., Oktavianus, J., Wang, S., & Lu, F. (2022). The role of influence of presumed influence and anticipated guilt in evoking social correction of COVID-19 misinformation. *Health Communication*, *37*(11), 1368–1377. http://dx.doi.org/10.1080/10410236.2021.1888452

Tajfel, H., & Turner, J. C. (1979). An integrative theory of intergroup conflict. In W. G. Austin & S. Worchel (Eds.), *The social psychology of intergroup relations* (pp. 33–48). Brooks/Cole.

van der Linden, S. (2022). Misinformation: Susceptibility, spread, and interventions to immunize the public. *Nature Medicine*, *28*(3), 460–467. http://dx.doi.org/10.1038/s41591-022-01713-6

Vosoughi, S., Roy, D., & Aral, S. (2018). The spread of true and false news online. *Science*, *359*(6380), 1146–1151. http://dx.doi.org/10.1126/science.aap9559

Vraga, E. K., Tully, M., & Bode, L. (2020). Empowering users to respond to misinformation about Covid-19. *Media and Communication*, *8*(2), 475–479. http://dx.doi.org/10.17645/mac.v8i2.3200

Walter, N., Brooks, J. J., Saucier, C. J., & Suresh, S. (2021). Evaluating the impact of attempts to correct health misinformation on social media: A meta-analysis. *Health Communication*, *36*(13), 1776–1784. http://dx.doi.org/10.1080/10410236.2020.1794553

Wang, Y., McKee, M., Torbica, A., & Stuckler, D. (2019). Systematic literature review on the spread of health-related misinformation on social media. *Social Science & Medicine*, *240*, 1–12. http://dx.doi.org/10.1016/j.socscimed.2019.112552

Wardle, C., & Derakhshan, H. (2017, October 31). *Information Disorder: An interdisciplinary framework*. First Draft. https://firstdraftnews.org:443/articles/coe-report

Wolters, E. A., & Steel, B. S. (2017). *When ideology trumps science: Why we question the experts on everything from climate change to vaccinations*. Bloomsbury.

World Economic Forum. (2023). *Global risks report 2023*. https://www.weforum.org/reports/global-risks-report-2023

World Health Organization. (2023). *Infodemic*. https://www.who.int/health-topics/infodemic

Xu, S., Coman, I. A., Yamamoto, M., & Najera, C. J. (2022). Exposure effects or confirmation bias? Examining reciprocal dynamics of misinformation, misperceptions, and attitudes toward COVID-19 vaccines. *Health Communication*, *38*(10), 2210–2220. http://dx.doi.org/10.1080/10410236.2022.2059802

Yan, K., Barbati, J. L., Duncan, K. L., Warner, E. L., & Rains, S. A. (2023). Russian troll vaccine misinformation dissemination on Twitter: The role of political partisanship. *Health Communication*, *38*(8), 1591–1600. http://dx.doi.org/10.1080/10410236.2021.2021692

Zhang, J., Featherstone, J. D., Calabrese, C., & Wojcieszak, M. (2021). Effects of fact-checking social media vaccine misinformation on attitudes toward vaccines. *Preventive Medicine*, *145*, 1–6. http://dx.doi.org/10.1016/j.ypmed.2020.106408

Zhao, S., Hu, S., Zhou, X., Song, S., Wang, Q., Zheng, H., Zhang, Y., & Hou, Z. (2023). The prevalence, features, influencing factors, and solutions for COVID-19 vaccine misinformation: Systematic review. *JMIR Public Health and Surveillance*, *9*, 1–23. http://dx.doi.org/10.2196/40201

9

Misinformation Identification and Correction

Rongwei Tang, Caitlin B. Neal, and Emily K. Vraga

Hubbard School of Journalism and Mass Communication, University of Minnesota Twin Cities

On February 3, 2023, a freight train carrying hazardous materials and operated by Norfolk Southern Railway derailed in East Palestine, Ohio, near the border of Pennsylvania. Thirty-eight railcars went off the tracks, 11 of which were carrying hazardous materials. As a result of the crash, several railcars burned for more than two days. Three days later, on February 6, Norfolk Southern partnered with local authorities to conduct a controlled burn of the derailed cars in order to avert an explosion. While an explosion was avoided, the controlled burn emitted hydrogen chloride and phosgene into the air, raising concerns about air quality. Between February 5 and February 6, residents within a one-mile by two-mile radius of the burn site were officially ordered by the Ohio governor Mike DeWine and the Pennsylvania governor Josh Shapiro to evacuate, with DeWine citing "a matter of life and death" (Orsagos & Seewer, 2023).

As residents of East Palestine sought accurate information about whether their homes and families were safe, a conspiratorial storm was brewing on social media (Taft, 2023). Incorrect claims surfaced that acid rain had caused contamination of a major river (Swenson, 2023; Taft, 2023; Tolentino & Sung, 2023), effectively expanding the zone of potential toxic exposure to span the entire Ohio River basin area. Online commentators on social media such as Telegram and Twitter wildly speculated that the event had been a planned attack or a vast "Chernobyl 2.0" cover-up (Thompson, 2023).

But while inaccuracies and mischaracterizations abounded, they were underpinned by some key truths. The derailment and resulting controlled burn did indeed impact the local natural environment, as confirmed by the Ohio Department of Natural Resources (Bendix & Li, 2023), with 43,000 aquatic animals found dead near the derailment (Grandoni & Koh, 2023). Prior to the derailment, Norfolk Southern and other major freight companies also had a well-documented history of padding profits at the expense of safety (Hurley & Boyle, 2023)—decisions that were made possible in part by the federal government's loosening of railroad safety regulations and its interference in the collective bargaining process of 12 unions representing railroad workers in the preceding months and years (Sainato, 2022; Taft, 2023). Residents reported lingering odors (Bendix & Li, 2023), headaches and chest pains (Bendix & Ede-Osifo, 2023), ailments, and even the death of pets and farm animals (Grandoni & Koh, 2023). By February 9, the Ohio Environmental Protection Agency was

Communication and Misinformation: Crisis Events in the Age of Social Media, First Edition.
Edited by Kevin B. Wright.
© 2025 John Wiley & Sons, Inc. Published 2025 by John Wiley & Sons, Inc.

reporting that air quality readings had returned to normal levels and that drinking water, which had not beenimpacted by the affected waterways, was confirmed to be safe (Taft, 2023).

During a crisis situation such as this, the study of misinformation and correction is especially fraught for the following reasons. First, the known information is constantly changing during a crisis, making it hard to distinguish misinformation from what is true, which is often defined as "the best available evidence from relevant experts *at the time*" (Vraga & Bode, 2020b, p. 138; emphasis added). Serious evaluation of environmental disasters also takes time: It can take weeks or longer to collect, monitor, and verify data (Taft, 2023), creating an information void where misinformation can flourish (Austin et al., 2012), especially online.

Second, when crisis strikes, it's often not immediately clear who is responsible for getting messages out to the public and what groups or actors should be considered experts who can vet and share accurate information. This early confusion reinforces the information voids that emerge in these situations. While pressure mounted for Norfolk Southern to engage with local residents on the progress of the cleanup, the company also faced criticism that it was incentivized to minimize the crisis and exercise damage control, which made it an unreliable narrator. Governmental agencies also faced the challenge of communicating information about an evolving situation: Even as air and water quality test results returned to normal and safe levels, many residents remained understandably apprehensive about returning home; online spectators from afar likewise expressed skepticism. Finally, the changing media environment—and especially the rise of social media sites—must also be considered when evaluating how best to respond to misinformation during a crisis.

Additionally, individuals are increasingly turning to social media sites for news (Newman et al., 2017) and information on crisis causes, backgrounds, and inside perspectives (Austin et al., 2012). Altogether, this chapter examines the scholarship regarding the spread of misinformation and efforts to correct it, especially on social media, and considers the various ways in which these lessons apply in different crisis situations. To do so, we first consider crisis communication as a framework, before reviewing how the correction of social media misinformation remains a particularly important strategy for mitigating the negative effects of misinformation during a crisis situation. We conclude by considering the limitations of corrective efforts and where future work is needed to better unite the fields of correction with crisis communication.

Crisis Communication as a Framework

A foundational understanding of crisis communication can be useful to a variety of organizations interested in misinformation and correction. Crisis communication can be defined as what an organization says and does in response to a crisis, or "the collection, processing, and dissemination required to address a crisis situation" (Coombs & Holladay, 2012, p. 20). While originally a topic among practitioners of crisis management—business executives might trade "war stories" of how they responded to such and such a crisis—public relations and communication scholars began to embrace and apply theoretical foundations and frameworks to advance our understanding of crisis communication beginning in the late 1980s to early 1990s (Coombs & Holladay, 2022). In keeping with its industry roots, most of the field's history has been dominated by how organizations can repair the reputational damage caused by the crisis. Quantitative analyses of crisis communication research from 1991 to 2009 showed that image repair theory and situational crisis communication theory (SCCT) dominate the landscape (Avery et al., 2010). Image repair theory involves several strategies for the accused party to evade responsibility for its wrongdoing, such as through simple denial, shifting the blame, and minimizing the seriousness of the act (Glantz & Benoit, 2018). SCCT is similarly concerned with addressing various crisis response strategies, chiefly by matching the type of crisis (ranging from minimal to high crisis responsibility) to the appropriate response (Coombs, 2018). While reputation management remains an important concern within the field of crisis communication, Liu and Fraustino (2014) recommend that researchers move "beyond image repair" by considering a wider variety of key publics affected by the crisis.

Another aspect pushing the field of crisis communication to new heights is the evolving media landscape and proliferation of social media. With these changes has come a concerted effort to raise social media to a level of higher theoretical importance within crisis communication theory. The subfield of social-mediated crisis communication (SMCC) emerged as a response to this need. Within this framework, the goal of SMCC is not simply to retrofit social media into an existing theory but to establish a new theory that supports how social media has fundamentally shifted the way in which organizations and publics communicate (Austin & Jin, 2018). Central to this burgeoning field is the question of how social media is used to communicate or learn about risks and crises (Hornmoen & Backholm, 2018). Separating self-inflicted internal crises from external crises also offers opportunities to develop disaster communication, an area of research that is particularly underexplored in a social-mediated landscape (Fraustino et al., 2018). While crisis communication deems misinformation to be threats to an organization's image, disaster communication contends with misinformation that has the potential to cause widespread harm to affected communities.

Studying crises in the context of major health and science events that seriously disrupt whole communities or societies—disasters, in other words—offers a unique space to unite the crisis communication and correction literature because the response to a disaster does not involve safeguarding reputation and minimizing organizational operations as its sole objectives, at least from the perspective of health and science agencies. Instead, health and science crises often require the transmission of crucial updates and recommendations regarding public health and safety. In this context, correction is of paramount importance. Furthermore, within the domain of science and health, definitions of misinformation are usually clear but tend to become less so during times of crisis. As a result, these two aspects are in a state of tension amid health or science crises.

The spread of misinformation on social media presents challenges for effective crisis management, and the field of crisis communication is still adjusting to the era of social media. For starters, misinformation in crisis communication literature has historically been conceptualized as incorrect information about a company, and there are several different approaches to combating this type of misinformation. SCCT, for example, emphasizes the need for organizations to aggressively combat inaccurate information by taking on various postures: deny, diminish, rebuild, or bolster (Coombs, 2014). In the model, each posture strategy can be useful to correct misinformation about an organization. Similarly, Benoit (1995) offers several strategies for organizations, but his model defines corrective action not as corrective action to combat misinformation but as an effort by an organization to repair the situation by promising change. However, both models are less applicable when it comes to correcting misinformation about public health and environmental disasters and the various risks and hazards present in those situations, as shifting the blame or minimizing the crisis are hardly helpful strategies when lives are at stake. Instead, providing alternative explanations, such as quickly contradicting misinformation with accurate information, is considered the best practice in correction research (Bode & Vraga, 2018). Recent major health events such as the 2015–2016 Zika virus outbreak and the COVID-19 pandemic have led to greater integration of misinformation and correction literature within crisis and risk communication frameworks (Malecki et al., 2021). Research at this intersection is still very much an active scene.

Thus, misinformation research can be a useful and valuable addition to crisis communication frameworks. Specifically, during science and health crises, misinformation can quickly spread, endangering democratic decision making and causing confusion among citizens and crisis managers (Lee et al., 2022; McKay & Tenove, 2021). Researchers argue that "global health crises are also *information* crises" (Xie et al., 2020). Misinformation is especially likely to go viral during natural disasters (King & Wang, 2023) and health crises (Erku et al., 2021) when there are information voids (Mheidly & Fares, 2020) filled with public confusion and information spreading quickly (Huang et al., 2015), allowing misinformation to thrive (Purnat et al., 2021). Crisis misinformation, defined as "false information about any aspect of an ongoing crisis or any incorrect information that can lead to a crisis according to factual evidence from credible source(s)" (Jin et al., 2020, p. 2), takes various forms and is often shared through social media platforms (Starbird et al., 2014). The prevalence of misinformation on social media (Southwell & Thorson, 2015), coupled with users' reliance on it for sensemaking in uncertain situations (Tandoc & Lee, 2022), may increase people's susceptibility and exposure to misinformation during crises. For example, a content analysis shows that Zika rumors received three times as many shares as verified stories (Sommariva et al., 2018). It is essential to address this issue in a timely manner (Purnat et al., 2021; Walter & Tukachinsky, 2020) because the impact of misinformation can be amplified by users' negative emotions, such as anxiety and anger, on social media platforms (Jin et al., 2016) and confusion may contribute to a lower intention to vet misinformation (Lu et al., 2022). But the uncertain situations also open up an opportunity for misinformation to be corrected because research indicates that correction could be more effective when people feel uncertain (Yang & Overton, 2022).

Defining Correction in a Crisis

Correction represents an important strategy for combating misinformation, especially during a crisis. We take an inclusive approach to defining correction (which we use interchangeably with debunking) to refer to any effort to respond directly to concrete pieces of misinformation to explain why that information is wrong or to provide accurate information (Ecker et al., 2022, Vraga & Bode, 2020a; Walter & Murphy, 2018; Walter et al., 2021). Broadly speaking, a number of meta-analysis have supported the power of corrections (Chan et al., 2017; Janmohamed et al., 2021; Walter & Murphy, 2018; Walter et al., 2021) and fact checking (Walter et al., 2020; Wood & Porter, 2019) in reducing misperceptions on the specific topic being debunked, although a more recent content analysis cast doubt on the ability of corrections to mitigate science misinformation specifically (Chan & Albarracín, 2023). This points to the need for ongoing research into what features of health and science crises may contribute to corrections being a more or less effective strategy for debunking misinformation.

Correction can take many different forms, but the two most common types of correction are logic-based and fact-based corrections. Notably, these two approaches—logical and factual—apply not just to corrections but also to other attempts to mitigate misinformation spread such as prebunking or inoculation. A fact-based correction explains the factual errors in the misinformation and provides the best available evidence on the topic, while a logic-based correction explains the misleading rhetorical strategies employed in the misinformation, often by pointing to common misleading tactics that are used across misinformation campaigns, such as those summarized by FLICC (fake experts, logical fallacies, impossible expectations, cherry-picking, and conspiracy theories; Cook, 2020) or DEPICT (discrediting, emotion, polarization, impersonation, conspiracy, and trolling; van der Linden, 2023). Both factual and logical corrections have been shown to be effective in reducing misperceptions (Schmid & Betsch, 2019; Vraga et al., 2020).

During crisis communication, however, the facts on the ground are often unknown or rapidly changing. In this kind of *emerging* misinformation environment (e.g., Vraga & Bode, 2020b), an expert consensus may not yet exist and little if any evidence may be easily available, making a fact-based correction difficult. In these scenarios, a logic-based correction may be more effective, especially if the misinformation is leveraging well-known misinformation tropes. For example, scholars have identified several common strategies of scientific denial (Diethelm & McKee, 2009; Hansson, 2017; Hoofnagle, 2007; Schmid & Betsch, 2019) and applied these to climate change denial (Coan et al., 2021; Cook, 2020) and COVID-19 issues (Hansson et al., 2021). For example, the strategies that denigrate existing experts on a topic or tap into conspiracies (Sell et al., 2020) may be prominent during a crisis situation, so being prepared to respond to and to describe these problematic scientific attacks may make corrections more effective.

Importantly, correction is a flexible strategy not only because it can take various forms (fact based versus logic based) but also because it can come from a wide variety of actors. While some research suggests that expert corrections may be more effective in reducing misperceptions than nonexperts (van der Meer & Jin, 2020; Vraga & Bode, 2017; Walter et al., 2021), others have found that trust matters more than expertise as a source of correction (Ecker & Antonio, 2021; Guillory & Geraci, 2013). But, while the question of who is *most* effective as a corrector is a matter of some debate, there is broad agreement that corrections do not *have* to come from experts and that peers can often effectively reduce beliefs in misinformation when they confront it (Bode & Vraga, 2018; Margolin et al., 2018; Vraga & Bode, 2018; Vraga, Tully, & Bode, 2022). As such, this opens up a wide range of possibilities: If corrections can come from anyone, many more people can participate in improving the quality of online discourse (Bode & Vraga, 2021b). This means that corrections during a crisis situation can come not only from official organizations but also from everyday people. And personal narratives—such as lived experiences with the crisis situation—that can work across other domains (Krishna & Amazeen, 2022; Lazić & Žeželj, 2021) may also be particularly useful during a crisis if people in an impacted area or scenario can share accurate information with others.

Finally, crisis situations may also offer special cases where corrections—especially if offered quickly—can be particularly powerful. Misinformation can be sticky, especially once it becomes entrenched in an individual's belief system (Ecker et al., 2022; Walter & Tukachinsky, 2020). What is especially important in a crisis situation is a rapidly offered correction that can reduce counterarguing (Kim & Lim, 2022) and prevent misinformation from being deeply encoded in the memory, hence making it easier to correct (Garrett & Weeks, 2013).

Correction on Social Media

The digital age has given rise to a dynamic environment driven by an influx of information where truth and fact are often blurred or distorted. Misinformation spreads easily in this landscape, dominated by social media platforms. Consequently, it has become increasingly important to consider not just how correction can limit misperception in a particular individual but also to reach broader groups that are impacted by misinformation.

Social media offers a space where misinformation can spread rapidly and often does (Vosoughi et al., 2018), but corrections are also scalable. Consider the potential size of an audience for a public correction of misinformation on social media, which can number in the hundreds or even thousands. Vraga and Bode (2017) originally used the term *observational correction*—which we call *observed correction* here—to describe how witnesses receive accurate information as a correction on social media and form more accurate attitudes as a result.

Observed correction plays a pivotal role in addressing and mitigating the spread of misperceptions and false narratives. Walter et al.'s (2021) meta-analysis provides robust evidence that observed correction can significantly reduce misperceptions. When individuals are exposed to the correction of misinformation in others, this leads to a reassessment and adjustment of their own beliefs. This helps create an environment on social media where the accuracy of information is valued and promoted.

A notable aspect of observed correction is its broad applicability. Existing research demonstrated its effectiveness across a multitude of topics from health, politics, and science to social issues and current affairs (Vraga et al., 2019; Walter & Murphy, 2018). Observed correction has worked to reduce misperceptions and bolster scientific knowledge in the early days of two recent pandemics, in relation to the spread of the Zika virus in the spring of 2016 and a false cure for COVID-19 (taking a hot bath) in the spring of 2020 (Bode & Vraga, 2018; Vraga & Bode, 2018, 2021). That observed correction was adaptable to health crisis situations suggests that it may be a versatile tool for handling misinformation during crisis situations regardless of the subject matter. Porter et al. (2023) also highlighted that observed correction of fact was effective across 10 different countries. This is important because misinformation is a global concern that transcends national boundaries. Irrespective of geographical, cultural, or linguistic differences, observed correction can serve as a powerful tool in the global fight against misinformation.

Observed correction's efficacy is not limited to a particular social media platform either. Previous research (Bode & Vraga, 2018; Kuru et al., 2022; Rossini et al., 2021; Smith & Seitz, 2019; Vijaykumar et al., 2021; Vraga & Bode, 2017; Vraga et al., 2020) showed its consistent effectiveness across various platforms such as Twitter, Facebook, Instagram, and WhatsApp. This underscores its resilience and adaptability to different digital contexts. It is also a potent approach to combat crisis misinformation. For instance, Janmohamed et al. (2021) found that during the COVID-19 pandemic observed correction was instrumental in combating the wave of misinformation that threatened public health efforts.

Importantly, people tend to like and appreciate corrections on social media across countries and contexts. A study by Bode and Vraga (2021a) highlighted that a significant number of Americans appreciated the value of correction on social media during the early days of the COVID-19 pandemic, suggesting a collective consciousness in ensuring the authenticity of information. This appreciation can be attributed to an understanding of the impact of misinformation on society and democracy at large, including inciting fear, causing confusion, and eroding trust in institutions. Similarly, Malhotra's (2023) exploration of urban Indian young adults' attitudes suggested a connection between the desire for correction and normative values. The importance social media users attach to the correction of misinformation may suggest that this practice is a matter not only of accuracy but also of moral duty. As social beings who depend on accurate information for sound decision making, people may find that observing correction reaffirms their ethical responsibility to share truthful information. Parallel results emerged from South Korea, where a study by Rich (2022) indicated that over 70 percent of participants appreciated observing corrections on social media. These findings emphasize the universal appeal and importance of accuracy in information exchange. The value people place on observed correction on social media therefore reflects a global commitment to truth and accuracy.

In conclusion, the importance of observed correction, especially on social media during crises, is multifold. Its broad applicability across topics, countries, and platforms, as well as its effectiveness regardless of the source or type of correction, positions it as an indispensable tool in the fight against misinformation. Particularly during times of crisis when misinformation can have serious consequences, observed correction can be used as a valuable approach to combat the spread of false narratives and reduce people's misperceptions.

Correction Strategies During Crises

Cognitive Factors

Efforts to correct misinformation in a crisis should consider the cognitive processes involved. Researchers argue that in a crisis, once misinformation is accepted, it is hard to correct the misperception (van der Meer & Jin, 2020) and people still rely on misinformation, which is often termed the *continued influence effect* (Lewandowsky et al., 2012). Cognitive accounts such as the integration account (where correction fails to encode sufficiently and cannot link to misinformation within memory) and selective retrieval account (greater familiarity with misinformation or a failure to retrieve correction) shed light on the persistence of misinformation effects (Ecker et al., 2022). At the same time, the knowledge revision components framework highlights principles such as encoding, passive activation, co-activation, integration, and competing activation to achieve knowledge revision (Kendeou & O'Brien, 2014). The memory for change framework integrates these theories and emphasizes the moderating role of recollection-based retrieval (remembering misinformation being corrected upon retrieval) in correction effects (Kemp et al., 2022). Thus, to counteract the continued influence effect of misinformation, corrections for crisis misinformation should be continually shared over time so that it becomes more familiar and easily retrievable (selective retrieval account). These corrections should also clearly reference the misinformation that is being addressed and explain why the correct information is more accurate, which can help individuals to mentally link the misinformation with the correction (the integration account). At the same time, by applying the memory for change framework, people will be reminded not just of the correct information but also that a correction has taken place. This may involve reinforcing the message that the initial information was incorrect and has since been updated or corrected.

Biases in how memory is created and stored, including those arising from inattention, transience, and misattribution, contribute to the continued influence of misinformation (Newman et al., 2022). For example, correction efforts are often forgotten, leading to belief regression, whereby misperceptions re-emerge over time (Swire-Thompson et al., 2023). During a crisis, when misinformation may be quite emotive and thus memorable, care must be taken to make sure that corrections are just as memorable to ensure their longevity. Likewise, reminding individuals of the misinformation before correction may improve short-term recall and belief accuracy (Wahlheim et al., 2020). Repeated corrections may also contribute to long-term memorability and counteract the influence of misinformation over time (Sanderson et al., 2022; Swire-Thompson et al., 2023).

Social Factors

Social norms and social and cultural contexts also play a critical role when considering how best to correct misinformation during crises, especially in terms of motivating more people to engage in corrective action. Social norms are a fundamental building block in many models predicting behavior, most notably the theory of planned behavior (Ajzen, 1991). Social norms (both injunctive and descriptive norms) can not only help to update people's health-related beliefs directly (Cookson et al., 2021; Ecker et al., 2023; Prike et al., 2023; Vlasceanu & Coman, 2022) but also influence their behavioral intentions.

This work on social norms has been increasingly applied to efforts to mitigate misinformation and its effects. Social norms are associated with a range of mitigation strategies such as the intention to correct (Koo et al., 2021), higher reporting rates for fake news (Gimpel et al., 2021), and lower intentions to share misinformation (Andı & Akesson, 2021). The power of social norms is not just limited to members of the public; one study found that among health- care professionals, beliefs that their colleagues are correcting misinformation (i.e., descriptive norms) mediate the effects of perceived organizational support on heightening their intentions to correct healthcare(Bautista et al., 2022).

However, social norms do not just exist in the wild but may be leveraged to encourage more people to perform corrections during a crisis. Social norms interventions have been shown to work, including when targeting injunctive norms (one *should* correct) and descriptive norms (others *do* correct) to predict willingness to counter misinformation (Roozenbeek et al., 2022). However, it is noteworthy that one study indicates that descriptive norms interventions alone may not be enough to increase sharing discernment but a combined intervention—social norms plus literacy tips or social norms plus an importance prime (i.e., priming people about the importance of sharing accurate news)— works to increase sharing discernment (Epstein et al., 2021). Clearly, more work is needed to understand how to utilize social norms to encourage correction, especially in crisis situations where galvanizing a broad public to respond to quickly circulating misinformation is essential, especially if professionals are busy managing the crisis itself and cannot focus on communication efforts.

In addition to social norms, other sociocultural factors such as trust in others, conflict avoidance, and relational factors may also influence whether and how people correct (Chadwick et al., 2023; Malhotra, 2023; Malhotra & Pearce, 2022). Politeness norms, for instance, can influence the approach to correction, as shown by young Indian adults using indirect methods when correcting older adults (Malhotra & Pearce, 2022). The norm of conflict avoidance also influences how individuals interact on social media, often leading to misinformation going unchallenged to avoid potential violence (Chadwick et al., 2023; Elsaesser et al., 2021; Malhotra, 2023; Soto-Vásquez et al., 2021). To avoid conflict for the corrector and to save face for the misinformation sender, the corrector can use certain strategies to perform corrections, such as correcting via a one-to-one private message and in indirect ways (e.g., sending fact checks) (Ng & Neyazi, 2022). In addition, trust in WhatsApp group members is also positively related to correction behaviors (Kuru et al., 2022).

Finally, social identity and group affiliation, and trust in institutions, also matter in the context of correcting crisis misinformation. For example, people's affiliations with different social, political, or religious groups can influence their acceptance of corrections (Nan et al., 2022). Individuals may resist correction because of motivated reasoning, a psychological phenomenon whereby they prioritize information that aligns with their pre-existing beliefs (Lewandowsky et al., 2012) or if the misinformation aligns with the beliefs or ideologies of a group they identify with (Ecker & Ang, 2019). In such cases, using trusted figures from within their group to deliver the correction can be beneficial. In addition, the level of trust in institutions such as government, science, and media can greatly influence the acceptance of correct messages (Swire-Thompson & Lazer, 2020). Communities with low trust in these institutions may disregard corrections from them. In these contexts collaborating with trusted community leaders or influencers to correct misinformation would be a more effective strategy.

Emotional Factors

Emotions play a significant role in the dissemination of misinformation during crises. During public health crises, Na et al. (2018) found that emotionally evocative crisis misinformation was more readily accepted by the public compared to less emotionally evocative misinformation. The spread of misinformation is accelerated through social media platforms, where users amplify emotionally charged messages, contributing to the sensemaking process in uncertain situations (Huang et al., 2015; Starbird, 2020). However, this influx of emotion-laden information can complicate problem solving, trigger unnecessary confusion, and potentially lead to ill-informed decision making among the public (Liu & Kim, 2011). Negative emotions such as anxiety, anger, and sadness can become salient during crises (Kim & Cameron, 2011), further motivating people to engage in heuristic processing (Wong et al., 2021). Research indicates that during a health crisis people are more susceptible to fear-arousing misinformation compared to fear-neutral misinformation (Lee, 2022). When people become reliant on misinformation, they are more susceptible to misinformation (Martel et al., 2020), and emotion regulation interventions such as emotional suppression or emotion reappraisal techniques don't seem to work (Bago et al., 2022).

Acknowledging the role of emotions in the context of a crisis is crucial for effectively addressing and correcting false information during crises. First, to counter crisis misinformation, it is important when performing correction to address the emotional element of misinformation and the public's fears and concerns, in addition to providing accurate information (Gesser-Edelsburg et al., 2018). Thus, it is crucial to acknowledge that it's normal for people to be misinformed or to believe misinformation, particularly in high-stress crisis situations. Corrective messages should be crafted with empathy and respect so as to maintain a connection with the audience. At the same time, self-efficacy messages could be integrated into corrective messages to help people better manage their fear (Sandman, 2006). Researchers have also argued that, in response to emotional misinformation, we should consider using narrative correction, which may be more engaging and make people sympathize with the corrector (Lee et al., 2021). Empirical evidence suggests that narrative correction may be effective at correcting misperceptions and narrative correction with emotional endings could be more effective in correcting people's attitudes compared with a simple correction (Sangalang et al., 2019).

However, emotion may also play a crucial role in the correction of misinformation during crises by reducing misperceptions caused by misinformation and motivating people to engage in corrective behaviors. Incorporating emotions into correction efforts can enhance their effectiveness and increase the likelihood of information being shared. Emotional messages capture the audience's attention and are more easily remembered (Lang et al., 1995). Emotion may also serve as motivation to correct misinformation (Yeo & McKasy, 2021). Fear appeals, for example, can be persuasive by emphasizing the severity of the threat and the importance of accurate information and are effective in motivating health professionals to engage in correction efforts (Chen & Tang, 2022). Moreover, during a crisis, factual elaboration correction is better than a simple rebuttal at motivating people to engage in preventive action by stimulating their negative emotions such as fear and anxiety (van der Meer & Jin, 2020). Furthermore, the presence of correction reduces people's misperceptions of the perceived severity of a crisis when misinformation downplays the risk by triggering people's fear (van der Meer & Jin, 2020).

Two theoretical models can help explain how emotional appeals work. First, the extended parallel process model explains how fear appeals work, highlighting the role of perceived threat (including perceived severity and perceived susceptibility), combined with efficacy messages in motivating behavior change (Witte, 1992). Similarly, anger appeals can elicit strong emotional responses and drive individuals to take action (Valentino et al., 2011). The anger activism model holds that people with higher anger levels and higher efficacy are the most motivated to engage in activism behaviors compared to other groups of people (Turner, 2007), and empirical evidence has shown that people with higher anger levels are more likely to support misinformation regulation (Sun et al., 2022). However, it is important to design emotional messages and emotional corrections carefully to avoid unintended negative outcomes by ensuring that they are tailored to the specific context and audience.

In summary, the correction of beliefs and behaviors during a crisis can be approached from cognitive, social, and emotional perspectives. Cognitively, correction counters biases and encourages critical thinking, employing strategies such as prebunking, fact checking, and technocognition. Socially, it leverages social norms and relationships to influence behavior and counter misinformation, albeit balancing politeness and conflict avoidance norms. Emotionally, correction harnesses emotions such as anger and fear as catalysts for change.

Limitations of Correction

Despite this work on the potential power of correction during the crisis, we must acknowledge its limitations. First and foremost, a lot of the work in the correction space has focused narrowly on reducing misperceptions or people's inaccurate beliefs on the topic

(Nyhan & Reifler, 2010). And changing beliefs matter: Many of our theories of behavioral change recognize the important role that beliefs (or attitudes) play in predicting behavior (Ajzen, 1991, 2020; Carpenter, 2010; Janz & Becker, 1984; Rosenstock, 1974; van der Linden, 2021). But none of these theories argue that beliefs are the *only* force that predicts behaviors. For example, the famous theory of planned behavior recognizes that attitudes serve as one of the antecedents of behavioral intentions, alongside perceptions of social norms and behavioral control (or self-efficacy) (Ajzen, 1991; Pundir et al., 2021), while the health belief model also considers the role of cues for action as well as self-efficacy (Carpenter, 2010; Janz & Becker, 1984).

The tenuous link between attitudes and behavior is echoed in the correction literature. Often, even successfully correcting a single belief (e.g., that a political candidate lied) does not change people's more holistic perceptions of an issue (e.g., whether or not they like that candidate; Porter & Wood, 2019; Swire-Thompson et al., 2019; Thorson, 2016), and the effects of corrections on related behaviors are mixed (Carey et al., 2020; Vraga, Bode, & Tully, 2022; Walter et al., 2021). However, this is not always the case—the gateway belief model suggests that correcting misperceptions of scientific consensus is of particular importance in shifting both attitudes and behaviors (Bode et al., 2020; Dixon, 2016; van der Linden, 2021). This means that efficient campaigns should probably identify the most important types of misinformation and target them. More attention needs to be paid to not just helping people develop accurate attitudes in a singular case but also supporting the appropriate behaviors that may be of special importance in an evolving crisis situation. This means that we should also consider whether so-called effective corrections also strengthen social norms, a sense of self-efficacy, or cues to take action that will work with more accurate attitudes to encourage social behaviors.

Finally, the narrow focus on the ability of correction to affect attitudes may miss other potential downstream effects. For example, Brian Southwell and colleagues (among others) have written persuasively about the potential for unintended consequences from misinformation correction, including potential distrust toward organizations (either those doing the correction or others), reallocation of resources away from other activities, and stigmatizing those holding misperceptions (Krause et al., 2023; Schmid & Betsch, 2022; Southwell et al., 2019; van der Meer et al., 2023) and decrease the accuracy of other beliefs (Carey et al., 2020). Likewise, research into the presentation of conflicting health information—which correction might create the perception of—also suggests the potential for backlash against health professionals and their recommendations (Nagler, 2014; Nagler et al., 2022). Given the quickly changing information environment, crisis situations may exacerbate these downstream risks of correction, and much more research is needed that goes beyond thinking of correction efficacy solely in terms of the targeted misperceptions.

Fortunately, new research has suggested that one area of early concern about the potential for corrections to backfire may have been overstated. Foundational research by Brendan Nyhan and Jason Reifler suggested that corrections of misinformation could actually lead people predisposed to believe the misinformation even more convinced of its veracity (Nyhan & Reifler, 2010, 2015). But more recent work across a range of topics suggested that, while corrections do not always work and may not influence behaviors as described, they very rarely backfire (Nyhan, 2021; Porter & Wood, 2019; Swire-Thompson et al., 2022; Wood & Porter, 2019). Therefore, corrections remain a valuable strategy for addressing misinformation albeit not a panacea.

Conclusion

"Be first, be right, be credible" (Centers for Disease Control and Prevention, n.d.). Such is the risk communication mantra of the US Centers for Disease Control and Prevention. Sage advice, but today's fractured and largely user-generated media environment presents unique challenges. There are many unknowns in a crisis, and the known information is constantly evolving, creating information voids where misinformation can flourish. Particularly in the context of crises that emerge in health, science, and environmental spaces, there is an inherent tension in how we define and thus respond to misinformation. Scientific endeavors often lead to bright lines between what is true and what is false (misinformation), based on scientific consensus and available data (Vraga & Bode, 2020b), but health and science crises blur these lines, further complicating the challenge of responding to misinformation. The rapid evolution of a crisis, especially when it involves an emerging health threat or a complex environmental disaster, can challenge established facts or create situations where there is not yet a consensus in the scientific community. It becomes more difficult to distinguish between misinformation and emerging information that has yet to be verified.

Social media are frequently pointed to as a space where misinformation can spread rapidly during crises (Lee et al., 2022). Social-mediated crisis communication theory, which emerged as a response to how social media has fundamentally shifted how organizations and publics communicate, can offer important insights for those working to correct misinformation in these spaces. People who are interested in studying misinformation and correction during crisis situations need to consider how best to leverage the insights from these two often distinct but increasingly interconnected fields of study.

As an approach that has broad applicability and is highly valued (Bode & Vraga, 2021a), the correction of misinformation on social media is an important and useful strategy to address misinformation during a crisis. The real-time, dynamic nature of crises, particularly those of health and science, necessitates timely and accurate information, which can sometimes only be offered as a correction (van der Meer & Jin, 2020). The damage that can be inflicted by misinformation, if not checked and corrected promptly, can severely disrupt crisis management efforts (Carlson et al., 2018), with potential dire consequences for affected communities (Tran et al., 2020). The need for quick, effective responses puts correction strategies at front and center in crisis communication. Using fact-based or logic-based correction, diverse actors (professionals, official authorities, or laypeople) can get involved in correcting misinformation and combating crisis misinformation. Their collective efforts, especially when effectively coordinated, can create a powerful counterweight to the misinformation spreading on social media platforms.

Effective crisis communication that successfully corrects misinformation requires a multifaceted approach that takes into account cognitive, sociocultural, and emotional factors. It's about not just providing accurate information but also how this information is communicated. Cognitively, to counter the continued influence of misinformation, corrections for crisis misinformation need to be made memorable, provided repeatedly over time, and be explicitly linked to crisis misinformation. From a sociocultural perspective, social norms (injunctive or descriptive norms) intervention could be used during a crisis to motivate people to engage in corrective efforts (King & Wang, 2023; Koo et al., 2021) and information-sharing discernment (Epstein et al., 2021). Given that people are more susceptible to emotionally evocative crisis misinformation (Gesser-Edelsburg et al., 2018), corrections need to address the emotional element of misinformation, such as using narratives and being crafted with empathy, in addition to providing accurate information.

In conclusion, this chapter underscores the urgent need for an intersectional dialogue between the fields of crisis communication and misinformation correction, as reflected in the real-world example of the Norfolk Southern Railway derailment. As we have illustrated, in moments of crisis, the urgency for accurate information escalates (Roche et al., 2013), as does the potential damage from misinformation. Consequently, the existing crisis communication theories may fail to address the crisis misinformation. The unique, complex, and evolving nature of crises requires a comprehensive understanding of the dynamics of misinformation within these contexts. Therefore, crisis communication can benefit immensely from the evolving understanding of how to correct misinformation, especially in our age of social media. By integrating these fields, we can formulate more effective, context-specific strategies to combat misinformation in real time, thereby reducing the associated risks and improving crisis management. We hope this chapter serves as a catalyst for researchers, policymakers, and crisis communicators to bring together these often siloed fields in a united front against misinformation during crises. The freight train derailment example is a stark reminder of the real-world stakes and why bridging these disciplines is not just an intellectual exercise but a societal imperative.

References

Ajzen, I. (1991). The theory of planned behavior. *Organizational Behavior and Human Decision Processes*, *50*(2), 179–211. http://dx.doi.org/10.1016/0749-5978(91)90020-T

Ajzen, I. (2020). The theory of planned behavior: Frequently asked questions. *Human Behavior and Emerging Technologies*, *2*(4), 314–324. http://dx.doi.org/10.1002/hbe2.195

Andı, S., & Akesson, J. (2021). Nudging away false news: Evidence from a social norms experiment. *Digital Journalism*, *9*(1), 106–125. http://dx.doi.org/10.1080/21670811.2020.1847674

Austin, L., Fisher Liu, B., & Jin, Y. (2012). How audiences seek out crisis information: Exploring the social-mediated crisis communication model. *Journal of Applied Communication Research*, *40*(2), 188–207. http://dx.doi.org/10.1080/00909882.2012.654498

Austin, L., & Jin, Y. (2018). *Social media and crisis communication*. Routledge.

Avery, E. J., Lariscy, R. W., Kim, S., & Hocke, T. (2010). A quantitative review of crisis communication research in public relations from 1991 to 2009. *Public Relations Review*, *36*(2), 190–192. http://dx.doi.org/10.1016/j.pubrev.2010.01.001

Bago, B., Rosenzweig, L. R., Berinsky, A. J., & Rand, D. G. (2022). Emotion may predict susceptibility to fake news but emotion regulation does not seem to help. *Cognition and Emotion*, *36*(6), 1166–1180. http://dx.doi.org/10.1080/02699931.2022.2090318

Bautista, J. R., Zhang, Y., & Gwizdka, J. (2022). Predicting healthcare professionals' intention to correct health misinformation on social media. *Telematics and Informatics*, *73*, 101864. https://doi.org/10.1016/j.tele.2022.101864

Bendix, A., & Ede-Osifo, U. (2023, February 18). *As residents near Ohio train derailment begin to file lawsuits, some report coughs or chest pain*. NBC News. https://www.nbcnews.com/news/us-news/lawsuits-filed-ohio-train-derailment-rcna71192

Bendix, A., & Li, D. (2023, February 14). *Residents near Ohio train derailment report dead fish and chickens as authorities say it's safe to return*. NBC News. https://www.nbcnews.com/health/health-news/residents-ohio-train-derailment-report-dead-fish-chickens-rcna70378

Benoit, W. L. (1995). Sears' repair of its auto service image: Image restoration discourse in the corporate sector. *Communication Studies*, *46*(1–2), 89–105. http://dx.doi.org/10.1080/10510979509368441

Bode, L., & Vraga, E. K. (2018). See something, say something: Correction of global health misinformation on social media. *Health Communication*, *33*(9), 1131–1140. http://dx.doi.org/10.1080/10410236.2017.1331312

Bode, L., & Vraga, E. K. (2021a). Value for correction: Documenting perceptions about peer correction of misinformation on social media in the context of COVID-19. *Journal of Quantitative Description: Digital Media*, *1*. https://doi.org/10.51685/jqd.2021.016

Bode, L., & Vraga, E. K. (2021b). People-powered correction: Fixing misinformation on social media. In H. Tumber & S. Waisbord (Eds.), *The Routledge companion to media disinformation and populism* (pp. 498–506). Routledge.

Bode, L., Vraga, E. K., & Tully, M. (2020). Correcting misperceptions about genetically modified food on social media: Examining the impact of experts, social media heuristics, and the gateway belief model. *Science Communication*, *43*(2), 1075547020981375. http://dx.doi.org/10.1177/1075547020981375

Carey, J. M., Chi, V., Flynn, D. J., Nyhan, B., & Zeitzoff, T. (2020). The effects of corrective information about disease epidemics and outbreaks: Evidence from Zika and yellow fever in Brazil. *Science Advances*, *6*(5), eaaw7449. http://dx.doi.org/10.1126/sciadv.aaw7449

Carlson, M., Jakli, L., & Linos, K. (2018). Rumors and refugees: How government-created information vacuums undermine effective crisis management. *International Studies Quarterly*, *62*(3), 671–685. http://dx.doi.org/10.1093/isq/sqy018

Carpenter, C. J. (2010). A meta-analysis of the effectiveness of health belief model variables in predicting behavior. *Health Communication*, *25*(8), 661–669. http://dx.doi.org/10.1080/10410236.2010.521906

Centers for Disease Control and Prevention. (n.d.). *Risk communication*. https://www.cdc.gov/healthcommunication/risk_communication.html

Chadwick, A., Vaccari, C., & Hall, N.-A. (2023). What explains the spread of misinformation in online personal messaging networks? Exploring the role of conflict avoidance. *Digital Journalism*, *12*(5), 1–20. http://dx.doi.org/10.1080/21670811.2023.2206038

Chan, M. S., & Albarracín, D. (2023). A meta-analysis of correction effects in science-relevant misinformation. *Nature Human Behaviour*, *7*, 1514–1525. http://dx.doi.org/10.1038/s41562-023-01623-8

Chan, M. S., Jones, C. R., Hall Jamieson, K., & Albarracín, D. (2017). Debunking: A meta-analysis of the psychological efficacy of messages countering misinformation. *Psychological Science*, *28*(11), 1531–1546. http://dx.doi.org/10.1177/0956797617714579

Chen, L., & Tang, H. (2022). Examining the persuasion process of narrative fear appeals on health misinformation correction. *Information, Communication & Society*, *26*(15), 2923–2941. https://doi.org/10.1080/1369118X.2022.2128849

Coan, T. G., Boussalis, C., Cook, J., & Nanko, M. O. (2021). Computer-assisted classification of contrarian claims about climate change. *Scientific Reports*, *11*(1), 22320. http://dx.doi.org/10.1038/s41598-021-01714-4

Cook, J. (2020). Deconstructing climate science denial. In D. C. Holmes & L. M. Richardson (Eds.), *Research handbook on communicating climate change* (pp. 62–78). Edward Elgar. https://doi.org/10.4337/9781789900408.00014

Cookson, D., Jolley, D., Dempsey, R. C., & Povey, R. (2021). A social norms approach intervention to address misperceptions of anti-vaccine conspiracy beliefs amongst UK parents. *PLoS ONE*, *16*(11), e0258985. http://dx.doi.org/10.1371/journal.pone.0258985

Coombs, W. T. (2014). State of crisis communication: Evidence and the bleeding edge. *Research Journal of the Institute for Public Relations*, *1*(1), 1–12. https://www.instituteforpr.org/wp-content/uploads/CoombsFinalWES.pdf

Coombs, W. T. (2018). Revising situational crisis communication theory: The influences of social media on crisis communication. In Y. Jin & L. L. Austin (Eds.), *Social media and crisis communication* (pp. 21–37). Routledge.

Coombs, W. T., & Holladay, S. J. (2012). The paracrisis: The challenges created by publicly managing crisis prevention. *Public Relations Review*, *38*(3), 408–415. http://dx.doi.org/10.1016/j.pubrev.2012.04.004

Coombs, W. T., & Holladay, S. J. (2022). *The handbook of crisis communication* (2nd ed.). Wiley.

Diethelm, P., & McKee, M. (2009). Denialism: What is it and how should scientists respond? *European Journal of Public Health*, *19*(1), 2–4. https://doi.org/10.1093/eurpub/ckn139

Dixon, G. (2016). Applying the gateway belief model to genetically modified food perceptions: New insights and additional questions. *Journal of Communication*, *66*(6), 888–908. https://doi.org/10.1111/jcom.12260

Ecker, U. K. H., & Ang, L. C. (2019). Political attitudes and the processing of misinformation corrections. *Political Psychology*, *40*(2), 241–260. http://dx.doi.org/10.1111/pops.12494

Ecker, U. K. H., & Antonio, L. M. (2021). Can you believe it? An investigation into the impact of retraction source credibility on the continued influence effect. *Memory & Cognition*, *49*(4), 631–644. http://dx.doi.org/10.3758/s13421-020-01129-y

Ecker, U. K. H., Lewandowsky, S., Cook, J., Schmid, P., Fazio, L. K., Brashier, N., Kendeou, P., Vraga, E. K., & Amazeen, M. A. (2022). The psychological drivers of misinformation belief and its resistance to correction. *Nature Reviews Psychology*, *1*(1), 13–29. http://dx.doi.org/10.1038/s44159-021-00006-y

Ecker, U. K. H., Sanderson, J. A., McIlhiney, P., Rowsell, J. J., Quekett, H. L., Brown, G. D., & Lewandowsky, S. (2023). Combining refutations and social norms increases belief change. *Quarterly Journal of Experimental Psychology*, *76*(6), 1275–1297. http://dx.doi.org/10.1177/17470218221111750

Elsaesser, C. M., Patton, D. U., Kelley, A., Santiago, J., & Clarke, A. (2021). Avoiding fights on social media: Strategies youth leverage to navigate conflict in a digital era. *Journal of Community Psychology*, *49*(3), 806–821. http://dx.doi.org/10.1002/jcop.22363

Epstein, Z., Berinsky, A. J., Cole, R., Gully, A., Pennycook, G., & Rand, D. G. (2021, May 18). Developing an accuracy-prompt toolkit to reduce COVID-19 misinformation online. *Harvard Kennedy School Misinformation Review*, *2*(3). https://doi.org/doi.org/10/gkdg8b

Erku, D. A., Belachew, S. A., Abrha, S., Sinnollareddy, M., Thomas, J., Steadman, K. J., & Tesfaye, W. H. (2021). When fear and misinformation go viral: Pharmacists' role in deterring medication misinformation during the "infodemic" surrounding COVID-19. *Research in Social and Administrative Pharmacy*, *17*(1), 1954–1963. http://dx.doi.org/10.1016/j.sapharm.2020.04.032

Fraustino, J. D., Liu, B. F., & Jin, Y. (2018). Social media use during disasters: A research synthesis and roadmap. In Y. Jin & L. L. Austin (Eds.), *Social media and crisis communication* (pp. 283–295). Routledge.

Garrett, R. K., & Weeks, B. E. (2013). The promise and peril of real-time corrections to political misperceptions. In *CSCW '13: Proceedings of the 2013 Conference on Computer Supported Cooperative Work* (pp. 1047–1058). Association for Computing Machinery. https://doi.org/10.1145/2441776.2441895

Gesser-Edelsburg, A., Diamant, A., Hijazi, R., & Mesch, G. S. (2018). Correcting misinformation by health organizations during measles outbreaks: A controlled experiment. *PLoS ONE*, *13*(12), e0209505. http://dx.doi.org/10.1371/journal.pone.0209505

Gimpel, H., Heger, S., Olenberger, C., & Utz, L. (2021). The effectiveness of social norms in fighting fake news on social media. *Journal of Management Information Systems*, *38*(1), 196–221. http://dx.doi.org/10.1080/07421222.2021.1870389

Glantz, M., & Benoit, W. L. (2018). The world's all atwitter: Image repair discourse on social media. In Y. Jin & L. L. Austin (Eds.), *Social media and crisis communication* (pp. 168–179). Routledge.

Grandoni, D. & Koh, J. (2023, February 23). *More than 43,000 aquatic animals are dead near Ohio train derailment*. The Washington Post. https://www.washingtonpost.com/climate-environment/2023/02/23/ohio-train-derailment-animals-deaths

Guillory, J. J., & Geraci, L. (2013). Correcting erroneous inferences in memory: The role of source credibility. *Journal of Applied Research in Memory and Cognition*, *2*(4), 201–209. http://dx.doi.org/10.1016/j.jarmac.2013.10.001

Hansson, S., Orru, K., Torpan, S., Bäck, A., Kazemekaityte, A., Meyer, S. F., Ludvigsen, J., Savadori, L., Pigrée, A., & Galvagni, A. (2021). COVID-19 information disorder: Six types of harmful information during the pandemic in Europe. *Journal of Risk Research*, *24*(3–4), 380–393. https://doi.org/10.1080/13669877.2020.1871058

Hansson, S. O. (2017). Science denial as a form of pseudoscience. *Studies in History and Philosophy of Science Part A*, *63*, 39–47. http://dx.doi.org/10.1016/j.shpsa.2017.05.002

Hoofnagle, M. (2007, April 30). Hello ScienceBlogs. https://scienceblogs.com/denialism/2007/04/30/hello-to-scienceblogs

Hornmoen, H., & Backholm, K. (2018). Social media use in crisis and risks: An introduction to the collection. In H. Hornmoen & K. Backholm (Eds.), *Social media use in crisis and risk communication: Emergencies, concerns and awareness* (pp. 1–12). Emerald. https://doi.org/10.1108/978-1-78756-269-120181018

Huang, Y. L., Starbird, K., Orand, M., Stanek, S. A., & Pedersen, H. T. (2015). Connected through crisis: Emotional proximity and the spread of misinformation online. In *CSCW '15: Proceedings of the 18th ACM Conference on Computer Supported Cooperative Work & Social Computing* (pp. 969–980). Association for Computing Machinery. http://dx.doi.org/10.1145/2675133.2675202

Hurley, B., & Boyle, L. (2023, February 16). The controversial company behind Ohio's toxic train disaster. *The Independent*. www.independent.co.uk/climate-change/news/ohio-train-derailment-chemicals-east-palestine-b2283132.html

Janmohamed, K., Walter, N., Nyhan, K., Khoshnood, K., Tucker, J. D., Sangngam, N., Altice, F. L., Ding, Q., Wong, A., Schwitzky, Z. M., Bauch, C. T., De Choudhury, M., Papakyriakopoulos, O., & Kumar, N. (2021). Interventions to mitigate COVID-19 misinformation: A systematic review and meta-analysis. *Journal of Health Communication*, *26*(12), 846–857. http://dx.doi.org/10.1080/10810730.2021.2021460

Janz, N. K., & Becker, M. H. (1984). The health belief model: A decade later. *Health Education Quarterly*, *11*(1), 1–47. http://dx.doi.org/10.1177/109019818401100101

Jin, Y., Fraustino, J. D., & Liu, B. F. (2016). The scared, the outraged, and the anxious: How crisis emotions, involvement, and demographics predict Publics' conative coping. *International Journal of Strategic Communication*, *10*(4), 289–308. http://dx.doi.org/10.1080/1553118X.2016.1160401

Jin, Y., van der Meer, T. G. L. A., Lee, Y.-I., & Lu, X. (2020). The effects of corrective communication and employee backup on the effectiveness of fighting crisis misinformation. *Public Relations Review*, *46*(3), 101910. http://dx.doi.org/10.1016/j.pubrev.2020.101910

Kemp, P. L., Alexander, T. R., & Wahlheim, C. N. (2022). Recalling fake news during real news corrections can impair or enhance memory updating: The role of recollection-based retrieval.

Cognitive Research: Principles and Implications, *7*(1), 85. http://dx.doi.org/10.1186/s41235-022-00434-1

Kendeou, P., & O'Brien, E. J. (2014). The knowledge revision components (KReC) framework: Processes and mechanisms. In D. N. Rapp & J. L. G. Braasch (Eds.), *Processing inaccurate information: Theoretical and applied perspectives from cognitive science and the educational sciences* (pp. 353–377). MIT Press. http://dx.doi.org/10.7551/mitpress/9737.001.0001

Kim, H. J., & Cameron, G. T. (2011). Emotions matter in crisis: The role of anger and sadness in the publics' response to crisis news framing and corporate crisis response. *Communication Research*, *38*(6), 826–855. http://dx.doi.org/10.1177/0093650210385813

Kim, Y., & Lim, H. (D.) (2022). Debunking misinformation in times of crisis: Exploring misinformation correction strategies for effective internal crisis communication. *Journal of Contingencies and Crisis Management*, *31*(3). http://dx.doi.org/10.1111/1468-5973.12447

King, K. K., & Wang, B. (2023). Diffusion of real versus misinformation during a crisis event: A big data-driven approach. *International Journal of Information Management*, *71*, 102390. http://dx.doi.org/10.1016/j.ijinfomgt.2021.102390

Koo, A. Z.-X., Su, M.-H., Lee, S., Ahn, S.-Y., & Rojas, H. (2021). What motivates people to correct misinformation? Examining the effects of third-person perceptions and perceived norms. *Journal of Broadcasting & Electronic Media*, *65*(1), 111–134. http://dx.doi.org/10.1080/08838151.2021.1903896

Krause, N. M., Beets, B., Howell, E. L., Tosteson, H., & Scheufele, D. A. (2023). Collateral damage from debunking mRNA vaccine misinformation. *Vaccine*, *41*(4), 922–929. http://dx.doi.org/10.1016/j.vaccine.2022.12.045

Krishna, A., & Amazeen, M. A. (2022). Narrative counters: Understanding the efficacy of narratives in combating anecdote-based vaccine misinformation. *Public Relations Review*, *48*(5), 102251. https://doi.org/10.1016/j.pubrev.2022.102251

Kuru, O., Campbell, S. W., Bayer, J. B., Baruh, L., & Ling, R. (2022). Encountering and correcting misinformation on WhatsApp. In *H. Wasserman & D. Madrid-Morales (Eds.), Disinformation in the global south* (pp. 88–107). Wiley. http://dx.doi.org/10.1002/9781119714491.ch7

Lang, A., Dhillon, K., & Dong, Q. (1995). The effects of emotional arousal and valence on television viewers' cognitive capacity and memory. *Journal of Broadcasting & Electronic Media*, *39*(3), 313–327. http://dx.doi.org/10.1080/08838159509364309

Lazić, A., & Žeželj, I. (2021). A systematic review of narrative interventions: Lessons for countering anti-vaccination conspiracy theories and misinformation. *Public Understanding of Science*, *30*(6), 644–670. http://dx.doi.org/10.1177/09636625211011881

Lee, J. (2022). When web add-on correction comes with fear-arousing misinformation in public health crisis: Focusing on the role of risk perception in belief in misinformation. *Journal of Applied Communication Research*, *50*(1), 70–90. https://doi.org/10.1080/00909882.2021.1964574

Lee, J., Britt, B. C., & Kanthawala, S. (2022). Taking the lead in misinformation-related conversations in social media networks during a mass shooting crisis. *Internet Research*, *33*(2), 638–663. http://dx.doi.org/10.1108/INTR-02-2021-0120

Lee, J., Kanthawala, S., Britt, B. C., Deavours, D. F., & Ott-Fulmore, T. (2021). Prevalence of anger, engaged in sadness: Engagement in misinformation, correction, and emotional tweets during mass shootings. *Online Information Review*, *46*(3), 422–440. http://dx.doi.org/10.1108/OIR-03-2021-0121

Lewandowsky, S., Ecker, U. K. H., Seifert, C. M., Schwarz, N., & Cook, J. (2012). Misinformation and its correction: Continued influence and successful debiasing. *Psychological Science in the Public Interest*, *13*(3), 106–131. https://doi.org/10.1177/1529100612451018

Liu, B. F., & Fraustino, J. D. (2014). Beyond image repair: Suggestions for crisis communication theory development. *Public Relations Review*, *40*(3), 543–546. http://dx.doi.org/10.1016/j.pubrev.2014.04.004

Liu, B. F., & Kim, S. (2011). How organizations framed the 2009 H1N1 pandemic via social and traditional media: Implications for U.S. health communicators. *Public Relations Review*, *37*(3), 233–244. http://dx.doi.org/10.1016/j.pubrev.2011.03.005

Lu, X., Vijaykumar, S., Jin, Y., & Rogerson, D. (2022). Think before you share: Beliefs and emotions that shaped COVID-19 (Mis)information vetting and sharing intentions among WhatsApp users in the United Kingdom. *Telematics and Informatics*, *67*, 101750. http://dx.doi.org/10.1016/j.tele.2021.101750

Malecki, K. M. C., Keating, J. A., & Safdar, N. (2021). Crisis communication and public perception of COVID-19 risk in the era of social media. *Clinical Infectious Diseases*, *72*(4), 697–702. http://dx.doi.org/10.1093/cid/ciaa758

Malhotra, P. (2023). Misinformation in WhatsApp family groups: Generational perceptions and correction considerations in a meso-news space. *Digital Journalism*, *12*(5), 594–612. http://dx.doi.org/10.1080/21670811.2023.2213731

Malhotra, P., & Pearce, K. (2022). Facing falsehoods: Strategies for polite misinformation correction. *International Journal of Communication*, *16*. https://ijoc.org/index.php/ijoc/article/view/18361/3762

Margolin, D. B., Hannak, A., & Weber, I. (2018). Political fact-checking on twitter: When do corrections have an effect? *Political Communication*, *35*(2), 196–219. https://doi.org/10.1080/10584609.2017.1334018

Martel, C., Pennycook, G., & Rand, D. G. (2020). Reliance on emotion promotes belief in fake news. *Cognitive Research: Principles and Implications*, *5*(1), 47. http://dx.doi.org/10.1186/s41235-020-00252-3

McKay, S., & Tenove, C. (2021). Disinformation as a threat to deliberative democracy. *Political Research Quarterly*, *74*(3), 703–717. http://dx.doi.org/10.1177/1065912920938143

Mheidly, N., & Fares, J. (2020). Leveraging media and health communication strategies to overcome the COVID-19 infodemic. *Journal of Public Health Policy*, *41*(4), 410–420. http://dx.doi.org/10.1057/s41271-020-00247-w

Na, K., Garrett, R. K., & Slater, M. D. (2018). Rumor acceptance during public health crises: Testing the emotional congruence hypothesis. *Journal of Health Communication*, *23*(8), 791–799. https://doi.org/10.1080/10810730.2018.1527877

Nagler, R. H. (2014). Adverse outcomes associated with media exposure to contradictory nutrition messages. *Journal of Health Communication*, *19*(1), 24–40. http://dx.doi.org/10.1080/10810730.2013.798384

Nagler, R. H., Vogel, R. I., Gollust, S. E., Yzer, M. C., & Rothman, A. J. (2022). Effects of prior exposure to conflicting health information on responses to subsequent unrelated health messages: Results from a population-based longitudinal experiment. *Annals of Behavioral Medicine*, *56*(5), 498–511. http://dx.doi.org/10.1093/abm/kaab069

Nan, X., Wang, Y., & Thier, K. (2022). Why do people believe health misinformation and who is at risk? A systematic review of individual differences in susceptibility to health misinformation. *Social Science & Medicine*, *314*, 115398. http://dx.doi.org/10.1016/j.socscimed.2022.115398

Newman, E. J., Swire-Thompson, B., & Ecker, U. K. H. (2022). Misinformation and the sins of memory: False-belief formation and limits on belief revision. *Journal of Applied Research in Memory and Cognition*, *11*(4), 471–477. http://dx.doi.org/10.1037/mac0000090

Newman, N., Fletcher, R., Kalogeropoulos, A., Levy, D. A. L., & Kleis Nielsen, R. (2017). *Reuters Institute digital news report 2017*. Reuters Institute. https://www.digitalnewsreport.org/survey/2017/

Ng, S. W. T., & Neyazi, T. A. (2022). Self- and social corrections on instant messaging platforms. *International Journal of Communication*, *17*. https://ijoc.org/index.php/ijoc/article/view/19142/4005

Nyhan, B. (2021). Why the backfire effect does not explain the durability of political misperceptions. *PNAS*, *118*(15), e1912440117. http://dx.doi.org/10.1073/pnas.1912440117

Nyhan, B., & Reifler, J. (2010). When corrections fail: The persistence of political misperceptions. *Political Behavior*, *32*(2), 303–330. http://dx.doi.org/10.1007/s11109-010-9112-2

Nyhan, B., & Reifler, J. (2015). Does correcting myths about the flu vaccine work? An experimental evaluation of the effects of corrective information. *Vaccine*, *33*(3), 459–464. https://doi.org/10.1016/j.vaccine.2014.11.017

Orsagos, P., & Seewer, J. (2023, February 7). Crews release toxic chemicals from derailed tankers in Ohio. *AP News*. https://apnews.com/article/ohio-train-derailment-updates-bf5a60de2243cd6f7f730096aa33294c

Porter, E., Velez, Y., & Wood, T. J. (2023). Correcting COVID-19 vaccine misinformation in 10 countries. *Royal Society Open Science*, *10*(3), 221097. https://doi.org/10.1098/rsos.221097

Porter, E., & Wood, T. J. (2019). *False alarm: The truth about political mistruths in the Trump era*. Cambridge University Press. http://dx.doi.org/10.1017/9781108688338

Prike, T., Butler, L., & Ecker, U. (2023). Source-credibility information and social norms improve truth discernment and reduce engagement with misinformation online. *PsyArXiv*. http://dx.doi.org/10.31234/osf.io/dhx6f

Pundir, V., Devi, E. B., & Nath, V. (2021). Arresting fake news sharing on social media: A theory of planned behavior approach. *Management Research Review*, *44*(8), 1108–1138. https://doi.org/10.1108/MRR-05-2020-0286

Purnat, T. D., Vacca, P., Czerniak, C., Ball, S., Burzo, S., Zecchin, T., Wright, A., Bezbaruah, S., Tanggol, F., Dubé, È., Labbé, F., Dionne, M., Lamichhane, J., Mahajan, A., Briand, S., & Nguyen, T. (2021). Infodemic signal detection during the COVID-19 pandemic: Development of a methodology for identifying potential information voids in online conversations. *JMIR Infodemiology*, *1*(1), e30971. http://dx.doi.org/10.2196/30971

Rich, T. S. (2022). South Korean perceptions of misinformation on social media: The limits of a consensus? *Journal of Asian and African Studies*. http://dx.doi.org/10.1177/00219096221137662

Roche, S., Propeck-Zimmermann, E., & Mericskay, B. (2013). GeoWeb and crisis management: Issues and perspectives of volunteered geographic information. *GeoJournal*, *78*(1), 21–40. http://dx.doi.org/10.1007/s10708-011-9423-9

Roozenbeek, J., Suiter, J., & Culloty, E. (2022). Countering misinformation: Evidence, knowledge gaps, and implications of current interventions. *European Psychologist*, *28*(3), 189–205. https://doi.org/10.1027/1016-9040/a000492

Rosenstock, I. M. (1974). The health belief model and preventative health behavior. *Health Education Monographs*, *2*(4), 354–386. http://dx.doi.org/10.1177/109019817400200405

Rossini, P., Stromer-Galley, J., Baptista, E. A., & Veiga de Oliveira, V. (2021). Dysfunctional information sharing on WhatsApp and Facebook: The role of political talk, cross-cutting exposure and social corrections. *New Media & Society*, *23*(8), 2430–2451. http://dx.doi.org/10.1177/1461444820928059

Sainato, M. (2022, December 16). Railroad workers pressure Congress and Biden to address working conditions. The Guardian. https://www.theguardian.com/us-news/2022/dec/16/railroad-workers-unions-congress-biden-working-conditions

Sanderson, J. A., Bowden, V., Swire-Thompson, B., Lewandowsky, S., & Ecker, U. K. H. (2022). Listening to misinformation while driving: Cognitive load and the effectiveness of (repeated) corrections. *Journal of Applied Research in Memory and Cognition*, *12*(3), 325–334. http://dx.doi.org/10.1037/mac0000057

Sandman, P. M. (2006). Crisis communication best practices: Some quibbles and additions. *Journal of Applied Communication Research*, *34*(3), 257–262. http://dx.doi.org/10.1080/00909880600771619

Sangalang, A., Ophir, Y., & Cappella, J. N. (2019). The potential for narrative correctives to combat misinformation. *Journal of Communication*, *69*(3), 298–319. http://dx.doi.org/10.1093/joc/jqz014

Schmid, P., & Betsch, C. (2019). Effective strategies for rebutting science denialism in public discussions. *Nature Human Behaviour*, *3*(9), 931–939. https://doi.org/10.1038/s41562-019-0632-4

Schmid, P., & Betsch, C. (2022). Benefits and pitfalls of debunking interventions to counter mRNA vaccination misinformation during the COVID-19 pandemic. *Science Communication*, *44*(5), 531–558. http://dx.doi.org/10.1177/10755470221129608

Seeger, M. W., Sellnow, T. L., & Ulmer, R. R. (1998). Communication, organization, and crisis. In M. E. Roloff (Ed.), *Communication yearbook* (Vol. *21*, pp. 231–275)). Greenwood.

Sell, T. K., Hosangadi, D., & Trotochaud, M. (2020). Misinformation and the US Ebola communication crisis: Analyzing the veracity and content of social media messages related to a fear-inducing infectious disease outbreak. *BMC Public Health*, *20*(1), 550. http://dx.doi.org/10.1186/s12889-020-08697-3

Smith, C. N., & Seitz, H. H. (2019). Correcting misinformation about neuroscience via social media. *Science Communication*, *41*(6). http://dx.doi.org/10.1177/1075547019890073

Sommariva, S., Vamos, C., Mantzarlis, A., Đào, L. U.-L., & Martinez Tyson, D. (2018). Spreading the (fake) news: Exploring health messages on social media and the implications for health professionals using a case study. *American Journal of Health Education*, *49*(4), 246–255. http://dx.doi.org/10.1080/19325037.2018.1473178

Soto-Vásquez, A. D., Gonzalez, A. A., Shi, W., Garcia, N., & Hernandez, J. (2021). COVID-19: Contextualizing misinformation flows in a US Latinx border community (media and communication during COVID-19). *Howard Journal of Communications*, *32*(5), 421–439. http://dx.doi.org/10.1080/10646175.2020.1860839

Southwell, B. G., Niederdeppe, J., Cappella, J. N., Gaysynsky, A., Kelley, D. E., Oh, A., Peterson, E. B., & Chou, W.-Y. S. (2019). Misinformation as a misunderstood challenge to public health. *American Journal of Preventive Medicine*, *57*(2), 282–285. https://doi.org/10/gjm96b

Southwell, B. G., & Thorson, E. A. (2015). The prevalence, consequence, and remedy of misinformation in mass media systems. *Journal of Communication*, *65*(4), 589–595. http://dx.doi.org/10.1111/jcom.12168

Starbird, K. (2020, April 27). *How to cope with an infodemic.* Brookings. https://www.brookings.edu/techstream/how-to-cope-with-an-infodemic

Starbird, K., Maddock, J., Orand, M., Achterman, P., & Mason, R. M. (2014). Rumors, false flags, and digital vigilantes: Misinformation on Twitter after the 2013 Boston Marathon bombing. In *iConference 2014 proceedings*. http://dx.doi.org/10.9776/14308

Sun, Y., Chia, S. C., Lu, F., & Oktavianus, J. (2022). The battle is on: Factors that motivate people to combat anti-vaccine misinformation. *Health Communication*, *37*(3), 327–336. http://dx.doi.org/10.1080/10410236.2020.1838108

Swenson, A. (2023, February 15). Posts misuse Ohio River map to distort contamination area. *AP News*. https://apnews.com/article/fact-check-ohio-contamination-map-411989877238

Swire-Thompson, B., Dobbs, M., Thomas, A., & DeGutis, J. (2023). Memory failure predicts belief regression after the correction of misinformation. *Cognition*, *230*, 105276. http://dx.doi.org/10.1016/j.cognition.2022.105276

Swire-Thompson, B., Ecker, U. K. H., Lewandowsky, S., & Berinsky, A. J. (2019). They might be a liar but they're my liar: Source evaluation and the prevalence of misinformation. *Political Psychology*, *41*(1), 21–34. http://dx.doi.org/10.1111/pops.12586

Swire-Thompson, B., & Lazer, D. (2020). Public health and online misinformation: Challenges and recommendations. *Annual Review of Public Health*, *41*(1), 433–451. http://dx.doi.org/10.1146/annurev-publhealth-040119-094127

Swire-Thompson, B., Miklaucic, N., Wihbey, J. P., Lazer, D., & DeGutis, J. (2022). The backfire effect after correcting misinformation is strongly associated with reliability. *Journal of Experimental Psychology: General*, *151*(7), 1655–1665. http://dx.doi.org/10.1037/xge0001131

Taft, M. (2023, February 16). The Ohio train derailment is a disaster of misinformation. *Gizmodo*. https://gizmodo.com/ohio-toxic-train-derailment-misinformation-conspiracies-1850119412

Tandoc, E. C., & Lee, J. C. B. (2022). When viruses and misinformation spread: How young Singaporeans navigated uncertainty in the early stages of the COVID-19 outbreak. *New Media & Society*, *24*(3), 778–796. http://dx.doi.org/10.1177/1461444820968212

Thompson, S. A. (2023, February 16). "Chernobyl 2.0"? Ohio Train Derailment Spurs Wild Speculation. *The* New York Times. https://www.nytimes.com/2023/02/16/technology/ohio-train-derailment-chernobyl.html

Thorson, E. A. (2016). Belief echoes: The persistent effects of corrected misinformation. *Political Communication*, *33*(3), 460–480. http://dx.doi.org/10.1080/10584609.2015.1102187

Tolentino, D., & Sung, M. (2023, February 23). How the East Palestine train derailment fueled fear on TikTok. *NBC News*. https://www.nbcnews.com/tech/east-palestine-ohio-train-derailment-tiktok-misinformation-rcna71853

Tran, T., Valecha, R., Rad, P., & Rao, H. R. (2020). An investigation of misinformation harms related to social media during humanitarian crises. In S. K. Sahay, N. Goel, V. Patil, & M. Jadliwala (Eds.), *Secure knowledge management in artificial intelligence era* (pp. 167–181). Springer. http://dx.doi.org/10.1007/978-981-15-3817-9_10

Turner, M. M. (2007). Using emotion in risk communication: The anger activism model. *Public Relations Review*, *33*(2), 114–119. http://dx.doi.org/10.1016/j.pubrev.2006.11.013

Valentino, N. A., Brader, T., Groenendyk, E. W., Gregorowicz, K., & Hutchings, V. L. (2011). Election night's alright for fighting: The role of emotions in political participation. *The Journal of Politics*, *73*(1), 156–170. http://dx.doi.org/10.1017/s0022381610000939

van der Linden, S. (2021). The gateway belief model (GBM): A review and research agenda for communicating the scientific consensus on climate change. *Current Opinion in Psychology*, *42*, 7–12. http://dx.doi.org/10.1016/j.copsyc.2021.01.005

van der Linden, S. (2023). *Foolproof: Why misinformation infects our minds and how to build immunity*. Norton.

van der Meer, T. G. L. A., Hameleers, M., & Ohme, J. (2023). Can fighting misinformation have a negative spillover effect? How warnings for the threat of misinformation can decrease general news credibility. *Journalism Studies*, *24*(6), 803–823. http://dx.doi.org/10.1080/1461670X.2023.2187652

van der Meer, T. G. L. A., & Jin, Y. (2020). Seeking formula for misinformation treatment in public health crises: The effects of corrective information type and source. *Health Communication*, *35*(5), 560–575. http://dx.doi.org/10.1080/10410236.2019.1573295

Vijaykumar, S., Rogerson, D. T., Jin, Y., & de Oliveira Costa, M. S. (2021). Dynamics of social corrections to peers sharing COVID-19 misinformation on WhatsApp in Brazil. *Journal of the American Medical Informatics Association*, *29*(1), 33–42. https://doi.org/10.1093/jamia/ocab219

Vlasceanu, M., & Coman, A. (2022). The impact of social norms on health-related belief update. *Applied Psychology. Health and Well-Being*, *14*(2), 453–464. http://dx.doi.org/10.1111/aphw.12313

Vosoughi, S., Roy, D., & Aral, S. (2018). The spread of true and false news online. *Science*, *359*(6380), 1146–1151. http://dx.doi.org/10.1126/science.aap9559

Vraga, E. K., & Bode, L. (2017). Using expert sources to correct health misinformation in social media. *Science Communication*, *39*(5), 621–645. https://doi.org/10.1177/1075547017731776

Vraga, E. K., & Bode, L. (2018). I do not believe you: How providing a source corrects health misperceptions across social media platforms. *Information, Communication & Society*, *21*, 1337–1353. https://doi.org/10.1080/1369118X.2017.1313883

Vraga, E. K., & Bode, L. (2020a). Correction as a solution for health misinformation on social media. *American Journal of Public Health*, *110*(S3), S278–S280. https://doi.org/10/gjmhgh

Vraga, E. K., & Bode, L. (2020b). Defining misinformation and understanding its bounded nature: Using expertise and evidence for describing misinformation. *Political Communication*, *37*(1), 136–144. http://dx.doi.org/10.1080/10584609.2020.1716500

Vraga, E. K., & Bode, L. (2021). Addressing COVID-19 misinformation on social media preemptively and responsively. *Emerging Infectious Diseases*, *27*(2), 396–403. http://dx.doi.org/10.3201/eid2702.203139

Vraga, E. K., Bode, L., & Tully, M. (2022). The effects of a news literacy video and real-time corrections to video misinformation related to sunscreen and skin cancer. *Health Communication*, *37*(13), 1622–1630. https://doi.org/10.1080/10410236.2021.1910165

Vraga, E. K., Kim, S. C., & Cook, J. (2019). Testing logic-based and humor-based corrections for science, health, and political misinformation on social media. *Journal of Broadcasting & Electronic Media*, *63*(3), 393–414. https://doi.org/10.1080/08838151.2019.1653102

Vraga, E. K., Kim, S. C., Cook, J., & Bode, L. (2020). Testing the effectiveness of correction placement and type on Instagram. *The International Journal of Press/Politics*, *25*(4), 632–652. https://doi.org/10.1177/1940161220919082

Vraga, E. K., Tully, M., & Bode, L. (2022). Assessing the relative merits of news literacy and corrections in responding to misinformation on Twitter. *New Media & Society*, *24*(10), 2354–2371, 691

Wahlheim, C. N., Alexander, T. R., & Peske, C. D. (2020). Reminders of everyday misinformation statements can enhance memory for and beliefs in corrections of those statements in the short term. *Psychological Science*, *31*(10), 1325–1339. http://dx.doi.org/10.1177/0956797620952797

Walter, N., Brooks, J. J., Saucier, C. J., & Suresh, S. (2021). Evaluating the impact of attempts to correct health misinformation on social media: A meta-analysis. *Health Communication*, *36*(13), 1776–1784. https://doi.org/10.1080/10410236.2020.1794553

Walter, N., Cohen, J., Holbert, R. L., & Morag, Y. (2020). Fact-checking: A meta-analysis of what works and for whom. *Political Communication*, *37*(3), 350–375. https://doi.org/10.1080/10584609.2019.1668894

Walter, N., & Murphy, S. T. (2018). How to unring the bell: A meta-analytic approach to correction of misinformation. *Communication Monographs*, *85*(3), 423–441. http://dx.doi.org/10.1080/03637751.2018.1467564

Walter, N., & Tukachinsky, R. (2020). A meta-analytic examination of the continued influence of misinformation in the face of correction: How powerful is it, why does it happen, and how to stop it? *Communication Research*, *47*(2), 155–177. http://dx.doi.org/10.1177/0093650219854600

Witte, K. (1992). Putting the fear back into fear appeals: The extended parallel process model. *Communication Monographs*, *59*(4), 329–349. http://dx.doi.org/10.1080/03637759209376276

Wong, J. C. S., Yang, J. Z., Liu, Z., Lee, D., & Yue, Z. (2021). Fast and frugal: Information processing related to the coronavirus pandemic. *Risk Analysis*, *41*(5), 771–786. http://dx.doi.org/10.1111/risa.13679

Wood, T., & Porter, E. (2019). The elusive backfire effect: Mass attitudes' steadfast factual adherence. *Political Behavior*, *41*(1), 135–163. https://doi.org/10.1007/s11109-018-9443-y

Xie, B., He, D., Mercer, T., Wang, Y., Wu, D., Fleischmann, K. R., Zhang, Y., Yoder, L. H., Stephens, K. K., Mackert, M., & Lee, M. K. (2020). Global health crises are also information crises: A call to action. *Journal of the Association for Information Science and Technology*, *71*(12), 1419–1423. http://dx.doi.org/10.1002/asi.24357

Yang, F., & Overton, H. (2022). What if unmotivated is more dangerous? The motivation-contingent effectiveness of misinformation correction on social media. *International Journal of Communication*, *16*. https://ijoc.org/index.php/ijoc/article/view/17510

Yeo, S. K., & McKasy, M. (2021). Emotion and humor as misinformation antidotes. *PNAS*, *118*(15), e2002484118. http://dx.doi.org/10.1073/pnas.2002484118

10

Message Strategies for Misinformation Correction: Current Research, Challenges, and Opportunities

Yan Huang[1] *and Weirui Wang*[2]

[1] *Jack J. Valenti School of Communication, University of Houston*
[2] *Department of Communication, Florida International University*

The digital age has brought about an unprecedented influx of information. While this has paved the way for enriching exchanges of knowledge and insights, it has simultaneously given rise to a chaotic information environment rife with misinformation. The ramifications of such misinformation are far-reaching, from distorted perceptions of important social issues to ill-formed public decision making (Ecker et al., 2022). Misinformation has seeped into almost every aspect of society, disrupting democratic systems, economic activities, public health programs, and even international relations (Jamieson & Albarracin, 2020; Nisbet et al., 2021; Schaffner & Roche, 2016; Wang & Huang, 2023). We have witnessed how misinformation acts as a significant barrier to the effective management of the COVID-19 pandemic, impairing the public's ability to accurately understand the risks associated with the coronavirus disease and the adoption of necessary preventive measures (Huang & Liu, 2022). Not only does misinformation pose challenges to addressing public crises, but it can also be the very cause of crises. A case in point is the misinformation surrounding vaccines, which fueled anti-vaccine sentiments, decreased the uptake of childhood vaccines, and culminated in measles outbreaks (Larson, 2018).

The proliferation of misinformation and its adverse impacts have motivated scholarly research on effective correction strategies. While a number of strategies have been proposed and empirically tested, researchers have also uncovered significant challenges to misinformation correction. The continued influence phenomenon, for instance, suggests that even debunked misinformation can continue to hamper individuals' beliefs and decisions (Walter & Tukachinsky, 2020). Moreover, the literature has highlighted psychological barriers that drive undesirable responses to misinformation correction, including cognitive dissonance (Wang et al., 2020), experienced as mental discomfort when individuals face conflicting information, and confirmation bias (Zhou & Shen, 2021), characterized by a propensity to avoid or downplay information that challenges one's existing beliefs or deeply held values. These psychological barriers underscore the complexities of misinformation correction and emphasize the need for carefully developed correction strategies.

A pressing question thus arises: How can we design misinformation correction programs that effectively counteract false claims and resonate with a wide array of audiences? Delving into different aspects of correction message design may be crucial in the battle against

Communication and Misinformation: Crisis Events in the Age of Social Media, First Edition.
Edited by Kevin B. Wright.
© 2025 John Wiley & Sons, Inc. Published 2025 by John Wiley & Sons, Inc.

misinformation. As an enduring topic in persuasion research, message construction is believed to play a role in influencing attitudes, beliefs, and behaviors (Perloff, 2020). Each facet of a message—from overarching aspects such as its content, structure, and format to specific phrasing and language features—can shape its efficacy (Shen & Bigsby, 2013). In an age where misinformation can swiftly spread via a simple click and become deeply rooted, merely broadcasting correction messages may not suffice. Paying close attention to the nuances of how correction messages are drafted and presented is crucial for optimal correction outcomes.

This chapter provides a review of current research on message strategies for misinformation correction. We begin by assessing the effects and features of argument-based messages, emotional appeals, and narratives in this context. We then reflect on the challenges in this area, while also highlighting opportunities for future research.

Argument-Based Correction

Argument-based messages aim to influence audiences using factual statements, empirical data, and expert opinions (Krakow et al., 2018). At the heart of any argument-based message is the claim being made, the evidence used to support it, and the logical reasoning that ties them together. Since the inception of persuasion research, scholars have been intrigued by how various features of argument-based messages, from more macro aspects such as message content and structure to more nuanced elements such as language features and word choices, shape persuasion outcomes (Shen & Bigsby, 2013). In this section, we review literature that examines the effects of these design features of argument-based messages in misinformation correction.

Simple Rebuttal vs. Factual Elaboration

Early research on misinformation correction suggests that, to better capture attention and avoid any possible backfire effect, correction messages should remain simple and concise and feature fewer arguments (Lewandowsky et al., 2012). The same research also highlights the importance of emphasizing facts. Guided by these insights, empirical research has developed and compared two types of correction messages: "simple rebuttal," which contains a straightforward refutation of the misinformation, and "factual elaboration," which counterargues against misinformation with detailed factual information and statistics (van der Meer & Jin, 2020).

Drawing from the elaboration likelihood model (Petty & Cacioppo, 1986), we might anticipate that factual elaboration would be more effective than simple rebuttal, as the inclusion of additional details and evidence would strengthen the overall argument quality. When individuals take the central route, they are more inclined to be persuaded by messages with robust argumentation. However, for individuals on the peripheral route, the presence of facts, details, and the extended message length may serve as peripheral cues signaling message quality, thereby enhancing persuasion outcomes. Consistent with this prediction, an experiment conducted within the context of a public health crisis demonstrated that a message corrective containing factual elaboration led to greater intentions to adopt protective actions than a corrective with a simple rebuttal (van der Meer & Jin, 2020). A similar pattern was found in another study replicating this comparison in the context of an organizational crisis (Jin et al., 2020), such that factual elaboration raised perceived message quality, which subsequently increased perceived organizational reputation. A meta-analysis further supported the persuasive advantages of correction messages including detailed information over correction messages that merely label misinformation as incorrect (Chan et al., 2017).

Message Sidedness

Sidedness pertains to the reference of opposing opinions. While one-sided messages include merely supportive information, two-sided messages also acknowledge the existence of opposing views (Shen & Bigsby, 2013). A meta-analysis suggests that two-sided messages are generally perceived to be more credible and persuasive than one-sided messages but only when they are refutational (O'Keefe, 1999), that is, they not only mention the opposing views but also provide counterarguments to them. Research indicates that the effectiveness of two-sided messages varies based on certain conditions (Eisend, 2006). They tend to be more persuasive when the audience is more educated, is aware of opposing views, or is not strongly in favor of the advocated position.

Empirical findings on the efficacy of two-sided messages in misinformation correction have been mixed. Featherstone and Zhang (2020) found that two-sided refutational messages effectively raised pro-vaccine attitudes and anger toward vaccine misinformation. However, their study compared these messages to misinformation exposure rather than to a one-sided corrective message. When two-sided corrections are directly compared with one-sided corrections, empirical evidence suggests that their efficacy is influenced by individual differences. For instance, two-sided corrections resonated more with individuals holding milder misperceptions, while one-sided corrections were more impactful for those with stronger misperceptions (Xiao & Su, 2021). Further, one-sided corrections were found to be more persuasive when individuals employed an online processing style, that is, they formed judgments instantly on receiving new information; conversely, two-sided corrections were effective when individuals used a memory-based processing style, integrating new information into long-term memory and drawing from this reservoir when forming judgments later (Carnahan & Garrett, 2019). Such findings highlight the need to tailor the sidedness strategy based on audience characteristics.

Discrediting the Source of Misinformation

Notably, a significant portion of misinformation disseminated online can be attributed to specific sources (Ecker et al., 2022). For instance, anti-vaccine misinformation often originates from vocal anti-vaxxer groups (Shelby & Ernst, 2013). Likewise, during the COVID-19 pandemic, some politicians weaponized misinformation for their own interests (Luengo & García-Marín, 2020). Drawing from dual processing models, research indicates that source credibility plays a crucial role in shaping judgments, particularly for individuals with low issue involvement or low cognitive capacity (Chaiken, 1980; Petty & Cacioppo, 1986). Accordingly, messages criticizing the credibility of misinformation sources may serve as an alternative correction strategy, especially for low involvement groups. Highlighting a source's lack of expertise, questionable intentions, or motives to mislead may reduce the persuasive influence of misinformation and enhance the coherence of debunking messages (Walter & Tukachinsky, 2020).

Empirical research on this "source attacking" strategy is still nascent. One study (Wood et al., 2023) compared this approach to factual rebuttals but demonstrated that discrediting the misinformants did not significantly change existing beliefs. It is worth noting, however, that the study's operationalization of this strategy was intertwined with a strongly condemnatory tone toward the misinformants, which might confound the findings. There are indeed some concerns that the tactic of ridiculing and condemning misinformation sources may elicit a defensive stance or reactance in individuals with similar misconceptions (Henkel et al., 2023). Moreover, it may inadvertently erode public trust and interest, ultimately stifling healthy public discussions on important social issues (Jennings & Russell, 2019). More empirical research is necessary to understand the efficacy of this strategy and to elucidate boundary conditions.

Inoculation and Exposing Argumentative Fallacies

Over half a century of research on inoculation theory suggests a more proactive approach to misinformation correction (McGuire, 1961). This involves forewarning audiences about potential misinformation they may encounter, providing a weak dose of it, and then arming them with counterarguments to resist the misinformation when they come across it (Maertens et al., 2021). Given the unpredictability of the specific false claims individuals might face at a later time, some researchers recommend that preemptive correction messages highlight the misleading techniques, rhetorical features, and argumentative fallacies often present in misinformation (Cook et al., 2023). For instance, misinformation frequently exhibits certain rhetorical features, such as assertive claims, the extensive use of declarative statements, emotional appeals, and the referencing of dubious sources (Zheng et al., 2021). Moreover, misinformation often contains various argumentative fallacies, including misrepresenting sources, drawing baseless conclusions, making claims without evidence, and constructing ambiguous narratives (Musi & Reed, 2022).

Longitudinal research lends support to the efficacy of inoculation messages exposing fallacies in misinformation (Maertens et al., 2021). The study suggests that, even though the effects of inoculation messages may diminish over time, exposure to them provides an immediate safeguard against subsequent misinformation, prompting individuals to approach it with a more skeptical lens.

Fact-Checking

Fact-checking has emerged as a popular and distinct message strategy in contemporary journalism to correct misinformation. Primarily employed by journalists and other gatekeepers, fact-checkers scrutinize and rectify false claims disseminated by public figures and institutions (Shin & Thorson, 2017). Fact-checkers have two unique content features: (a) a thorough and objective evaluation of claims grounded in evidence from reputable sources and rigorous research; and (b) the use of truth scales—a rating system that quickly and directly communicates the veracity of scrutinized public statements, aiding audiences who might lack the requisite background or motivation to sift through detailed analyses (Amazeen et al., 2018). While a meta-analysis supports the overall positive effects of fact-checkers on beliefs (Walter et al., 2020), it also indicates a nuanced interaction effect with partisanship; specifically, Republicans or conservatives may be less receptive to fact-checking when it challenges their ideology, compared to their Democrat or liberal counterparts.

Message Framing

As one of the most prolific areas in persuasion, framing research posits that selective emphasis on certain aspects of an issue (known as emphasis framing) or the subtle linguistic choices made in delivering logically equivalent messages (referred to as equivalence framing) may dramatically influence perceptions and judgments (Huang et al., 2022). Although the literature has proposed a variety of message frames (Hallahan, 1999), empirical testing of their applicability in misinformation correction is nascent.

Originating from the prospect theory, the notion of *gain versus loss framing* suggests that messages can emphasize either the positive outcomes of adhering to the advocacy or the adverse consequences of disregarding it (O'Keefe & Nan, 2012). Borah et al. (2022) examined the relative effectiveness of gain versus loss framing in correcting human papillomavirus vaccine misperceptions. Their findings revealed a minimal difference between the two frames when participants engaged in low levels of reflection, processing new information by incorporating it into their existing cognitive framework. However, among those with high reflection, loss framing was more successful in reducing misperceptions.

Another study focused on the efficacy of *individual versus collective framing* in correcting misinformation regarding mask-wearing during the pandemic (Xiao et al., 2023). The correction with individual framing emphasized the personal benefits of mask-wearing, whereas collective framing highlighted the broader community benefits of this protective measure. The study findings showed that argument-based messages utilizing individual framing were more effective in motivating participants to engage in discussions and share correction messages on social media platforms.

Jargon or Lexical Complexity

The effective communication of scientific concepts and professional terminology to the public has been a focal point of discussion among researchers (Bullock et al., 2019). Central to this debate is the role of jargon, those technical terms used in specialized areas. Some suggest that the specificity and nuance afforded by jargon can ensure clarity and reduce ambiguities in discussions on complex topics (Sharon & Baram Tsabari, 2014). This is important, especially considering the uncertainty and confusion caused by rampant misinformation in the public space (Huang & Liu, 2022). However, there is evidence suggesting that the use of jargon may hinder the information-processing and comprehension of non-expert audiences, potentially alienating the public from vital scientific discussions (Shulman et al., 2020). With the increasing importance of science communication in policymaking, education, and public opinion, the role of jargon and its effects on public understanding demand careful consideration.

Fact-checking practices often encounter this dilemma. The very nature of rigorous verification often necessitates the use of complex language. However, a meta-analysis indicates that lexical complexity, including the use of jargon, can adversely influence the effectiveness of fact-checkers (Walter et al., 2020). Notably, research suggests that the impact of jargon may not be uniformly detrimental in misinformation correction. Huang and Wang (2023) highlighted a nuanced perspective through an experiment and found that, without inducing a specific motive for information-processing, jargon use hindered persuasion among participants with misbeliefs regarding climate change. Yet, when participants were directed to process information for accurate judgments, jargon was not only tolerated but also led to more positive correction outcomes by mitigating feelings of anger and enhancing the perceived credibility of the correction message. This suggests potential strategies that pair an emphasis on accuracy with judicious jargon use, especially for intervention programs targeting audiences with misbeliefs.

Language Intensity

This term encompasses a range of linguistic elements, from controlling language—described as direct, domineering, or forceful—to its opposite, which is characterized by politeness, deference, or hedging (Miller et al., 2007). The psychological reactance theory posits that, when persuasive messages use strong or intense language, audiences may perceive an overly controlling intent and feel their autonomy or freedom is under threat. This perception can lead to undesirable responses such as anger and counterarguments, which ultimately result in message rejection (Brehm, 1966).

An interview study suggests that politeness and respect in delivering correction messages may be crucial in reducing the influence of misinformation, especially among elderly people (Malhotra & Pearce, 2022). In line with this observation, an experimental study showed that participants had a more positive perception of hedged correction messages than those employing direct language, which was perceived as more aggressive and less respectful (Martel et al., 2021). However, this study did not find a direct effect of language intensity on message acceptance. The flip side of the story may be that, while polite language might not be as threatening as controlling language, it can sometimes diminish the credibility or authority of a message or its source (Burgoon et al., 1975). If a message is presented too tentatively, it may lack the conviction needed to sway skeptics.

Emotional Appeals and Misinformation Correction

Early research on misinformation correction has focused on argument-based messages and logical reasoning, potentially related to the assumption that appealing to emotions may lead to less effortful information-processing and, consequently, less accurate judgments or undesirable correction outcomes (Li et al., 2022; Martel et al., 2020). In recent years, scholars have increasingly recognized the importance of emotions in misinformation correction.

First, research suggests that misinformation often evokes stronger emotions than correction messages, leveraging the influence of emotions to spread among audiences. For example, YouTube videos promoting COVID-19 conspiracy theories contained a higher proportion of fear-inducing content, which was also linked to a much higher number of views. Similarly, tweets spreading misinformation about the El Paso and Dayton mass shootings were heavily infused with negative emotions such as anger, sadness, and anxiety.

Second, research has highlighted the link between emotions and susceptibility to misinformation. For example, during the COVID-19 pandemic, individuals who reported heightened emotionality, including both positive and negative emotions, were more prone to believing and disseminating misinformation (Li et al., 2022). In a study where participants were presented with a fictitious public health crisis, those who had been induced to feel anger were more susceptible to accepting anger-related rumors.

Several theories shed light on the link between emotions and misinformation susceptibility. One primary explanation is the feeling as information theory. This theory posits that individuals often rely on their emotions as informational cues for judgments. Particularly during crises, when reliable and timely information may be scarce and uncertainty heightened, individuals may lean on their emotions for guidance. In line with the feeling as information theory, as emotions are often more accessible and easier to retrieve in memory, the perceptual fluency of processing emotions may drive individuals to evaluate the information as truthful, regardless of its actual accuracy (Martel et al., 2020). Similarly, the emotional congruence hypothesis suggests that, when the emotion conveyed by a message aligns with an individual's current emotional state, they are more likely to accept the information as true because of the ease of processing it. Such scenarios resonate especially during crises when individuals commonly feel anxious, fearful, or angry, and misinformation exploits these emotions to foster misbeliefs.

Given the role of emotions within the misinformation context, there is growing interest in leveraging emotional appeals—messages designed to evoke specific emotions to enhance persuasion—in debunking misinformation. For instance, research has shown that messages concluding with appeals to negative emotions can effectively counter misbeliefs and reduce positive attitudes toward organic tobacco (Sangalang et al., 2019).

Empirical research has investigated the correction effects of appeals to specific discrete emotions. An experimental study found that fear appeals embedded in a story motivated participants who reported high efficacy through character identification to generate a greater intention to correct health misinformation. Humor appeal has also received a good deal of scholarly attention. Using an eye-ing approach, scholars found that humorous correction increased attention to visual appeals of correction messages, which in turn reduced the credibility of misinformation and decreased misperceptions related to the HPV vaccine. However, the study did not provide evidence of the advantages of humorous correction over nonhumorous correction because it also reduced misperceptions by increasing perceived credibility of the correction message. It is generally believed that the persuasive advantages of humor appeal lie in its capacity to capture attention, enhance recall, and foster engagement, particularly among those who are less interested in the topic being addressed (Becker & Waisanen, 2013). Another notable advantage of humor appeal in misinformation correction is its capability to inhibit psychological reactance (Moyer-Gusé et al., 2018). Since humor demands cognitive effort to decode and comprehend jokes and can thus prevent individuals from critically scrutinizing the arguments, correction messages containing humor appeal are less likely to face counterarguments. However, humor appeal comes with potential drawbacks: Individuals may consider the issue addressed as being of less concern (Cook et al., 2023; Vraga et al., 2019) and may not engage in high levels of cognitive elaboration on the correction message, dismissing it as lighthearted rather than taking it seriously.

Research has also examined the potential effect of guilt appeal in misinformation correction. Guilt is an emotional response that arises when individuals perceive a violation of their moral standards or normative expectations (Antonetti et al., 2018). While some emotions drive individuals to attribute blame to others, anticipated guilt usually compels them to internalize blame for harmful actions and their subsequent negative outcomes. Researchers have explored the role of anticipated guilt in misinformation correction by prompting individuals to consider the potential repercussions of failing to address false information and the harm it may cause. This is an approach to motivating social correction against misinformation. Research shows that threat-based appeals can induce anticipated guilt, subsequently encouraging individuals to rectify misinformation (Sun et al., 2022).

Narrative Correction

Narratives are defined as messages containing stories that depict characters and plots, featuring a clear beginning, middle, and end (Hinyard & Kreuter, 2007). Narratives are powerful tools for persuasion because they convey causal claims subtly by weaving them into story events arranged chronologically and present these claims with less overt persuasive intent, which reduces the perceived threat to individual freedom (Dal Cin et al., 2004). Well-constructed narratives possess notable psychological appeals, transporting individuals to the narrative world and allowing them to connect with story characters and to vicariously experience what they have gone through (Green, 2006). This process involves a temporary detachment from the real world and a deep immersive experience that triggers emotional engagement. This immersion often reduces the tendency to use the facts and knowledge acquired in the real world to critically analyze and counterargue against the narratives (Green & Brock, 2000).

Recently, researchers have recognized the potential of narratives to address two primary challenges in misinformation correction. The first pertains to the tenacity of misinformation effects. Despite corrections, many individuals continue to hold onto and to act on the basis of misinformation (Walter & Tukachinsky, 2020). This continued influence often arises from motivated reasoning and a defensive motive where individuals gravitate to information consistent with their preexisting beliefs and resist opposing viewpoints (Hart & Nisbet, 2012). The second challenge concerns the cognitive structures people use to process information. Once an individual accepts misinformation, it often gets integrated into their knowledge structure through mental models (Lewandowsky et al., 2012). If the misinformation is later debunked, gaps will appear in their mental models. However, individuals, prefer complete mental models even if it means holding onto recognized falsehoods (Susmann & Wegener, 2022). This preference complicates the task of misinformation correction.

Given these hurdles, narratives emerge as a promising solution. They can help counter motivated reasoning and defensive motives and offer a compelling alternative to misinformation in mental models. Theories of narrative persuasion highlight the superiority of narratives over other message formats in inhibiting audience resistance, which they attribute largely to the deeply immersive and affect-laden nature of narrative experience (Dal Cin et al., 2004; Ratcliff & Sun, 2020). This experience demands significant cognitive engagement, which diminishes the capacity for critical message evaluation and the tendency to counterargue. Additionally, narratives can adeptly address the gaps in mental models created when misinformation is debunked. They offer detailed, coherent alternative explanations by meticulously mapping out causal relationships through story events (Sangalang et al., 2019).

While theoretical accounts highlight the positive impact of narratives in misinformation correction, empirical studies offer a more nuanced picture. For example, Sangalang et al. (2019) found that, compared to a no-correction condition, narrative correction effectively decreased positive attitudes and intentions related to organic tobacco that had been bolstered by misinformation. In three experiments, Ecker et al. (2020) found that narrative correction was not more effective than nonnarrative correction. This remained consistent across different misinformation types and topics: fictitious issues, false health claims, and real-world misinformation linked to worldviews. Importantly, this pattern held whether the correction outcomes were assessed immediately after exposure to the correction or two days later. Huang and Wang (2022) added another layer of complexity and showed that correction mechanisms on social media could condition the efficacy of narrative correction. It was more effective than nonnarrative correction if it was delivered to participants through algorithmic recommendation with explicit endorsement cues indicating agreement from a collective body of Internet users. In contrast, where participants were told that the correction was from their social media contacts, nonnarrative correction produced more favorable correction outcomes.

The mixed empirical findings underscore the call for a second generation of narrative research to identify distinct elements and characteristics of narrative messages and explore their moderating impacts (Huang & Green, 2023). The current literature has investigated the effects of the following narrative features in misinformation correction.

Narratives with Emotional Endings

The previous section of this chapter explains why emotions are important in misinformation correction. Scholars are also interested in integrating emotional appeals into narrative correction. For instance, Sangalang et al. (2019) designed narratives that end by inducing discrete emotions such as fear and anger. They found that narratives with negative emotional endings were more effective than narratives without emotional endings.

Narratives with Characters' Self-Persuasion

Building on literature on both self-persuasion—where individuals shift attitudes by generating their own pro-advocacy arguments—and narrative persuasion theories, Huang and Green (2023) developed a type of narrative focusing on a character's self-persuasion process. In particular, the narrative featured a character who initially hesitated to receive mRNA vaccines but, after thoroughly researching scientific evidence and consulting expert opinions, opted to get vaccinated. The study aimed to determine whether this type of narrative could elicit a vicarious self-persuasion experience and amplify narrative effects among vaccine-hesitant individuals. The findings indicate that the narrative revolving around a character's self-persuasion process was more persuasive than the narrative featuring a consistently pro-vaccine character. It enhanced pro-vaccine attitudes and intentions by increasing participants' empathy toward the character and their self-referencing thoughts. The effects were especially pronounced among participants with a lower trust in science. While the study is not directly about misinformation correction, it underscores the potential of narratives showcasing a character's self-persuasion in reshaping the attitudes of individuals who have previously held misbeliefs.

Refutational Narratives

As previously mentioned, narratives can convey persuasive arguments implicitly through the causal links implied by story events. While information in a narrative format is typically easier to process than information in nonnarrative formats, there is a trade-off: Subtly embedded persuasive messages may sometimes be overlooked or misinterpreted (Moyer-Gusé et al., 2019). Researchers consider this to be a potential limitation of narrative correction (Ecker et al., 2020).

Building on the insights from research on epilogues in entertainment education programs (Moyer-Gusé et al., 2012), Wang and Huang (2023) devised a strategy to enhance the clarity and strength of persuasive messages embedded in narrative correction by adding a refutational ending to narratives. This refutational ending serves as a direct counterpoint to challenge and refute the erroneous claims propagated by misinformation, reinforcing the core persuasive messages implied through story events. Results from the study reveal that the effect of a refutational ending depends on the timing of correction exposure. Specifically, narratives equipped with refutational endings may be more effective as a prebunking or inoculation tool that prepares audiences to counter upcoming misinformation. Conversely, in a debunking scenario (post-misinformation exposure) simple narratives without refutational endings may generate more positive correction outcomes.

Moreover, informed by the research on the sidedness of argument-based messages (O'Keefe, 1999), Wang and Huang (2021) explored the impact of sidedness in narrative correction. They crafted two-sided refutational narratives that not only recognized potential counterarguments against the advocacy but also offered means of rebuttal. Experiment results indicate that two-sided refutational narratives do not necessarily outperform one-sided simple narratives. However, the two-sided approach may be advantageous among audiences who are already familiar with the issue or who are deeply engaged with it.

These recent findings suggest that narrative correction can effectively mitigate the influence of misinformation but that its efficacy does not consistently surpass that of nonnarrative correction. Leveraging the inherent strengths of narratives, such as amplifying their emotional resonance or featuring relatable characters, can enhance their effectiveness. Introducing supplementary elements to narratives, whether a refutational conclusion or strategies to fend off potential counterarguments, yields varied results depending on the context and the placement of correction messages. Moreover, the efficacy of narrative correction depends on a range of audience factors, such as their prior knowledge or issue involvement.

Challenges and Opportunities

After an extensive review of the literature on argument-based messages, emotional appeals, and narratives within the context of misinformation correction, it is evident that the topic is both intricate and multifaceted. Research on correction messages is about not just identifying effective strategies but also understanding the nuances that influence their efficacy. It is important to discuss the challenges and opportunities that await scholars in this area of research.

Theories and Research on Competitive Message Effects

Current studies on misinformation correction have borrowed extensive insights from traditional persuasion research. However, a major theoretical challenge emerges: Our conventional understanding of message effects is largely anchored in theories that assume single message exposure. Most classical persuasion theories were framed within contexts where individuals' beliefs and attitudes were influenced in isolation, without the interference of conflicting messages. However, today's information-saturated digital age presents a more complex picture.

The essence of misinformation correction lies in navigating a more dynamic and competitive information environment. The audience of a correction message is not a blank slate but is influenced by an intricate interplay of previously received misinformation, established beliefs, and the social and psychological contexts that shape their perception and reception of new information (Ecker et al., 2022). Every correction message is competing not just with misinformation but also for attention amid a cacophony of information from myriad sources.

This presents an urgent need and also an opportunity for either the development of existing theories or the birth of new paradigms that are able to encompass the complexities and nuances of message effects in competitive information environments. Theory development must appreciate the dynamics of multiple message exposures, whereby information is constantly weighed against existing beliefs and challenged by messages presenting conflicting viewpoints. Theoretical frameworks should also pay special attention to the influence of various cognitive processes such as confirmation bias, cognitive dissonance, and motivated reasoning when determining competitive message effects (Walter & Tukachinsky, 2020).

Given these directions for theory development, it is crucial to address the obstacles faced during actual theory testing. Central to these challenges are the limitations intrinsic to controlled experiments and the self-report measures of message responses. Testing competitive message effects may involve exposing participants to multiple message stimuli and asking them to report their responses to each message. This may inadvertently sensitize them to the study's objectives and skew their self-reported responses. This in turn limits the broader applicability of experimental findings to real-world contexts. However, the silver lining is the emergence of advanced experimental methods, such as eye-tracking and neuroimaging. These techniques promise deeper insights, beyond what can be captured from self-reports alone, into more spontaneous cognitive processes activated during the processing of competitive messages.

Moreover, big data analytics and natural language processing help pave the way for field experiments in real-time digital landscapes instead of relying solely on controlled lab-based experiments. Researchers may capture authentic audience responses as they interact naturally with multiple competing messages online, pinpointing emotions or biases triggered by competing messages. This makes the findings on correction message strategies more applicable in real-world misinformation intervention programs.

Audience Segmentation and Tailored Correction

A key insight gleaned from examining argument-based messages, emotional appeals, and narratives in the context of misinformation correction is the absence of a one-size-fits-all solution. To achieve the best results in misinformation correction, it is crucial to tailor correction messages to the specific characteristics of the target audience.

The notion of audience segmentation and message tailoring involves categorizing subgroups within a population based on shared characteristics and needs (Noar et al., 2007). This approach enables more targeted strategies and tailored messages directly addressing the specific information needs of an audience. This can be instrumental in persuading and guiding them toward desired attitudes and behaviors. Nonetheless, the success of this approach relies heavily on an in-depth understanding of the target audience. Messages that resonate on deeper levels, including aligning with audiences' attitudes, beliefs, norms, and cultural values, are more impactful than merely tailoring messages on the basis of more superficial demographic factors (Huang & Shen, 2016; Huang et al., 2023).

Understanding the target audience on a deeper level is paramount, particularly when crafting misinformation correction messages. Rooted in the notion of motivated reasoning, individuals tend to process new correction information in ways that align with their existing beliefs (Hart & Nisbet, 2012). Consequently, they either selectively expose themselves to, or process in a biased manner, any information that deviates from their existing viewpoints or ideology. Recognizing this challenge, scholars underscore the need for correction messages tailored to specific audience segments based on their political, cultural, and value orientations (Nan et al., 2022).

Pioneering work indicates that tailored approaches in misinformation correction are not just a theoretical ideal but can be practiced effectively. Dixon et al. (2017) exemplified this by crafting messages promoting a free-market solution to climate change, targeting conservatives' apprehensions about governmental interference in the market. This approach was found to effectively enhance beliefs regarding climate change among conservatives, outperforming other correction message strategies (Dixon et al., 2017). Similarly, Lunz Trujillo et al. (2021) first designed a survey identifying psychological barriers to vaccine acceptance, such as concerns about needle and blood sensitivity as well as about moral purity. Armed with this detailed insight, they crafted messages that specifically addressed these concerns, resulting in a significant reduction in misinformation acceptance. These findings underscore the benefits of adopting a tailored approach to misinformation correction.

However, a major challenge in implementing tailored correction is the need for a deep understanding of the various factors that may influence individuals' processing and reception of correction messages. The rapid spread of misinformation often necessitates an immediate response, leaving little time for comprehensive audience research and the development of carefully tailored messages (Huang & DiStaso, 2020). Professionals are thus often constrained to deploy simple, general, one-size-fits-all rebuttals.

Looking ahead, the key to unlocking the full potential of tailored correction strategies lies not only in the creation of tailored correction messages but also in their strategic placement, ensuring that they reach the right audiences at the right time. This necessitates integrating nuanced audience data from web analytics with advanced placement algorithms (Huang & Wang, 2022). The advancements in real-time data analytics and artificial intelligence could be instrumental in this endeavor, facilitating the swift development and distribution of messages attuned to the unique informational needs, cultural preferences, and psychological antecedents of distinct audience segments. Scholarly investigations into the persuasive roles of AI and algorithms can shed light on how to make correction messages more compelling and how to position them effectively.

On the placement front, collaborations between researchers and social media platforms can lead to algorithms that prioritize the display of these tailored corrections, ensuring that they reach audiences when they are most receptive. Such strategies can be augmented by scholarly research on the optimal times, contexts, and digital environments for correction message exposure. The partnership between social media platforms and governmental organizations is also important. Together, they can create an ecosystem where tailored correction messages are not just seen but deeply accepted and acted on.

Conclusion

This chapter has delved into the message strategies for misinformation correction, highlighting the roles of argument-based messages, emotional appeals, and narratives. Each strategy brings unique strengths and challenges to the table, and their efficacy can be both potent and nuanced. One profound realization that has emerged from this review is that, while traditional persuasion theories offer valuable insights, the rapidly evolving digital environment requires us to consider the dynamics of competitive message effects. The sheer volume and velocity of information today necessitate a more complex understanding of how messages compete, complement, or conflict. Moreover, the vast diversity of audiences calls for a more sophisticated approach, emphasizing segmentation and tailored correction. As we navigate the complexities of misinformation correction in competitive information environments, it is crucial that we consistently and rigorously refine our theoretical frameworks and methodological approaches to ensure that they remain relevant and effective.

References

Amazeen, M. A., Thorson, E., Muddiman, A., & Graves, L. (2018). Correcting political and consumer misperceptions: The effectiveness and effects of rating scale versus contextual correction formats. *Journalism & Mass Communication Quarterly*, *95*(1), 28–48. http://dx.doi.org/10.1177/1077699016678186

Antonetti, P., Baines, P., & Jain, S. (2018). The persuasiveness of guilt appeals over time: Pathways to delayed compliance. *Journal of Business Research*, *90*, 14–25. http://dx.doi.org/10.1016/j.jbusres.2018.03.030

Becker, A. B., & Waisanen, D. J. (2013). From funny features to entertaining effects: Connecting approaches to communication research on political comedy. *Review of Communication*, *13*(3), 161–183. https://doi.org/10.1080/15358593.2013.826816

Borah, P., Kim, S., Xiao, X., & Lee, D. K. L. (2022). Correcting misinformation using theory-driven messages: HPV vaccine misperceptions, information seeking, and the moderating role of reflection. *Atlantic Journal of Communication*, *30*(3), 316–331. http://dx.doi.org/10.1080/15456870.2021.1912046

Brehm, J. W. (1966). *A theory of psychological reactance*. Academic Press. http://dx.doi.org/10.1002/hrdq.20027

Bullock, O. M., Colón Amill, D., Shulman, H. C., & Dixon, G. N. (2019). Jargon as a barrier to effective science communication: Evidence from metacognition. *Public Understanding of Science*, *28*(7), 845–853. http://dx.doi.org/10.1177/0963662519865687

Burgoon, M., Jones, S. B., & Stewart, D. (1975). Toward a message-centered theory of persuasion: Three empirical investigations of language intensity. *Human Communication Research*, *1*(3), 240–256. https://doi.org/10.1111/j.1468-2958.1975.tb00271.x

Carnahan, D., & Garrett, R. K. (2019). Processing style and responsiveness to corrective information. *International Journal of Public Opinion Research*, *32*(3), 530–546. http://dx.doi.org/10.1093/ijpor/edz037

Chaiken, S. (1980). Heuristic versus systematic information processing and the use of source versus message cues in persuasion. *Journal of Personality and Social Psychology*, *39*(5), 752–766. http://dx.doi.org/10.1037/0022-3514.39.5.752

Chan, M. P. S., Jones, C. R., Hall Jamieson, K., & Albarracín, D. (2017). Debunking: A meta-analysis of the psychological efficacy of messages countering misinformation. *Psychological Science*, *28*(11), 1531–1546. http://dx.doi.org/10.1177/0956797617714579

Cook, J., Ecker, U. K. H., Trecek-King, M., Schade, G., Jeffers-Tracy, K., Fessmann, J., Kim, S. C., Kinkead, D., Orr, M., Vraga, E., Roberts, K., & McDowell, J. (2023). The cranky uncle game—Combining humor and gamification to build student resilience against climate misinformation. *Environmental Education Research*, *29*(4), 607–623. http://dx.doi.org/10.1080/13504622.2022.2085671

Dal Cin, S., Zanna, M. P., & Fong, G. T. (2004). Narrative persuasion and overcoming resistance. In E. S. Knowles & J. A. Linn (Eds.), *Resistance and persuasion* (pp. 175–191). Lawrence Erlbaum.

Dixon, G., Hmielowski, J., & Ma, Y. (2017). Improving climate change acceptance among U.S. conservatives through value-based message targeting. *Science Communication*, *39*(4), 520–534. http://dx.doi.org/10.1177/1075547017715473

Ecker, U. K. H., Butler, L. H., & Hamby, A. (2020). You don't have to tell a story! A registered report testing the effectiveness of narrative versus non-narrative misinformation corrections. *Cognitive Research: Principles and Implications*, *5*(64), 1–26. http://dx.doi.org/10.1186/s41235-020-00266-x

Ecker, U. K. H., Lewandowsky, S., Cook, J., Schmid, P., Fazio, L. K., Brashier, N., Kendeou, P., Vraga, E. K., & Amazeen, M. A. (2022). The psychological drivers of misinformation belief and its resistance to correction. *Nature Reviews Psychology*, *1*(1), 13–29. http://dx.doi.org/10.1038/s44159-021-00006-y

Eisend, M. (2006). Two-sided advertising: A meta-analysis. *International Journal of Research in Marketing*, *23*(2), 187–198. http://dx.doi.org/10.1016/j.ijresmar.2005.11.001

Featherstone, J. D., & Zhang, J. (2020). Feeling angry: The effects of vaccine misinformation and refutational messages on negative emotions and vaccination attitude. *Journal of Health Communication*, *25*(9), 692–702. http://dx.doi.org/10.1080/10810730.2020.1838671

Green, M. C. (2006). Narratives and cancer communication. *Journal of Communication*, *56*(Suppl.1), S163–S183. http://dx.doi.org/10.1111/j.1460-2466.2006.00288.x

Green, M. C., & Brock, T. C. (2000). The role of transportation in the persuasiveness of public narratives. *Journal of Personality and Social Psychology*, *79*(5), 701–721. http://dx.doi.org/10.1037/0022-3514.79.5.701

Hallahan, K. (1999). Seven models of framing: Implications for public relations. *Journal of Public Relations Research*, *11*(3), 205–242. http://dx.doi.org/10.1207/s1532754xjprr1103_02

Hart, P. S., & Nisbet, E. C. (2012). Boomerang effects in science communication: How motivated reasoning and identity cues amplify opinion polarization about climate mitigation policies. *Communication Research*, *39*(6), 701–723. http://dx.doi.org/10.1177/0093650211416646

Henkel, L., Sprengholz, P., Korn, L., Betsch, C., & Böhm, R. (2023). The association between vaccination status identification and societal polarization. *Nature Human Behaviour*, *7*(2), 231–239. http://dx.doi.org/10.1038/s41562-022-01469-6

Hinyard, L. J., & Kreuter, M. W. (2007). Using narrative communication as a tool for health behavior change: a conceptual, theoretical, and empirical overview. *Health Education & Behavior*, *34*(5), 777–792. http://dx.doi.org/10.1177/1090198106291963

Huang, Y., & DiStaso, M. (2020). Responding to a health crisis on Facebook: The effects of response timing and message appeal. *Public Relations Review*, *46*(3), 1–8. http://dx.doi.org/10.1016/j.pubrev.2020.101909

Huang, K. Y., Fung, H. H., & Sun, P. (2023). The effect of audience–character similarity on identification with narrative characters: A meta-analysis. *Current Psychology*, *43*, 7026–7043. http://dx.doi.org/10.1007/s12144-023-04842-4

Huang, Y., & Green, M. C. (2023). Reducing COVID-19 vaccine hesitancy among African Americans: The effects of narratives, character's self-persuasion, and trust in science. *Journal of Behavioral Medicine*, *46*(1–2), 290–302. http://dx.doi.org/10.1007/s10865-022-00303-8

Huang, Y., & Liu, W. (2022). Promoting COVID-19 vaccination: The interplay of message framing, psychological uncertainty, and public agency as a message source. *Science Communication*, *44*(1), 3–29. http://dx.doi.org/10.1177/10755470211048192

Huang, Y., & Shen, F. (2016). Effects of cultural tailoring on persuasion in cancer communication: A meta-analysis. *Journal of Communication*, *66*(4), 694–715. http://dx.doi.org/10.1111/jcom.12243

Huang, Y., & Wang, W. (2022). When a story contradicts: Correcting health misinformation on social media through different message formats and mechanisms. *Information, Communication and Society*, *25*(8), 1192–1209. http://dx.doi.org/10.1080/1369118X.2020.1851390

Huang, Y., & Wang, W. (2023, August). *Overcoming confirmation bias in misinformation correction: Effects of processing motive and jargon on climate change policy support.* Paper presented at the 106th annual conference of the Association for Education in Journalism and Mass Communication (AEJMC), Washington, DC.

Huang, Y., Wang, W., & Yang, C. (2022). Framing: Equivalency. In E. Y. Ho, C. L. Bylund, & J. C. M. van Weert (Eds.), *The international encyclopedia of health communication* (pp. 1–6). Wiley. http://dx.doi.org/10.1002/9781119678816.iehc0640

Jamieson, K. H., & Albarracin, D. (2020). The relation between media consumption and misinformation at the outset of the SARS-CoV-2 pandemic in the US. *The Harvard Kennedy School Misinformation Review*, *1*(2). https://doi.org/10.37016/mr-2020-012

Jennings, F. J., & Russell, F. M. (2019). Civility, credibility, and health information: The impact of uncivil comments and source credibility on attitudes about vaccines. *Public Understanding of Science*, *28*(4), 417–432. http://dx.doi.org/10.1177/0963662519837901

Jin, Y., van der Meer, T. G. L. A., Lee, Y.-I., & Lu, X. (2020). The effects of corrective communication and employee backup on the effectiveness of fighting crisis misinformation. *Public Relations Review*, *46*(3), 101910. http://dx.doi.org/10.1016/j.pubrev.2020.101910

Krakow, M. M., Yale, R. N., Jensen, J. D., Carcioppolo, N., & Ratcliff, C. L. (2018). Comparing mediational pathways for narrative- and argument-based messages: Believability, counterarguing, and emotional reaction. *Human Communication Research*, *44*(3), 299–321. http://dx.doi.org/10.1093/hcr/hqy002

Larson, H. J. (2018). The biggest pandemic risk? Viral misinformation. *Nature*, *562*(7727), 309. http://dx.doi.org/10.1038/d41586-018-07034-4

Lewandowsky, S., Ecker, U. K. H., Seifert, C. M., Schwarz, N., & Cook, J. (2012). Misinformation and its correction: Continued influence and successful debiasing. *Psychological Science in the Public Interest*, *13*(3), 106–131. http://dx.doi.org/10.1177/1529100612451018

Li, M. H., Chen, Z., & Rao, L. L. (2022). Emotion, analytic thinking and susceptibility to misinformation during the COVID-19 outbreak. *Computers in Human Behavior*, *133*, 107295. https://doi.org/10.1016/j.chb.2022.107295

Luengo, M., & García-Marín, D. (2020). The performance of truth: Politicians, fact-checking journalism, and the struggle to tackle COVID-19 misinformation. *American Journal of Cultural Sociology*, *8*, 405–427. http://dx.doi.org/10.1057/s41290-020-00115-w

Lunz Trujillo, K., Motta, M., Callaghan, T., & Sylvester, S. (2021). Correcting misperceptions about the MMR vaccine: Using psychological risk factors to inform targeted communication strategies. *Political Research Quarterly*, *74*(2), 464–478. http://dx.doi.org/10.1177/1065912920907695

Maertens, R., Roozenbeek, J., Basol, M., & van der Linden, S. (2021). Long-term effectiveness of inoculation against misinformation: Two longitudinal experiments. *Journal of Experimental Psychology*, *27*(1), 1–16. http://dx.doi.org/10.1037/xap0000315

Malhotra, P., & Pearce, K. (2022). Facing falsehoods: Strategies for polite misinformation correction. *International Journal of Communication Systems, 16*, 2303–2324. https://ijoc.org/index.php/ijoc/article/view/18361

Martel, C., Pennycook, G., & Rand, D. G. (2020). Reliance on emotion promotes belief in fake news. *Cognitive Research: Principles and Implications, 5*, 1–20. https://doi.org/10.1186/s41235-020-00252-3

Martel, C., Mosleh, M., & Rand, D. G. (2021). You're definitely wrong, maybe: Correction style has minimal effect on corrections of misinformation online. *Media and Communication, 9*(1), 120–133. http://dx.doi.org/10.17645/mac.v9i1.3519

McGuire, W. J. (1961). Resistance to persuasion conferred by active and passive prior refutation of the same and alternative counterarguments. *Journal of Abnormal and Social Psychology, 63*(2), 326–332. http://dx.doi.org/10.1037/h0048344

Miller, C. H., Lane, L. T., Deatrick, L. M., Young, A. M., & Potts, K. A. (2007). Psychological reactance and promotional health messages: The effects of controlling language, lexical concreteness, and the restoration of freedom. *Human Communication Research, 33*, 219–240. http://dx.doi.org/10.1111/j.1468-2958.2007.00297.x

Moyer-Gusé, E., Jain, P., & Chung, A. H. (2012). Reinforcement or reactance? Examining the effect of an explicit persuasive appeal following an entertainment-education narrative. *Journal of Communication, 62*(6), 1010–1027. http://dx.doi.org/10.1111/j.1460-2466.2012.01680.x

Moyer-Gusé, E., Robinson, M. J., & Mcknight, J. (2018). The role of humor in messaging about the MMR vaccine. *Journal of Health Communication, 23*(6), 514–522. https://doi.org/10.1080/10810730.2018.1473533

Moyer-Gusé, E., Tchernev, J. M., & Walther-Martin, W. (2019). The persuasiveness of a humorous environmental narrative combined with an explicit persuasive appeal. *Science Communication, 41*(4), 422–441. http://dx.doi.org/10.1177/1075547019862553

Musi, E., & Reed, C. (2022). From fallacies to semi-fake news: Improving the identification of misinformation triggers across digital media. *Discourse & Society, 33*(3), 349–370. http://dx.doi.org/10.1177/09579265221076609

Nan, X., Wang, Y., & Thier, K. (2022). Why do people believe health misinformation and who is at risk? A systematic review of individual differences in susceptibility to health misinformation. *Social Science & Medicine, 314*, 115398. http://dx.doi.org/10.1016/j.socscimed.2022.115398

Nisbet, E. C., Mortenson, C., & Li, Q. (2021). The presumed influence of election misinformation on others reduces our own satisfaction with democracy. *Harvard Kennedy School Misinformation Review, 1*(7), 1–16. https://doi.org/10.37016/mr-2020-59

Noar, S. M., Benac, C. N., & Harris, M. S. (2007). Does tailoring matter? Meta-analytic review of tailored print health behavior change interventions. *Psychological Bulletin, 133*(4), 673–693. http://dx.doi.org/10.1037/0033-2909.133.4.673

O'Keefe, D. J. (1999). How to handle opposing arguments in persuasive messages: A meta-analytic review of the effects of one-sided and two-sided messages. *Annals of the International Communication Association, 22*(1), 209–249. http://dx.doi.org/10.1080/23808985.1999.11678963

O'Keefe, D. J., & Nan, X. (2012). The relative persuasiveness of gain- and loss-framed messages for promoting vaccination: A meta-analytic review. *Health Communication, 27*(8), 776–783. http://dx.doi.org/10.1080/10410236.2011.640974

Perloff, R. M. (2020). *The dynamics of persuasion: Communication and attitudes in the 21st century*. Routledge.

Petty, R. E., & Cacioppo, J. T. (1986). The elaboration likelihood model of persuasion. *Advances in Experimental Social Psychology, 19*, 123–181. http://dx.doi.org/10.1016/S0065-2601(08)60214-2

Ratcliff, C. L., & Sun, Y. (2020). Overcoming resistance through narratives: Findings from a meta-analytic review. *Human Communication Research*, *46*(4), 412–443. http://dx.doi.org/10.1093/hcr/hqz017

Sangalang, A., Ophir, Y., & Cappella, J. N. (2019). The potential for narrative correctives to combat misinformation. *Journal of Communication*, *69*(3), 298–319. http://dx.doi.org/10.1093/joc/jqz014

Schaffner, B. F., & Roche, C. (2016). Misinformation and motivated reasoning: Responses to economic news in a politicized environment. *Public Opinion Quarterly*, *81*(1), 86–110. http://dx.doi.org/10.1093/poq/nfw043

Sharon, A. J., & Baram-Tsabari, A. (2014). Measuring mumbo jumbo: A preliminary quantification of the use of jargon in science communication. *Public Understanding of Science*, *23*(5), 528–546. http://dx.doi.org/10.1177/0963662512469916

Shelby, A., & Ernst, K. (2013). Story and science: How providers and parents can utilize storytelling to combat anti-vaccine misinformation. *Human Vaccines & Immunotherapeutics*, *9*(8), 1795–1801. http://dx.doi.org/10.4161/hv.24828

Shen, L., & Bigsby, E. (2013). The effects of message features. In *The SAGE handbook of persuasion: Developments in theory and practice* (pp. 20–35). SAGE.

Shin, J., & Thorson, K. (2017). Partisan selective sharing: The biased diffusion of fact-checking messages on social media. *Journal of Communication*, *67*(2), 233–255. http://dx.doi.org/10.1111/jcom.12284

Shulman, H. C., Dixon, G. N., Bullock, O. M., & Colón Amill, D. (2020). The effects of jargon on processing fluency, self-perceptions, and scientific engagement. *Journal of Language and Social Psychology*, *39*(5–6), 579–597. http://dx.doi.org/10.1177/0261927X20902177

Sun, Y., Oktavianus, J., Wang, S., & Lu, F. (2022). The role of influence of presumed influence and anticipated guilt in evoking social correction of COVID-19 misinformation. *Health Communication*, *37*(11), 1368–1377. https://doi.org/10.1080/10410236.2021.1888452

Susmann, M. W., & Wegener, D. T. (2022). The role of discomfort in the continued influence effect of misinformation. *Memory & Cognition*, *50*(2), 435–448. http://dx.doi.org/10.3758/s13421-021-01232-8

van der Meer, T. G. L. A., & Jin, Y. (2020). Seeking formula for misinformation treatment in public health crises: The effects of corrective information type and source. *Health Communication*, *35*(5), 560–575. http://dx.doi.org/10.1080/10410236.2019.1573295

Vraga, E. K., Kim, S. C., & Cook, J. (2019). Testing logic-based and humor-based corrections for science, health, and political misinformation on social media. *Journal of Broadcasting & Electronic Media*, *63*(3), 393–414. https://doi.org/10.1080/08838151.2019.1653102

Walter, N., Cohen, J., Holbert, R. L., & Morag, Y. (2020). Fact-checking: A meta-analysis of what works and for whom. *Political Communication*, *37*(3), 350–375. http://dx.doi.org/10.1080/10584609.2019.1668894

Walter, N., & Tukachinsky, R. (2020). A meta-analytic examination of the continued influence of misinformation in the face of correction: How powerful is it, why does it happen, and how to stop it? *Communication Research*, *47*(2), 155–177. http://dx.doi.org/10.1177/0093650219854600

Wang, R., He, Y., Xu, J., & Zhang, H. (2020). Fake news or bad news? Toward an emotion-driven cognitive dissonance model of misinformation diffusion. *Asian Journal of Communication*, *30*(5), 317–342. http://dx.doi.org/10.1080/01292986.2020.1811737

Wang, W., & Huang, Y. (2021). Countering the "harmless e-cigarette" myth: The interplay of message format, message sidedness, and prior experience with e-cigarette use in misinformation correction. *Science Communication*, *43*(2), 170–198. http://dx.doi.org/10.1177/1075547020974384

Wang, W., & Huang, Y. (2023). Comparing the effects of simple and refutational narratives in misinformation correction: The moderating roles of correction placement and issue involvement. *Public Understanding of Science*, *32*(8). http://dx.doi.org/10.1177/09636625231168995

Wood, R. M., Juanchich, M., Ramirez, M., & Zhang, S. (2023). Promoting COVID-19 vaccine confidence through public responses to misinformation: The joint influence of message source and message content. *Social Science & Medicine*, *324*, 115863. http://dx.doi.org/10.1016/j.socscimed.2023.115863

Xiao, X., Borah, P., Lee, D. K. L., Su, Y., & Kim, S. (2023). A story is better told with collective interests: An experimental examination of misinformation correction during the COVID-19 pandemic. *American Journal of Health Promotion*, *37*(7), 915–923. http://dx.doi.org/10.1177/08901171231184075

Xiao, X., & Su, Y. (2021). Integrating reasoned action approach and message sidedness in the era of misinformation: The case of hpv vaccination promotion. *Journal of Health Communication*, *26*(6), 371–380. http://dx.doi.org/10.1080/10810730.2021.1950873

Zheng, X., Wu, S., & Nie, D. (2021). Online health misinformation and corrective messages in China: A comparison of message features. *Communication Studies*, *72*(3), 474–489. http://dx.doi.org/10.1080/10510974.2021.1917437

Zhou, Y., & Shen, L. (2021). Confirmation bias and the persistence of misinformation on climate change. *Communication Research*, *49*(4). http://dx.doi.org/10.1177/00936502211028049

11

Understanding the Role of Attention to Misinformation and Correction Mechanisms on Social Media with Eye-Tracking Technology: Implications for Climate Change Crisis Communication

Sojung Claire Kim[1], Emily K. Vraga[2], John Cook[3], and Sydney Carver[4]

[1] *Department of Communication, George Mason University*
[2] *Hubbard School of Journalism and Mass Communication, University of Minnesota Twin Cities*
[3] *Melbourne Centre for Behaviour Change, University of Melbourne*
[4] *Department of Communication, George Mason University*

Health and science misinformation are prevalent online, and scholars recognize this as a public concern (Chou et al., 2018). The purposeful dissemination of false or misleading information, the amplification of rumors and conspiracy theories, and the manipulation of emotions and values are all characteristics of misinformation (Krause et al., 2020). Misinformation can have negative societal consequences, including decreased public trust in government institutions, increased polarization and division among the public, and ineffective responses to crisis events such as climate change.

There has been much discourse around how to communicate the climate change crisis to the public effectively, including how to reduce or debunk misinformation around this topic. Specifically, the denial and misrepresentation of scientific facts relating to climate change is a major example of crisis misinformation that has been promoted by a variety of individuals and organizations, including government leaders, fossil fuel industries, and ideologically driven corporations and interest groups (Basseches et al., 2022). To address this challenge, the United Nations acknowledges the risk of climate change misinformation online and provides resources and communication tips aimed at tackling deceptive or misleading content that contributes to the misperceptions of the climate consensus and scientific solutions (United Nations, 2023).

Social media has become an influential medium for the spread of both knowledge and misinformation. On social media platforms such as X/Twitter, misinformation has been found to spread faster and more broadly than accurate information (Broniatowski et al., 2018; Vosoughi et al., 2018). Users may further distribute false information by reposting, retweeting, and commenting, which can encourage more attention to such information on social media. While social media can contribute to increasing the reach and impact of misinformation, it also has the capacity to rectify and counteract misinformation (Bode & Vraga, 2021a; Tandoc et al., 2020). In other words, the ability to reach large and diverse audiences, the possibility for dynamic and participatory engagement, and the hazards of amplifying disinformation or creating information bubbles are all potential benefits as well as challenges of utilizing social media to correct misinformation.

Communication and Misinformation: Crisis Events in the Age of Social Media, First Edition.
Edited by Kevin B. Wright.
© 2025 John Wiley & Sons, Inc. Published 2025 by John Wiley & Sons, Inc.

A few strategies and interventions have been proposed and tested to correct misinformation on social media, including fact-checking, debunking, prebunking, and user-generated observational corrections (Bode & Vraga, 2021a; Kim et al., 2021; Margolin et al., 2018; Vraga & Bode, 2017, 2020). But there is a need for further research to optimize the effective use of social media as a tool or platform to correct misinformation and promote accurate, reliable, and trustworthy information.

The existing literature tells us that direct corrections to misinformation on social media can be effective in reducing misperceptions, especially when these corrections are witnessed by a large audience of bystanders (Bowles et al., 2020; Smith & Seitz, 2019; Vraga & Bode, 2020; Walter et al., 2021). But this is by no means always the case, and corrections can sometimes fail to reduce misperceptions (Nyhan & Reifler, 2010; Vraga et al., 2019) or produce belief echoes whereby the directly targeted misperceptions are reduced but their effects on related attitudes (such as candidate evaluations) linger (Thorson, 2016; Walter & Tukachinsky, 2020).

If this is the case, what explains these diverse findings with regard to the efficacy of correction on social media? There are many possible explanations and, given the scope and diversity of the misinformation problem, we would not expect a single solution to mitigate misperceptions effectively across all topics (Bode & Vraga, 2021b; Southwell et al., 2019). A major limitation in much of the existing research on the value of correction is that it does not explicitly examine the role that *attention* plays in explaining the effectiveness (or lack thereof) of corrections. Existing research also does not measure attention as a crucial mediating concept between misinformation or correction message exposure and misperception reduction (Bode & Vraga, 2015; Lewandowsky et al., 2012; Nyhan & Reifler, 2010). For this reason, we argue that studying attention to misinformation and its correction messages on social media should be the first reasonable step to further parse how this understudied cognitive process might influence their ability to shape related (mis)perceptions, attitudes, and behavioral intentions.

Literature Review

Relevant Theories and Approaches to Correcting Misinformation

Once misinformation has taken hold, it is notoriously difficult to dislodge (Chan et al., 2017). To address this challenge, relevant theories have been adopted and applied to misinformation correction from various disciplines (Lewandowsky et al., 2012). First, inoculation has been proposed as a method to preemptively expose individuals to weakened or distorted arguments before they encounter the real thing and thereby build resistance to misinformation and reduce its persuasive power (McGuire & Papageorgis, 1961). Inoculation originally applied the metaphor of vaccination to the knowledge acquisition process. Just as a vaccine builds immunity by exposing people to a weakened form of a disease, inoculation messages strengthen immunity to misinformation by exposing people to misinformation in a weakened form together with counterarguments including highlighting the flaws in the misinformation and encouragements to actively engage with information.

Alternatively, Lewandowsky et al. (2012) proposed debunking as a complementary approach to inoculation, which involves correcting misinformation after it has been encountered. Debunking can be achieved by providing corrective information that is coherent, simple, and memorable and by targeting the underlying cognitive and motivational processes that contribute to the persistence of misinformation (Lewandowsky et al., 2020).

Both strategies have shown promise in experimental settings, but their relative effectiveness in real-world contexts and for different types of misinformation remains uncertain (Tay et al., 2022; Vraga et al., 2020). Nevertheless, the development and testing of such correction strategies with different analytical methods are crucial for managing and reducing the negative consequences of crisis misinformation, including its potential impact on public health (e.g., vaccination uptake) and environmental sustainability (e.g., public support for policies to mitigate climate change).

The two most common approaches used to correct misinformation, fact-based and logic-based corrections, are grounded in these theories. *Fact-based corrections*, also described as topic-based (Schmid & Betsch, 2019) or issue-based (Basol et al., 2021) corrections, involve demonstrating how misinformation is false through factual explanations. In contrast, logic-based corrections, also known as technique-based (Schmid & Betsch, 2019) corrections, involve explaining the misleading rhetorical techniques or logical fallacies in misinformation (Banas & Miller, 2013).

Most misinformation corrections have taken a fact-based approach, as evidenced by the descriptor *fact-checking*. However, fact-based corrections are applicable only to specific pieces and/or context of misinformation, whereas logic-based corrections can be applied to different misinforming arguments that use the same misleading techniques or logical fallacies across different topics. For instance, an inoculation targeting the fake expert technique used in tobacco misinformation was found to reduce the influence of climate misinformation using the same misleading technique (Cook et al., 2017).

Another aspect of fact-based corrections is that their educational benefits can potentially be canceled out when they are presented along with misinformation (van der Linden et al., 2017), while logic-based corrections are robust when they are seen alongside conflicting information (Vraga et al., 2020). Another advantage of the logic-based approach is that it can be used when misinformation is difficult to define (Vraga & Bode, 2020), such as with statements about the future (Nieminen & Sankari, 2021), paltering statements that are strictly true but also misleading (Rogers et al., 2017), and arguments with hidden assumptions (Birks, 2019).

Unique Characteristics of Social Media When Correcting Misinformation

Social media is a prolific source of rampant misinformation during periods such as the 2016 US presidential election (Bovet & Makse, 2019) and the 2020 COVID pandemic (Ahmed et al., 2020). However, social media also offers a platform for observational correction, whereby people update their attitudes or beliefs after seeing another person corrected on social media (Vraga & Bode, 2017). However, the effectiveness and impact of observational corrections depends on the character of the correction source. Credibility is an influential factor: corrections from high credibility institutions such as the Centers for Disease Control and Prevention are more effective in reducing misperceptions in ordinary users (Vraga & Bode, 2017). While both fact-checkers and ordinary citizens may post corrections to social media misinformation, the vast majority of corrections are posted by citizens, most of which tend to be rude and/or opinion-based (Micallef et al., 2020).

The relatively small number of professional fact-checking organizations has led to explorations of other solutions such as crowdsourced fact-checking, with a wisdom-of-crowds approach yielding similar results to expert fact-checkers (Bhuiyan et al., 2020; Epstein et al., 2020). Crowdsourcing can provide faster responses, address non-English misinformation more comprehensively, and address potential political bias by creating politically biased crowds (Martel et al., 2022). Recently, generative AI has also been offering solutions to the automated detection of misinformation and the generation of corrections in real time. For example, ChatGPT has been shown to be effective in assessing the credibility of news outlets (Yang & Menczer, 2023), although its usefulness in generating fact-checking messages yielded mixed results (DeVerna et al., 2023). While the use of generative AI to automate misinformation correction shows technical promise on social media, it has created further challenges, with tools such ChatGPT able to provide more compelling misinformation across various topics (Spitale et al., 2023).

Attention as an Essential Factor to Understanding Misinformation Correction

Although it has not yet been widely studied in the misinformation correction literature, attention should be explored as an essential factor for understanding the correction of misinformation. Across a wide range of theories of information-processing, persuasion, and attitude formation, attention serves as a necessary (but rarely) sufficient condition. For example, Zaller's receive–accept–sample model holds that people must receive (and thus pay attention to) information before it can affect their beliefs (Zaller, 1992); while *attention* is not named as a part of the model, it is implied in both the exposure and the acceptance (or rejection) portion of the model. Similarly, the elaboration likelihood model lays out two different pathways by which attitude change can occur, depending on the amount of elaboration (which requires attention) paid to the stimuli (Petty & Cacioppo, 1986). Finally, the limited capacity model of mediated message processing explores how people process media messages, a process that starts with *encoding* the information that people attend to either deliberately or incidentally (Lang, 2000, 2006). These communication models all speak to the role that attention plays in shaping how media messages are able to affect people's knowledge and beliefs—a process that should be replicated when people are exposed to misinformation and corrections that require them to update their attitudes in response.

Moreover, understanding how attention is allocated should be of particular importance when we consider the processing of correction messages on social media. Attention is a scarce and valued commodity (Feng et al., 2015; Franck, 2019; Stroud, 2017), and nowhere more so than on social media, where content from a seemingly endless array of sources compete for our attention in the same space, a phenomenon known as context collapse (Davis & Jurgenson, 2014; Marwick & Boyd, 2011). Unlike other mediated environments where a single source commands our attention, misinformation and correction on social media are inherently swept up in the cacophony of voices, making understanding *which* content receives attention of special importance.

Beyond its theoretical value, emerging literature has highlighted the importance that attention plays specifically in the context of misinformation and correction. One study found that when attention is diverted—in this case, when people listened to corrections while in a driving simulator—the corrections were less effective among those with a higher cognitive load (i.e., less attention to devote to the correction) than those with a lower cognitive load (Sanderson et al., 2022), although a separate study found that multitasking did not limit the effectiveness of corrections (Szumowska et al., 2021). Attention can also be directed to information accuracy—and doing so tends to make people better able to distinguish truth from fiction (Pennycook et al., 2020, 2021).

Misinformation Correction Research with Eye-Tracking to Study Attention

Thus far, we have theoretical and empirical reasons to believe that attention is important to understanding misinformation correction on social media. The question thus becomes "How can we best understand people's attention patterns to misinformation and its corrections on social media?" This is where leveraging eye-tracking technology can help us understand precisely *what* types of content people are paying attention to on social media and *how* that shapes their impact on attitudes.

Eye-tracking is a technology that uses nearly infrared light to identify people's attention to stimuli with to a less than a millisecond of precision (Tobii, 2023). While such visual gaze data cannot distinguish between conscious and unconscious attention—for example, an individual may be looking at a particular post deliberately, have their attention drawn to salient elements unconsciously, or be looking at something without being fully aware of their gaze—it still speaks to what information is entering the visual stream.

As such, eye-tracking offers several clear advantages to deepen our understanding of how people process misinformation and correction on social media and how such a process influences subsequent attitudes and behaviors. Previous studies have demonstrated the value of eye-tracking technology in the space of misinformation and correction. One eye-tracking study found that people paid more attention to nonevidence-based (misinformation) images than on evidence-based images on a simulated Facebook feed, which they attributed to the "more shocking, attention grabbing, novel, or provocative" nature of the misinformation images (Chou et al., 2020, p. 1164). This finding aligns with earlier research suggesting that misinformation travels more quickly and widely on social media as a result of its novelty and emotionality (Vosoughi et al., 2018). A second study of a simulated Facebook feed found that people spent more time looking at news posts that agreed with them, especially if the comments under that post disagreed with it (Sülflow et al., 2019). Another study outside of the social media domain suggested that attention was higher to schema-inconsistent information, regardless of its factual accuracy (Coronel et al., 2019).

Our own previous eye-tracking research also examined understudied information-processing or attention mechanisms when individuals reviewed misinformation and correction messages on social media (Kim et al., 2021). In the case of human papillomavirus vaccination misinformation (claiming that the HPV vaccine causes autoimmune symptoms), we compared two logic-based corrections—one humorous and one not—in response to a HPV misinformation tweet. The study findings suggested that attention to a humorous correction (compared to a nonhumorous correction) increased attention to the misinformation tweet it was responding to—and in doing so reduced the HPV misperceptions in line with the correction. Further analyses using the same dataset studied visual attention and visual saliency for the images and textual components of the HPV messages and found that, compared to the nonhumorous correction, the humorous correction generated more attention to the text and also to the image of the correction message that contained the logical explanation of the misinformation's fallacy. Additionally, people's attention paths were consistent with left-to-right and top-to-bottom viewing patterns when reading the social media messages.

Purpose of the Study

There is a lot to learn from eye-tracking studies regarding not just whether correction works but the mechanisms by which it is effective. Therefore, the current study builds from previous eye-tracking work in this domain to consider how fact-based versus logic-based message strategies to respond to misinformation can shape attention to both the misinformation and the corrective response. We explore this question using the climate change crisis as a topic because of its importance, impact, and implications for the social, economic, political, and public health aspects of society and the prevalence of climate misinformation on social media. This eye-tracking study examines individuals' message viewing patterns on Twitter and how different correction strategies would encourage (or discourage) attention to the visual and textual elements of the misinformation (RQ1) and response messages (RQ2).

Methods

Experimental Design

This study used a between-subjects design with two different climate crisis correction strategies, fact-based ($n = 28$) and logic-based ($n = 21$) corrections. No correction was also included as a control condition ($n = 27$). Participants were randomly assigned to one of the three conditions and instructed to review one manipulated tweet with eight dummy tweets. The dummy tweets were unrelated to climate change and included random texts and images on topics such as nature, hiking, cookies, or an aquarium. The dummy tweets were included to mask the study purpose from participants so that they were not primed to answer in any particular way. The viewing order was randomized to avoid potential order effects. Twitter was selected as a social media platform to convey climate misinformation and its corrections because of its popularity and ability to spread false information more widely and quickly than real news (Vosoughi et al., 2018).

For each condition, the manipulated messages contained an original tweet that conveyed misinformation about climate change prediction models—"Climate models do not and cannot include everything. They're based on a set number of variables. So if the models don't include everything, they aren't right. And we shouldn't make decisions until the models are right"—and a reply tweet that included its correction with a relevant image. In the fact-based correction the reply tweet included scientific facts arguing against the false claim in the original misinformation tweet, while in the logic-based correction the tweet focused on unveiling the logical fallacies (e.g., impossible expectations) in the misinformation argument. In the control condition, the reply tweet contained unrelated information about the Minecraft game and how a random Twitter user spent time playing the game around Christmas time. The message layout and format were consistent across different conditions and the same username and icon, along with similar word counts, were used to avoid potential biases and confounding effects.

Participants

Participants aged 18 years or older who were able to speak and understand English were recruited from a large eastern US public university using different recruitment methods.

Participants were offered extra credit in their participating course on completion of the study, which included a visit to an eye-tracking research lab on campus.

The final sample included 76 participants. The average age of the participants was 20.20 years old ($SD = 3.62$), with 60.5 percent of them being female and 44.7 percent White.

Eye-Tracking Setup and Procedures

The study was conducted in three stages, lasting approximately 30–40 minutes in total. Participants were first asked to complete a short online pretest survey in Qualtrics regarding their social media use and attitudes on various social issues. Upon the completion, they were asked to set up an appointment with an eye-tracking research lab within one week. On arrival participants were randomly assigned to one of the three experimental conditions and viewed nine tweet messages on a 17-inch computer screen. The monitor was placed on a desk and the participant seated in a stationary chair so that they had a comfortable setting in which to browse. The eye-tracker that was used enabled participants to move their heads and bodies freely while reviewing the messages.

Before participants viewed the messages, the eye-tracking software calibrated their eye movements to ensure correct capturing of their eye gaze. Participants whose calibration failed three times were excluded from the study. During the eye-tracking experiment, participants' eye movements were captured and recorded with the Tobii Pro X3-120 screen-based portable eye-tracker while they reviewed the social media messages (Tobii, 2023). Participants viewed each tweet for 15 seconds before being automatically advanced to the next tweet. We chose to limit the amount of time participants could spend on a given tweet to reflect actual social media browsing behaviors, where attention to a single post is often fleeting. This limit exceeds the average time participants spent on social media stimuli according to previous research (e.g., Kim et al., 2021; Vraga et al., 2016). After completion of the eye-tracking experiment, an online posttest survey was conducted through Qualtrics in the lab as the last step. The posttest survey included questions on topics such as climate attitudes and demographics.

Measuring Attention through Eye-Tracking Measures

With eye-tracking technology, we were able to attain an objective evaluation of visual behavior, which included eye gaze and positioning data. When collecting such data, it is important to choose an area of interest (AOI), a predefined area that researchers are interested in exploring within a given message (Holmqvist et al., 2011). Selection of the AOI is based on proposed research questions or hypotheses, and for this project we wanted to examine how the different correction strategies would encourage (or discourage) visual attention to the text and image portions of the original misinformation and reply correction tweets. See Figure 11.1 for the predefined AOIs within the message stimuli.

We used one of the most common eye-tracking metrics to measure attention: total fixation duration (TFD). TFD is defined as the total duration of the (eye gaze) fixations inside an AOI (Tobii 2023). All TFD data were measured and collected in milliseconds from the Tobii Pro Lab software but reported in seconds for improved readability.

Attention to misinformation tweet. TFD was measured to capture visual attention to the text ($M = 2.63$, Mdn = 2.38, $SD = 1.98$) and image ($M = 0.84$, Mdn = 0.78, $SD = 0.62$) portions of the original misinformation tweet. However, there were some participants for whom we recorded no time spent on the misinformation text ($n = 4$) and image ($n = 7$) AOIs.

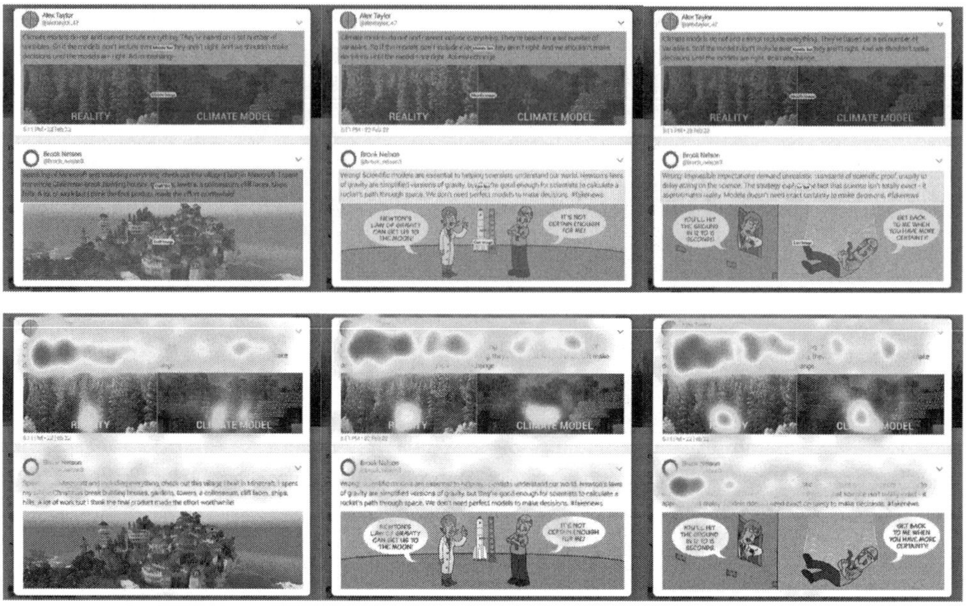

Figure 11.1 Message stimuli with AOIs and heat maps. Note: Misinformation control, fact-based correction, and logic-based corrrection conditions, respectively (red and darker colors in the heat maps suggest longer fixations).

Attention to correction tweet. TFD was measured to capture visual attention to the text ($M = 0.73$, Mdn $= 0.09$, $SD = 1.11$) and image ($M = 0.16$, Mdn $= 0.00$, $SD = 0.37$) portions of the reply correction tweet. There were also participants for whom we recorded no time spent on the correction text ($n = 34$) and image ($n = 48$) AOIs.

Analytical Strategy

The eye-tracking data was collected and exported to SPSS using the Tobii Pro Lab software (Version 1.217) (Tobii, 2023). A series of one-way analyses of variance (ANOVAs) were performed to examine the proposed research questions. Aggregated heat maps were also acquired from the Tobii Pro Lab software for descriptive qualitative analyses.

Results

The aim of our research questions was to examine individuals' message viewing patterns and how two different correction strategies, the fact-based and logic-based corrections, along with the no correction control, encourage visual attention to the climate change crisis misinformation (RQ1) and its correction messages (RQ2) in Twitter.

Our RQ1 asked whether the presence and type of corrective response would affect people's attention to the misinformation post. No significant effects of the correction strategies were found on attention to either the misinformation text or the misinformation image.

Our RQ2 examined attention to the response correction post, which varied between an unrelated (control) response, a fact-based response, and a logic-based response. We again found no significant differences between the three conditions in terms of the attention to the correction image. However, the results did reveal a significant effect of the correction strategies on attention to the correction tweet text AOI, $F(2, 73) = 11.44$, $p < 0.001$, $\eta^2 = 0.24$. To parse the specific differences, Games-Howell post hoc tests were performed, considering the significance of the Levene test for the homogeneity of variance. There was a significant mean difference between the logic-based correction ($M = 1.60$, $SD = 1.39$) and the control condition ($M = 0.46$, $SD = 0.91$), and between the logic-based correction and the fact-based correction condition ($M = 0.35$, $SD = 0.60$). There was no significant difference between the fact-based correction and the control condition. See Figures 11.2 (misinformation) and 11.3 (correction) for the visualization of these findings.

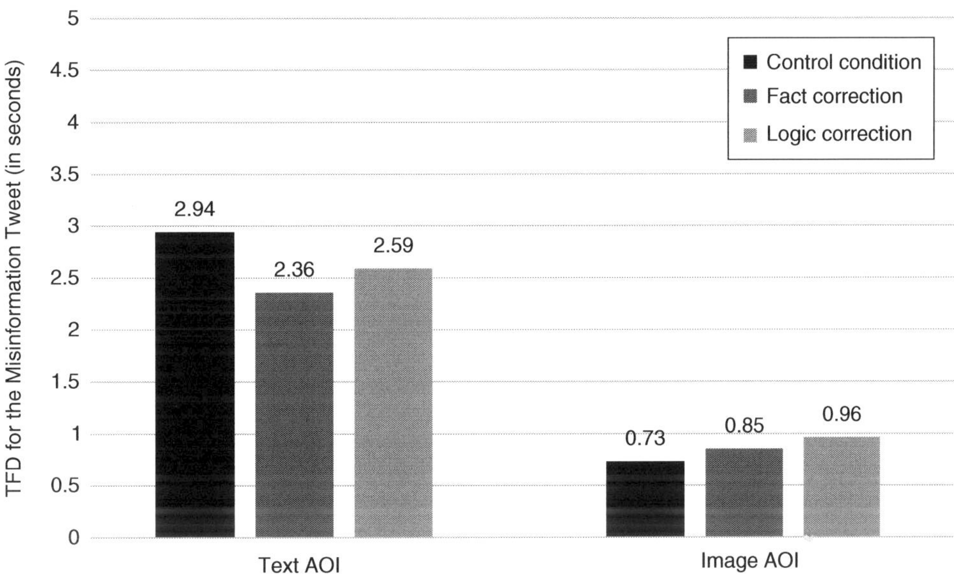

Figure 11.2 TFD for the misinformation tweet by experimental condition ($n = 76$).

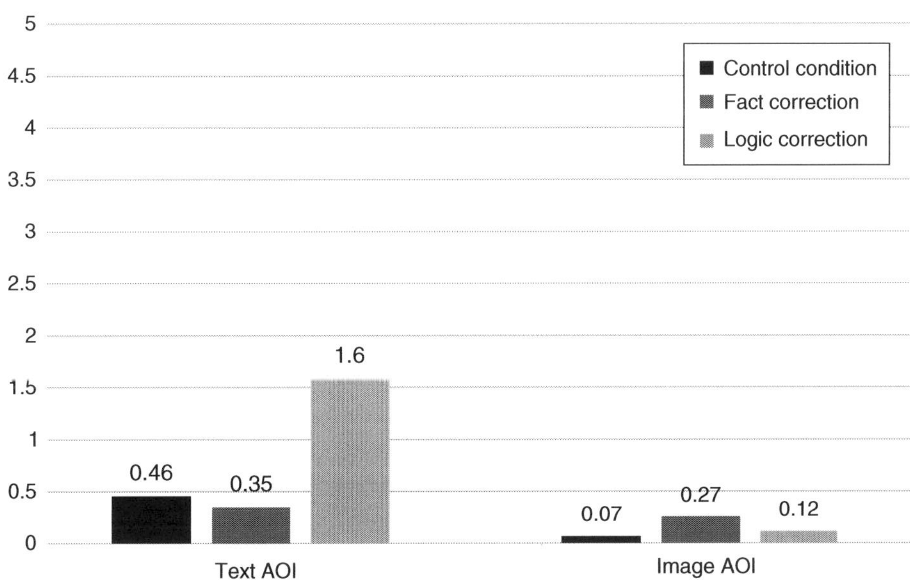

Figure 11.3 TFD for the correction tweet by experimental condition ($n = 76$).

We had many participants who had no recorded attention time for the correction message and so had to interpret these results with caution. Additionally, we ran the same ANOVA analysis with only 42 participants (who spent any time on the correction text AOI) to see if the same results held. The same statistical significance was observed, such that a significant effect of the correction strategies on attention to the correction tweet text AOI was found, $F(2, 39) = 5.65$, $p < 0.01$, $\eta^2 = 0.23$, with the same viewing patterns. That is, the logic-based correction worked better than the fact-based correction with regard to paying attention to the correction text area. Similarly, we found no significant effects of the correction strategies on attention to either the misinformation text, the misinformation image, or the correction image.

Finally, the qualitative heat map data revealed the visual attention of participants by condition and shared similar and consistent patterns. The visualization indicated that the text area of the correction tweet received the most attention in the logic-based correction compared to the fact-based correction or the control condition. The image area of the correction tweet seemed to generate less attention than its text area and this pattern seemed consistent across all conditions. For the misinformation tweet, across all corrections, the text area generated higher visual attention compared to the image area of the message. See Figure 11.1 for the heat maps.

Discussion

This study used eye-tracking technology to examine the effectiveness of fact-based and logic-based correction interventions, compared to an irrelevant (control) response, in generating visual attention to climate change crisis misinformation and the correction message itself on Twitter. Our results suggest that different types of response strategies to misinformation on Twitter can elicit quite different attention patterns. Understanding how people allocate their attention, the most valuable commodity on social media, is of critical importance in developing best practices in responding to and mitigating harmful climate change misinformation.

First, we note that, in general, people paid little attention to the correction messages overall. Roughly half of our participants spent no attention on the correction message. We suspect that this lack of attention may be an artifact of our study design, which included a preset viewing time of 15 seconds per tweet. This may have hindered some participants from reviewing the contents of the manipulated tweets fully, and the top-down reading style adopted on social media suggests that the correction was less viewed. In deciding the preset time, we considered the normal reading speed of an adult and emulated the actual time individuals spend reading a tweet. To ensure full attention to and digestion of the messages, future research may permit participants to read the messages at their own speed. However, attention to the misinformation tweet is in line with previous research, which found that Twitter users spend only three seconds reading a simple tweet that is of interest to them (Counts & Fisher, 2011). If this result holds, however, it reinforces the advantage that misinformation has compared to corrective messages on social media. If people spend twice as long viewing a misinformation message as a corrective response, as they did in this study, the difficulties faced by those seeking to mitigate the negative impact of misinformation is further highlighted.

Importantly, we did not find any differences in attention to the misinformation tweet regardless of whether or how the response debunked its inaccurate claims. Our previous eye-tracking study had found that a humorous logic-based correction directed more attention to a misinformation message, compared to a nonhumorous logic-based correction on social media (Kim et al., 2021). However, we did find that the logic-based correction was the most successful at capturing audience attention, at least to the text area of the correction tweet. People paid significantly more attention to the text of the correction tweet compared to both the fact-based and control (in which the response to the misinformation tweet did not directly address the misinformation) conditions. This may suggest that the correction strategy of pinpointing the logical fallacies in the original climate misinformation message was more interesting to participants or required greater attention to cognitively process than the correction strategy of offering a factual explanation of the scientific prediction models of climate change. That people appear to pay more attention to the correction text when it uses a logic-based approach contributes to the ongoing conversation about the value of logic-based compared to fact-based correction strategies (Kim et al., 2021; Schmid & Betsch, 2019; Vraga et al., 2020).

However, there was little difference between the fact-based correction and the control condition in terms of the amount of visual attention paid to the correction text. We suspect that the participants may perceive the content of the random reply tweet in the control condition (about playing the Minecraft game around Christmas) to be as interesting and/or memorable as the content of the correction tweet in the fact-based correction condition.

Moreover, both the descriptive results from the eye-tracking data and the heat map visualization emphasize that the text areas of the misinformation and correction tweets received more attention than the image areas of both posts across all conditions. This is interesting and unexpected given the nature of social media platforms—quick and convenient processing of information, information overload, and therefore attraction to visual cues rather than details in text (e.g., Vraga et al., 2016).

Finally, this study reinforces not only the benefits of studying attention with eye-tracking but also the challenges associated with it. Eye-tracking technologies are increasingly available for academic and consumer research and offer an opportunity to gather unique gaze data by unobstructively measuring individuals' visual attention or information-processing patterns (King et al., 2019). However, challenges exist with any use of technology and difficult decisions must be made when creating message stimuli for eye-tracking protocols that maintain both internal and external validity. Each of these choices has important consequences for the interpretation of the results. In this study, we attempted to simulate social media environments more closely by forcing the limited attention that social media posts often receive. But in doing so we lost valuable data about what people may have paid attention to within the response post in particular. While we hope that the study highlights the important ways in which eye-tracking studies add to the field of misinformation and correction research, especially with regard to the climate change crisis, from our experience we would also urge that these studies be carefully designed and interpreted to improve clarity on the topic.

Our study acknowledges several limitations. First, we have no way of confirming that full attention was what was taking place while participants' eyes were being tracked. Participants may have been skimming through the misinformation and correction messages and paying only partial attention (King et al., 2019). In other words, eye gaze measures don't offer details about the depth of visual attention (e.g., full versus partial) or the valence (positive versus negative) of individuals' message engagement, unless they are combined with other psycho-physiological or self-reported measures (Casado-Aranda et al., 2023). Past research with eye-tracking, however, has shown that attention captured with eye gaze metrics reflects careful review or cognitive processing of a message (e.g., Duchowski, 2007; Eckstein et al., 2017; Rayner, 1998).

Second, the controlled lab setting and the constraints of the message viewing condition when conducting an eye-tracking experiment may affect the ecological validity of the study (King et al., 2019). Thanks to the advancement of eye-tracking technologies, however, our eye-tracker, Tobii X3-120, was able to allow people to move freely rather than be awkwardly positioned without moving in front of a computer screen. This level of freedom among participants helped to reduce the artificiality of the lab setting and improve the external validity of the study.

Third, this study included only one specific type of climate change crisis misinformation: the complexity of the scientific climate change prediction model. While we picked this topic because of the prevalence of misinformation on the topic (Coan et al., 2021), we are not sure if the same findings will hold for other climate misinformation or for different topics with high misinformation penetration rates (e.g., COVID-19, vaccination).

Fourth, we relied on a convenient sample of US college students, but different cultures may interpret and react to the same climate crisis misinformation correction messages differently. For example, how and to what degree participants drawn from different contexts would respond to the humorous logic-based correction may differ.

Despite these limitations, the study contributes to the existing literature by offering unique insights on theory, methodology and analysis, and practice. In the misinformation literature, attention has been much understudied but an essential mechanism to understand *what* and *how* different correction interventions work, especially in the social media environment. Given the abundance (and overload) of information on social media, messages compete for people's attention. Considering how social media users paying attention to a message or any given component in a message (e.g., text, image, username) is the first step before any discussion of perceptual, attitudinal, or behavioral intention changes.

An eye-tracking study has a competitive advantage methodologically because eye-tracking data allow us to look at objective and unobtrusive visual behavioral data in the form of eye gaze positioning and movement to study message attention (King et al., 2019). Analytically, the study included the most well-established fixation-based eye-tracking metric, TFD, to accurately operationalize attention to, or cognitive information-processing of, climate crisis misinformation and correction messages.

Finally, the study findings have much to offer various stakeholders including scholars, educators, and practitioners. In communicating the climate change crisis, it is crucial to understand how attention is paid to related misinformation and its correction messages and to develop a targeted, effective intervention strategy to reduce misperceptions and encourage positive crisis prevention and management behaviors. The logic-based correction should be incorporated into any strategy to encourage visual attention to the corrective arguments to counter misinformation about climate change. Given the unique characteristics of the social media environment and its growing popularity for message creation and consumption, future research should continue to test various correction strategies and their effectiveness in encouraging attention mechanisms, so that we can ultimately reduce climate change misperceptions and facilitate proenvironmental attitudes and behavioral changes.

References

Ahmed, W., Vidal-Alaball, J., Downing, J., & Seguí, F. L. (2020). COVID-19 and the 5G conspiracy theory: Social network analysis of Twitter data. *Journal of Medical Internet Research*, *22*(5), e19458.

van der Linden, S., Leiserowitz, A., Rosenthal, S., & Maibach, E. (2017). Inoculating the public against misinformation about climate change. *Global Challenges*, 1(2), 1600008. https://doi.org/10.1002/gch2.201600008

Banas, J. A., & Miller, G. (2013). Inducing resistance to conspiracy theory propaganda: Testing inoculation and metainoculation strategies. *Human Communication Research*, *39*(2), 184–207.

Basol, M., Roozenbeek, J., Berriche, M., Uenal, F., McClanahan, W. P., & Linden, S. V. D. (2021). Towards psychological herd immunity: Cross-cultural evidence for two prebunking interventions against COVID-19 misinformation. *Big Data & Society*, *8*(1). https://doi.org/10.1177/20539517211013868

Basseches, J. A., Bromley-Trujillo, R., Boykoff, M. T., Culhane, T., Hall, G., Healy, N., Hess, D. J., Hsu, D., Krause, R. M., Prechel, H., Roberts, J. T., & Stephens, J. C. (2022). Climate policy conflict in the U.S. states: A critical review and way forward. *Climatic Change*, *170*(3–4), 32.

Bhuiyan, M. M., Zhang, A. X., Sehat, C. M., & Mitra, T. (2020). Investigating differences in crowdsourced news credibility assessment: Raters, tasks, and expert criteria. *Proceedings of the ACM on Human–Computer Interaction*, *4*(CSCW2), 1–26.

Birks, J. (2019) Fact-checking journalism and political argumentation: A British perspective.

Bode, L., & Vraga, E. K. (2015). In related news, that was wrong: The correction of misinformation through related stories functionality in social media. *Journal of Communication*, *65*(4), 619–638.

Bode, L., & Vraga, E. K. (2021a). Correction experiences on social media during COVID-19. *Social Media+ Society*, *7*(2), 20563051211008829.

Bode, L., & Vraga, E. K. (2021b). The Swiss cheese model for mitigating online misinformation. *Bulletin of the Atomic Scientists*, *77*(3), 129–133. https://doi.org/10.1080/00963402.2021.1912170

Bovet, A., & Makse, H. A. (2019). Influence of fake news in Twitter during the 2016 US presidential election. *Nature Communications*, *10*(1), 7.

Bowles, J., Larreguy, H., & Liu, S. (2020). Countering misinformation via WhatsApp: Preliminary evidence from the COVID-19 pandemic in Zimbabwe. *PLoS ONE*, *15*(10), e0240005. http://dx.doi.org/10.1371/journal.pone.0240005

Broniatowski, D. A., Jamison, A. M., Qi, S., AlKulaib, L., Chen, T., Benton, A., Quinn, S. C., & Dredze, M. (2018). Weaponized health communication: Twitter bots and Russian trolls amplify the vaccine debate. *American Journal of Public Health*, *108*(10), 1378–1384.

Casado-Aranda, L. A., Sánchez-Fernández, J., & Ibáñez-Zapata, J. Á. (2023). Evaluating communication effectiveness through eye tracking: Benefits, state of the art, and unresolved questions. *International Journal of Business Communication*, *60*(1), 24–61.

Chan, M. P. S., Jones, C. R., Hall Jamieson, K., & Albarracín, D. (2017). Debunking: A meta-analysis of the psychological efficacy of messages countering misinformation. *Psychological Science*, *28*(11), 1531–1546.

Chou, W. S., Trivedi, N., Peterson, E., Gaysynsky, A., Krakow, M., & Vraga, E. (2020). How do social media users process cancer prevention messages on Facebook? An eye-tracking study. *Patient Education and Counseling*, *103*(6), 1161–1167. http://dx.doi.org/10.1016/j.pec.2020.01.013

Chou, W. Y. S., Oh, A., & Klein, W. M. (2018). Addressing health-related misinformation on social media. *JAMA*, *320*(23), 2417–2418.

Coan, T. G., Boussalis, C., Cook, J., & Nanko, M. O. (2021). Computer-assisted classification of contrarian claims about climate change. *Scientific Reports*, *11*(1), 22320.

Cook, J., Lewandowsky, S., & Ecker, U. K. (2017). Neutralizing misinformation through inoculation: Exposing misleading argumentation techniques reduces their influence. *PLoS ONE*, *12*(5), e0175799.

Coronel, J. C., Poulsen, S., & Sweitzer, M. D. (2019). Investigating the generation and spread of numerical misinformation: A combined eye movement monitoring and social transmission approach. *Human Communication Research*, *46*(1), 25–54. https://doi.org/10.1093/hcr/hqz012

Counts, S., & Fisher, K. (2011). Taking it all in? Visual attention in microblog consumption. *Proceedings of the International AAAI Conference on Web and Social Media*, *5*(1). https://doi.org/10.1609/icwsm.v5i1.14103

Davis, J. L., & Jurgenson, N. (2014). Context collapse: Theorizing context collusions and collisions. *Information, Communication & Society*, *17*(4), 476–485. https://doi.org/10.1080/1369118X.2014.888458

DeVerna, M. R., Yan, H. Y., Yang, K. C., & Menczer, F. (2023). Artificial intelligence is ineffective and potentially harmful for fact checking. *arXiv*, 2308.10800.

Duchowski, A. (2007). *Eye tracking methodology: Theory and practice*. Springer.

Eckstein, M. K., Guerra-Carrillo, B., Singley, A. T. M., & Bunge, S. A. (2017). Beyond eye gaze: What else can eyetracking reveal about cognition and cognitive development? *Developmental Cognitive Neuroscience*, *25*, 69–91.

Epstein, Z., Pennycook, G., & Rand, D. (2020, April). Will the crowd game the algorithm? Using layperson judgments to combat misinformation on social media by downranking distrusted sources. In *Proceedings of the 2020 CHI Conference on Human Factors in Computing Systems* (pp. 1–11). Association for Computing Machinery.

Feng, L., Hu, Y., Li, B., Stanley, H. E., Havlin, S., & Braunstein, L. A. (2015). Competing for attention in social media under information overload conditions. *PLoS ONE*, *10*(7), e0126090. http://dx.doi.org/10.1371/journal.pone.0126090

Franck, G. (2019). The economy of attention. *Journal of Sociology*, *55*(1), 8–19. http://dx.doi.org/10.1177/1440783318811778

Holmqvist, K., Nyström, M., Andersson, R., Dewhurst, R., Jarodzka, H., & Van de Weijer, J. (2011). Eye tracking: A comprehensive guide to methods and measures. Oxford University Press.

Kim, S. C., Vraga, E. K., & Cook, J. (2021). An eye tracking approach to understanding misinformation and correction strategies on social media: The mediating role of attention and credibility to reduce HPV vaccine misperceptions. *Health Communication*, *36*(13), 1687–1696. http://dx.doi.org/10.1080/10410236.2020.1787933

King, A. J., Bol, N., Cummins, R. G., & John, K. K. (2019). Improving visual behavior research in communication science: An overview, review, and reporting recommendations for using eye-tracking methods. *Communication Methods and Measures*, *13*(3), 149–177.

Krause, N. M., Freiling, I., Beets, B., & Brossard, D. (2020). Fact-checking as risk communication: The multi-layered risk of misinformation in times of COVID-19. *Journal of Risk Research*, *23*(7–8), 1052–1059. http://dx.doi.org/10.1080/13669877.2020.1756385

Lang, A. (2000). The limited capacity model of mediated message processing. *Journal of Communication*, *50*(1), 46–70. http://dx.doi.org/10.1111/j.1460-2466.2000.tb02833.x

Lang, A. (2006). Using the limited capacity model of motivated mediated message processing to design effective cancer communication messages. *Journal of Communication*, *56*(s1), S57–S80. http://dx.doi.org/10.1111/j.1460-2466.2006.00283.x

Lewandowsky, S., Cook, J., Ecker, U., Albarracín, D., Kendeou, P., Newman, E. J., Pennycook, G., Porter, E., Rand, D. G., Rapp, D. N., Reifler, J., Roozenbeek, J., Schmid, P., Seifert, C. M., Sinatra, G. M., Swire-Thompson, B., van der Linden, S., Wood, T. J., & Zaragoza, M. S. (2020). The debunking handbook 2020. https://skepticalscience.com/debunking-handbook-2020-downloads-translations.html

Lewandowsky, S., Ecker, U. K. H., Seifert, C. M., Schwarz, N., & Cook, J. (2012). Misinformation and its correction: Continued influence and successful debiasing. *Psychological Science in the Public Interest*, *13*, 106–131.

Margolin, D. B., Hannak, A., & Weber, I. (2018). Political fact-checking on Twitter: When do corrections have an effect? *Political Communication*, *35*(2), 196–219.

Martel, C., Allen, J., Pennycook, G., & Rand, D. G. (2022). Crowds can effectively identify misinformation at scale. *Perspectives on Psychological Science*, *19*(2), 477–488. https://doi.org/10.1177/17456916231190388

Marwick, A. E., & Boyd, D. (2011). I tweet honestly, I tweet passionately: Twitter users, context collapse, and the imagined audience. *New Media & Society*, *13*(1), 114–133. https://doi.org/10.1177/1461444810365313

McGuire, W. J., & Papageorgis, D. (1961). The relative efficacy of various types of prior belief-defense in producing immunity against persuasion. *The Journal of Abnormal and Social Psychology*, *62*(2), 327–337.

Micallef, N., He, B., Kumar, S., Ahamad, M., & Memon, N. (2020). The role of the crowd in countering misinformation: A case study of the COVID-19 infodemic. In *In 2020 IEEE international conference on big data* (pp. 748–757). IEEE.

Nieminen, S., & Sankari, V. (2021). Checking PolitiFact's fact-checks. *Journalism Studies*, *22*(3), 358–378.

Nyhan, B., & Reifler, J. (2010). When corrections fail: The persistence of political misperceptions. *Political Behavior*, *32*(2), 303–330. http://dx.doi.org/10.1007/s11109-010-9112-2

Pennycook, G., Epstein, Z., Mosleh, M., Arechar, A. A., Eckles, D., & Rand, D. G. (2021). Shifting attention to accuracy can reduce misinformation online. *Nature*, *592*(7855), 590–595.

Pennycook, G., McPhetres, J., Zhang, Y., Lu, J. G., & Rand, D. G. (2020). Fighting COVID-19 misinformation on social media: Experimental evidence for a scalable accuracy-nudge intervention. *Psychological Science*, *31*(7), 770–780. http://dx.doi.org/10.1177/0956797620939054

Petty, R. E., & Cacioppo, J. T. (1986). The elaboration likelihood model of persuasion. In R. E. Petty & J. T. Cacioppo (Eds.), *Communication and persuasion: Central and peripheral routes to attitude change* (pp. 1–24). Springer.

Rayner, K. (1998). Eye movements in reading and information processing: 20 years of research. *Psychological Bulletin*, *124*(3), 372–422.

Rogers, T., Zeckhauser, R., Gino, F., Norton, M. I., & Schweitzer, M. E. (2017). Artful paltering: The risks and rewards of using truthful statements to mislead others. *Journal of Personality and Social Psychology*, *112*(3), 456–473.

Sanderson, J. A., Bowden, V., Swire-Thompson, B., Lewandowsky, S., & Ecker, U. K. H. (2022). Listening to misinformation while driving: Cognitive load and the effectiveness of (repeated)

corrections. *Journal of Applied Research in Memory and Cognition*, *12*(3), 325–334. http://dx.doi.org/10.1037/mac0000057

Schmid, P., & Betsch, C. (2019). Effective strategies for rebutting science denialism in public discussions. *Nature Human Behaviour*, *3*(9), 931–939.

Smith, C. N., & Seitz, H. H. (2019). Correcting misinformation about neuroscience via social media. *Science Communication*, *41*(6). http://dx.doi.org/10.1177/1075547019890073

Southwell, B. G., Niederdeppe, J., Cappella, J. N., Gaysynsky, A., Kelley, D. E., Oh, A., Peterson, E. B., & Chou, W.-Y. S. (2019). Misinformation as a misunderstood challenge to public health. *American Journal of Preventive Medicine*, *57*(2), 282–285. https://doi.org/10.1016/j.amepre.2019.03.009

Spitale, G., Biller-Andorno, N., & Germani, F. (2023). AI model GPT-3 (dis)informs us better than humans. *Science Advances*, *9*(26). http://dx.doi.org/10.1126/sciadv.adh1850

Stroud, N. J. (2017). Attention as a valuable resource. *Political Communication*, *34*(3), 479–489. http://dx.doi.org/10.1080/10584609.2017.1330077

Sülflow, M., Schäfer, S., & Winter, S. (2019). Selective attention in the news feed: An eye-tracking study on the perception and selection of political news posts on Facebook. *New Media & Society*, *21*(1), 168–190.

Szumowska, E., Czarnek, G., Dragon, P., & Keersmaecker, J. D. (2021). Correction after misinformation: Does engagement in media multitasking affect attitude adjustment? *Comprehensive Results in Social Psychology*, *4*(2), 199–226. https://doi.org/10.1080/23743603.2021.1884495

Tandoc, E. C., Jr., Lim, D., & Ling, R. (2020). Diffusion of disinformation: How social media users respond to fake news and why. *Journalism*, *21*(3), 381–398.

Tay, L. Q., Hurlstone, M. J., Kurz, T., & Ecker, U. K. (2022). A comparison of prebunking and debunking interventions for implied versus explicit misinformation. *British Journal of Psychology*, *113*(3), 591–607.

Thorson, E. (2016). Belief echoes: The persistent effects of corrected misinformation. *Political Communication*, *33*(3), 460–480. http://dx.doi.org/10.1080/10584609.2015.1102187

Tobii. (2023). *What is eye tracking?* https://www.tobii.com/learn-and-support/get-started/what-is-eye-tracking

United Nations. (2023). *Communicating on climate change*. https://www.un.org/en/climate change/communicating-climate-change

Vosoughi, S., Roy, D., & Aral, S. (2018). The spread of true and false news online. *Science*, *359*(6380), 1146–1151.

Vraga, E. K., & Bode, L. (2017). Using expert sources to correct health misinformation in social media. *Science Communication*, *39*(5), 621–645.

Vraga, E. K., & Bode, L. (2020). Correction as a solution for health misinformation on social media. *American Journal of Public Health*, *110*(S3), S278–S280. http://dx.doi.org/10.2105/AJPH.2020.305916

Vraga, E. K., Bode, L., & Troller-Renfree, S. (2016). Beyond self-reports: Using eye tracking to measure topic and style differences in attention to social media content. *Communication Methods and Measures*, *10*(2–3), 149–164. https://doi.org/10.1080/19312458.2016.1150443

Vraga, E. K., Kim, S. C., & Cook, J. (2019). Testing logic-based and humor-based corrections for science, health, and political misinformation on social media. *Journal of Broadcasting & Electronic Media*, *63*(3), 393–414. https://doi.org/10.1080/08838151.2019.1653102

Vraga, E. K., Kim, S. C., Cook, J., & Bode, L. (2020). Testing the effectiveness of correction placement and type on Instagram. *The International Journal of Press/Politics*, *25*(4), 632–652.

Walter, N., Brooks, J. J., Saucier, C. J., & Suresh, S. (2021). Evaluating the impact of attempts to correct health misinformation on social media: A meta-analysis. *Health Communication*, *36*(13), 1776–1784. https://doi.org/10.1080/10410236.2020.1794553

Walter, N., & Tukachinsky, R. (2020). A meta-analytic examination of the continued influence of misinformation in the face of correction: How powerful is it, why does it happen, and how to stop it? *Communication Research*, *47*(2), 155–177. https://doi.org/10.1177/0093650219854600

Yang, K. C., & Menczer, F. (2023). Large language models can rate news outlet credibility. *arXiv*, 2304.00228.

Zaller, J. R. (1992). *The nature and origins of mass opinion*. Cambridge University Press.

12

Inoculation Approaches to Science Misinformation Correction

Josh Compton

Department of Speech Communication, Dartmouth College

Inoculation theory explains how a position, such as an attitude or a belief, can be made more resistant to misinformation (see Compton, 2013; McGuire, 1964), and, as its name suggests, the process looks a lot like a preventive medical intervention. With medical inoculations, people are preexposed to weakened forms of offending agents such as viruses, and this controlled preexposure motivates defenses to gear up for future stronger viral attacks. With misinformation inoculations, people are preexposed to weakened forms of offending agents—ranging from specific messages that might contain false or misleading information to larger strategies such as propaganda campaigns—and this controlled preexposure motivates the defenses to gear up for future stronger persuasive attacks.

With a proven track record of over 60 years informing scholarship, theory development, and application across issues and contexts, inoculation theory remains a robust theory and messaging strategy. Much of its application has been in two main areas: politics (see Compton & Ivanov, 2013, for a review) and health (see Compton et al., 2016, for a review). But more recently inoculation theory has been applied with increased scope and intensity to issues of science communication (see Compton et al., 2021), including as an antidote to science misinformation through informing campaigns to combat climate misinformation, vaccine myths, and more. Much of this work leverages the reach and speed of social media—a source of misinformation but also a source of interventions to mitigate misinformation. This chapter explores some of this work and looks forward to some areas that inoculation theory might explore next in the context of science communication and crisis misinformation correction on social media.

Inoculation Theory

Inoculation theory's name goes a long way toward explaining the theory. An attitude or belief, or other position or state, can be protected against influence in much the same way as a body can be protected against viruses through preexposure to weakened forms of the challenges (Compton, 2013; McGuire, 1964). Exposure to the weakened challenge is strong enough to be unsettling but not so strong as to overcome, and so there is motivation to shore up defenses for the impending attack.

Communication and Misinformation: Crisis Events in the Age of Social Media, First Edition.
Edited by Kevin B. Wright.
© 2025 John Wiley & Sons, Inc. Published 2025 by John Wiley & Sons, Inc.

A conventional inoculation theory-based message has two key components: a forewarning and refutational preemption (see Compton, 2013). A forewarning usually appears at the beginning of an inoculation message, and the main goal of a forewarning is to announce impending challenges to a desired state (e.g., a valued belief). A typical forewarning message might read: "You have the right position on this issue, but there are people who are going to try to change your mind, and some of their strategies are so effective you might be misled." In some iterations of an inoculation message forewarning, message recipients are also warned that many other people have been influenced by these strategies. Some inoculation interventions also repeat the forewarning at the end of the inoculation message—a re-reminder that attacks against a position are on the horizon.

The main purpose of a forewarning in an inoculation message is to generate threat (Compton, 2013, 2021). Threat has a particular meaning in inoculation theory, which does not necessarily match up with conventional understandings of threat. Instead of conceptualizing threat as a thing—someone or something that is dangerous—inoculation scholars conceptualize threat as a message response or a reaction. Threat in inoculation is a realization that a held belief (or attitude or value) is vulnerable (Compton, 2013; McGuire, 1964).

Forewarnings are not required for threat to be elicited. The mere presence of counterattitudinal content in an inoculation message, or the weakened form of the impending threat, can be enough to elicit threat (Compton, 2013; McGuire, 1964). But, when forewarnings are used in an inoculation message, they do generate threat. When they are used, forewarnings actually generate most of the threat from an inoculation message (Compton & Ivanov, 2012).

The other part of a conventional inoculation message is refutational preemption. Usually, refutational preemption is in the form of a two-sided message: counterarguments are raised and counterarguments are refuted (Compton, 2013). A typical inoculation message will raise and refute two or three counterarguments and, importantly, the resistance conferred by an inoculation message is not limited to the specific counterarguments that were raised and refuted. That is, even if a counterargument is encountered later that was not preempted in the inoculation intervention message, an inoculation message can confer resistance to it (see Banas & Rains, 2010; McGuire, 1964). Inoculation, then, is unleashing a robust response to future persuasive attacks, one not limited to remembering a few refutations of a few counterarguments.

Instead of, or in addition to, raising and refuting specific counterarguments, refutational preemption can also take the form of teaching people how to identify and refute propaganda strategies (e.g., Roozenbeek & van der Linden, 2019) and reasoning fallacies (e.g., Cook et al., 2017). Yet another preemptive refutational approach is to warn of the influence of specific mediated channels such as television news visuals (e.g., Pfau et al., 2008); of psychological responses such as reactance (e.g., Richards & Banas, 2015); or of genres such as narrative (e.g., Compton & Mason, 2020) or humor (e.g., Compton, 2018a). This preexposure to weakened challenges can take many forms, but the constant across these examples of refutational preemption is that potentially influential challenges (e.g., specific counterarguments, reasoning fallacies, message modes) are weakened in some way, rendering them safe enough to generate a healthy protective response.

Among inoculation theory's notable strengths as a resistance intervention are (a) its efficacy in protecting against a wide range of attacks and (b) its adaptability. First, inoculation interventions can have an umbrella effect, conferring resistance beyond the issue and arguments included in the inoculation intervention message. As McGuire and colleagues established in some of inoculation theory's earliest research (e.g., McGuire, 1961), raising and refuting a few specific counterarguments extends resistance to counterarguments that are not mentioned in the inoculation treatment (Banas & Rains, 2010). Other research has found that inoculating against certain risky behaviors can confer resistance to other risky behaviors, even when those other risky behaviors are not mentioned in the inoculation intervention (e.g., Parker et al., 2012). Inoculation can confer an umbrella of protection against many attacks across many issues.

Inoculation messaging is also highly adaptable. Although most inoculation treatment messages and attack messages used in the early decades of inoculation theory research were often in the form of printed communications (e.g., essays, editorials, articles), more contemporary research has established inoculation's efficacy across a range of media and channels, including social media (e.g., Haigh & Wigley, 2015), videos (e.g., Pfau et al., 1992), websites (e.g., Salmon et al., 2023), and online games (e.g., Basol et al., 2020). This strength of inoculation is especially relevant in a discussion of how inoculation theory could address misinformation on social media.

These strengths—inoculation theory's umbrella effects and inoculation theory's adaptability—make inoculation theory a popular and effective messaging strategy across issues and contexts and across media and forms. As previously mentioned, much of this work has explored the contexts of political campaigns (see Compton & Ivanov, 2012, for a review) and health campaigns (see Compton et al., 2016). More recent work has also established inoculation's efficacy in the context of science communication, including conferring resistance to science communication misinformation in times of crisis through the use of social media. Some key studies in this context are reviewed next.

Inoculation Theory, Science Communication, and Crisis Misinformation

As my colleagues and I put it, "better communication—better writing, better speaking, better listening, better reading, better reporting, and throughout it all, better *thinking* is critical" when addressing contested science (Compton et al., 2021, p. 2). Inoculation can promote such better communication, and consequently inoculation can help to confer resistance to misinformation.

Ideally, such theory-guided efforts can preempt the misinformation before it is even encountered, that is, inoculation as prophylactic (Compton, 2020b). But, even when misinformation cannot be preempted, an inoculation approach can help by correcting attitudes and beliefs and then making these newly corrected attitudes and beliefs more resistant to future change, that is, inoculation as therapeutic (Compton, 2020b). Either way, inoculation theory can guide a robust, effective science communication strategy to combat misinformation before, during, and/or after crises. This section offers a sample of some of the work done with inoculation theory and science communication in times of crises—from longstanding crises such as climate change to more contemporary crises such as the COVID-19 pandemic—including work that explores misinformation within the context of social media and the Internet.

Climate Change

Climate change is one of the most studied issues in science-related inoculation scholarship (Compton et al., 2021). Misinformation abounds about climate change's causes, its significance, and even its very existence. For example, climate change deniers have raised doubts about whether there is consensus regarding human-caused climate change in the scientific community. There is—one study found that 97 percent of climate scientists agree (Cook et al., 2016)—so how can inoculation-informed science communication efforts push back on this misinformation and to address the climate crisis (see Pierrehumbert, 2019)?

Van der Linden et al. (2017) wielded inoculation-based interventions against a specific source of consensus misinformation: a debunked yet influential online misinformation campaign called the Global Warming Petition Project, which claims that over 30,000 scientists disagree about human-caused climate change. Two inoculation interventions were tested. In one, people were simply warned that politically motivated voices would try to convince them that scientists disagree about human-caused climate change. In another, people were warned of impending challenges and given a detailed refutation of the misinformation, for example, that many of the names on the petition, which included Star Wars characters, were fictional. Both inoculation efforts were able to confer resistance to the misleading petition, an effect that has been replicated in follow-up registered studies (Maertens et al., 2020; Williams & Bond, 2020).

In another study, Cook et al. (2017) also tested inoculation's efficacy against the misinformation of the Global Warming Petition Project. They found some similar effects as van der Linden et al. (2017) but approached their inoculation intervention in a different way. Instead of providing a factual preemptive refutation of the claims made by the Global Warming Petition Project, Cook et al. (2017) explained the reasoning fallacies undergirding the Global Warming Petition Project's influence. This logic-based approach to inoculation messaging conferred protection to misinformation. In another climate change study, Vraga et al. (2020) looked at a different piece of climate change misinformation: the false idea that the increased production of CO_2 is actually good for the planet. When fact- and logic-based inoculation treatments were compared, logic-based inoculation messages were found to be the more effective; this supported the benefits of inoculating against logical fallacies (see also Cook et al., 2017).

Together, these studies support inoculation theory as a messaging strategy to address the climate crisis, especially in reinforcing scientific consensus about the causes of climate change (Cook et al., 2017; van der Linden et al., 2017). Scholars have used these findings to develop inoculation-informed climate communication campaigns, including an innovative online game called Cranky Uncle (https: //crankyuncle.com; see also Cook et al., 2023)

But what about other issues of science misinformation such as those that circulate during public health crises? We explore inoculation theory's approach to the COVID-19 pandemic—the disease and the vaccination—in the following sections.

COVID-19

Soon after the COVID-19 pandemic was identified, inoculation scholars began to study inoculation messaging as a way to promote a more accurate, healthier understanding of the virus itself and of preventive strategies, including—aptly enough in the context of this chapter—inoculation. As van der Linden and colleagues put it:

> There is an urgent need to counter the growing wave of COVID-19 vaccine misinformation by (a) taking more pre-emptive action via inoculation messages—especially around the medical consensus on safety and efficacy—and (b) by unveiling and defanging the manipulation techniques used to dupe people with vaccine-related misinformation. (van der Linden et al., 2021, p. 2; see also van der Linden et al., 2020)

Efforts to marshal inoculation interventions to combat COVID-19 vaccine misinformation have been successful, as demonstrated in a brief summary of findings to follow.

Amazeen et al. (2022) confirmed inoculation's potential as a COVID-19 vaccination promotion strategy. Their study tested two types of inoculation messages: (a) a generic inoculation message that warned of COVID-19 misinformation in general and encouraged careful scrutiny; and (b) a specific inoculation message that also raised some specific misinformation in conjunction with rebuttals of that information. The specific inoculation intervention was successful in protecting positive attitudes toward COVID-19 vaccination—that is, they had a prophylactic effect. The specific inoculation intervention was not effective, however, with those who did not have positive attitudes toward COVID-19 vaccination, that is, there were no observed therapeutic benefits. Generic inoculation messages fared better with those with negative and moderate attitudes toward COVID-19 vaccination. (Interestingly, these therapeutic benefits did not hold up when debunking messages followed the inoculation intervention and attack messages.)

Jiang et al. (2022) tested inoculation's efficacy in promoting COVID-19 vaccines to college students in Hong Kong. Inoculation interventions worked better than conventional one-sided health advocacy messages (but, surprisingly, not statistically better than the control, or no-message, condition). The one-sided health advocacy message—supportive arguments about inoculation with no mention of counterarguments—actually backfired, resulting in lower support for vaccines than the control or no-message condition.

Piltch-Loeb et al. (2022) delivered their COVID-19 vaccine inoculation messages in the form of 30-second short videos using narrative, fact, or both. The inoculation videos resulted in better identification of rhetorical strategies used in misinformation and increased willingness to get vaccinated, and discouraged intentions to share misinformation with others. In another study employing videos, Ramirez et al. (2022) tested two-minute inoculation-based video ads on Facebook aimed at users in rural counties in South Texas, in a pilot study. The videos featured peers modeling COVID-19 vaccine acceptance. The English- and Spanish-language videos worked better than conventional vaccine promotion ads from the Centers for Disease Control and Prevention as measured by clicking the "find a vaccine near you" link.

Inoculation scholars have also looked at inoculation-based campaigns in the form of online games. For example, Basol et al. (2021) found that the online game *Go Viral!* protected against misinformation. *Go Viral!* is a choice-based game that took about five minutes to play, with gameplayers learning about common misinformation strategies—fearmongering, fake experts, and conspiracy theories—and then had experience wielding these misinformation strategies to gain likes and credibility points. Those who played the game were more likely to recognize the manipulation strategies at work in COVID-19 misinformation, and importantly their increased confidence in their ability to spot misinformation seemed justified. That is, "people only became more confident in their ability when they correctly rated misinformation as manipulative" (Basol et al., 2021, p. 13). The game version worked better than a more passive inoculation message—an infographic—and people were more likely to share the game with others than the infographic. Notably, this research team assessed inoculation's efficacy cross-culturally, in French, English, and German languages.

In another game-based inoculation intervention, Ma et al. (2023) tested a gamified version delivered via the WeChat social media platform in China. In their game, players could earn points by accurately and speedily identifying misinformation. The game helped confer resistance to misinformation, with evidence that persuasion knowledge—an understanding of the persuasive tactics at work—played a key role.

Collectively, these studies offer encouraging evidence that inoculation theory can be a successful messaging strategy to combat COVID-19 misinformation, including by harnessing the reach and expediency of social media and online platforms. Specific messages seem to work best to protect positive attitudes toward COVID-19 vaccines, and general messages seem to work best to change neutral or negative attitudes (Amazeen et al., 2022). Inoculation-based messages work better than one-sided messages (Jiang et al., 2022). Inoculation messages can be effective in the form of 30-second videos (Piltch-Loeb et al., 2022) and longer (e.g., two-minute) videos (Ramirez et al., 2022). Gamified inoculation messages seem to hold particular promise (Basol et al., 2021; Ma et al., 2023). Evidence of inoculation theory-based COVID-19 messaging is encouraging, but what about other types of vaccines? We review some information on this possibility next.

Other Vaccinations

One of the first vaccines to receive attention from inoculation scholars was the human papillomavirus vaccine. Attention to combating misinformation or misperceptions about HPV vaccination is needed. Despite being recommended for adolescents and young adults, "HPV vaccine coverage remains suboptimal, and lags behind that of other routinely recommended adolescent vaccines" (Bednarczyk, 2019, p. 1628). Often, HPV vaccine hesitancy is based on myths about the vaccine, including its efficacy in protecting against cancer and its safety (Bednarczyk, 2019). Additionally, the HPV vaccine has been highly politicized, and as Chido-Amajuoyi et al. (2023) noted, "many parents' first exposure to information about HPV came through partisan news outlets, which may have influenced their attitudes toward the vaccine" (p. 5). Clearly, an effective messaging strategy that helps people work through information about HPV vaccination is needed. Might inoculation theory help?

Wong (2016) and Wong and Harrison (2014) looked at whether inoculation-based interventions could help protect positive attitudes toward HPV vaccines among young women in the face of antivaccination rhetoric. The intervention worked. Compared to a control condition (no inoculation message), those inoculated retained their positive attitudes toward HPV vaccination after exposure to counterarguments. More specifically, they tested two types of inoculation messages. One message raised and refuted arguments against vaccination in general, and the other arguments against HPV vaccination in particular. Both types of inoculation messages worked. More recently, Park et al. (2022) examined inoculation efficacy against HPV rumors and found inoculation messages to be more effective than supportive (one-sided) messages in relation to parental vaccine attitudes, parental vaccine intentions, and parental intention to speak in support of HPV vaccination.

Inoculation scholars have also assessed inoculation interventions in communicating information about other vaccines, including fictitious diseases. For example, Okuno et al. (2022) assessed inoculation messaging related to three types of vaccines: subcutaneous influenza vaccine, intranasal influenza vaccine, and "novel severe infectious disease" (a fictitious disease). They conducted their study in Japan. Refutational two-sided messages—those that raised concerns about vaccines and offered refutations of those concerns—worked best in communicating novel vaccination information that boosted willingness to get vaccinated.

Jolley and Douglas (2017) also looked at a fictitious disease and vaccine. In their study, participants read a fictional scenario about a disease threatening their children, with rather severe symptoms, and a vaccination that could protect them. When they were prepared beforehand with an inoculation message, they were more likely to express their intention to have their children vaccinated against the threat. But when they were not prepared beforehand they were less likely to do so.

In general, then, inoculation as a vaccination-promotion strategy has established efficacy across types of vaccines and message content and strategies. Also of note is that vaccination inoculation theory research reflects a broad geographical reach, with success not only in the United States but also in Canada (Vivion et al., 2022), Japan (Okuno et al., 2022), and Hong Kong (Jiang et al., 2022). With continuing efforts to design inoculation messaging for online media, including the game Bad Vax! (https://www.goviralgame.com), the reach of inoculation-informed interventions continues to grow.

Biotechnology and Animal Experimentation

Other work in inoculation theory and science has turned to scientific processes and industry. For example, Wood (2007) tested inoculation messages on attitudes toward agricultural biotechnology prior to exposure to antibiotechnology arguments (inadequate testing and health and environmental risks). Inoculation messages had a number of effects. Those who already had positive attitudes toward agricultural biotechnology were protected in their attitudes by inoculation messages. Those who had neutral or negative attitudes toward agricultural biotechnology had their attitudes moved in a more positive direction by inoculation messages. Inoculation both had a persuasive effect and helped confer resistance to future counterpersuasion.

Nabi (2003) assessed inoculation's efficacy with attitudes toward animal experimentation in scientific research in the face of criticism against it (e.g., that it is cruel). In addition to extending inoculation theory to a new issue (animal experimentation) and an underexplored domain (science communication), this work was also innovative in that it used videos to both inoculate and attack attitudes toward medical experimentation. The inoculation video that worked best was one that matched the level of emotional intensity of the attack message (e.g., a high-intensity inoculation video protected best against a high-intensity attack video).

Summary

This brief review of inoculation and science communication supports inoculation theory's strength as a message strategy and as a way to understand attitudes and beliefs about scientific issues, topics, and challenges (see also Compton et al., 2021; Ivanov & Parker, 2021). In these instances, inoculation shows an alternative—or addition—to retroactive responses to science misinformation, at times by harnessing the speed and efficiency of online media. With these encouraging results in mind, we conclude with some ideas for where inoculation theory and science crisis communication could go next.

Future Directions

Modes

Early work in inoculation theory used text-based inoculation intervention messages, including essays and editorials. Later work extended inoculation modes, successfully employing videos, cartoons, and online games to deliver inoculation theory-informed messaging, including some of the work mentioned in this chapter. Additional modes warrant increased attention in future inoculation theory work. For example, inoculation treatments in the form of tweetorials—"collections of threaded tweets with an educational mission" (Graham, 2021, p. 8)—could be tested to leverage social media platforms. Even with word and/or character limits, social media posts can be threaded together to advance a more nuanced argument, including the two-sided messaging format often used in inoculation messaging. Research should also explore online platforms that have been understudied in inoculation research, including TikTok—a content-sharing platform that can be used to promote misinformation (see Feijoo et al., 2023), but also, perhaps a platform that can also be used to promote resistance to health misinformation through inoculation-based interventions.

As another example, inoculation theory could guide applications of AI-based chat services (e.g., ChatGPT), which have inherent features of dialogue (e.g., raising of and responding to questions and prompts). Inoculation too has inherent features of dialogue, for example, the raising of and responding to counterarguments. Scholars have pointed out how a conventional inoculation message models dialogue (e.g., Compton & Mason, 2020), and future work could explore how such dialogic interfaces can offer an interactive inoculation experience, for example, by asking AI-based chat services to refute myths and misinformation, which would pair counterarguments (myths, misinformation) with refutations (AI-based chat responses).

Finally, the role and impact of word-of-mouth communication on inoculation-conferred resistance should not be overlooked. Inoculation scholars have made great strides in capturing how inoculation messages are particularly effective at motivating more talk about the target issue (Compton & Pfau, 2009), a type of talk called postinoculation talk, or PIT (e.g., Ivanov et al., 2012). Not only do inoculation-based messages seem to motivate more talk about the issue but this talk also strengthens the resistance effects of inoculation messages (Ivanov et al., 2012). That is, the more people talk about the issue after exposure to the inoculation intervention, the more robust their position becomes on that issue. To this point, work with PIT has explored myriad policy issues, including legalizing marijuana (Ivanov et al., 2012, 2015); restricting depictions of violence on television (Ivanov et al., 2012, 2015); banning handguns (Ivanov et al., 2012, 2015); legalizing gambling (Ivanov et al., 2012, 2015); making decisions on investments (Dillingham & Ivanov, 2016); and restoring confidence in government protective agencies after terrorism (Ivanov et al., 2018). Less attention has been paid to PIT in the context of science misinformation. More work in this area could build on encouraging research about the role of word-of-mouth communication in addressing scientific and health issues, including climate change (e.g., Connor et al., 2016), vaccinations (e.g., Xin et al., 2021), and other crises. Additionally, PIT research is particularly promising in the context of social media, where "talk" could take the form of chats, comments, emails, and other social media posts.

Scientist (and Science) Credibility

Inoculation theory has been established as a messaging strategy to protect against attacks on credibility (i.e., character assassination: see Compton, 2020a), mostly in the context of politics (e.g., Pfau & Burgoon, 1988). Inoculation campaigns can preemptively raise and refute character attacks, conferring resistance to stronger attacks launched in the future. Next, inoculation theory should continue to be assessed as a way to mitigate attacks against the credibility of science and scientists, perhaps functioning as a means of "proactivity in addressing prevalent misconceptions and biases regarding the field" (Sonmez et al., 2023, p. 16) or even tailoring the messages to specific types of attacks on credibility (see Samoilenko & Cook, 2023). A meta-analysis reveals that inoculation-based interventions are effective in guiding credibility assessments (Lu et al., 2023).

Some research has shown that the war-on-science framing can derogate perceptions of scientific credibility, especially among conservatives (Hardy et al., 2019); perhaps inoculation theory messaging can help dispel the negative effects of this framing. Other examples in this area include inoculating against misperceptions of what it means to do one's own research to build and preserve the credibility of scientific research (see Chinn & Hasell, 2023) and inoculating against backlash related to the inherent uncertainty of scientific forecasting such as weather forecasting (see Compton, 2018b).

Future research should also consider how to counter inoculation-based messaging when it is used to harm scientific credibility, that is, when inoculation messaging is used to build resistance to "healthy" persuasion. Inoculation theory is like any tool: It can be used for benefit or for harm. Much as inoculation was explored as an antidote to "bad" persuasion (see McGuire, 1970), we must also consider antidotes to "bad" inoculation. Banas and Miller (2013) propose one possibility: metainoculation, or inoculating against inoculation as an influence strategy. They found that warning of an impending inoculation-informed message mitigated the effectiveness of the message. Additional investigations of inoculation and credibility should continue, as an agent to both build and protect credibility (Compton, 2020a). The area of science and misinformation offers many opportunities for inoculation messaging to protect credibility perceptions, from communicating the credibility of specific scientists (e.g., Anthony Fauci, former director of the National Institute of Allergy and Infectious Diseases) to better explaining how science works in general (e.g., the scientific method).

Emotions

Inoculation theory was long thought to be a mostly cognitive process. Exposure to inoculation messages were thought to motivate counterarguing efforts against attack messages, or messages that ran counter to the fortified belief or attitude (see Compton, 2013; McGuire, 1964), and this was characterized as a cognitive process. Later, inoculation scholars uncovered powerful emotional processes of inoculation-conferred resistance to influence (see Compton et al., 2022, for a review), including how anger seems to boost resistance (Pfau et al., 2001) and how inoculation unleashes a number of emotional responses, emotions that endure even after a position has been attacked (Ivanov et al., 2020).

Inoculation theory and affect research could build on recent findings about the role(s) of emotions in science misinformation. For example, Featherstone and Zhang (2020) found that vaccine misinformation can elicit anger, but two-sided refutational messages can diminish this anger. Refutational content is a common feature of inoculation messaging. Counterarguments are often raised and refuted to generate threat and offer refutational content against future misinformation (see Compton, 2013; McGuire, 1964). At the same time, anger—something to be mitigated against in the context of Featherstone and Zhang's (2020) study—can function as a booster to resistance in inoculation. Future research should take a closer look at how inoculation-based messaging works with and/or against anger in contexts such as vaccine misinformation, which may be one way to "leverage emotions" in vaccination communication campaigns (Chou & Budenz, 2020, p. 1719).

Likewise, inoculation research can build on recent theorizing and research on emotions and climate change communication. As Chapman et al. (2017) urge:

> Rather than treat emotion as a lever or switch to be directly calibrated and pulled for a desired effect, the climate change communication community should adopt a more nuanced, evidence-based understanding of the multiple and sometimes counterintuitive ways that emotion, communication and issue engagement are intertwined. (p. 850)

Inoculation theory research could be one way to answer this call, with its attention to how affect and cognitions function in resistance. Such research could also further explore positive emotions and inoculation-conferred resistance to influence, including hope (see Shen et al., 2023).

Another aspect of inoculation-conferred resistance to influence that seems particularly promising for continued work in science misinformation correction is threat. As previously discussed, threat is a core part of inoculation theory if not *the* core part of inoculation theory. As Compton and others have argued, threat is what makes an inoculation intervention an inoculation intervention (Compton, 2009, 2021; Pfau, 1997). An inoculation message—through the use of a forewarning of impending challenges, or bringing up potential counterarguments and preemptively refuting them, or both—motivates an active process of resistance (Compton, 2013; McGuire, 1964). And yet, despite threat's importance in inoculation, there remains much more to learn about what threat is, how threat works, when threat works, and more (see Compton, 2021; Ivanov, 2017). Science misinformation resistance is a prime area for exploring this construct, since science misinformation often consists of affective and cognitive argumentation (see Compton et al., 2021), and threat seems to be an amalgamation of affective and cognitive responses (Compton, 2009, 2021).

Of course, there remain many other potential directions for ongoing and future inoculation theory research beyond what we have covered here, including whether (and under what conditions) inoculation enhances discernment rather than a more heuristically based resistance response (see Banas & Miller, 2013; Modirrousta-Galian & Higham, 2023) and whether—or under what conditions—logic-based inoculation (e.g., Cook et al., 2017; Vraga et al., 2020) outperform fact-based inoculation. In relation to the latter, Banas and Miller (2013) found, in contrast to findings from Cook et al. (2017) and Vraga et al. (2020) in their work described earlier in this chapter, that fact-based inoculation interventions were more effective than logic-based inoculation interventions in conferring resistance to a September 11 conspiracy film. As with the areas of possibility outlined, science misinformation—and more to the point, science misinformation on social media—is a promising area for these inoculation theory investigations.

Conclusion

Inoculation theory has been established as a consistently effective and powerful means of mitigating persuasive attacks through over 60 years of steady empirical investigation. Inoculation research output shows no signs of abating either. Indeed, if the last few years are an indication, we may be on the verge of another resurgence of inoculation theory application and development, especially as it relates to misinformation and disinformation, propaganda, and conspiracy in crisis situations.

This newer work is exciting, with large-scale efforts to distribute inoculation-based messages through innovative means such as online games (e.g., Bad News game: Basol et al., 2020). At the same time, we benefit from recognizing that, although the newest work is pushing inoculation theory forward in both application and theoretical development, it is part of a long historic story of resistance research, building on a theory that, since its inception, has been empirically tested, theoretically stretched, and widely applied across contexts and issues, including controversial issues in science.

References

Amazeen, M. A., Krishna, A., & Eschmann, R. (2022). Cutting the bunk: Comparing the solo and aggregate effects of prebunking and debunking COVID-19 vaccine misinformation. *Science Communication*, *44*(4), 387–417. http://dx.doi.org/10.1177/10755470221111558

Banas, J., & Miller, G. (2013). Inducing resistance to conspiracy theory propaganda: Testing inoculation and metainoculation strategies. *Human Communication Research*, *39*(2), 184–207. http://dx.doi.org/10.1111/hcre.12000

Banas, J., & Rains, S. (2010). A meta-analysis of research on inoculation theory. *Communication Monographs*, *77*(3), 281–331. http://dx.doi.org/10.1080/03637751003758193

Basol, M., Roozenbeek, J., Berriche, M., Uenal, F., McClanahan, W. P., & van der Linden, S. (2021). Towards psychological herd immunity: Cross-cultural evidence for two prebunking interventions against COVID-19 misinformation. *Big Data & Society*, *8*(1). 20539517211013868. http://dx.doi.org/10.1177/20539517211013868

Basol, M., Roozenbeek, J., & van der Linden, S. (2020). Good news about bad news: Gamified inoculation boosts confidence and cognitive immunity against fake news. *Journal of Cognition*, *3*(1). http://dx.doi.org/10.5334/joc.91

Bednarczyk, R. A. (2019). Addressing HPV vaccine myths: Practical information for healthcare providers. *Human Vaccines and Immunotherapeutics*, *15*(7–8), 1628–1638. http://dx.doi.org/10.1080/21645515.2019.1565267

Chapman, D. A., Lickel, B., & Markowitz, E. M. (2017). Reassessing emotion in climate change communication. *Nature Climate Change*, *7*(12), 850–852. http://dx.doi.org/10.1038/s41558-017-0021-9

Chido-Amajuoyi, O. G., Onyeaka, H., Amonoo, H. L., & Shete, S. (2023). The influence of political ideology on awareness of HPV and HPV vaccine among adults in the United States. *Human Vaccines and Immunotherapeutics*, *19*(2), 2232706. http://dx.doi.org/10.1080/21645515.2023.2232706

Chinn, S., & Hasell, A. (2023). Support for "doing your own research" is associated with COVID-19 misperceptions and scientific mistrust. *Harvard Kennedy School Misinformation Review*, *4*(3). http://dx.doi.org/10.37016/mr-2020-117

Chou, W. Y. S., & Budenz, A. (2020). Considering emotion in COVID-19 vaccine communication: Addressing vaccine hesitancy and fostering vaccine confidence. *Health Communication*, *35*(14), 1718–1722. http://dx.doi.org/10.1080/10410236.2020.1838096

Compton, J. (2009). Threat explication: What we know and don't yet know about a key component of inoculation theory. *STAM Journal*, *39*, 1–18.

Compton, J. (2013). Inoculation theory. In J. P. Dillard & L. Shen (Eds.), *The SAGE handbook of persuasion: Developments in theory and practice* (2nd ed., pp. 220–236). SAGE. http://dx.doi.org/10.4135/9781452218410.n14

Compton, J. (2018a). Inoculating against/with political humor. In J. Baumgartner & A. B. Becker (Eds.), *Political humor in a changing media landscape: A new generation of research* (pp. 95–114). Lexington Books.

Compton, J. (2018b). When weather forecasters are wrong: Image repair and public rhetoric after severe weather. *Science Communication, 40*(6), 778–788. http://dx.doi.org/10.1177/1075547018799101

Compton, J. (2020a). Inoculation against/as character assassination. In M. Icks, J. Keohane, E. Shiraev, & S. Samoilenko (Eds.), *The Routledge handbook of character assassination and reputation management* (pp. 25–35). Routledge.

Compton, J. (2020b). Prophylactic versus therapeutic inoculation treatments for resistance to influence. *Communication Theory, 30*(3), 330–343. http://dx.doi.org/10.1093/ct/qtz004

Compton, J. (2021). Threat and/in inoculation theory. *International Journal of Communication, 15*, 1–13. https://ijoc.org/index.php/ijoc/article/view/17634/3565

Compton, J., & Ivanov, B. (2012). Untangling threat during inoculation-conferred resistance to influence. *Communication Reports, 25*(1), 1–13. http://dx.doi.org/10.1080/08934215.2012.661018

Compton, J., & Ivanov, B. (2013). Vaccinating voters: Surveying political campaign inoculation scholarship. *Annals of the International Communication Association, 37*(1), 251–283. http://dx.doi.org/10.1080/23808985.2013.11679152

Compton, J., Ivanov, B., & Hester, E. (2022). Inoculation theory and affect. *International Journal of Communication, 16*, 3470–3483. https://ijoc.org/index.php/ijoc/article/view/19094

Compton, J., Jackson, B., & Dimmock, J. A. (2016). Persuading others to avoid persuasion: Inoculation theory and resistant health attitudes. *Frontiers in Psychology, 7*(122). http://dx.doi.org/10.3389/fpsyg.2016.00122

Compton, J., & Mason, A. (2020). Narrative and the inoculation theory of resistance to influence. In S. G. Schartel Dunn & G. S. Nisbett (Eds.), *Innovations and implications of persuasive narrative* (pp. 23–42). Peter Lang. http://dx.doi.org/10.3726/b17049

Compton, J., & Pfau, M. (2009). Spreading inoculation: Inoculation, resistance to influence, and word-of-mouth communication. *Communication Theory, 19*, 9–28. http://dx.doi.org/10.1111/j.1468-2885.2008.01330.x

Compton, J., van der Linden, S., Cook, J., & Basol, M. (2021). Inoculation theory in the post-truth era: Extant findings and new frontiers for contested science, misinformation, and conspiracy theories. *Social and Personality Psychology Compass, 15*, 1–16. http://dx.doi.org/10.1111/spc3.12602

Connor, P., Harris, E., Guy, S., Fernando, J., Shank, D. B., Kurz, T., Bain, P. G., & Kashima, Y. (2016). Interpersonal communication about climate change: How messages change when communicated through simulated online social networks. *Climatic Change, 136*, 463–476. http://dx.doi.org/10.1007/s10584-016-1643-z

Cook, J., Ecker, U. K., Trecek-King, M., Schade, G., Jeffers-Tracy, K., Fessmann, J., Kim, S. C., Kinkead, D., Orr, M., Vraga, E., Roberts, K., & McDowell, J. (2023). The cranky uncle game: Combining humor and gamification to build student resilience against climate misinformation. *Environmental Education Research, 29*(4), 607–623. http://dx.doi.org/10.1080/13504622.2022.2085671

Cook, J., Lewandowsky, S., & Ecker, U. K. H. (2017). Neutralizing misinformation through inoculation: Exposing misleading argumentation techniques reduces their influence. *PLoS ONE, 12*(5). http://dx.doi.org/10.1371/journal.pone.0175799

Cook, J., Oreskes, N., Doran, P. T., Anderegg, W. R., Verheggen, B., Maibach, E. W., & Nuccitelli, D. (2016). Consensus on consensus: A synthesis of consensus estimates on human-caused global warming. *Environmental Research Letters*, *11*(4), 048002. http://dx.doi.org/10.1088/1748-9326/11/4/048002

Dillingham, L. L., & Ivanov, B. (2016). Using postinoculation talk to strengthen generated resistance. *Communication Research Reports*, *33*(4), 295–302. http://dx.doi.org/10.1080/08824096.2016.1224161

Featherstone, J. D., & Zhang, J. (2020). Feeling angry: The effects of vaccine misinformation and refutational messages on negative emotions and vaccination attitude. *Journal of Health Communication*, *25*(9), 692–702. http://dx.doi.org/10.1080/10810730.2020.1838671

Feijoo, B., Sádaba, C., & Zozaya, L. (2023). Distrust by default: Analysis of parent and child reactions to health misinformation exposure on TikTok. *International Journal of Adolescence and Youth*, *28*(1), 2244595. http://dx.doi.org/10.1080/02673843.2023.2244595

Graham, S. S. (2021). Misinformation inoculation and literacy support tweetorials on COVID-19. *Journal of Business and Technical Communication*, *35*(1), 7–14. http://dx.doi.org/10.1177/1050651920958505

Haigh, M. M., & Wigley, S. (2015). Examining the impact of negative, user-generated content on stakeholders. *Corporate Communications*, *20*(1), 63–75. http://dx.doi.org/10.1108/CCIJ-02-2013-0010

Hardy, B. W., Tallapragada, M., Besley, J. C., & Yuan, S. (2019). The effects of the "war on science" frame on scientists' credibility. *Science Communication*, *41*(1), 90–112. http://dx.doi.org/10.1177/1075547018822081

Ivanov, B. (2017). Inoculation theory applied in health and risk messaging. In J. Nussbaum (Ed.), *Oxford research encyclopedia of communication* (pp. 278–304). Oxford University Press. http://dx.doi.org/10.1093/acrefore/9780190228613.013.254

Ivanov, B., Hester, E. B., Martin, J. C., Silberman, W., Slone, A. R., Goatley-Soan, S., Geegan, S., Parker, K. A., Herrington, T. F., Riker, S., & Anderson, A. (2020). Persistence of emotion in the process of inoculation: Experiencing post-attack threat, fear, anger, happiness, sadness, and surprise. *Communication Quarterly*, *68*(5), 560–582. http://dx.doi.org/10.1080/01463373.2020.1850492

Ivanov, B., Miller, C. H., Compton, J., Averbeck, J. M., Robertson, K. J., Sims, J. D., Parker, K. A., & Parker, J. L. (2012). Effects of post-inoculation talk on resistance to influence. *Journal of Communication*, *62*, 701–718. http://dx.doi.org/10.1111/j.1460-2466.2012.01658.x

Ivanov, B., & Parker, K. A. (2021). Science communication and inoculation: Mitigating the effects of the coronavirus outbreak. In H. D. O'Hair & M. J. O'Hair (Eds.), *Communicating science in times of crisis: COVID-19 pandemic* (pp. 302–320). Wiley Blackwell. http://dx.doi.org/10.1002/9781119751809.ch13

Ivanov, B., Sellnow, T., Getchell, M., & Burns, W. (2018). The potential for inoculation messages and postinoculation talk to minimize the social impact of politically motivated acts of violence. *Journal of Contingencies and Crisis Management*, *26*(4), 414–424. http://dx.doi.org/10.1111/1468-5973.12213

Ivanov, B., Sims, J. D., Compton, J., Miller, C. H., Parker, K. A., Parker, J. L., Harrison, K. J., & Averbeck, J. M. (2015). The general content of post-inoculation talk: Recalled issue-specific conversations following inoculation treatments. *Western Journal of Communication*, *79*(2), 218–238. http://dx.doi.org/10.1080/10570314.2014.943423

Jiang, L. C., Sun, M., Chu, T. H., & Chia, S. C. (2022). Inoculation works and health advocacy backfires: Building resistance to COVID-19 vaccine misinformation in a low political trust context. *Frontiers in Psychology*, *13*. http://dx.doi.org/10.3389/fpsyg.2022.976091

Jolley, D., & Douglas, K. M. (2017). Prevention is better than cure: Addressing anti-vaccine conspiracy theories. *Journal of Applied Social Psychology*, *47*(8), 459–469. http://dx.doi.org/10.1111/jasp.12453

Lu, C., Hu, B., Li, Q., Bi, C., & Ju, X. D. (2023). Psychological inoculation for credibility assessment, sharing intention, and discernment of misinformation: Systematic review and meta-analysis. *Journal of Medical Internet Research*, *25*, e49255. http://dx.doi.org/10.2196/49255

Ma, J., Chen, Y., Zhu, H., & Gan, Y. (2023). Fighting COVID-19 misinformation through an online game based on the inoculation theory: Analyzing the mediating effects of perceived threat and persuasion knowledge. *International Journal of Environmental Research and Public Health*, *20*(2), 980. http://dx.doi.org/10.3390/ijerph20020980

Maertens, R., Anseel, F., & van der Linden, S. (2020). Combatting climate change misinformation: Evidence for longevity of inoculation and consensus messaging effects. *Journal of Environmental Psychology*, *70*, 101455. https://doi.org/10.%201016/j.jenvp.2020.101455

McGuire, W. J. (1961). Resistance to persuasion conferred by active and passive prior refutation of the same and alternative counterarguments. *The Journal of Abnormal and Social Psychology*, *63*(2), 326–332. http://dx.doi.org/10.1037/h0048344

McGuire, W. J. (1964). Inducing resistance to persuasion: Some contemporary approaches. In L. Berkowitz (Ed.), *Advances in experimental social psychology* (pp. 191–229). Academic Press. http://dx.doi.org/10.1016/S0065-2601(08)60052-0

McGuire, W. J. (1970). A vaccine for brainwash. *Psychology Today*, *3*(9), 37–64.

Modirrousta-Galian, A., & Higham, P. A. (2023). Gamified inoculation interventions do not improve discrimination between true and fake news: Reanalyzing existing research with receiver operating characteristic analysis. *Journal of Experimental Psychology: General*, *152*(9), 2411–2437. http://dx.doi.org/10.1037/xge0001395

Nabi, R. (2003). "Feeling" resistance: Exploring the role of emotionally evocative visuals in inducing inoculation. *Media Psychology*, *5*(2), 199–223. http://dx.doi.org/10.1207/S1532785XMEP0502_4

Okuno, H., Arai, S., Suzuki, M., & Kikkawa, T. (2022). Impact of refutational two-sided messages on attitudes toward novel vaccines against emerging infectious diseases during the COVID-19 pandemic. *Frontiers in Public Health*, *10*, 166. http://dx.doi.org/10.3389/fpubh.2022.775486

Park, E., Kim, S., & Cameron, G. T. (2022). Immunize the HPV vaccine rumors: Effects of inoculation messages and tone of voice on parental intention to vaccinate their children. *Journal of Community Health*, *47*(5), 790–799. http://dx.doi.org/10.1007/s10900-022-01100-9

Parker, K. A., Ivanov, B., & Compton, J. (2012). Inoculation's efficacy with young adults' risky behaviors: Can inoculation confer cross-protection over related but untreated issues? *Health Communication*, *27*(3), 223–233. http://dx.doi.org/10.1080/10410236.2011.575541

Pfau, M. (1997). The inoculation model of resistance to influence. In G. A. Barnett & F. J. Boster (Eds.), *Progress in communication sciences: Advances in persuasion* (Vol. 13, pp. 133–171). Ablex.

Pfau, M., Bockern, S. V., & Kang, J. G. (1992). Use of inoculation to promote resistance to smoking initiation among adolescents. *Communication Monographs*, *59*(3), 213–230. http://dx.doi.org/10.1080/03637759209376266

Pfau, M., & Burgoon, M. (1988). Inoculation in political campaign communication. *Human Communication Research*, *15*(1), 91–111. http://dx.doi.org/10.1111/j.1468-2958.1988.tb00172.x

Pfau, M., Haigh, M. M., Shannon, T., Tones, T., Mercurio, D., Williams, R., Binstock, B., Diaz, C., Dillard, C., Browne, M., Elder, C., Reed, S., Eggers, A., & Melendez, J. (2008). The influence of television news depictions on the images of war on viewers. *Journal of Broadcasting & Electronic Media*, *52*(2), 303–322. http://dx.doi.org/10.1080/08838150801992128

Pfau, M., Szabo, E. A., Anderson, J., Morrill, J., Zubric, J., & Wan, H.-H. (2001). The role and impact of affect in the process of resistance to persuasion. *Human Communication Research*, *27*(2), 216–252. http://dx.doi.org/10.1111/j.1468-2958.2001.tb00781.x

Pierrehumbert, R. (2019). There is no Plan B for dealing with the climate crisis. *Bulletin of the Atomic Scientists*, *75*(5), 215–221. http://dx.doi.org/10.1080/00963402.2019.1654255

Piltch-Loeb, R., Su, M., Hughes, B., Testa, M., Goldberg, B., Braddock, K., Miller-Idriss, C., Maturo, V., & Savoia, E. (2022). Testing the efficacy of attitudinal inoculation videos to enhance COVID-19 vaccine acceptance: Quasi-experimental intervention trial. *JMIR Public Health and Surveillance*, *8*(6), e34615. http://dx.doi.org/10.2196/34615

Ramirez, A. G., Despres, C., Chalela, P., Weis, J., Sukumaran, P., Munoz, E., & McAlister, A. L. (2022). Pilot study of peer modeling with psychological inoculation to promote coronavirus vaccination. *Health Education Research*, *37*(1), 1–6. http://dx.doi.org/10.1093/her/cyab042

Richards, A. S., & Banas, J. A. (2015). Inoculating against reactance to persuasive health messages. *Health Communication*, *30*(5), 451–460. http://dx.doi.org/10.1080/10410236.2013.867005

Roozenbeek, J., & van der Linden, S. (2019). Fake news game confers psychological resistance against online misinformation. *Palgrave Communications*, *5*, 65. http://dx.doi.org/10.1057/s41599-019-0279-9

Salmon, D. A., Dudley, M. Z., Brewer, J., Shaw, J., Schuh, H. B., Proveaux, T. M., Jamison, A. M., Forr, A., Goryn, M., Breiman, R. F., Orenstein, W. A., Kao, L.-S., Josiah, Willock, R., Cantu, M., Decea, T., Mowson, R., Tsubata, K., Bucci, L. M., et al. (2023). *LetsTalkShots*: Personalized vaccine risk communication. *Frontiers in Public Health*, *11*. http://dx.doi.org/10.3389/fpubh.2023.1195751

Samoilenko, S. A., & Cook, J. (2023). Developing an *ad hominem* typology for classifying climate misinformation. *Climate Policy*, *24*(1), 138–151. http://dx.doi.org/10.1080/14693062.2023.2245792

Shen, L., Li, S. S., Sweeney, K., & Lee, D. (2023). Re-visiting hope as a discrete emotion and its role in persuasion. *Communication Quarterly*, *71*(3), 322–341. http://dx.doi.org/10.1080/01463373.2023.2203827

Sonmez, B., Makarovs, K., & Allum, N. (2023). Public perception of scientists: Experimental evidence on the role of sociodemographic, partisan, and professional characteristics. *PLoS ONE*, *18*(7), e0287572. http://dx.doi.org/10.1371/journal.pone.0287572

van der Linden, S., Dixon, G., Clarke, C., & Cook, J. (2021). Inoculating against COVID-19 vaccine misinformation. *eClinicalMedicine*, *33*. http://dx.doi.org/10.1016/j.eclinm.2021.100772

van der Linden, S., Leiserowitz, A., Rosenthal, S., & Maibach, E. (2017). Inoculating the public against misinformation about climate change. *Global Challenges*, *1*(2), 1600008. http://dx.doi.org/10.1002/gch2.201600008

van der Linden, S., Roozenbeek, J., & Compton, J. (2020). Inoculating against fake news about COVID-19. *Frontiers in Psychology*, 11. http://dx.doi.org/10.3389/fpsyg.2020.566790

Vivion, M., Anassour Laouan Sidi, E., Betsch, C., Dionne, M., Dubé, E., Driedger, S. M., Gagnon, J., Graham, J., Greyson, D., Hamel, D., Lewandowsky, S., MacDonald, N., Malo, B., Meyer, S. B., Schmid, P., Steenbeek, A., van der Linden, S., Verger, P., Witteman, H. O., et al. (2022). Prebunking messaging to inoculate against COVID-19 vaccine misinformation: An effective strategy for public health. *Journal of Communication in Healthcare*, *15*(3), 232–242. http://dx.doi.org/10.1080/17538068.2022.2044606

Vraga, E. K., Kim, S. C., Cook, J., & Bode, L. (2020). Testing the effectiveness of correction placement and type on Instagram. *The International Journal of Press/Politics*, *25*(4), 632–652. http://dx.doi.org/10.1177/1940161220919082

Williams, M. N., & Bond, C. M. (2020). A preregistered replication of "inoculating the public against misinformation about climate change". *Journal of Environmental Psychology*, *70*, 101456. http://dx.doi.org/10.1016/j.jenvp.2020.101456

Wong, N. C. H. (2016). "Vaccinations are safe and effective": Inoculating positive HPV vaccine attitudes against antivaccination attack messages. *Communication Reports*, *29*(3), 127–138. http://dx.doi.org/10.1080/08934215.2015.1083599

Wong, N. C. H., & Harrison, K. J. (2014). Nuances in inoculation: Protecting positive attitudes toward the HPV vaccine and the practice of vaccinating children. *Journal of Women's Health, Issues and Care*, *3*(6). http://dx.doi.org/10.4172/2325-9795.1000170

Wood, M. L. M. (2007). Rethinking the inoculation analogy: Effects on subjects with differing preexisting attitudes. *Human Communication Research*, *33*, 357–378. http://dx.doi.org/10.1111/j.1468-2958.2007.00303.x

Xin, M., Luo, S., She, R., Chen, X., Li, L., Li, L., Chen, X., & Lau, J. T. (2021). The impact of social media exposure and interpersonal discussion on intention of COVID-19 vaccination among nurses. *Vaccine*, *9*(10), 1204. http://dx.doi.org/10.3390/vaccines9101204

13

Big Data Approaches to Identifying Crisis Misinformation

Haoning Xue[1] *and Cuihua (Cindy) Shen*[2]

[1] *Department of Communication, University of Utah*
[2] *Department of Communication, University of California, Davis*

Our complex information ecosystem is characterized by the increasing volume and rapid dissemination of both accurate and false information (Vosoughi et al., 2018). To address the challenge of crisis misinformation, a critical first step is the prompt and reliable detection of misinformation, for several reasons. First, misinformation identification informs the extent, nature, and themes of falsehoods. This knowledge is crucial in shaping the scale and focus of countermeasures, such as debunking false claims with factual information or addressing underlying biases and fears. Second, early identification can curb the wider dissemination of misinformation. The more rapidly false information is recognized and addressed, the less chance it has to take hold and spread across networks. Third, identifying specific instances of misinformation provides tangible examples that can be used to educate the public about its presence and nature, especially in crisis situations. For news outlets, educational platforms, and governments, clear identification of misinformation is a prerequisite for building trust with their audience and developing effective policies and regulations to combat it.

To date, misinformation detection has been done using several strategies and by different stakeholders. For example, there are various independent and editorial fact-checking organizations worldwide dedicated to verifying the accuracy of viral claims and statements (IFCN, 2023), such as http://snopes.com, an independent fact-checking website, and Reuters Fact Check, an in-house fact-checking division at Reuters news agency. Ordinary citizens can also play a pivotal role in the battle against misinformation through crowdsourced and collaborative fact-checking efforts. For instance, in Taiwan, ordinary citizens voluntarily collaborate to inquire, identify, and validate questionable statements in collaborative efforts on Cofacts, an online crowdsourced fact-checking community (Cofacts, 2023). In 2021 the social media platform Twitter launched its Birdwatch platform, allowing Twitter users to provide additional or contextual information for tweets that may contain potentially misleading content (Coleman, 2021). In addition to fact-checking efforts, Poynter, a nonprofit media institute, has launched MediaWise, a project that focuses on digital literacy among teenagers and older adults. MediaWise has initiated a series of courses on media literacy to empower individuals with the essential skills to discern misinformation and remain vigilant in this intricate information environment (MediaWise, 2023).

Communication and Misinformation: Crisis Events in the Age of Social Media, First Edition.
Edited by Kevin B. Wright.
© 2025 John Wiley & Sons, Inc. Published 2025 by John Wiley & Sons, Inc.

These human-led approaches have proven effective in combating misinformation, but they are not without limitations in the era of big data, where misinformation is produced and spread on a colossal scale and at an unprecedented pace. Social media accelerates and complicates the spread and impact of misinformation (Altay & Acerbi, 2023). While misinformation is not a brand-new phenomenon and often thrives in times of crises and uncertainty, social media significantly amplifies the problem of misinformation by enabling the broadcasting of misinformation to billions of people within an exceptionally short period of time. This viral spread of misinformation also greatly magnifies the detrimental impact of misinformation on public health and safety. In addition, social media complicates the problem of misinformation, with various actors involved, including ordinary users, malicious actors, and social bots, all of whom can potentially produce and disseminate misinformation (Broniatowski et al., 2018; Shao et al., 2018). Ordinary users may unintentionally be involved in the misinformation propagation process. Malicious actors, however, deliberately create and spread misinformation, while social bots can generate and distribute misinformation automatically at a large scale, even forming coordinated, weaponized networks to spread misinformation (Zhang et al., 2023).

The conventional fact-checking approach by media organizations relies on professional journalists to manually gather contextual information and verify claims, while the crowdsourced community approach also relies on the voluntary labor of a dedicated group of informed citizens. Regardless of their scale, these human-led methods demand substantial time, personnel, and financial resources for manual verification. This case-by-case approach also struggles to yield generalizable insights on misinformation characteristics at a larger scale. There is an urgent need for a more efficient way to promptly identify and stem the spread of misinformation and to mitigate the detrimental impacts of misinformation on the whole society.

Given the intricacies of misinformation on social media, it becomes urgent to adopt the big data approaches to intercept misinformation at its early stages and prevent its dissemination to a wider social network or its impact on a broader public. Big data refers to "the information assets characterized by such a high volume, velocity and variety to require specific technology and analytical methods for its transformation into value" (De Mauro et al., 2015, p. 103). When applied to the context of misinformation detection, the big data approaches are involved in the process from data collection to data processing and analysis to detect and analyze misinformation in the current information-rich environment. The advantage of these approaches extends beyond its cost efficiency; they are a more appropriate misinformation detection approach, especially given the virality of information on social media and the emergence of multimodal misinformation. Compared to conventional human-led fact-checking approaches, the big data approaches are capable of detecting misinformation at its early stages at a much larger scale and at a much lower cost (Torabi Asr & Taboada, 2019). Further, big data allows for the exploration of misinformation propagation patterns and content-level attributes, which enhances our understanding of the misinformation phenomenon.

Technological advances complicate the problem of misinformation at the content level. However, multimodal misinformation is increasingly prevalent, with the wide usage of devices and platforms centered on multimedia including but not limited to images and videos. Multimodal misinformation poses an even greater threat to public health and safety during crises because, on the one hand, multimodal misinformation that functions as arguments, heuristics, and attention determinants can be more persuasive and damaging than textual misinformation (Y. Peng et al., 2023; Shen et al., 2019), and, on the other hand, it presents technological challenges to traditional fact-checking efforts, which struggle with the verification of synthesized multimodal misinformation (Walker et al., 2023; Weikmann & Lecheler, 2023).

Multimodal misinformation falls into three broad categories: out-of-context misinformation, manipulated misinformation, and synthetic/fabricated misinformation (Kasra et al., 2018; Qian et al., 2023). *Out-of-context misinformation*, also known as *misattribution*, refers to "the use of unedited and authentic images in a false context to misrepresent reality" through a recompression process (Cao et al., 2020; Qian et al., 2023). *Manipulated multimodal misinformation* refers to photoshopped visual information, with key elements removed, created, or edited (Kasra et al., 2018). These two kinds of misinformation are relatively straightforward to identify and correct when the source of the visual information is already known. Lastly, *synthetic misinformation* poses a greater challenge, involving images or videos fully or partially generated by technology (J. Zhou et al., 2023). Various AI generators empowered by generative adversarial networks (GAN; Goodfellow et al., 2020), such as ChatGPT, DALL-E, and Synthesia can automatically generate textual and multimodal information based on user description. Depending on the fabrication of multimodal features, synthetic multimodal misinformation can be categorized into the following types: (a) face-swap, (b) lip-synching, (c) puppet-master (i.e., facial expression reenactment), (d) face synthesis and attribute manipulation, and (e) audio-only deepfake (see Masood et al., 2023). In addition, AI-generative technologies can take snippets of existing media featuring a person and automatically generate new multimodal information for that person. For example, Jordan Peele used AI to generate a deepfake video of President Obama delivering fake news in 2018 (Vincent, 2018). This instance illustrates the growing sophistication and danger of synthetic misinformation, demonstrating the inadequacy of the conventional human-led approach and the urgent need for detection and intervention using big data approaches. Such an approach excels by (a) enabling automated detection that reduces the need for intensive labor, (b) conducting real-time and cross-platform misinformation monitoring and detection, and (c) providing insights into content and user patterns that humans may not notice with advanced computational analysis.

In what follows, we introduce state-of-the-art big data approaches to identifying misinformation, including content- and context-based detection, based on a systematic review of misinformation detection-related literature from January 2021 to August 2023 ($N = 157$). We then discuss existing challenges and future directions for effectively and appropriately leveraging big data in the battle against misinformation, including misinformation related to crises.

The Basics of the Big Data Approaches

Prior to discussing various big data approaches to misinformation detection, this section provides an introductory overview of relevant definitions, processes, and evaluation metrics. Machine learning is central of using big data for misinformation detection. It is defined as the process of "coaching computers to intelligently perform tasks beyond traditional number crunching by learning the surrounding environment through repeated examples" (El Naqa & Murphy, 2015, p. 6). In other words, machine learning is the process of teaching computers to learn from data and to make decisions (in this case, determining whether or not to classify a piece of information as misinformation). Three key steps are usually involved in developing misinformation detection models: (a) data collection and preprocessing; (b) feature engineering; and (c) model selection, training, and testing.

First, the prerequisite of misinformation detection models involves data collection, data labeling, and data preprocessing. To develop a misinformation detector, input data is needed for computers to identify data patterns. Researchers often rely on social media data (e.g., Twitter, Weibo, Facebook, TikTok) and datasets from professional fact-checking organizations to study misinformation characteristics. It is noteworthy that the data that can be used to train misinformation detection models is not exclusively restricted to misinformation claims; networks delineating the propagation of (mis)information and additional contextual data also serve as valuable training resources. For example, W. Y. Wang (2017) collected a dataset of fact-checked true and false news with six-class verdicts from PolitiFact, a fact-checking organization in which professional journalists research and determine the verdicts of claims in question. The input data often comes with labels that indicate the veracity of the input data, serving as the target outcome in machine-learning models to differentiate between true and false information. Depending on the data label availability, machine learning can be categorized as supervised or unsupervised machine learning (El Naqa & Murphy, 2015). Supervised machine learning refers to the scenario where the input data is paired with a known classification label or outcome variable. In this case, misinformation claims are usually paired with fact-checking labels. By contrast, the classification labels are unknown in the case of unsupervised machine learning, where computers identify patterns and relationships of the input data without the restriction of labels. In misinformation detection, supervised machine learning is most common and applicable where the verdicts of misinformation claims are provided.

Second, featuring engineering is the process of "formulating the most appropriate features given the data, the model, and the task" (Zheng & Casari, 2018). Features are characteristics or attributes of input data that can be useful for machine learning tasks. On the one hand, researchers may define and handpick features that are theoretically pertinent to the task. For example, bag-of-words (BoW) representations are common features used in natural language processing tasks (Zheng & Casari, 2018). The BoW representation gives information on the presence of frequency of vocabularies in a given document, which can be used for text classification and thematic understanding, without considering semantic structures or meanings. Features considering more semantic contexts can be used as well. For example, since contextual features such as topics and misinformation-sharing intentions are related to misinformation characteristics and dissemination patterns (Chung & Kim, 2021; Vosoughi et al., 2018), these features have been selected and integrated into misinformation detection models (e.g., X. Zhou et al., 2020). Such manually selected features are also referred to as handcrafted features. At the same time, neural networks—networks that consist of layers of neurons—are capable of automatically conducting matrix transformation of input data. This is the process where computers transform any kind of input data, from texts to videos, into computer-understandable numeric values, represented as matrices. This process produces complex and latent features that can significantly improve model performance, although these deep features are less theory driven or interpretable by humans, compared with handcrafted features (S.-C. Wang, 2003). Notable neural network models such as convolutional neural networks (CNNs) and recurrent neural networks (RNNs) produce deep layers that are matrix representations of training data.

The last step of machine learning revolves around model selection, training, and testing, a process that is significantly influenced by the nature of input data and the task at hand. For example, CNNs achieve the best performance with two-dimensional data such as images, while RNNs are suitable for sequential data such as texts and are therefore selected for natural language understanding tasks (Goodfellow et al., 2016, p. 367). When a model has been trained on input data, it is crucial to evaluate the model's performance, that is, how well it can make correct predictions with unseen data. This is usually achieved with a train–test split, where a model is trained by learning from the training set (e.g., 80 percent of all input data) and is evaluated with its prediction performance with the remaining unseen testing set. A more systematic and robust model evaluation technique is called cross-validation, which involves training and evaluating the model with different subsets of input data. This is an iterative process in which every bit of data is used for training and evaluation rather than depending on a particular data subset where input data usually happens with only one iteration, which usually happens with only one iteration. For categorical classification tasks such as misinformation detection, several performance evaluation metrics are prevalent: (a) accuracy; (b) precision, recall, and F1 score; and (c) areas under the curve (AUC) (see Zheng, 2015, for a review). Accuracy is the simplest evaluation metric, calculating the proportion of true predictions out of all predictions made by the model (true positives and true negatives out of all predictions). However, given the inherent imbalance of misinformation datasets in which misinformation is rare, accuracy alone has its limitation in providing more nuanced information on model performance. Therefore, precision, recall, and F1 scores are more insightful in accounting for data imbalance and providing additional information on false positives or true negatives. Precision refers to the percentage of true positive predictions of all positive predictions (the sum of both true positives and false positives), with a high precision representing low false positive rates. Recall refers to the percentage of true positive predictions of all positive cases in the sample (the sum of true positives and false negatives), with high recall representing high true positive rates. The F1 score is a harmonic mean of precision and recall, capturing the precision–recall trade-off and providing a more balanced evaluation of model performance, considering both precision and recall. Lastly, AUC illustrates the relationship between recall and false positives, representing model performance at the cost of false positives. A successful machine-learning model for misinformation detection should aim to achieve both high precision and recall (Zheng, 2015).

In the sections that follow, we introduce three types of big data-based misinformation detection approaches: content-based (i.e., textual and multimodal misinformation), context-based (i.e., user, propagation, and metadata), and feature fusion approaches (see Table 13.1 for a summary of misinformation detection approaches). To present an overview of state-of-the-art misinformation detection approaches, we conducted a systematic review from January 2021 to August 2023. Using the Web of Science application programming interface (API) (Clarivate, 2023), we searched 52 relevant keywords (e.g., synthetic misinformation detection; see Table 13.2 for the full list), retrieving 157 peer-reviewed publications. In addition, we reviewed additional publications cited by these articles, aiming to provide a more comprehensive and robust understanding of the literature in misinformation detection.

Content-Based Misinformation Detection

Misinformation and true information possess distinctive features related to the content itself, which makes the content-based approaches the mainstream in misinformation detection. In this section, we discuss different approaches to detecting both textual and multimodal misinformation.

Table 13.1 Summary of Big-data Approaches for Misinformation Detection.

Category			Example study
Content-based approach	Textual information	Handcraft features	Rashkin et al. (2017) Shu et al. (2017)
		Deep features	Hu et al. (2020)
		Knowledge graph	Ciampaglia et al. (2015)
	Multimodal information	Out-of-context misinformation	Aneja et al. (2021)
		Synthetic misinformation	McCloskey and Albright (2019)
Context-based approach	Social media user information		Zhou et al. (2022b)
	Propagation information		Davoudi et al. (2022)
	Situational information		Liao et al. (2022)
Feature-fusion approach			Huang et al. (2023)

Table 13.2 A List of Search Terms Used in Literature Search, as a Combination of Context Keywords and Misinformation-related Keywords.

Context keywords (13)	Misinformation keywords (4)	Search terms (52)
Automatic, early stage, spreader, contextual cue, textual, semantic, visual, image, multimodal, video, synthetic, deepfake, bot	Misinformation, disinformation, fake news, rumor	Context keyword + misinformation keyword + detection (e.g., multimodal fake news detection)

Detection of Textual Misinformation

The detection of textual misinformation relies on (a) handcrafted style-based features, (b) deep features, and (c) knowledge graphs.

Handcrafted Style-Based Features

Drawing from social science research in linguistics, communication, and psychology, handcrafted style-based features can be broadly categorized into linguistic and psycholinguistic features, where psycholinguistic features focus on the psychology-related attributes in addition to linguistic features (X. Zhou et al., 2020). First, linguistic features include both lexical and syntactic features, such as the presence and recurrence of specific vocabularies, phrases, or expressions, as well as linguistic rules and vocabulary functions. Text preprocessing is a common technique to transform unstructured textual information into more structured data formats that highlight lexical and syntactic meanings. A prevalent and fundamental method employed for this transformation is the BoW model, which constructs matrices of word frequency (Zhang et al., 2010). Additionally, part-of-speech tagging is extensively used to identify the grammar functionality of words and sentence structures (Ratnaparkhi, 1996). Research on linguistic features has revealed distinctive linguistic patterns that differentiate misinformation from true information, such that misinformation tends to have a shorter length and use more swear words, action verbs, and first-person singular compared to true information (Giachanou et al., 2022; Horne & Adali, 2017; Rashkin et al., 2017).

Second, psycholinguistic features are particularly informative in understanding the psychological, emotional, and cognitive characteristics of misinformation. Dictionary-based linguistic tools such as linguistic inquiry and word count are often used to extract and compute vocabulary associated with specific psychological, cognitive, emotional, and perceptive processes such as positive and negative emotions, certainty, and analytical thinking. Moreover, human annotation is often employed to provide human perceptions of psycholinguistic features as training data. For example, in a recent study, X. Zhou et al. (2022) instructed research assistants to categorize the perceived intentions of (mis)information spreaders as either intentional or unintentional, which serves as training data for developing misinformation detection models. A considerable amount of research in this domain has concentrated on sentiment analysis, finding that misinformation tends to be more negative than of true information (Horne & Adali, 2017). In addition to sentiments, psycholinguistic features such as perceived information novelty (Kumari et al., 2021) and expressions of skepticism (Kwon et al., 2017) have been included in developing misinformation detectors. Including these social science-informed style-based features can significantly improve the performance of misinformation detection models (Shu et al., 2017).

Deep Features

Deep learning-based approaches automatically capture latent textual features from unstructured text data. One prominent approach is transformers, a specific type of neural network that incorporates a self-attention mechanism in processing sequential data in natural language processing. Transformers are commonly used as pretrained models to enhance language comprehension and task-specific model performance. Bidirectional encoder representations from transformers (BERT; Devlin et al., 2019) is one of the most prevalent transformers. BERT has undergone extensive training on a large amount of text data and showcases exceptional proficiency in language representation as pretrained models in various NLP scenarios. For example, FakeBERT, a model based on BERT that has been trained and fine-tuned, achieved an accuracy of 98.90 percent in misinformation detection (Kaliyar et al., 2021).

Beyond BERT, various neural networks have been used to build misinformation detectors. Hu et al. (2020) developed a CNN-based misinformation detector, attaining an accuracy of 91.67 percent. It is also common to adopt an ensemble approach, combining different neural network models to boost performance. Nasir et al. (2021) introduced a hybrid CNN–RNN model that outperforms other existing models on the test dataset. A comprehensive evaluation of ensemble approaches found that fine-tuning BERT-based language models can achieve the highest accuracy of 98.41 percent, a substantial improvement over the BERT benchmark with an accuracy of 93.32 percent (Wani et al., 2021). Given BERT's power in understanding and representing language, BERT-based models that are fine-tuned based on specific context (e.g., COVID-19 misinformation, vaccine misinformation) can achieve the best performance in textual misinformation detection.

Knowledge Graphs

In addition to handcrafted and deep features derived from unstructured text data, knowledge graphs offer structured and interpretable data that can be useful for misinformation detection tasks. Knowledge graphs are "semantic nets that integrate various and heterogeneous information sources to represent knowledge about certain domains of discourse" (Fensel et al., 2020, p. 6), with nodes representing entities of interest and edges presenting entity relationships (C. Peng et al., 2023). For instance, in a scenario where vaccines and autism are two separate entities, knowledge graphs could illustrate that these two entities are not related, linking vaccines with preventive effects and linking autism with genetic and environmental causes. Therefore, when it comes to a misinformation claim that says vaccines cause autism, knowledge graphs can clearly inform fact-checking efforts by showing that there is no relationship. Knowledge graphs such as Google Knowledge Graphs have been extensively used in manual fact-checking processing; knowledge graphs also serve as a useful knowledge base for automated fact-checking (Ciampaglia et al., 2015). As the example illustrates, knowledge graphs can automatically verify whether or not two entities are related, without relying on human fact-checkers to manually determine information truthfulness. Knowledge graphs can not only achieve high accuracy in misinformation detection but also provide transparent and interpretable insights by tracing the decision-making paths (Shi & Weninger, 2016). This approach is particularly useful for domains with established and clear ground truths such as medicine. However, it is crucial to note that truths are constantly evolving, and knowledge graphs are often incomplete, imprecise, and belated (Pan et al., 2018).

Multilingual Misinformation

Multilingual misinformation presents a significant challenge to textual misinformation detection. Misinformation transcends languages, yet there are insufficient resources to detect misinformation across languages, especially for low-resource languages in the global south (Gereme et al., 2021). Big data emerges as a valuable asset for multilingual misinformation detection, offering a cost-efficient solution to improve information accessibility and equity for low-resource languages.

First, big data enable the creation and preservation of large-scale misinformation datasets, serving as crucial resources for developing language-specific language models and conducting misinformation detection in that particular language context. For example, researchers have developed word embeddings for Amharic and developed a misinformation detection model using an Amharic misinformation database (Gereme et al., 2021). In addition, big data facilitate the creation of multilingual misinformation datasets related to COVID-19, providing a valuable training dataset for future research (Y. Li et al., 2020).

Second, an alternative approach to multilingual misinformation detection relies on language models with cross-lingual capacities. For example, multilingual BERT has been trained using monolingual corpora in 104 languages (Devlin et al., 2019). Such multilingual language models can be integrated into misinformation detection models as the basis for fine-tuning to detect multilingual misinformation. Leveraging multilingual BERT, researchers have developed a misinformation detector that can detect misinformation across different languages and topical domains (De et al., 2021). Although this approach may not be suitable for culture-specific misinformation, it is useful for detecting universal misinformation, such as misinformation related to COVID-19, that has been transmitted in different languages and across different countries during the pandemic. Utilizing this big data approach holds promise in curbing the cross-linguistic spread of misinformation.

Detection of Multimodal Misinformation

The approaches to multimodal misinformation detection are closely tied to specific multimodal misinformation categories (i.e., out of context, manipulated, or synthetic). The key to detecting out-of-context multimodal misinformation is multimodal information inconsistency with text captions because out-of-content multimodal media are unmanipulated. At the same time, detecting manipulated and synthetic multimodal misinformation demands uncovering signals of synthetic features with machine-learning methods.

Out-of-Context Multimodal Misinformation

The detection task of out-of-context multimodal misinformation typically involves two elements: (a) comparing visual–textual information consistency; and (b) comparing visual information with existing visual evidence. Aneja et al. (2021) used a self-supervised learning approach to develop an out-of-context multimodal misinformation detector on image-caption data. They examined the consistency between visual information and captions, achieving an accuracy of 85 percent. Abdelnabi et al. (2022) proposed the Consistency-Checking Network (CCN) to assist and improve human evaluation of misinformation. This is because CCN not only compares image–caption consistency but also checks textual and visual information against existing textual and visual evidence. Further, Qi and colleagues (2021) incorporated embedded text in images in their detector, reaching an accuracy of 97.5 percent. Since images are usually copied and pasted in out-of-context misinformation, block artifact grids, the grid-like byproduct patterns that are generated in the process of image compression, are useful for detection as well (W. Li et al., 2009).

Manipulated and Synthetic Multimodal Misinformation

Similar to the detection of textual misinformation, the detection of manipulated and synthetic multimodal features draws on both handcrafted and deep features. Handcrafted features in computer vision include image edges and textures (Nanni et al., 2017), which can be extracted using techniques such as the scale-invariant feature transform (SIFT; Lowe, 2004). For example, inconsistencies in lighting and missing reflections can be extracted as signals of visual manipulation (Matern et al., 2019). Specifically, GAN-generated visuals are particularly saturated compared to authentic images, making saturation cues effective indicators of synthesized misinformation with an AUC of 0.92 (McCloskey & Albright, 2019). Similar forensic approaches have been applied to synthetic audio detection. For example, language-specific phonetic features have been used to detect lip-synching discrepancies with an equal error rate as low as 4.5 percent (Korshunov et al., 2019). These features are widely used in speech recognition and now serve as cues to detect speech–audio inconsistency. However, rapid advancements in speech generation and AI voiceovers present significant challenges to maintaining high detection performance in synthetic audio (Masood et al., 2023).

Despite their effectiveness, handcrafted features are less commonly used in multimodal misinformation detection due to their high computational cost. In contrast, deep learning-based approaches directly extract more comprehensive features from raw multimodal information and provide more information and greater robustness (Nanni et al., 2017). CNNs are predominantly used in computer vision and multimodal information-processing for their advantage in processing two-dimensional data. FaceForensics++ (Rossler et al., 2019) provides benchmarks and datasets for deepfake detection research, with CNN-based models demonstrating accuracies exceeding 90 percent. Yu et al. (2019) developed a CNN-based detector of GAN-generated visuals with an accuracy of 99.43 percent. Montserrat et al. (2020) developed a deepfake detector based on both CNN and RNN, achieving a validation accuracy of 92.61 percent.

Context-Based Misinformation Detection: Users, Networks, and Metadata

The discussion has largely resolved around detection methods based on the content characteristics of misinformation. However, it is crucial to incorporate contextual factors, including the source and propagation structure. A large amount of misinformation is created and disseminated deliberately, in which malicious human users and bots could engage in coordinated misinformation operations with distinctive features (Ferrara, 2017; Zhang et al., 2023). These distinctions could be reflected in user activities, metadata, propagation structures, and other contextual cues. In this section, we provide an overview of how these contextual cues have been incorporated in detecting misinformation.

Social Media User Information

First, examining the characteristics of social media users engaged in spreading misinformation is crucial for identifying false information. This approach stems from the premise that individuals disseminating misinformation exhibit distinct behaviors compared to those sharing authentic information (Shu et al., 2017). On the one hand, these users can be categorized into either human users or social bots. Bots have become a crucial part of the digital information ecosystem, taking on the role of efficient information dissemination and congregation. However, malicious bots intentionally propagating misinformation pose substantial risks. Research has found that malicious social bots have played a significant role in disseminating misinformation from low-credibility sources on social media (Shao et al., 2018). Especially at the early stage of propagation, before misinformation is widely circulated, social bots are primary contributors to the distribution and reinforcement of misinformation. By analyzing user characteristics and content features, researchers have successfully distinguished malicious bots from human users or legitimate bots (Barbon et al., 2018).

On the other hand, human users can be categorized as misinformation creators, spreaders, and recipients (Shahid et al., 2022). Identifying users on the basis of their unique roles and behavior patterns in the misinformation spread process is instrumental to its detection. For example, PageRank (Gupta et al., 2012) is the first credibility algorithm that leverages user data to determine page credibility. The PageRank algorithm incorporates events, tweets, and user information on Twitter and iteratively updates user credibility with new events. Inspired by this algorithm, a novel misinformation detector has been developed, considering both the credibility and influence of misinformation creators: credibility is determined by the portion of credible post history, while influence is determined by the potential reach of a user's post (Jarrahi & Safari, 2023). Similar approaches have been used in more recent studies by considering more nuances in user data. For example, Chen et al. (2022) deconstructed user features in three ways: user profile (i.e., user metadata), structural features (i.e., network characteristics among users), and temporal features (i.e., the temporal patterns of user engagement). These features are further integrated into a comprehensive model for misinformation detection that achieved an accuracy of over 90 percent. Researchers also captured the nuances of user intention in the propagation process (X. Zhou et al., 2022). Human annotation data on user intention (i.e., malicious, not malicious) was included and significantly improved the accuracy of the misinformation detector with an AUC score of around 0.9.

Propagation Information

Second, propagation structures provide useful information for identifying differences between the spread of misinformation and authentic information. Misinformation tends to spread faster and to a wider audience than real news, considering both structural and temporal information cascade features (Vosoughi et al., 2018). In addition, misinformation tends to show more specific propagation temporal patterns because malicious misinformation spreaders target specific events with specific timelines, in contrast to authentic users who have relatively stable activity patterns on a daily or weekly basis (Shahid et al., 2022). Propagation structures refer not only to the structural and temporal features of the cascade that spreads a piece of misinformation on social media but also consider networks of friending, stance, and co-occurrences of user engagement (Shu et al., 2017). For example, using issue-specific stances of retweets as information cascades can increase misinformation detection accuracy (Jin et al., 2016). Friendship networks as a macrolevel propagation network can help identify malicious users and misinformation (Shu et al., 2020); for example, misinformation spreaders tend to have fewer followers (Kwon et al., 2017). The structural relationships between hashtags can be used as indicators of news credibility and detection tasks (X. Zhou, Zafarani, & Ferrara, 2022).

These structural networks can also be altered or fused to increase the accuracy of misinformation detection, as propagation features are often intertwined and related, and not all propagation features are informative for detection tasks. Propagation2Vec is a misinformation detection network that is specifically designed for early detection when the complete propagation network is not available (Silva et al., 2021). This detector can achieve state-of-the-art performance in early detection tasks by identifying informative nodes in the propagation networks and reconstructing the partial networks of the complete propagation networks. In addition, researchers developed a hybrid detector that fused both propagation and stance networks, which has proved to be an effective early detection method (Davoudi et al., 2022).

Situational/Circumstantial Information

Lastly, the context in which misinformation is disseminated matters. Misinformation does not exist in a vacuum but constantly interacts with different entities in the information ecosystem. For example, both the misinformation and its comments can be used for misinformation detection because users may debunk it or provide additional contextual information in the comments section. Shu et al. (2019) incorporated a user–news interaction embedding in the misinformation detection model, in addition to separate user, news, and publisher embeddings. The user–news interaction embedding captures how users in the comments interact with misinformation, and this significantly improves the accuracy of misinformation detection, especially for detection at the early stages. Researchers also rely on news contextual information such as topic labels for the detection tasks, providing additional contextual information for misinformation detection models to adjust according to domain-specific characteristics (Liao et al., 2022). These contextual features, while supplementary, can greatly complement the main features of misinformation and improve the performance of misinformation detection models.

Feature Fusion and Ensemble Approach

The prior discussion has focused primarily on misinformation detection using individual features or individual models based on either content or context information. Feature fusion is the combination of different feature layers as an integrated input feature (Dai et al., 2021). This approach can be applied across various classes of features, including content and contextual features. The raw data on content, propagation, and user information can be transformed into embeddings in lower-dimensional spaces for processing.

By integrating a range of features, we can achieve a more comprehensive understanding of the training data, which in turn improves the robustness, generalizability, and overall performance of misinformation detection models. Feature fusion also allows for the exploration of relationships between different feature embeddings by creating correlation matrices and weight loadings, which are not considered in the single-feature approach. Within the content level, feature fusion is commonly employed by integrating textual, visual, and audio information into a fusion layer in multimodal information-processing (Xue et al., 2021). For example, to detect misinformation on short video platforms, researchers integrate captions, visual features, and audio features of TikTok videos, which significantly improves the model performance (Shang et al., 2021). Similarly, researchers also integrated both textual and visual information on social media posts to detect misinformation on Weibo and Twitter (Khattar et al., 2019; H. Zhou et al., 2022). Within the propagation features, the structural and temporal features are often fused together, which is a more fine-grained feature fusion approach to differentiate similar cascade structures with different temporal features (Huang et al., 2023). Further, content and context features can also be fused to the same model; for example, a tri-relationship embedding is built based on news content, user and publisher features, and how they interact with news content (e.g., Shu et al., 2019). Content and propagation features can be integrated as well: content embedding and a node embedding of misinformation on Twitter are integrated to jointly detect misinformation (Tu et al., 2021). Fusing different features can indeed provide additional information and improve the misinformation detection performance.

Challenges and Future Directions

Despite the large body of research on early-stage misinformation detection using big data in the computer science and information science literature, several challenges remain. Below, we discuss these challenges and some potential future directions for this line of research. Interdisciplinary research that incorporates both social science research on misinformation impacts and dynamics and computer science research on advanced machine-learning models is needed, especially since misinformation detection research can benefit greatly from social science theory input.

The biggest challenge in early-stage misinformation detection revolves around information veracity in terms of (a) the complexity of misinformation label decisions and (b) the availability of ground truth. On the one hand, all studies reviewed in this chapter try to detect factually false misinformation. These studies use existing baseline databases from fact-checking organizations, with misinformation claims fact-checked to be true or false. However, information veracity is often a continuum rather than a binary category. In addition to misinformation that has been fact-checked and shown to be factually false, many variations exist, such as unverifiable information during a crisis or (mis)information that is partly true and partly false, including out-of-context misinformation, miscaptioned misinformation, and misattributed misinformation. These nuances present a huge challenge for expert journalists in the fact-checking process, yet they are largely ignored in the automated misinformation detection research. In addition, recent communication studies have found that there are inconsistencies in the ruling of misinformation across fact-checking organizations (Lelo, 2023), which means that the ground truth is often controversial and contested. Different fact-checking organizations indeed have different editorial and fact-checking practices and guidelines. It is a huge problem for misinformation detection tasks that require straightforward labeled data, while ground truth is a challenge in itself.

In addition, misinformation detection also faces the challenge of data availability and quality (Torabi Asr & Taboada, 2019). First, as misinformation is only a very small part of the whole information ecosystem, the training dataset is inherently imbalanced. Researchers have tried to overcome this problem with a balanced design or algorithms that can handle imbalanced data, but this solution still has limitations in overfitting and bias. Second, data quality is a huge concern. Beyond the inconsistency of verdicts between fact-checking organizations, there are other problems with data sources and human-annotated data. Most misinformation datasets come from Twitter, and the overreliance on Twitter data means that the nuances in misinformation on other open or more closed information-sharing spaces, such as Facebook and WhatsApp, are not captured in the extant misinformation detection research. Therefore, detection models trained on Twitter data would not perform well on other platforms. Further, it is very common for computer scientists to rely on human annotation of misinformation as handcrafted features for detection tasks. However, there are no universal guidelines on human annotation, especially when it comes to psycholinguistic features where subjective evaluations can vary across individuals. The annotated data may not be accurate if the annotation is done without a consistent codebook or by research assistants without proper training. Computer scientists often rely on human annotation data in the model training process. However, when it comes to theoretical concepts in social science, collaboration with social scientists is needed to produce robust annotation data, otherwise there is a high risk of the "garbage in, garbage out" scenario with poor-quality and inaccurate data undermining the performance of the misinformation detection model.

The integration of social science insights into misinformation detection is increasingly critical, particularly during times of public crisis. We have reviewed some detection research that has achieved state-of-the-art accuracy by employing theory-informed handcrafted features (X. Zhou & Zafarani, 2020). For example, social desirability bias (Grimm, 2010) and the third-person effect (Davison, 1983) have informed the involvement of contextual information such as user comments in misinformation detection studies. Despite the outstanding performance of deep learning models, there is still a need for theory-informed handcrafted features to guide computers' attention and enhance human understanding of misinformation characteristics. For example, communication theories related to message sensation value (Palmgreen et al., 1991) and the activation model and information exposure (Donohew et al., 1980) have informed multimodal information-processing, which can provide theoretical input for the development of multimodal misinformation detectors. These social science theories highlight theoretical concepts that are useful for misinformation detection, but their application in computer and information science is still limited. There is an urgent need for social scientists to provide actionable implications for misinformation detection methods. Similarly, early stage the input of social science research, especially in the areas of crisis communication and public relations, is needed to detect misinformation at its early stages. For example, situational crisis communication Theory (Coombs, 2007) highlights the contextual understanding of the crisis, which can inform the integration of more contextual information in early misinformation detection tasks. Misinformation detection research can rely on this input to better address the problem of detecting misinformation in its early stages.

References

Abdelnabi, S., Hasan, R., & Fritz, M. (2022). Open-domain, content-based, multi-modal fact-checking of out-of-context images via online resources. Proceedings of the IEEE/CVF Conference on Computer Vision and Pattern Recognition (CVPR), 14940–14949.

Altay, S., & Acerbi, A. (2023). People believe misinformation is a threat because they assume others are gullible. *New Media & Society*. 14614448231153379. http://dx.doi.org/10.1177/14614448231153379

Aneja, S., Bregler, C., & Nießner, M. (2021). COSMOS: Catching out-of-context misinformation with self-supervised learning. *arXiv*:2101.06278

Barbon, S., Jr., Campos, G. F. C., Tavares, G. M., Igawa, R. A., Proença, M. L., Jr., & Guido, R. C. (2018). Detection of human, legitimate bot, and malicious bot in online social networks based on wavelets. *ACM Transactions on Multimedia Computing Communications and Applications, 14*(1S). http://dx.doi.org/10.1145/3183506

Broniatowski, D. A., Jamison, A. M., Qi, S., AlKulaib, L., Chen, T., Benton, A., Quinn, S. C., & Dredze, M. (2018). Weaponized health communication: Twitter bots and Russian trolls amplify the vaccine debate. *American Journal of Public Health, 108*(10), 1378–1384. http://dx.doi.org/10.2105/AJPH.2018.304567

Cao, J., Qi, P., Sheng, Q., Yang, T., Guo, J., & Li, J. (2020). Exploring the role of visual content in fake news detection. In K. Shu, S. Wang, D. Lee, & H. Liu (Eds.), *Disinformation, misinformation, and fake news in social media: Emerging research challenges and opportunities* (pp. 141–161). Springer. http://dx.doi.org/10.1007/978-3-030-42699-6_8

Chen, X., Zhou, F., Trajcevski, G., & Bonsangue, M. (2022). Multi-view learning with distinguishable feature fusion for rumor detection. *Knowledge-Based Systems, 240*, 108085. http://dx.doi.org/10.1016/j.knosys.2021.108085

Chung, M., & Kim, N. (2021). When I learn the news is false: How fact-checking information stems the spread of fake news via third-person perception. *Human Communication Research, 47*(1), 1–24. http://dx.doi.org/10.1093/hcr/hqaa010

Ciampaglia, G. L., Shiralkar, P., Rocha, L. M., Bollen, J., Menczer, F., & Flammini, A. (2015). Computational fact checking from knowledge networks. *PLoS ONE, 10*(6), e0128193. http://dx.doi.org/10.1371/journal.pone.0128193

Clarivate. (2023). Web of Science APIs. https://clarivate.com/products/scientific-and-academic-research/research-analytics-evaluation-and-management-solutions/web-of-science-apis

Cofacts. (2023, October 5). *Cofacts—Message reporting chatbot and crowd-sourced fact-checking community*. https://en.cofacts.tw

Coleman, K. (2021, January 25). Introducing Birdwatch, a community-based approach to misinformation. X. https://blog.x.com/en_us/topics/product/2021/introducing-birdwatch-a-community-based-approach-to-misinformation

Coombs, W. T. (2007). Protecting organization reputations during a crisis: The development and application of situational crisis communication theory. *Corporate Reputation Review*, *10*(3), 163–176. http://dx.doi.org/10.1057/palgrave.crr.1550049

Dai, Y., Gieseke, F., Oehmcke, S., Wu, Y., & Barnard, K. (2021). Attentional feature fusion. In 2021 IEEE Winter Conference on Applications of Computer Vision (WACV), 3560–3569. IEEE. https://doi.org/10.1109/WACV48630.2021.00360

Davison, W. P. (1983). The third-person effect in communication. *Public Opinion Quarterly*, *47*(1), 1–15. http://dx.doi.org/10.1086/268763

Davoudi, M., Moosavi, M. R., & Sadreddini, M. H. (2022). DSS: A hybrid deep model for fake news detection using propagation tree and stance network. *Expert Systems with Applications*, *198*, 116635. http://dx.doi.org/10.1016/j.eswa.2022.116635

De, A., Bandyopadhyay, D., Gain, B., & Ekbal, A. (2021). A transformer-based approach to multilingual fake news detection in low-resource languages. *ACM Transactions on Asian and Low-Resource Language Information Processing*, *21*(1). http://dx.doi.org/10.1145/3472619

De Mauro, A., Greco, M., & Grimaldi, M. (2015). What is big data? A consensual definition and a review of key research topics. *AIP Conference Proceedings*, *1644*(1), 97–104. http://dx.doi.org/10.1063/1.4907823

Devlin, J., Chang, M.-W., Lee, K., & Toutanova, K. (2019). BERT: Pre-training of deep bidirectional transformers for language understanding. *arXiv*:1810.04805. http://arxiv.org/abs/1810.04805

Donohew, L., Palmgreen, P., & Duncan, J. (1980). An activation model of information exposure. *Communication Monographs*, *47*(4), 295–303. http://dx.doi.org/10.1080/03637758009376038

El Naqa, I., & Murphy, M. J. (2015). What is machine learning? In I. El Naqa, R. Li, & M. J. Murphy (Eds.), *Machine learning in radiation oncology: Theory and applications* (pp. 3–11). Springer. http://dx.doi.org/10.1007/978-3-319-18305-3_1

Fensel, D., Şimşek, U., Angele, K., Huaman, E., Kärle, E., Panasiuk, O., Toma, I., Umbrich, J., & Wahler, A. (2020). Introduction: What is a knowledge graph? In D. Fensel, U. Şimşek, K. Angele, E. Huaman, E. Kärle, O. Panasiuk, I. Toma, J. Umbrich, & A. Wahler (Eds.), *Knowledge graphs: Methodology, tools and selected use cases* (pp. 1–10). Springer. http://dx.doi.org/10.1007/978-3-030-37439-6_1

Ferrara, E. (2017). Disinformation and social bot operations in the run up to the 2017 French presidential election. *arXiv*:1707.00086.

Gereme, F., Zhu, W., Ayall, T., & Alemu, D. (2021). Combating fake news in "low-resource" languages: Amharic fake news detection accompanied by resource crafting. *Information*, *12*(1). http://dx.doi.org/10.3390/info12010020

Giachanou, A., Ghanem, B., Ríssola, E. A., Rosso, P., Crestani, F., & Oberski, D. (2022). The impact of psycholinguistic patterns in discriminating between fake news spreaders and fact checkers. *Data & Knowledge Engineering*, *138*, 101960. http://dx.doi.org/10.1016/j.datak.2021.101960

Goodfellow, I., Bengio, Y., & Courville, A. (2016). *Deep learning*. MIT press.

Goodfellow, I., Pouget-Abadie, J., Mirza, M., Xu, B., Warde-Farley, D., Ozair, S., Courville, A., & Bengio, Y. (2020). Generative adversarial networks. *Communications of the ACM*, *63*(11), 139–144. http://dx.doi.org/10.1145/3422622

Grimm, P. (2010). Social desirability bias. In J. N. Sheth & N. K. Malhotra (Eds.), *Wiley International Encyclopedia of Marketing*. Wiley. https://doi.org/10.1002/9781444316568.wiem02057

Gupta, M., Zhao, P., & Han, J. (2012). Evaluating event credibility on Twitter. In *Proceedings of the 2012 SIAM international conference on data mining (SDM)* (Vol. 1–0, pp. 153–164). Society for Industrial and Applied Mathematics. http://dx.doi.org/10.1137/1.9781611972825.14

Horne, B., & Adali, S. (2017). This just in: Fake news packs a lot in title, uses simpler, repetitive content in text body, more similar to satire than real news. *Proceedings of the International AAAI Conference on Web and Social Media*, *11*(1), 759–766. http://dx.doi.org/10.1609/icwsm.v11i1.14976

Hu, Q., Li, Q., Lu, Y., Yang, Y., & Cheng, J. (2020). Multi-level word features based on CNN for fake news detection in cultural communication. *Personal and Ubiquitous Computing*, *24*(2), 259–272. http://dx.doi.org/10.1007/s00779-019-01289-y

Huang, Q., Zhou, C., Wu, J., Liu, L., & Wang, B. (2023). Deep spatial–temporal structure learning for rumor detection on Twitter. *Neural Computing and Applications*, *35*(18), 12995–13005. http://dx.doi.org/10.1007/s00521-020-05236-4

IFCN. (2023). *IFCN Code of Principles*. https://ifcncodeofprinciples.poynter.org

Jarrahi, A., & Safari, L. (2023). Evaluating the effectiveness of publishers' features in fake news detection on social media. *Multimedia Tools and Applications*, *82*(2), 2913–2939. http://dx.doi.org/10.1007/s11042-022-12668-8

Jin, Z., Cao, J., Zhang, Y., & Luo, J. (2016). News Verification by Exploiting Conflicting Social Viewpoints in Microblogse. *Proceedings of the AAAI Conference on Artificial Intelligence*, *30*(1). http://dx.doi.org/10.1609/aaai.v30i1.10382

Kaliyar, R. K., Goswami, A., & Narang, P. (2021). FakeBERT: Fake news detection in social media with a BERT-based deep learning approach. *Multimedia Tools and Applications*, *80*(8), 11765–11788. http://dx.doi.org/10.1007/s11042-020-10183-2

Kasra, M., Shen, C., & O'Brien, J. F. (2018). Seeing Is Believing: How People Fail to Identify Fake Images on the Web. *Extended Abstracts of the 2018 CHI Conference on Human Factors in Computing Systems*, 1–6. http://dx.doi.org/10.1145/3170427.3188604

Khattar, D., Goud, J. S., Gupta, M., & Varma, V. (2019). MVAE: Multimodal variational autoencoder for fake news detection. *WWW '19: The World Wide Web Conference*, 2915–2921. http://dx.doi.org/10.1145/3308558.3313552

Korshunov, P., Halstead, M., Castan, D., Graciarena, M., McLaren, M., Burns, B., Lawson, A., & Marcel, S. (2019). Tampered speaker inconsistency detection with phonetically aware audio-visual features. *International Conference on Machine Learning*.

Kumari, R., Ashok, N., Ghosal, T., & Ekbal, A. (2021). Misinformation detection using multitask learning with mutual learning for novelty detection and emotion recognition. *Information Processing & Management*, *58*(5), 102631. http://dx.doi.org/10.1016/j.ipm.2021.102631

Kwon, S., Cha, M., & Jung, K. (2017). Rumor detection over varying time windows. *PLoS ONE*, *12*(1), e0168344. http://dx.doi.org/10.1371/journal.pone.0168344

Lelo, T. (2023). Assessing the consistency of fact-checking in political debates. *Journal of Communication*, *73*(6), 587–600. http://dx.doi.org/10.1093/joc/jqad028

Li, W., Yuan, Y., & Yu, N. (2009). Passive detection of doctored JPEG image via block artifact grid extraction. *Signal Processing*, *89*(9), 1821–1829. http://dx.doi.org/10.1016/j.sigpro.2009.03.025

Li, Y., Jiang, B., Shu, K., & Liu, H. (2020). MM-COVID: A Multilingual and Multimodal Data Repository for Combating COVID-19 Disinformation. *arXiv*: 2011.04088.

Liao, Q., Chai, H., Han, H., Zhang, X., Wang, X., Xia, W., & Ding, Y. (2022). An integrated multi-task model for fake news detection. *IEEE Transactions on Knowledge and Data Engineering*, *34*(11), 5154–5165. http://dx.doi.org/10.1109/TKDE.2021.3054993

Lowe, D. G. (2004). Distinctive image features from scale-invariant Keypoints. *International Journal of Computer Vision*, *60*(2), 91–110. http://dx.doi.org/10.1023/B:VISI.0000029664.99615.94

Masood, M., Nawaz, M., Malik, K. M., Javed, A., Irtaza, A., & Malik, H. (2023). Deepfakes generation and detection: State-of-the-art, open challenges, countermeasures, and way forward. *Applied Intelligence*, *53*(4), 3974–4026. http://dx.doi.org/10.1007/s10489-022-03766-z

Matern, F., Riess, C., & Stamminger, M. (2019). Exploiting visual artifacts to expose deepfakes and face manipulations. 2019 IEEE Winter Applications of Computer Vision Workshops (WACVW), 83–92. http://dx.doi.org/10.1109/WACVW.2019.00020

McCloskey, S., & Albright, M. (2019). Detecting GAN-Generated Imagery Using Saturation Cues. 2019 IEEE international conference on image processing (ICIP), 4584–4588. http://dx.doi.org/10.1109/ICIP.2019.8803661

MediaWise. (2023). Poynter. https://www.poynter.org/mediawise

Montserrat, D. M., Hao, H., Yarlagadda, S. K., Baireddy, S., Shao, R., Horvath, J., Bartusiak, E., Yang, J., Guera, D., Zhu, F., & Delp, E. J. (2020, June). Deepfakes detection with automatic face weighting. *Proceedings of the IEEE/CVF conference on computer vision and pattern recognition (CVPR) workshops.*

Nanni, L., Ghidoni, S., & Brahnam, S. (2017). Handcrafted vs. non-handcrafted features for computer vision classification. *Pattern Recognition*, *71*, 158–172. http://dx.doi.org/10.1016/j.patcog.2017.05.025

Nasir, J. A., Khan, O. S., & Varlamis, I. (2021). Fake news detection: A hybrid CNN-RNN based deep learning approach. *International Journal of Information Management Data Insights*, *1*(1), 100007. http://dx.doi.org/10.1016/j.jjimei.2020.100007

Palmgreen, P., Donohew, L., Lorch, E. P., Rogus, M., Helm, D., & Grant, N. (1991). Sensation seeking, message sensation value, and drug use as mediators of PSA effectiveness. *Health Communication*, *3*(4), 217–227. http://dx.doi.org/10.1207/s15327027hc0304_4

Pan, J. Z., Pavlova, S., Li, C., Li, N., Li, Y., & Liu, J. (2018). Content based fake news detection using knowledge graphs. In D. Vrandečić, K. Bontcheva, M. C. Suárez-Figueroa, V. Presutti, I. Celino, M. Sabou, L.-A. Kaffee, & E. Simperl (Eds.), *The semantic web – ISWC 2018* (pp. 669–683). Springer.

Peng, C., Xia, F., Naseriparsa, M., & Osborne, F. (2023). Knowledge graphs: Opportunities and challenges. *Artificial Intelligence Review*, *56*(11), 13071–13102. http://dx.doi.org/10.1007/s10462-023-10465-9

Peng, Y., Lu, Y., & Shen, C. (2023). An agenda for studying credibility perceptions of visual misinformation. *Political Communication*, *40*(2), 225–237. http://dx.doi.org/10.1080/10584609.2023.2175398

Qi, P., Cao, J., Li, X., Liu, H., Sheng, Q., Mi, X., He, Q., Lv, Y., Guo, C., & Yu, Y. (2021). Improving fake news detection by using an entity-enhanced framework to fuse diverse multimodal clues. Proceedings of the 29th ACM International Conference on Multimedia, 1212–1220. http://dx.doi.org/10.1145/3474085.3481548

Qian, S., Shen, C., & Zhang, J. (2023). Fighting cheapfakes: Using a digital media literacy intervention to motivate reverse search of out-of-context visual misinformation. *Journal of Computer-Mediated Communication*, *28*(1), zmac024. http://dx.doi.org/10.1093/jcmc/zmac024

Rashkin, H., Choi, E., Jang, J. Y., Volkova, S., & Choi, Y. (2017). Truth of varying shades: Analyzing language in fake news and political fact-checking. *Proceedings of the 2017 Conference on Empirical Methods in Natural Language Processing*, 2931–2937. https://doi.org/10.18653/v1/D17-1317

Ratnaparkhi, A. (1996). A maximum entropy model for part-of-speech tagging. Conference on Empirical Methods in Natural Language Processing, 133–142.

Rössler, A., Cozzolino, D., Verdoliva, L., Riess, C., Thies, J., & Niessner, M. (2019, October). FaceForensics++: Learning to Detect Manipulated Facial Images. 2019 IEEE/CVF International Conference on Computer Vision (ICCV), 1–11. https://doi.org/10.1109/ICCV.2019.00009

Shahid, W., Li, Y., Staples, D., Amin, G., Hakak, S., & Ghorbani, A. (2022). Are you a cyborg, bot or human?—A survey on detecting fake news spreaders. *IEEE Access*, *10*, 27069–27083.

Shang, L., Kou, Z., Zhang, Y., & Wang, D. (2021). A multimodal misinformation detector for COVID-19 short videos on TikTok. 2021 IEEE International Conference on Big Data (Big Data), 899–908. http://dx.doi.org/10.1109/BigData52589.2021.9671928

Shao, C., Ciampaglia, G. L., Varol, O., Yang, K.-C., Flammini, A., & Menczer, F. (2018). The spread of low-credibility content by social bots. *Nature Communications*, *9*(1), 4787. http://dx.doi.org/10.1038/s41467-018-06930-7

Shen, C., Kasra, M., Pan, W., Bassett, G. A., Malloch, Y., & O'Brien, J. F. (2019). Fake images: The effects of source, intermediary, and digital media literacy on contextual assessment of image credibility online. *New Media & Society*, *21*(2), 438–463. http://dx.doi.org/10.1177/1461444818799526

Shi, B., & Weninger, T. (2016). Ffact checking in heterogeneous information networks. Proceedings of the 25th International Conference Companion on World Wide Web, 101–102. http://dx.doi.org/10.1145/2872518.2889354

Shu, K., Mahudeswaran, D., Wang, S., & Liu, H. (2020). Hierarchical propagation networks for fake news detection: Investigation and exploitation. *Proceedings of the International AAAI Conference on Web and Social Media*, *14*(1), 626–637. http://dx.doi.org/10.1609/icwsm.v14i1.7329

Shu, K., Sliva, A., Wang, S., Tang, J., & Liu, H. (2017). Fake news detection on social media: A data mining perspective. *SIGKDD Explorations Newsletter*, *19*(1), 22–36. http://dx.doi.org/10.1145/3137597.3137600

Shu, K., Wang, S., & Liu, H. (2019). Beyond news contents: The role of social context for fake news detection. Proceedings of the Twelfth ACM International Conference on Web Search and Data Mining, 312–320. http://dx.doi.org/10.1145/3289600.3290994

Silva, A., Han, Y., Luo, L., Karunasekera, S., & Leckie, C. (2021). Propagation2Vec: Embedding partial propagation networks for explainable fake news early detection. *Information Processing & Management*, *58*(5), 102618. http://dx.doi.org/10.1016/j.ipm.2021.102618

Torabi Asr, F., & Taboada, M. (2019). Big data and quality data for fake news and misinformation detection. *Big Data & Society*, *6*(1). 2053951719843310. http://dx.doi.org/10.1177/2053951719843310

Tu, K., Chen, C., Hou, C., Yuan, J., Li, J., & Yuan, X. (2021). Rumor2vec: A rumor detection framework with joint text and propagation structure representation learning. *Information Sciences*, *560*, 137–151. http://dx.doi.org/10.1016/j.ins.2020.12.080

Vincent, J. (2018, April 17). Watch Jordan Peele use AI to make Barack Obama deliver a PSA about fake news. The Verge. https://www.theverge.com/tldr/2018/4/17/17247334/ai-fake-news-video-barack-obama-jordan-peele-buzzfeed

Vosoughi, S., Roy, D., & Aral, S. (2018). The spread of true and false news online. *Science, 359*(6380), 1146–1151. http://dx.doi.org/10.1126/science.aap9559

Walker, J., Thuermer, G., Vicens, J., & Simperl, E. (2023). AI art and misinformation: approaches and strategies for media literacy and fact checking. *Proceedings of the 2023 AAAI/ACM Conference on AI,* Ethics, and Society, 26–37. http://dx.doi.org/10.1145/3600211.3604715

Wang, S.-C. (2003). Artificial neural network. In S.-C. Wang (Ed.), *Interdisciplinary computing in Java programming* (pp. 81–100). Springer. http://dx.doi.org/10.1007/978-1-4615-0377-4_5

Wang, W. Y. (2017). "Liar, liar pants on fire": A new benchmark dataset for fake news detection. *arXiv*:1705.00648.

Wani, A., Joshi, I., Khandve, S., Wagh, V., & Joshi, R. (2021). Evaluating deep learning approaches for Covid19 fake news detection. In T. Chakraborty, K. Shu, H. R. Bernard, H. Liu, & M. S. Akhtar (Eds.), *Combating online hostile posts in regional languages during emergency situation* (pp. 153–163). Springer.

Weikmann, T., & Lecheler, S. (2023). Cutting through the hype: Understanding the implications of deepfakes for the fact-checking actor-network. *Digital Journalism*, 1–18. http://dx.doi.org/10.1080/21670811.2023.2194665

Xue, J., Wang, Y., Tian, Y., Li, Y., Shi, L., & Wei, L. (2021). Detecting fake news by exploring the consistency of multimodal data. *Information Processing & Management*, *58*(5), 102610. http://dx.doi.org/10.1016/j.ipm.2021.102610

Yu, N., Davis, L. S., & Fritz, M. (2019). Attributing fake images to GANs: Learning and analyzing GAN fingerprints. Proceedings of the IEEE/CVF International Conference on Computer Vision (ICCV). http://dx.doi.org/10.1109/ICCV.2019.00765

Zhang, Y., Jin, R., & Zhou, Z.-H. (2010). Understanding bag-of-words model: A statistical framework. *International Journal of Machine Learning and Cybernetics*, *1*(1), 43–52. http://dx.doi.org/10.1007/s13042-010-0001-0

Zhang, Y., Sharma, K., & Liu, Y. (2023). Capturing cross-platform interaction for identifying coordinated accounts of misinformation campaigns. In J. Kamps, L. Goeuriot, F. Crestani, M. Maistro, H. Joho, B. Davis, C. Gurrin, U. Kruschwitz, & A. Caputo (Eds.), *Advances in information retrieval* (pp. 694–702). Springer.

Zheng, A. (2015). *Evaluating machine learning models*. O'Reilly Media.

Zheng, A., & Casari, A. (2018). *Feature engineering for machine learning: Principles and techniques for data scientists*. O'Reilly Media.

Zhou, H., Ma, T., Rong, H., Qian, Y., Tian, Y., & Al-Nabhan, N. (2022). MDMN: Multi-task and domain adaptation based multi-modal network for early rumor detection. *Expert Systems with Applications*, *195*, 116517. http://dx.doi.org/10.1016/j.eswa.2022.116517

Zhou, J., Zhang, Y., Luo, Q., Parker, A. G., & De Choudhury, M. (2023). Synthetic lies: Understanding AI-generated misinformation and evaluating algorithmic and human solutions. *Proceedings of the 2023 CHI Conference on Human Factors in Computing Systems*. http://dx.doi.org/10.1145/3544548.3581318

Zhou, X., Jain, A., Phoha, V. V., & Zafarani, R. (2020). Fake news early detection: A theory-driven model. *Digital Threats*, *1*(2). http://dx.doi.org/10.1145/3377478

Zhou, X., Shu, K., Phoha, V. V., Liu, H., & Zafarani, R. (2022). "This is fake! Shared it by mistake": Assessing the intent of fake news spreaders. *Proceedings of the ACM Web Conference*, *2022*, 3685–3694. http://dx.doi.org/10.1145/3485447.3512264

Zhou, X., & Zafarani, R. (2020). A survey of fake news: Fundamental theories, detection methods, and opportunities. *ACM Computing Surveys*, *53*(5). http://dx.doi.org/10.1145/3395046

Zhou, X., Zafarani, R., & Ferrara, E. (2022). From fake news to #fakenews: Mining direct and indirect relationships among hashtags for fake news detection. *arXiv*:2211.1113.

Index

Communication and Misinformation: Crisis Events in the Age of Social Media, First Edition.
Edited by Kevin B. Wright.
© 2025 John Wiley & Sons, Inc. Published 2025 by John Wiley & Sons, Inc.

n

o

p

Printed and bound by CPI Group (UK) Ltd, Croydon, CR0 4YY
18/12/2024
14613877-0001